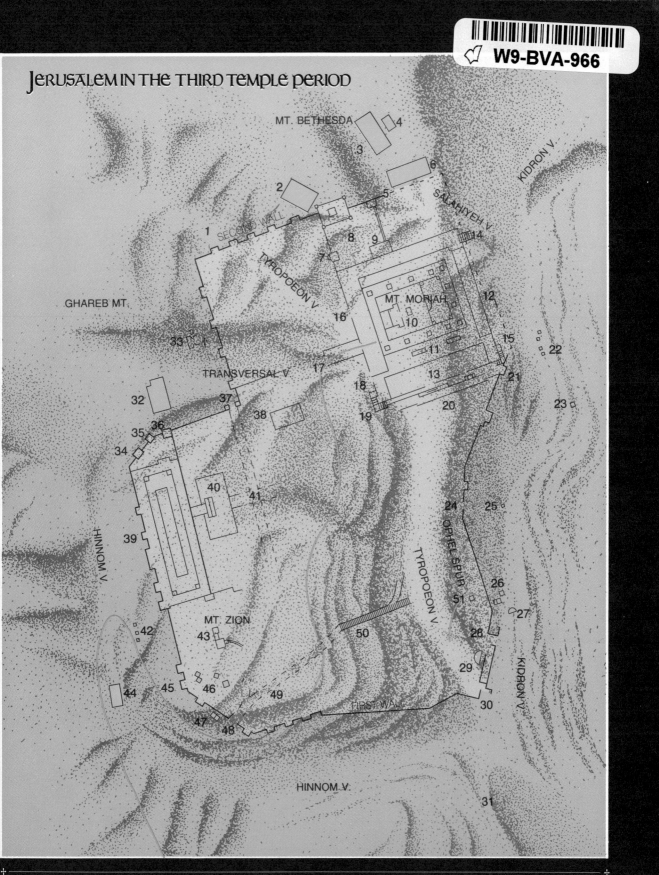

Jerusalem in the Third Temple Period

הרסו את ההיכל
הזה ובשלשה ימים אקימנו

SOLVITE TEMPLVM HOC ET IN TRIBVS
DIEBVS EXCITABO ILLVD

ΛΥΣΑΤΕ ΤΟΝ ΝΑΟΝ ΤΟΥΤΟΝ ΚΑΙ ΕΝ ΤΡΙΣΙΝ
ΗΜΕΡΑΙΣ ΕΓΕΡΩ ΑΥΤΟΝ

DESTROY THIS TEMPLE
AND IN THREE DAYS
I WILL RAISE IT UP AGAIN

John 2:19

Plate 1 (overleaf) Fourth-century mosaic "pictorial" map of Jerusalem in the Church of St. Pudentiana, Rome. Above the semicircular portico is perhaps one of the oldest "maps" of Jerusalem, with the mound of Calvary surmounted by a jeweled cross. The principal buildings on the left are the Baptistery, Anastasis, and the Martyrion built by Constantine in the fourth century. To the right of Golgotha are the church and Coenaculum on Mt. Zion. The gate on the extreme right may be one of the temple gates leading to the Mount of Olives, on which may be seen Constantine's basilica, the Eleona. Photographed by M. J. Prus, Loyola University of Chicago.

JERUSALEM
City of Jesus

An Exploration of the Traditions,
Writings, and Remains
of the Holy City
From the Time of Christ

TEXT BY
RICHARD M. MACKOWSKI, S.J.

PHOTOGRAPHY BY
GARO NALBANDIAN

WILLIAM B. EERDMANS PUBLISHING COMPANY
GRAND RAPIDS, MICHIGAN

DEDICATION   TO MY STUDENTS
In the Classroom
On the Study Tours
Around the Campus
IN GRATITUDE

IMPRIMI POTEST
Michael J. Lavelle, S.J.
Provincial, Detroit Province
of the Society of Jesus
February 1, 1978

Library of Congress Cataloging in Publication Data
Mackowski, Richard M   1929–
    Jerusalem.

    1. Jerusalem—Description. 2. Jerusalem—Antiquities.
I. Nalbandian, Garo.   II. Title.
DS109.M2   226'.09   79-28093
ISBN 0-8028-3526-0

The Author and Photographer wish to extend their personal gratitude to the Condon Fund for the generous subsidy to assist in the publication of this book.

TABLE OF CONTENTS

LIST OF ABBREVIATIONS

AASOR	Annual of the American Schools of Oriental Research	JBC	Jerome Biblical Commentary (1968)
ADAJ	Annual of the Department of Antiquities of Jordan	JBL	Journal of Biblical Literature
		JR	Jerusalem Revealed, ed. Y. Yadin (1975)
ANEP	Ancient Near East in Pictures, ed. J. B. Pritchard, 2nd ed. (1969)	LCL	Loeb Classical Library
		L&S	A Greek-English Lexicon, H.G. Liddell and R. Scott (1963)
ANET	Ancient Near Eastern Texts, ed. J. B. Pritchard, 3rd ed. (1969)	LS	A Latin Dictionary, C.T. Lewis and C. Short (1879)
Ant.	Josephus Antiquitates Judaeorum	LXX	Septuagint
BA	Biblical Archaeologist	MT	Massoretic Text
BAR	Biblical Archaeology Review	OGI(S)	Orientis Graeci Inscriptiones (Selectae), ed. E. W. Dittenberger (1903–5)
BASOR	Bulletin of the American Schools of Oriental Research		
		PEFQS	Palestine Exploration Fund Quarterly Statement
BGU	Berliner griechische Urkunden	PEQ	Palestine Exploration Quarterly
BJ	Josephus Bellum Judaicum	PG	Patrologia Graeca, ed. J. Migne
BTS	Bible et Terre Sainte	PL	Patrologia Latina, ed. J. Migne
CNI	Christian News from Israel	P Ox	Oxyrhynchus Papyri
DJD	Discoveries in the Judaean Desert of Jordan	P Petr	Flinders Petrie Papyri
ELS	Enchiridion Locorum Sanctorum, D. Baldi, O.F.M., 2nd ed. (1955)	QDAP	Quarterly of the Department of Antiquities in Palestine
HTR	Harvard Theological Review	RB	Revue Biblique
IDB	Interpreter's Dictionary of the Bible	RivB	Rivista Biblica
IEJ	Israel Exploration Journal	SBFLA	Studii Biblici Franciscani Liber Annuus
IES	Israel Exploration Society	SH	Studia Hierosolymitana
IG	Inscriptiones Graecae (1873–1891)	ZA	Zeitschrift für Assyriologie
ILN	Illustrated London News	ZDPV	Zeitschrift des deutschen Palästina-Vereins

PREFACE

SINCE NO AUTHOR writes a book by himself, because he is indebted to his many friends and colleagues for their encouragement and academic background, we wish to express our gratitude to all who have helped in this effort. We have been fortunate to be able to rely on the support of a number of scholars for their wisdom and many suggestions, sometimes by way of personal discussions or on-the-spot explorations. In many instances we have depended on their scholarly productions, with the hope that we have done justice, if even in a brief citation. Many of these works are in languages not always accessible to the general reader. In the presentation of Jerusalem of the time of Jesus as we envision it, we have drawn from many sources, sometimes reinterpreting them (we hope we have not misrepresented them), and sometimes forming our own conclusions. If Solomonic decisions had to be made with regard to certain aspects of this study, they were made because of our own personal convictions. Hence, our readers may perhaps discover not only points of disagreement, but perhaps even a stimulus for further research and discussion. We welcome such assistance.

It is quite difficult to acknowledge by name all who have helped in this pursuit. At the head of this litany of names of friends, scholars, and institutions, many sincere thanks are due to Prof. Nachman Avigad, Hebrew University of Jerusalem; Rev. Bellarmino Bagatti, O.F.M., Studium Biblicum Franciscanum, Jerusalem; M. Ben-Dov, Jerusalem Excavations; Rev. Pierre Benoit O.P., École Biblique et Archéologique Française, Jerusalem; Rev. Dr. and Mrs. Robert H. Boyd, Luther Theological Seminary, St. Paul, Minn.; Mr. Magen Broshi, The Shrine of the Book, Jerusalem; the Classical Museum, Istanbul; The Pictorial Archive of Middle Eastern History (especially for the following photographs: 12–13, 24, 26, 29–32, 34, 40, 46–47, 70, 83, 86, 88–90,

95, 97, 99, 102–3, 120, 149, 153), the late Rev. Charles Coüasnon, O.P., Latin architect for restoration of the Church of the Holy Sepulchre; Mr. Ibrahim Dakkak, Engineer, El-Aqsa Restoration Committee, Jerusalem; Miss Dia' Abou-Ghazi, Musée Égyptien, Service des Antiquités, Cairo; The Pontifical Biblical Institute, Jerusalem; Israel Exploration Society and Department of Antiquities; Rev. John R. Lee, C.S.B., St. John Fisher College, Rochester, N.Y.; Miss Mary Joan Madigan; Prof. Benjamin Mazar, Hebrew University of Jerusalem; Capt. Jean-Philippe Ollier, United Nations; Rev. Wolfgang E. Pax, O.F.M., Studium Biblicum Franciscarum, Jerusalem; Rev. Bar-Gil Pixner, O.S.B., Dormition Abbey, Jerusalem; Rev. Raymond V. Schroder, S.J., Loyola University of Chicago; National Aeronautics and Space Administration, Houston; Mr. Hassan Tahboub, Director of the Awqaf Department, Supreme Muslim Council, Jerusalem; the late Rev. Roland de Vaux, O.P., École Biblique, Jerusalem; the Ecumenical Institute for Advanced Theological Research, Jerusalem; Canon John Wilkinson, St. George Anglican Cathedral, Jerusalem; and Prof. Yigael Yadin, Hebrew University of Jerusalem.

Our very special gratitude and indebtedness for their constant assistance in this project we extend to the Very Rev. Paul H. Besanceney, S.J., and Michael J. Lavelle, S.J., Provincial Superiors of the Detroit Province of the Society of Jesus; Mr. Carl A. Klint, for the technical drawings of the maps and plans involved in this undertaking; to the Confraternity of Christian Doctrine, Inc., for the use of the excerpts from the New American Bible; Sr. Mary Demetria Lodge, B.V.M., for her great patience and generosity in typing out the manuscript; and Mr. Marlin J. Van Elderen of Wm. B. Eerdmans Publishing Company, for his special interest in this book.

Finally, this small tribute to Jerusalem would not

have become a reality if it had not been for the interest and support of photographer Mr. Garo Nalbandian. I thank him for his excellent photos, which took him over two years to produce. And I thank him for the many lessons he taught me about the city in which he himself was born.

We began this project at the Ecumenical Institute for Advanced Theological Research in Jerusalem. We consider it fitting that we should have brought it to completion at Loyola University of Chicago on this feast of Our Blessed Lady, Queen of the Society of Jesus.

April 22, 1977   RICHARD M. MACKOWSKI, S.J.

LIST OF MAPS AND FIGURES

LIST OF PLATES

JERUSALEM
City of Jesus

Plate 3 *(facing page) Artist's representation of the Herodian temple, showing the Court of the Women, the Gate of Nicanor, and the Debir or Holy of Holies the entrance to which is flanked by two pink columns, known since Solomonic times as Yakin (left), Boaz (right). This Temple Model, which depicts Jerusalem just before its fall to Titus in A.D. 70, is at the Holy Land Hotel in West Jerusalem. The late Prof. M. Avi-Yonah of the Hebrew University of Jerusalem is responsible for the topographical and archaeological data used in construction of this model.*

Plate 2 *Jerusalem from the Mount of Olives in the springtime. The magnificent golden cupola of the Muslim Dome of the Rock marks the site of the Jewish temple. All of the arrows of history, tradition, and archaeology point to this spot on which Solomon, Zerubbabel, and Herod the Great built splendid sanctuaries to the one true God.*

INTRODUCTION

A strong city have we;
he sets up walls and ramparts to protect us.
Open up the gates to let in a nation that is just,
one that keeps faith.
A nation of firm purpose you keep in peace;
in peace, for its trust in you.

Isa. 26:1–3

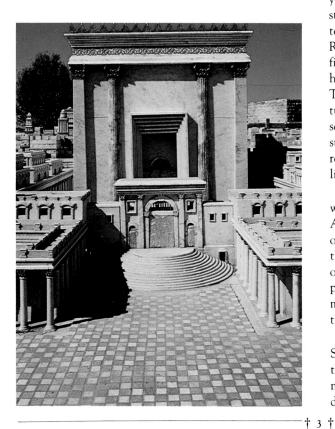

JERUSALEM was an extremely beautiful city in the time of Jesus. It is no wonder, then, that one of Jesus' disciples exclaimed: "Teacher, look at the huge blocks and the enormous buildings!" (Mark 13:1). Clearly, this is a reference to the large Herodian masonry which embellished the temple area, to the Temple of Yahweh itself, and to Herod the Great's own grandiose building program in the City of Jesus.

According to biblical exegetes and historians, the year was A.D. 27. The Temple had been "under construction for forty-six years" (John 2:20). It was the fifteenth year of the reign of Tiberius Caesar as emperor of Rome (Luke 3:1). By now the Temple proper was almost finished. The outer wall enclosing the sacred precinct had already been completed. The acropolis on which the Temple stood must have been a truly magnificent structure. We know this from biblical and extrabiblical sources, and archaeological explorations in the area, studied in the light of the literary sources, assist in a reconstruction of what the Temple must have looked like in the time of Jesus.

Herod the Great beautified the City of the Temple with many other splendid buildings. He rebuilt Fortress Antonia, strategically located in the northeastern corner of the city, to protect his subjects from an attack from the ominous northeast, a weak point in the topography of Jerusalem. In the northwest Herod built his royal palace with its three imposing towers and an adjacent military installation, to provide strong protection from the enemy advancing on the city from this direction.

There were also many other fine buildings in the city. Some had already existed before Herod ascended the throne of Judaea in 37 B.C.; some he rebuilt or remodeled, while some were new additions to the Herodian capital. There was an archives building, a theatre

Plate 4 Reading of the Torah, the Law, at the Western Wall, Judaism's most sacred shrine. The lower courses of Herodian masonry are the only extant remains of the Herodian temple enclosure. According to tradition a white dove representing the Holy Spirit or the Divine Presence is said to hover over the western side of the Temple and to mourn with the wailers. The dew drops on the stones in the morning are said to be the tears of those who weep over the destruction of the Temple. Since the Arab-Israeli war of 1967, many celebrations, such as that pictured here on the Feast of Simhath-Torah, "the rejoicing in the Law," now take place at the Wall. The upper layers of this wall are a mélange of Mamelukan and Turkish masonry, though some authorities also identify early Arabic and Crusader material.

Plate 5 Christians from every corner of the world pilgrimage to Jerusalem to the most sacred church in Christendom, which embraces within its historic walls the scenes of Jesus' crucifixion on Calvary and his glorious resurrection from the garden tomb. Here a Greek Orthodox woman kisses the columns of the main portal of the Church of the Holy Sepulchre.

and a hippodrome, a remodeled Xystos bridge from the Temple to the royal palace on Mt. Zion; and there were public squares, the largest of which was the city square in the Upper City opposite Herod's palace. The Hasmonaean palace, east of the royal residence, had already existed for at least several decades.

The Jerusalem Temple Model on the premises of the Holy Land Hotel in West Jerusalem offers the most splendid picture of what Jerusalem must have looked like in the first century. It illustrates in stone the Holy City towards the end of the Third Temple period, in the years just before Jerusalem was besieged by Titus' armies and finally destroyed in the year A.D. 70, less than a half of a century after Jesus' crucifixion and resurrection there.

Whether studying this model or contemplating

Jerusalem itself from the Mount of Olives, the pilgrim and scholar may recall the eloquent words of the Talmud, which describe Jerusalem as a unique city: "Ten measures of beauty descended from the heavens—nine were taken by Jerusalem and one by the rest of the world" (*Kiddushim* 49b). However, the beauty of the City of the Temple was not only in its physical appearance, hewn out of the royal stone of the area. Jerusalem is a uniquely sacred city. It was sacred to kings David and Solomon and their posterity, because the altar and Temple of God were situated in it. It was sacred to Jesus, who was born into the Davidic family, and to his followers, because Jerusalem is the birthplace of Christianity. From the earliest days of Islam Jerusalem was sacred, because it is connected so intimately with Muhammed's "night journey" to God's temple here.

Thus, today Jerusalem is a particularly holy city to the three great monotheistic religions of the world. It is the center and capital of Judaism. It is the birthplace of Christianity. And it is Islam's third most holy place after Mecca and Medina.

The Western Wall, formerly called the Wailing

Plate 6 *The third most sacred city in Islam, Jerusalem is called el-Quds, The Holy or The Sanctuary, in Arabic. Muslims from all over the world come to the Holy City on the great feast days in Islam. The golden Dome of the* *Rock in the background technically is not a mosque but a shrine. These worshipers are facing south towards the el-Aqsa Mosque, which is oriented towards Mecca and Medinah, the cities of Muhammed's birth and Hegirah.*

Wall, is Judaism's most important and most venerated shrine, surpassing in rank the Zealots' last stronghold at Masada or even the Shrine of the Book which houses the renowned Dead Sea Scrolls.

The Basilica of the Holy Sepulchre preserves the actual sites of Calvary and Jesus' tomb. It is the church par excellence in Christendom, outranking St. Peter's in Rome, the Hagia Sophia in Istanbul, or St. Paul's Cathedral in London.

Dating back to the dawn of Islam in the second half of the seventh century A.D., the inspiring Dome of the Rock stands on the site of Mt. Moriah, where a long tradition locates the would-be sacrifice of Isaac and the mount from which, according to Islamic theology, Muhammed, the messenger of God, ascended into the Seventh Heaven (Koran xvii). Jerusalem is also the scene of the famous el-Aqsa Mosque, the important Islamic house of prayer. Indeed, Jerusalem is called in Arabic el-Quds, the Holy.

No other city can claim such honors. At the sight of Jerusalem the pilgrim experiences the emotions of his predecessors. Christians are reminded of how Jesus wept over Jerusalem, because of the terrible fate the sanctuary would suffer. It would be desecrated and devastated. The Romans would surround it with ramparts and would attack it from almost every side. Jesus foretold this great destruction of Jerusalem: "They will wipe you out... and leave not a stone on a stone within you" (Luke 19:44).

But Jerusalem has always experienced a resurrection. Throughout its almost five thousand years of recorded history, the city suffered approximately ten sieges and sixteen destructions. Since the time of Jesus, Jerusalem was razed completely—by Titus in A.D. 70 and again by Hadrian in A.D. 135. In 1009 Sultan Hakim destroyed all of its churches. Nevertheless, Jerusalem survives today as very much a living and thriving city. It is a busy city, and the constant movement within its ancient fortifications reminds both pilgrim and scholar of the resplendent history to which the stones of Jerusalem give witness.

Plate 7 *Excavations beneath the el-Aqsa Mosque and the Crusader addition (left) have revealed how Jerusalem must have looked after its fall to Rome in A.D. 70. The columns are probably those of the Royal Portico just above the southern temple wall. Visible also are the ancient steps leading up to the (Double) Huldah Gate, whose lintel can be detected in the joint between the southern wall and the Crusader fortress below the silver dome of el-Aqsa.*

Plate 8 *Oldest map of the Holy Land from Madaba (biblical Medeba; Josh. 13:16; 1 Macc. 1:9, 31; Ant. xiii. 254; xiv. 18), a small village east of the Dead Sea. In the early Christian period it was the seat of a bishopric. The pictorial mosaic map was executed in the second half of the sixth century but was not discovered until ca. 1890 when it was almost completely destroyed during the rebuilding of the present church on the site. Nevertheless, it is of unlimited value with regard to the topography and toponomy of the Holy Land. The contours of the land are distinguishable by color: the mountains are in rather dark shades of maroon and red, the valleys in yellow or beige; the rivers and seas are bluish-gray. Jerusalem receives a special place of honor, in a cartouche, which is actually the walls of the city. Most of the Byzantine buildings shown in it are identifiable today.*

CHAPTER 1 GOING UP TO JERUSALEM

We will go up to the house of the Lord.
Ps. 122:1b

The Roads to Jerusalem

JERUSALEM is strategically located in the center of the world. Indeed ancient literary sources often speak of Jerusalem as the "navel of the earth."[1] Some of the earliest maps of the Holy Land, especially the famous Madaba Map of the sixth century A.D., illustrate how true this is.[2]

Throughout the ages Jerusalem has been revered as a uniquely holy city in the minds and hearts of literally thousands of pilgrims who worship the one true God there. For the Jews this God is Yahweh or El, the all-holy one who chose them as his people. It was in his special honor that they built the City of the Temple. For Christians this same God is called Theos or Deus, the one who sent his beloved Son for the redemption and sanctification of mankind. It was to perpetuate the memory of Jesus' preaching, of his passion, death, and crucifixion in Jerusalem, that his followers constructed the most important shrine in Christendom, the Church of the Holy Sepulchre. Muslims call this same God Allah (similar to Hebrew *El*); and it was because of the particular association of Allah and Muhammed that the followers of Islam embellished the Temple Mount with the el-Aqsa Mosque and the glorious Dome of the Rock. To worship in Jerusalem was and still is the goal of these monotheists, written deeply in their thoughts and aspirations. "Next year in Jerusalem," the now-fulfilled desire of the Jews, as they continue in the Diaspora to express this wish during their liturgical Passover meal, could also be uttered by Christians and Muslims alike, because they too are intimately related to the long, sacred history of Jerusalem. No other city in the religious history of mankind can rival the Holy City of Jerusalem!

Jerusalem is also at the center of the physical world from a geographical point-of-view as ancient pilgrims

Plate 9 *At the sound of the shofar or ram's horn, a throng of Jewish pilgrims winds its way across the Valley of Hinnom and up towards Mt. Zion to celebrate the feasts in the City of the Temple. The belfry of the Benedictine Church of the Dormition dominates the scene, which is close to the alleged Tomb of King David. From here the pilgrims continue through the Old City towards the Western Wall of the Temple.*

Figure 1 Azimuthal equidistant projection of the world, centered on Jerusalem, showing thirteen major cities of the world and their true distances to Jerusalem. Every point on the map is a true direction (azimuth) from the center point; such a projection is the only kind that can show the entire world with accurate distances rather than only one hemisphere.
(Courtesy CENTER FOR CARTOGRAPHIC RESEARCH AND SPATIAL ANALYSIS, MICHIGAN STATE UNIVERSITY)

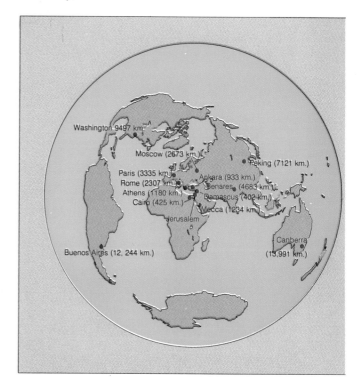

and geographers considered it. Geographically speaking, Jerusalem is located practically in the center of the Holy Land today, as it was in days past, despite the political vicissitudes of the ages. It is strategically positioned in the highlands, lying on the Judaean north-south watershed, on a natural plateau along the trunk road almost midway between the fertile plains of Galilee and the parched desert sands of the Negeb.

For centuries, even prior to recorded history, merchant caravans and invading armies have traversed this important highway through the central mountain range, the backbone of Palestine. This thoroughfare is also known as the historic "route of the patriarchs"—of Abraham, Isaac, and Jacob who, according to biblical accounts, traveled this way.

Ancient towns and cities mark the important trading stations along this caravan route leading to and from Jerusalem. The principal stations on this axis can still be identified, for they played an important role in antiquity. Many are living cities, towns, and villages today, though a few still lie buried beneath centuries of debris.

Ein-gannim, the modern town of Jennin, sixty-nine miles north of Jerusalem, is described in the Bible as "the spring of the gardens," assigned to the northern tribe of Issachar (Josh. 19:21). It was also the city of pasture lands that belonged to the Gershonite clan of Levites (Josh. 21:29). Ibleam (Khirbet Belame) was a Canaanite city, captured in the fifteenth century B.C. by Thutmoses III (1502–1448), no doubt one of the greatest Egyptian Pharaohs. Ibleam lay "in Issachar and in Asher," but it was later awarded to the tribe of Manasseh (Josh. 18:11; 1 Kgs. 9:27). Not far from Ibleam is the well-known site of Dothan (Tell Dothain),[3] situated in the luxuriant valley named after the historic site where Jacob's sons sold their brother Joseph for twenty silver pieces to a caravan of Ishmaelite merchants on their way to Egypt (Gen. 37:25–28).[4]

Turning eastwards for a relatively short distance through the mountain pass between Gerizim, the

mountain of blessings, and Ebal, the mountain of curses (Deut. 11:26–32; Josh. 8:30–35), caravans arrived at Shechem (Tell Shechem-Balatah),[5] forty miles north of Jerusalem. Here in 922 B.C. Solomon's rebellious son Rehoboam addressed the gathered Israelite tribes with such belligerent words that the kingdom split into two separate states, Israel in the north and Judah in the south (1 Kgs. 12:1–20; 1 Chr. 10:1–19). Almost a thousand years later, at Jacob's Well at the eastern end of this pass, Jesus conversed with a woman of Samaria, an event recorded by the Evangelist John (John 4:4–42).

Veering southwards again, the mountain road winds and twists through the picturesque valley of Lebona (Lubban) (Jgs. 21:19) north of Bethel and Ai, two sites mentioned in Joshua's capture of Canaan. However, Ai (et-Tell) did not exist as a city at this time.[6] Bethel (Beitin) was captured.[7] The area is evocative of Abraham's encampment here, and was the scene of the departure between Abraham and Lot (Gen. 13:1–18). A short distance to the south lay Michmash, Wadi Sweinit with the huge rocky crags of Seneh and Bozez inside it, Geba, and Gibeah of Saul. Jonathan's victory over the Philistines here is described in 1 Sam. 14:1–23. On the main road towards Jerusalem stand the modern twin cities of el-Bireh and Ramallah, ten miles

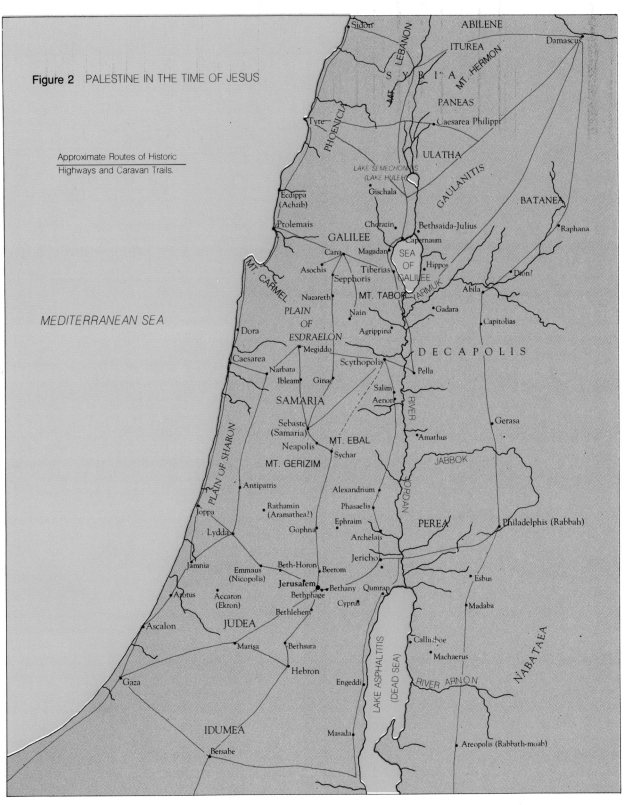

Figure 2   PALESTINE IN THE TIME OF JESUS

Approximate Routes of Historic
Highways and Caravan Trails.

from the Holy City. El-Bireh is identified by some as the Beeroth of the Gibeonite Confederacy, along with Chephirah, Gibeon, and Kiriath-yearim (Josh. 9:17).[8] It is also the traditional scene where Mary and Joseph noticed that the young Jesus was not in their midst after their pilgrimage to Jerusalem (Luke 2:41–47). Between el-Bireh–Ramallah and Jerusalem, only five miles north of Jerusalem, is another famous biblical city—Gibeon (el-Jib), over which "the sun stood still" while Joshua was fighting the Gibeonites (Josh. 10:1–6, 12–13). The deep pool of Gibeon[9] reminds one of Jeremiah's description of the "great waters of Gibeon" (Jer. 41:12). Most of these places were resettled by the Jews after their return from captivity in Babylon from 587 to 537. By the first century B.C. they were thriving cities, especially during the reign of Herod the Great (37–4 B.C.) and his successors until about A.D. 39. These, then, are the important cities, the great market towns or caravan stops, leading to Jerusalem from the north.

From Jerusalem southbound lay Bethlehem of Judah, Hebron of Caleb, and Beer-Sheba in the territory of Simeon. Bethlehem (Beit el-Lahami), which really means the "House of Laham," a Canaanite divinity (rather than the traditional "House of Bread"), is the home of David's royal family (1 Sam. 16:1–4). Here the young shepherd was anointed king of Israel (1 Sam. 16:3, 11–13). Another king of Israel was to be born in this city of David, of the same stock and of the same family. Around the year 6 B.C. Jesus of Nazareth was born in Bethlehem of Judaea, as this province was called after Pompey's conquest of Palestine in 63 B.C.

The distance from Bethlehem to Hebron is only about seventeen miles. The scenery along this road differs little from the scenery described in the hills of Ephraim and Samaria. However, there are fewer ample valleys in this part of the country, unlike the valleys of Dothan, Shechem, and Lebona. Nor are there as many important biblical sites along this southern portion of the route of the patriarchs as between Jennin and Jerusalem. Off this main road, however, situated in the eastern Judaean desert, looms the impressive site of the Herodium (Gebel Furdeis, "Paradise Mount"), which Herod the Great built commemorating his victory over the Parthians in 42 B.C., and which was intended as his

Plate 10 *Space photo of the lands of the Bible, with kind permission of the National Aeronautics & Space Administration, Houston. I am indebted to my cousin Dr. Theresa Krolikowski who obtained this rare photo. One is reminded of the wanderings of the patriarchs, the journey of Mary and Joseph, and the Nabataean trade routes which probably formed the background of the Matthaean account of the adoration of the Magi, of Jesus' ministry in Galilee and Judaea with Jerusalem as his goal, and of the spread of Christianity. Today the movement is back to Jerusalem!*

mausoleum, sixty stadia or roughly fifteen miles southeast from Jerusalem (*BJ* i. 265, 419, 673; xvii. 193–99).[10]

Hebron, which derives its name from Hebrew ḥaber, "friend," justifiably merits this name, for it is the place where Abraham, God's friend, is buried in the Cave of Machpelah, which he purchased for a family tomb from Ephron the Hittite for four hundred silver shekels (Gen. 23:10–17). The modern Arabic name is el-Khalil, which also means "the friend." The Arabs also revere Abraham and the other patriarchs and their wives once interred beneath the present Ibrahimi Mosque, the Mosque of Abraham, over the site of the Cave of Machpelah.[11]

Thirty-one miles farther is Beer-Sheba, another city associated with the patriarchs, in the rugged southern part of the land, the Negeb.

If, in general, armies descended upon Jerusalem from

the north, traders for the most part approached from the south, especially during Solomon's reign and in the time of Jesus. Traveling along the same patriarchal route from south to north towards the Holy City, we can vividly envision long, rich caravans of the wealthy Nabataean merchants from Southern Arabia. Historians agree that these Arab peoples formed one of the greatest civilizations in the ancient Near East, from at least the early second century B.C. to the reign of the Roman Emperor Trajan (A.D. 98–117).[12] These extremely gifted people built great cities in the desert. Archaeological explorations have revealed such magnificent sites as Nitzana (Nessana, identified with Auga el-Hafir),[13] Shivta (Subeita),[14] Avdat (Eboda),[15] and Mampsis (Kurnub).[16] Mampsis commanded perhaps the most important road junction in the Negeb leading north towards Jerusalem from Ezion-Geber (Eilath), approximately 142 miles south, and from the beautiful "rose city" of Petra, the Nabataean capital, west across the desert towards Beer-Sheba in the Negeb and Gaza on the Mediterranean. Within their vast empire the Nabataean Arabs proved themselves to be engineers, artists, agriculturists, scientists, astrologers, merchants, and traders dealing in rich perfumes, oils, wines, exotic spices, expensive oriental silks, as well as gold, frankincense, and myrrh, exported from the distant east. It must be against this background that Matt. 2:1–12 describes the adoration of the Magi.

The roads up to Jerusalem from either the east or the west were neither as direct nor as convenient as the main highway from the north to the south. The ascent from the Jordan Valley to Jerusalem was perhaps a bit more traversable than the steep ravines from the Mediterranean Sea to the capital of Judaea. Nevertheless, these two approaches to the Holy City are also historical.

From Nabataea and Edom farther to the southeast, oriental traders would have made their first important stop across the Jordan at Jericho (Tell es-Sultan, modern er-Riha),[17] reputed to be one of the world's oldest cities. Jericho is situated in the deep Jordan Valley, less than five miles northwest of the Dead Sea, and approximately twenty-one miles from Jerusalem. But the climb from Jericho to Jerusalem in this comparatively short space is

almost 4,000 feet. At Jericho camel caravans would then begin this steep ascent through the biblical pass known as Ma'ale-adummim (Josh. 15:7; 18:17), the so-called Ascent of Blood, Qa'alat ed-Damm in Arabic, derived from the red-colored ferriferous rock in this region. (Another possible derivation is from the road's ultimate destination, Edom, whose root means "red" in Semitic languages.) The modern highway follows almost exactly the course of the ancient road, which winds through precipitous Wadi el-Qelt, the biblical demarcation line between the territories of Benjamin in the north and Judah to the south. The modern name, the Ascent of Blood, suggests the frequent bloody raids by bandits along ancient roads; indeed, a long Christian tradition places Jesus' parable of the Good Samaritan (Luke 10:25–37) on just such a road. Today, pilgrims and tourists are shown the "Good Samaritan Inn," the Khan el-Hadrur (from the root meaning "caution"), about ten miles east of Jerusalem. From this point upwards the road to Jerusalem becomes comparatively easy, for Senonian chalk, the predominant geological composition here, is not as rough and craggy.

In the time of Jesus thousands of Jewish pilgrims from Perea, Decapolis, and Galilee would have come up to Jerusalem along this ancient road to celebrate the three great pilgrim feasts of Passover, Pentecost, and Tabernacles in the City of the Temple. Jesus, too, would have followed the same itinerary at times.

Actually, there were two approaches to Jerusalem from the west, but they were far more difficult than that from the east. Caravans and armies could make the climb from the Mediterranean coastal plain, then through the lowlands, the biblical Shephelah, and choose either the Shorek Valley (Wadi es-Surar) or the more famous, though more arduous, pass of Beth-Horon just above the plain of Ajalon. Both approaches directed the trader, traveler, soldier, or pilgrim to the Holy City from Joppa, Jerusalem's main port along the Mediterranean shoreline (2 Chr. 2:15; Ezr. 3:7; 1 Macc. 10:75; Acts 9:36–42; 10:7–22).

The road through the pass of Beth-Horon (Josh. 10:10), probably meaning the "House of [the god] Hurun," continues to the present in the names of two small villages situated on the hilltops along this historic pass: Beit-ʿUr et-Taḥta preserves the name of Lower Beth-Horon (Arabic *taḥt,* "Lower"); Beit-ʿUr el-Foqa perpetuates the name of Upper Beth-Horon (Arabic *foqa,* "upper"). Lower and Upper Beth-Horon were points on the boundary between the clans of Benjamin in the south and Ephraim in the north (Josh. 16:3, 5; 18:13). The pass of Beth-Horon also led up to Jerusalem through Gibeon. *Ca.* 918 B.C., in the fifth year of Rehoboam's reign of Judah from his capital in Jerusalem, the Egyptian Pharaoh Sheshonk (biblical Shishak) (955–914) of the Twenty-second Dynasty passed through on his way to Jerusalem; Beth-Horon appears on the Karnak list of Palestinian cities conquered by Shishak.[18] Just over two hundred years later the Assyrian monarch Sennacherib, who had established headquarters at Lachish in the Shephelah, strongly guarded this vital pass. Eventually, Jerusalem was forced to capitulate to Sennacherib in the early seventh century B.C., probably during the reign of Ethiopian Taharqa, Pharaoh of Egypt from 690–664, during the Twenty-fifth (Nubian) Dynasty. However, the second pass to Jerusalem is perhaps the more famous.

The Ark of the Covenant, which the Philistines placed on a cart drawn by cattle, passed through the steep ascent of the Vale of Shorek, leading upwards to Kiriath-Yearim (modern Abu Ghosh), which the Crusaders identified with New Testament Emmaus (Luke 24:13),[19] and still higher up towards the Mountain of God (Nebi Samwil), which geographers identify as the high place of Gibeon (1 Sam. 6:7–21). Nebi Samwil is also referred to as the Mountain of Joy (Mons Gaudii or Mont Joie of the Crusader period), for from its summit a panoramic view of the Holy City of Jerusalem could first be clearly seen by pilgrims. In August 1523, Iñigo of Loyola (later known as Ignatius), a Basque soldier turned Christian pilgrim, reports that two miles before reaching Jerusalem, a Spanish nobleman named Diego Manes encouraged the group of pilgrims that, since in a short while they would come to this inspiring point, it would be helpful for all to prepare their consciences and then continue to walk to Jerusalem in silence.[20] Such were also the traditions and spirits of the ancient pilgrims of both Old and New Testaments.

To summarize, the course of the principal north-

Plate 11 *Ark of the Covenant, as depicted in the synagogue at Capernaum. The synagogue is dated to at least the middle part of the fourth century A.D.; the synagogue school belongs to the fifth century. This fine piece of workmanship reminds us of the Old Testament passages 1 Sam. 4:1–11; 5:1–6:18; 2 Sam. 6:1–17.*

south road across the hill country of Palestine is certain. It followed the lines of the watershed from Galilee, through Samaria and Judaea, then down to the Negeb. The present road, whose lines are dictated by the same geographical contours, preserves the direction of this ancient trade route. Though there exists no concrete evidence of a paved road along this important highway, the towns and villages, the former caravan stations located along this route, are proof enough that an important thoroughfare existed here in ancient times, as it does in the present.

The west-east and east-west approaches to Jerusalem are also neatly established by sufficient material evidence. For example, some sections of an ancient Roman road can still be discerned along the west-east stretch from the coastal plain through Beth-Horon to Jerusalem. One such segment is clearly visible at Beit-ʿUr et-Taḥta; and another, perhaps a longer and more evident branch, appears closer to Jerusalem, a short distance east of el-Jib, Old Testament Gibeon. This section of the ancient road joins the modern highway at this juncture. It is the Via Romana traveled by Peter and Paul on their way to

Plate 12 Jerusalem from the south, from Gebel Mukabber (from Arabic kabir, "great," sometimes rendered Telescope Mount). Muslims explain that it was from this mountain that Omar Ibn el-Khattab exclaimed "God is great!" when he first beheld the city at his feet. The superb view from this place shows the deep Kidron Valley with Siloam village on its right and the traditional site of Haceldama to the left. The Lower and Upper cities are clearly distinguishable: Ophel, the original Jebusite and Davidic town, is on the right; Mt. Zion is the higher part of the city on the left. Visible also are a large segment of the southern wall and the two domes dominating the Haram esh-Sharif. The Jerusalem promontory is not very high nor even very large; yet, all must "go up" to the House of the Lord.

or from Lydda, Joppa, Caesarea, and Ptolemais (Acts 9:32–43; 10:1–48; 11:1–18; 21:8–25; 23:23–27:2). The Roman legions, after the fall of Jerusalem in A.D. 70, would have carried the spoils of war—the menorah or seven-branch candelabra and the altar of shewbread, as depicted on the Arch of Titus in the Imperial Forum (Pl. 152) at Rome—along this road from Jerusalem to Caesarea (BJ vi. 260, 271, 287–391, 403–8; vii. 63–74). This triumphal display took place in the spring of A.D. 71.

The east-west stretch preserves a few sections of the Roman road from Jericho to Jerusalem, along the Wadi el-Qelt. Concrete evidence is still visible on the eastern flank of the Mount of Olives and some other sections not far from Khan el-Hadrur, the traditional Inn of the Good Samaritan. We would locate the scene of Luke 2:44 along this road, because of the danger (political and religious) of traveling through "hostile" Samaritan territory. Moreover, the former Turkish road here, used until the period of the British Mandate over Palestine, follows the course of the preceding Crusader and Byzantine approaches to Jerusalem. Jesus would have traveled this road on his way up to the City of the Temple.

Songs of joy, the inspiring Psalms of Ascent (Pss. 120–134), were echoed by the pilgrims: "Mountains are round about Jerusalem; so the Lord is round about his people both now and forever"(125:2); "I lift up my eyes towards the mountains" (121:1); "I rejoiced because they said to me, we will go to the house of the Lord" (122:1). And again, "Lift up your hands toward the sanctuary, and bless the Lord" (134:2), because "we have set foot within your gates, O Jerusalem—Jerusalem, built as a city with compact unity!" (122:2–3).

Plate 13 *Jerusalem from the northeast. Surrounded by hills, the Jerusalem promontory is separated from these heights by two rather steep ravines: the Kidron Valley (left) and the southern portion of the Valley of Hinnom (above), south of the southern ramparts of the Old City. The Tyropoeon Valley which cuts through the walled city (from north to south) can be vividly traced from the Damascus Gate in the north wall in a southeasterly direction towards the Temple Mount on which stand today the golden Dome of the Rock and silver dome of the el-Aqsa Mosque. The Lower City lies to the left of the Tyropoeon Valley; the Upper City is to the right. Notice the flat plain north of the city walls, an excellent place for an invading army's encampment. Mt. Scopus, from which the enemy would descend upon the City of the Temple, is still farther north.*

The Geology of the Holy City

MUCH OF THE BEAUTY of Jerusalem can be attributed to its majestic hills and picturesque valleys. Nature
herself offers an internal, deeper reason why these hills
and valleys have taken on the shapes and forms they
have displayed from the timeless epochs of God's crea-
tive activity until the present. Thus, a study of the geology of Jerusalem, a survey analysis of the various rock
formations and their natural composition, is important
and even quite fascinating.

A study of geological formations will help to explain
in a remarkable manner both the topography, the
natural contours of Jerusalem's terrain, and its effect on
the way of life of the people in the Holy City.

The rather low plateau on which the city sits was
formed some 36 to 135 million years ago. These geological epochs are called the Cenozoic and Mesozoic
periods, known also as part of the Eocene and Creta-
ceous periods. They followed the settling of the Nubian
sandstone—now only evident in the rock formations on
the eastern plateau of Transjordan—and preceded the
Senonian chalk deposits, which form the rolling lowlands on either side of the central limestone ridge of
Palestine. But Cenomanian limestone is the foundation
of the entire east Judaean desert, and is the principal
geological material from which Jerusalem itself is
formed.

Essentially of calcium carbonate, the limestone of the
Holy Land is of two types: Cenomanian and Turonian.
Cenomanian is hard and quite capable of withstanding
erosion. It is composed mainly of dolomite and "indus-
trial" limestone mixed with some chalk. Difficult to
quarry, it is not usually employed as ordinary building
material. Indeed, only a few good quarries of this kind of
limestone exist in modern West Jerusalem. In Arabic,
Cenomanian limestone is called *mizzi aḥmar* and *mizzi
yehudi*—"red" and "Jewish" *mizzi*, respectively.

Turonian limestone, though also quite durable, is
made up of various strata or layers and, therefore, easier
to extract from its natural rocky source. It is generally
well aerated, especially when exposed to the circulation
of air, and in this way it also becomes purer and harder
stone, which is much more useful for building purposes.

*If they were to keep silence,
I tell you the very stones would cry out!*

Luke 19:40

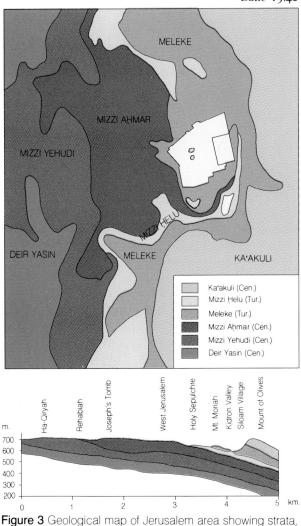

Figure 3 Geological map of Jerusalem area showing strata,
deposits, and contours of Jerusalem's terrain.

Because of the stratification in Turonian limestone dikes, this type of stone sustains moisture much more readily. Water sources originate in Turonian limestone layers, as do the Spring of Gihon and Ein-Rogel, just southeast of Jerusalem, and at Beit-Safafa southwest of the city.

The comparatively thin layers of Turonian limestone are technically called in Arabic *mizzi ḥelu* and *meleke*: *mizzi ḥelu* connotes "sweet," while *meleke* signifies "royal" stone. *Meleke* is the principal building material in Jerusalem. It was used for the city walls, the many public buildings and, appropriately, the Temple.

The entire Old City, furthermore, is one large Turonian limestone dike, running from north to south. Meleke is especially abundant in the Sidqiyahu Cave, the so-called Cave of Zedekiah or Solomon's Quarries, beneath the northeastern section of the Bethesda quarter. However, it is quarried in only very limited areas in West Jerusalem: in the Yemin-Moshe quarter opposite Mt. Zion, and the Sanhedria compound, northwest of the present walled city. A section of the Hill of Ghareb was also used as a quarry around the sixth and fifth centuries B.C.

The mixture of hard and soft geological ingredients in the Cenomanian and Turonian limestones explains the geological orientation of Jerusalem. It is why the entire Old City slopes from *ca.* 2587 feet in the northwest corner near the New Gate on the Hill of Ghareb, down to 2441 feet at the point called Mt. Moriah, from which there is a rather sudden southward decline to 2000 feet near Ein-Rogel. This is clearly why there is an "Upper" and a "Lower" city of Jerusalem. It also accounts for the valleys that were formed around and within it.

On the western side, upon which the Upper City is located, some of the hard Cenomanian and softer Turonian limestones split apart to form the Valley of Hinnom, stretching west-northwest, and running in a southerly direction beneath the present sixteenth-century ramparts of the Old City, then turning rather sharply eastwards and terminating at the spring Ein-Rogel. When split apart, these two kinds of limestones usually cause fairly deep gorges, as noticeable in the southeastern part of Ge-Hinnom in the craggy cliffs just below Abu-Thori.

On the east, where the Lower City is situated, hard

***Plate 14** Jerusalem is a city set on a hill; in fact, it is also surrounded by hills. Still, Jerusalem cannot be obscured, for "a city set on a hill cannot be hidden," Jesus told his listeners in the Sermon on the Mount (Matt. 5:14b). This picture shows a house not only set on rock but also solidly built of the same substance. It is a rather recent structure, but the walls built on the limestone rock belong to the sixteenth century, to Suleiman the Magnificent who built Jerusalem's defense system ca. 1538, as the inscription at the Jaffa Gate indicates. The picture also illustrates the strata or layers that are characteristic of Turonian limestone. Beneath these structures are the so-called Solomon's Quarries, though we do not think that they should be looked for in the subterranean passages below, but in the area (through which the modern Sultan Suleiman Street passes) between this artificially cut rocky spur of Bethesda and its counterpart (opposite it to the north) which forms a part of Gordon's Calvary and the traditional site of Jeremiah's Grotto.*

Turonian and rather soft Senonian chalk broke off to form the deep Kidron Valley. During this geological movement of some fifty to seventy million years ago, the entire promontory of the Old City was cut apart again, almost exactly from north to south, to form the Tyropoeon Valley, and from east to west to form the Transversal Valley from approximately the area of the Jaffa Gate down to the Tyropoeon itself. Likewise, the Salahiye Valley on Bethesda Hill is oriented northwest to southeast, beginning near the northeast extension of

Plate 15 *Excavations in the Holy City have intensified since the 1967 Arab-Israeli war. Shown here are the lower courses of stonework of a huge complex of palatial buildings of the Omayyad Caliphate of the seventh and eighth centuries A.D. The spring of Robinson's Arch can be seen jutting out of the Western Wall; the arch formed a part of a monumental stairway described by Josephus (Ant. xv. 410). Subsequent excavations revealed Christian, Byzantine, and Herodian material.*

the Tyropoeon and ending abruptly at St. Stephen's Gate, then dropping precipitously into the Kidron below.

Eastwards, across the Kidron Valley stands the Mount of Olives, an elevation that is geologically entirely different from the plateau on the west, across the Valley of Hinnom. The Mount of Olives is approximately 250 feet higher than the Moriah peak in the Old City. Its slope betrays its own geological composition, which is Cenomanian chalk (Arabic *Ka'akuli*). Standing on the top of the Mount of Olives and looking eastwards towards the Judaean desert below, one can easily discern the Senonian chalk hills as they swiftly fall down towards the Jordan Valley only some 21 miles to the east. Although these hills are round and gentle, the fall is quite precipitous. From 2691 feet above sea level the rocky terrain declines to 1291 feet below sea level at the Dead Sea, which is itself 1300 feet deep in its deepest northern half.

The lower slopes of the Mount of Olives are of Turonian limestone. Nary stone also forms the top of the adjacent Mt. Scopus. The limited presence of this type of stone naturally accounts for the "saddle" between the two mountains—which are, in fact, only one single range—between the Augusta Victoria Hospital on Mt. Scopus and the Greek Orthodox Patriarch's residence at Viri Galilaei on the Mount of Olives.

From a geological point-of-view, it is easy to understand why Jerusalem is further subdivided into four geographical sectors, according to the peaks of its hills: (a) the Ophel-Moriah spur in the southeast, separated from (b), the Bethesda hill by the shallower transversal valley on the northeast, separated from (c) Mt. Zion on the southwest, separated from (d), the Hill of Ghareb on the northwest by the Transversal Valley that runs between these two heights.

This geologico-geographical description further explains why Jerusalem is a naturally defensible fortress on the southeast; and it provides at least one reason why its

Plate 16 *Ripe olive berries. The olive tree (Olea europea, but probably indigenous to western Asia) is an evergreen that grows profusely throughout the Mediterranean area. In Palestine it is the most common and highly prized tree, which flourishes particularly in the rocky hill country from Samaria to Hebron. Although a cultivated olive tree may grow for about 1500 years, it is doubtful that these in Gethsemani survive from the time of Jesus. The ripened berries are harvested towards the end of November. They are edible and can be pressed for their rich oil which is used for many purposes, such as the anointing of a priest or king, for fuel and light, for medicine and massaging. From the gnarled trunk sprout numerous branches, which not only provide a certain amount of shade, but are used, like the palm branch and willow, for the roofs of the booths on the Feast of Tabernacles. The wood, whose grain forms a marblelike pattern, was and still is used in carpentry since it is very durable. The olive tree was a symbol of divine blessing, of strength and prosperity.*

Plate 17 *The olive blossom is practically microscopic and cannot be seen unless the branch is closely examined. (Photo by Mrs. J. Rose of the Ecumenical Institute for Advanced Theological Research, Tantur).*

earliest settlement began here. On the other hand, Jerusalem was open to an invasion from the north, as the prophets continually warned.

Jerusalem was not only founded upon a rock—the Turonian limestone described above—but its citizens' dwellings were also made from the same material, as was God's dwelling place among men. From ancient times until the present, Jerusalemites built their defense walls, their private homes and public buildings, their palaces, many shrines, and their great Temple, from the very substance upon which the city was built. Furthermore, the fertile soil in the valleys that surround it originates in the eroding process of the Cenomanian and Turonian limestone hills and cliffs around it. During the rainy season these rich deposits are washed down into the valleys around the Holy City.

In some parts of ancient Palestine the conditions were very much like those in Egypt and Mesopotamia. The Philistine coastal plain and the Jordan Valley are for the most part sandy regions, though the sand along the Philistine coast comes from Egypt, and the soil of the Jordan Valley is primarily alluvial deposits, originating from distant geological periods. Thus, sun-dried or

Plate 18 The large, thick leaves of the fig tree provide shade during the hot summer months. The early or green fig, which ripens before the appearance of its leaves, is picked in the spring, in June; it is especially sweet and juicy and is preferred over the later, purplish fig, which matures from late August until early winter. Native to Asia Minor and Syria, the fig is believed to have been introduced to Palestine at a very early date.

baked brick was the common building substance. Stone had to be quarried and transported with great difficulty.

But Jerusalem, like the rest of the hill country that forms the rocky limestone backbone of Palestine, is different. Archaeological excavations in and around the city have exhumed city walls, gates and towers, houses, and sacred shrines, all made of blocks of quite sizeable limestone rock. The walls of the Jebusite-Davidic Jerusalem were built of stones. The palace-fortresses of Herod the Great were constructed of huge ashlars of meleke Turonian limestone. The magnificent temples of Solomon, Zerubbabel, and Herod the Great were of the same royal stone.

Jerusalem had an ample water-supply in the southeast corner where the city began. The rich springs Gihon and Rogel, originating in the Turonian limestone strata, furnished enough water in this rather limited region through its very earliest prehistorical and historical stages. Later, as the city expanded, the growing population was forced to dig out immense public reservoirs, most of which are still visible today, and private cisterns to collect and store rainwater to provide this precious commodity particularly during the hot, dry season from the end of May until mid-October. While many private citizens hewed out their own cisterns in the natural limestone pavement of the small courtyards in their homes, wealthy rulers such as Simon the Hasmonaean and Herod the Great carved out very large reservoirs strategically placed in the more ample depressions of the

valleys of Jerusalem. The Pool of Siloam is naturally located in the Tyropoeon Valley in the southeastern part of the city, and the Sheep Pool and Pool of Israel are the natural product of the Wadi es-Salahiye in the northeastern sector called Bethesda. The Tower Pool is located very conveniently in the lower slope of Ghareb.

As for the flora of Jerusalem, the principal plants in the vicinity in biblical times must have been the olive and fig trees. An abundance of beautiful olive groves graced the western slopes of Mt. Olivet to the east of the city, hence its name. The geological composition of Turonian rock and nary stone, which erodes to form an excellent type of soil, is very conducive to the cultivation of olive trees. Though the climate in Jerusalem during the summer months may be extremely hot and dry, Turonian limestone preserves moisture very well. The olive flourishes in such geological and climatic conditions.

The olive would not have survived long on the eastern slopes of Mt. Olivet, for they are composed of an almost entirely different type of geological material. The Senonian chalk of which this flank is formed is neither firm nor does it hold water long enough, and it thus would neither encourage nor promote such plantations. In fact, as one descends the Mount of Olives eastwards into the Judaean wilderness, one immediately notices how the verdure almost abruptly disappears. A few pines and mimosas grow near Ein-el-haud, the traditional Spring of the Apostles near Jerusalem, but this is principally because of a limestone dike running through the region. By and large, the Senonian chalk hills east of the Holy City are barren. Only during the heavy rainy season from November to April do the undulating hills here take on a particular beauty, for the scrub and some wild

Plate 19 *The fertile bed of the Kidron Valley contrasts with the hills of Jerusalem above. Looking west, the hill on the left is Abu-Thori, the traditional Mount of Evil Counsel where the Jews met to plot Jesus' arrest. Haceldama is just below to the right. The silver dome of el-Aqsa (right) overlooks the Ophel spur south of the Haram enclosure.*

desert flowers burgeon only at this time. The same hills and valleys here are unbelievably parched and dry during the long summer season, and thus one can appreciate what the Palestinian desert is really like. Indeed, Zion (*sion,* from *ṣiyyen,* "to point out"), according to some interpretations, "points out" the difference between the desert and the sown.[1]

As for the fig tree, figs flourish in almost every part of the Holy Land, today as in ancient times, particularly in the stony regions of the hill country. Two types of figs are found: the early, green fig and the late fig, which is red or dark purple. Though the fruit of both is delicious, the "early fig" is much sweeter (Mic. 7:1; Nah. 3:12). Fig trees are sometimes planted in the gardens of the homes inside the city, but they grow in abundance in the lower part of the Kidron Valley just below Ophel. Wild figs like the olive used to form a part of the landscape of Jerusalem in general.

The Kidron Valley is exceptionally fertile, and many different kinds of trees, fruits, and vegetables thrive there. Besides olives and figs, there are also date palms, almonds, pomegranates, artichokes, and roses. Naturally, the waters of Ein-Gihon and Ein-Rogel contribute to the area's richness. No wonder, then, biblical scholars identify this region as the possible site of Solomon's royal gardens located just outside the "gate between the two walls" (2 Kgs. 25:4; cf. Jer. 39:4; 52:7).

Finally, Jerusalem's geological environment was a determining factor in the manner in which its people buried their dead. Unlike the residents of the coastal plain or the Jordan Valley who interred their dead in the sandy soil, the people of Jerusalem and other mountainous regions of Palestine buried their deceased in natural caves or sepulchres hewn out of the rock. The recently-discovered tombs cut in the side of the hill at Gebel Qaʿaqir, *ca.* 10 miles west of Hebron,[2] clearly illustrate this manner of burial during the Patriarchal or Middle Bronze Age in Palestine.[3] The custom continued into Hellenistic and Roman times, as shown at Beit-Guvrin (biblical Maresha or Marissa, Roman Eleutheropolis) and Masada. At Jerusalem, rock-hewn tombs were used by the Jebusites of the second millennium B.C.; David, Solomon, and the kings of Judah were interred in similar tombs in the City of David; and Jesus himself was laid to rest in just such a tomb.

As can be seen from this brief study, the Holy City of Jerusalem was not only built upon rock, but was entirely constructed of stone. This rock defined much of its people's way of life and determined much of the city's history.

Plate 20 *Ancient tombs cut into the rock on Ophel. The large tomb on the left is commonly called the Tomb of David.*

Plate 21 *Rock-hewn tombs along the western slope of the Tyropoeon Valley from the period of the later kings of Judah. These sepulchres were empty, for skeletons were removed from a burial ground when parts of the city were extended for public use. The tombs probably belonged to an upper class, perhaps officials.*

Plate 22 *Jerusalem panorama from the south. At the center is Ein-Rogel, where the Hinnom, Tyropoeon, and Kidron valleys meet. To the right is the Ophel-Moriah spur, site of the City of David and the Temple Mount. Mt. Zion and the Upper City are in the distance to the left.*

CHAPTER **11**

THE TOPOGRAPHY OF JERUSALEM

His Foundation upon the holy mountains the Lord loves.

Ps. 87:1

Plate 23 *Shepherd and flock on Gebel Mukabber, the highest point south of Jerusalem. From its southern slopes Bethlehem can also be seen.*

The Hills of Jerusalem

JERUSALEM is one of the five main basins formed by the main watershed route, which the patriarchs must have followed in their migrations from the north, southwards towards Hebron and on to Beer-sheba. In the vicinity of Jerusalem this watershed originates at Mt. Scopus and runs through the Sanhedriyeh Quarter, southwards through modern Romemah, Mahaneh Yehudah, and the Terra Sancta College at the Place de France, and then continues towards the YMCA just above the Valley of Ge-Hinnom. Its course continues toward Gebel Mukabber, directly opposite Jerusalem in the south, and finally to Ramat-Rachel, less than 3 miles south of Jerusalem.

An excellent view of the topography of this area is offered from the vicinity of Har-Giloh in the southwest, along whose eastern slopes the village of Beit-Jalah is located (incorrectly identified with Gallim of Judah, 1.5 miles west of Bethlehem). The view of Jerusalem from here is impressive—comparable only to that beheld from Nebi Samwil to the northwest of the Holy City. From here can be appreciated Jerusalem's much gifted position, which has enhanced its political, economic, and religious importance.

From a strategic and military point of view, Jerusalem is a natural fortress situated in a fairly small region between the mountains of Hebron and the hills of Bethel, despite being *ca.* 1050 feet lower in altitude. (Hebron and Bethel are approximately 3500 feet above sea level.) The Temple Mount is *ca.* 2441 feet above sea level. The Holy Sepulchre is approximately 2477; the area of the New Gate, the highest point of the walled Old City today, is 2587 feet above sea level.

The naturally defensible position of this elongated

promontory, the Mountain of the Lord, made Jerusalem a genuine stronghold since earliest times. "His holy mountain, fairest of heights, is the joy of all the earth" (Ps. 48:2). Here also lies the full meaning of the Psalmist's song "Mountains are round about Jerusalem; so the Lord is round about his people, both now and forever" (Ps. 125:2).

The prophet Isaiah speaks of Jerusalem as "a quiet abode," a city of peace (Isa. 33:20), but the strategic position and the character of the city itself compelled its inhabitants to transform it also into a veritable fortress. Its position on a caravan trail and military route invited attack, particularly from the north, where there were no steep ravines to protect it, and from the east and west, where important trade routes regularly passed. From Jerusalem to Jaffa (biblical Joppa), the ancient port of Jerusalem, is a distance of not more than 38 miles; and Jerusalem is only 21 miles northeast of the Dead Sea. It is *ca.* 130 miles from Dan in the north to Jerusalem, and 53 miles from the Holy City to Beer-Sheba in the south.

From the mountains directly above the Holy

Plate 24 *Spur of Ophel, seen from the southwest, running southwards from the Temple Mount (Haram esh-Sharif) and separated from the hills around it by the Kidron and the Tyropoeon (left). The Valley of Hinnom (Gehenna) can also be detected between the Upper City and the Hill of Evil Counsel (left). The three valleys meet near Ein-Rogel (lower right). Mt. Scopus is clearly visible in the background.*

Plate 25 *(right) Ophel, represented on the Jerusalem Temple Model. The city is entirely surrounded by a wall; the course of the western segment has not been determined (if, indeed, there was a wall along this ridge during the Third Temple period). Within the City of David are the Synagogue of the Freedmen and the palaces of the royal family of Adiabene. The southern wall of the Temple and the Huldah Gates are above. (This model has been modified since the excavations along the southern wall of the Haram.)*

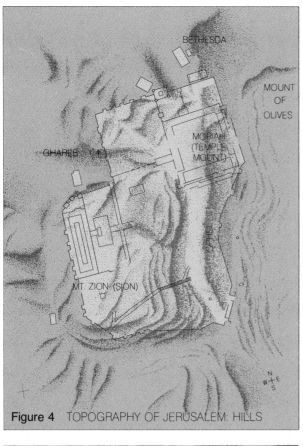

Figure 4 TOPOGRAPHY OF JERUSALEM: HILLS

City—Mt. Scopus in the north, the Mount of Olives to the east, or Gebel Mukabber, directly to the south—one notices that Jerusalem is a single large promontory separated from the surrounding mountains by two rather steep valleys on the east and west. These two valleys converge to form a triangle at the southeastern corner of the city.

Why did Jerusalem grow from a tiny spur on the southeast end of the promontory in David's time to a large walled city in the New Testament period[1]—to an even larger city today? For at least four and a half millennia Jerusalem was constantly inhabited, despite many sieges, plunderings, and almost complete devastation. The large promontory of approximately 250 acres that comprises the walled-in city today is not just a flat plateau. The city proper, like the mountains around it, is also made up of various degrees of elevation: Mt. Ophel, in the southeast, is just over 2000 feet above sea level; Mt. Moriah, actually the northern extension of Ophel, measures approximately 2441 feet; and Bethesda, the northeastern suburb above the Ophel-Moriah spur, is 2527 feet above sea level. Mt. Zion, which dominates the southwestern sector of Jerusalem, rises to a height of 2550 feet; and Mt. Ghareb, according to our interpretation of Jer. 31:39 the highest point within the Old City walls, climbs to an altitude of 2587 feet. The area around the Holy Sepulchre Church is approximately 2477 feet high; it is a part of the southeastern slope of the Hill of Ghareb.

Each of these hills or "mountains" of Jerusalem has its own special historical and biblical importance. Let us now consider them in the light of their Old Testament background and subsequent history in relation to the City of Jesus during the Third Temple period.

Ophel means a "mound" or "hill" in Hebrew (from the Semitic root ʿ-ph-l, "to swell"), but denoting a "fortified hill" or a "city," thus an acropolis or the highest point of the city. Jerusalem is itself situated on a high place. Technically speaking, Ophel Hill forms only the southeastern spur of the Jerusalem promontory, south of the sixteenth-century walled town. Ophlas was the name by which the first-century Jewish historian Flavius Josephus (*ca.* A.D. 38–100) knew this quarter of Jerusalem (*BJ* v. 145). Because of its position, protected

by the deep valleys on either side plus its natural water source in Spring Gihon, the Ophel was the original site of the Jebusite and later Davidic city from about the twelfth to tenth centuries B.C. But historical records prove that Jerusalem had been known as a town or city much earlier. A recently-discovered cuneiform tablet from the great city of Ebla[2] south of Aleppo in northern Syria bears the name Urusalim, along with such other biblical sites as Hazor, Megiddo, and Gaza. This tablet dates to the third millennium B.C., which makes it contemporary with the age of the pyramids in Egypt. The name Jerusalem also appears in Egyptian hieroglyphic writing in the Execration Texts of *ca.* 2000 B.C. ( ),[3] transliterated *Urusalim.* A third reference to the city occurs in the Assyrian cuneiform tablets of the Amarna correspondence (*ca.* 1350 B.C.), during the important Eighteenth Dynasty of Egypt. The Assyrian text reads *Urusalimmu* ( ).[4] From its earliest recorded history, therefore, Jerusalem or Jebus, as the city was named by some of its earliest known inhabitants, was a Canaanite stronghold built on a physi-

Plate 26 *Northern portion of the Ophel-Moriah spur, site of the ancient Lower City.*

Plate 27 *Theodotus Inscription of the second or third century A.D., discovered on Ophel in 1914. Our translation reads: "Theodotus Vettanos [or, son of Vettanos], priest and synagogue leader, son of a synagogue leader and grandson of a leader of a synagogue, built [restored?] this synagogue for the purpose of the reading of the Law and for the instruction of the commandments of the Law, the hostel and guest rooms, and the baths [ritual baths?] for foreigners who need them. This synagogue was established by his forefathers, the elders and Simonides." (Israel Exploration Society)*

Plate 28 *Bethesda hill in the northeast quarter of the Old City, from the Lutheran tower of the Erlöserkirche in the Muristan Quarter. Notice the sloping of the Bethesda hill (from north [left] to south [right]), as it drops towards the Arab Omariyyeh School overlooking the northern area of the Haram esh-Sharif. The tall minaret in the center stands in the vicinity of the school, the Convent of the Sisters of Sion, and, a little farther to the east, the site of St. Anne's Church where the remains of the Sheep Pool and Asclepieion were discovered.*

cally defensible mound. From this tiny spur both its physical growth and historical fame expanded to make it one of the greatest cities in the world.

In the time of Jesus the Ophlas-Ophel quarter was where the poorer and more conservative Jews had their homes, shops, synagogues, and gardens. This would have been the quarter of Jerusalem which Jesus entered on his triumphal Messianic entry into the City of David, riding through the steep walls of the Kidron Valley towards the southern city gate. The large crowds followed him through the ancient Casemate-wall Gate, popularly called "the gate between the two walls." This was the most convenient opening in the city's ramparts at this juncture, and the road through it led directly upwards toward the Temple Mount in the northern sector just above Ophel. It is also likely that this road passed by the royal palaces of Queen Helena and her household,[5] for the Adiabene family customarily built their palaces in the popular quarter of Jerusalem. Close by must have been the Synagogue of the Freedmen (Acts 6:9), built by the descendants of the Jews taken captive to Rome by Pompey in 63 B.C., who themselves now held Roman

citizenship. A few years after Jesus' death, some members of this synagogue engaged Stephen in a heated debate concerning observance of the Mosaic Law and the role of the Temple in Judaism and Christianity (Acts 6:8–7:53). Stephen would later become the first to sacrifice his life for the new faith.

Archaeologists, digging in the southern part of Ophel *ca.* 1914,[6] uncovered foundations of a building which they believe to have belonged to the Synagogue of the Freedmen. In a cistern nearby, the same team of archaeologists discovered a limestone inscription in Greek, the only relic of the many synagogues built in Jerusalem before the fall of the city to Rome in A.D. 70. Whether this inscription belonged to the same synagogue recorded in Acts 6:9 is still conjectural, though there is nothing to disprove it.

Moriah is the traditional name for the upper section of the Ophel spur. According to tradition, Moriah was the place where Abraham was to sacrifice his son Isaac. As recorded in Gen. 22:1–19, Abraham was told by God to go to "the land of Moriah" in order to offer his son to God. The author gives the following popular explanation for the name of the site: "Abraham named the site *'Yahweh yir'eh*' [meaning "God will see"]: hence people now say, 'On the mountain the Lord will see,'" (Gen. 22:14). The grammatical form of the Hebrew verb (*ra'ah,* "to see") is difficult, if not impossible, to parse.

Mt. Moriah is also the site of the threshing floor which David purchased from Araunah the Jebusite (2 Sam. 24:16) for his altar. It is the site David showed his son Solomon for the construction of the first temple of Yahweh in Jerusalem (2 Chr. 3:1). Solomon's temple lasted on this spot until its destruction by Nebuchadnezzar in 587 B.C. Zerubbabel built the second temple on this site, and it lasted until the first century B.C., when Herod the Great *ca.* 20/19 B.C. decided to raze it and built another, much more splendid temple on the exact site.

Bethesda is the name of both the hill and quarter in the northeastern corner of Jerusalem. In Aramaic the word means "House of Mercy" (Hebrew *Beth-hesed;* Greek *Bethsatha, Bezetha, Bezetho,* etc., but the correct transcription should be *Bethesda*).[7] In the first century,

Plate 29 *Jerusalem from the southwest. In the foreground can be seen Mt. Zion and the entire Upper City. The west and south branches of the Hinnom Valley are just below Mt. Zion. The Tyropoeon Valley, running from the northwest towards the southeast, separates the Lower City from the Upper. The mountains in the background are the Scopus and Olivet range, including the mountains in the territory of Benjamin. One need only study the contours and the ridge of Mt. Zion to trace the city walls of first-century Jerusalem and to locate the Armenian compound, where stood Herod's palace, later occupied by the Roman procurators and known as the Praetorium.*

as mentioned by Josephus (*BJ* v. 151–52), this quarter of the city was also known as *Kainopolis* or "New City." It was not yet enclosed within the city walls during the time of Jesus, though there must have been some dwellings and religious structures here at the time. Bethesda or *Kainopolis* was not incorporated into the city proper until the building of the "third wall" under Herod Agrippa I (41–44), about a decade or so after the crucifixion of Jesus. Bethesda, which was separated from Fortress Antonia and the Temple by a transversal valley and moat (*BJ* v. 149) running roughly from east to west, was the scene of John 5:1–13, where Jesus is described as having cured a paralytic at the shrine of the healing cult (see Chapter 5—Reservoirs).

Zion, or Mt. Zion, originally referred to the entire ancient city of Jerusalem, as it does again in modern times, though the city has greatly expanded in recent decades. Zion was the city of cities, the one "pointed out" (*ṣiyyen*) to the Hebrews, located on a hill separating the desert from the sown.[8] Others derive the name from Hebrew *ṣāyôn*, "parched ground" or a "dry place," following the interpretation of the word in Isa. 25:5; 32:2; Arabic *ṣāhweh* and *ṣāhyun* (*ṣihyûn*), "hillcrest" or "mountain ridge," also point to some kind of "dry or parched land" (cf. Syriac *ṣehyûn*). It has also been suggested that Zion be derived from Hurrian *ṣeya*, "brook" or "river," in which case the phrase "the stronghold of Zion" in 2 Sam. 5:7 would be identified with the City of David, and would point to the Jebusite stronghold situated above the brook Kidron in the region of Spring Gihon. Interestingly enough, this is the first biblical reference to the capture of Jerusalem by David (2 Sam. 5:6–10; 1 Chr. 11:4–9).

Mt. Zion today means only the southwestern spur of the Jerusalem promontory. This name erroneously—or perhaps by extension—was probably bestowed in the first century A.D. or later in the Byzantine period, by people who equated the Upper City with the stronghold captured by David, thinking that the southwestern hill of Jerusalem had indeed been the former Jebusite city. Josephus reports (*BJ* v. 137) that the hill on which the Upper City was located was much higher and had a flatter ridge, and so, owing to its strength, was named by King David "the Stronghold" (*phrouríon*).

Mt. Zion today contains many sacred shrines and historical sites which help in reconstructing that part of the Herodian city during the time of Jesus. The Citadel, for instance, marks the site of the three great Herodian towers and the barracks of the praetorian guard stationed here to protect the city from an attack from the northwest. The modern Armenian Orthodox Seminary is built over the site of Herod's palace, the Praetorium of the Gospels. St. James' Cathedral, also of the Armenian Orthodox Patriarchate, and the Armenian compound around it mark the site of the "upper agora" or the public square of first-century Jerusalem. These important sites

Plate 30 *Christian Quarter of the Old City on Mt. Ghareb. Included are the Church of the Holy Sepulchre (two domes) and the Lutheran Erlöserkirche (white tower). North (left) of the Holy Sepulchre is the Mosque el-Khanqeh near the site of the palace of the Catholic Patriarchate of the twelfth- and thirteenth-century Latin Kingdom of Jerusalem; south of the Basilica is the mosque of Caliph Omar.*

are contained within the sixteenth-century walled city of Suleiman the Magnificent. Outside these ramparts, to the south, are the Dormition Church and Abbey of the Benedictine monks of Cologne, the Franciscan chapel Ad Coenaculum adjacent to it, with the so-called room of the Last Supper and the traditional Tomb of David below it, the Greek Orthodox Seminary, the American School of Holy Land Studies, and the Protestant cemetery, whose gravestones are in themselves an impressive record of the important persons who lived and died in and for the Holy Land.

In the time of Jesus and up to the destruction of Jerusalem by the Romans, the city was divided by the Tyropoeon Valley into the Lower and the Upper City. There was occupation in the southeastern part of the city, within the Tyropoeon Valley, and on Mt. Zion. These parts were surrounded by city walls, as was also the temple area north of Ophel. However, there was only sparse occupation north of the walls, and practically none on the northwestern hill.

The northwestern hill of Jerusalem, occupied today by the Christian Quarter of the Old City, lay outside the city's defenses in the Old and New Testament periods. Its name, Ghareb, is based on a reference in Jer. 31:39, though the part intended was probably situated slightly lower than the entire extent of the quarter today. The name Ghareb, rendered also Gareb by assonance,[9] is derived from the Semitic root meaning "west." (The root is contained in the name of the Western Wall [*ha-Kotel ha-Magharabi*], the Wailing Wall of the Jews, and the western portal of the Dome of the Rock [*el-Bab el-Gharbi*], both of which face directly west.) This is the highest area of Jerusalem today, measuring 2587 feet above sea level in the vicinity of the New Gate (Bab Abdoul Hamid), which was opened only in 1889. Ghareb as such is not mentioned by Josephus. According to the

historian it is simply included in the "range" of the Upper City.[10] Josephus indicates that it was the scene of fierce fighting for Jerusalem on the part of the Tenth Roman Legion *Fretensis* stationed in the neighborhood of the Tower Pool (Amygdalon, from Hebrew *migdal*), which lay at its base.[11] (This pool is identified with the Birket el-Hamman el-Batrak, or the pool of the Patriarch's Bath, located on a southwest to northeast line between the Jaffa Gate and the Church of the Holy Sepulchre.) Ghareb was the site of a Jewish burial ground during the Third Temple period, as the rock-hewn tombs beneath the foundations of the Holy Sepulchre Church attest.

These, then, are the hills that form the topography of Jerusalem as known by Jesus in the first century. But Jerusalem is also a city surrounded by rather imposing eminences, particularly on the north, east, and south. (The rather high plateau on the west side, across the Valley of Hinnom, had no special significance at this time. It therefore lies outside the scope of this particular work.)

Mt. Scopus is the eminence that dominates the Holy City in the north. Its name is derived from the Greek verb *skópein*, meaning to "look out," or to "see," in the sense of "survey." Josephus indicates that it was named Mt. Scopus because both "Jerusalem and the Temple could be seen from this point" (*Ant.* xi. 329).[12] Indeed, Jerusalem was most vulnerable from the north, and throughout its entire history the city had always been besieged from the north. (The tunnel through which David's general Joab accomplished the capture of the Jebusite stronghold [2 Sam. 5:8] was a part of the Gihon Spring system which then lay in the northeastern part of the fortress on Ophel.) As the highest point in the proximity of Jerusalem in the north, Mt. Scopus served as the lookout from which subsequent armies advanced upon

Plate 31 *Ascension Mosque on the Mount of Olives, dating to the second half of the fourth century. Although it was transformed into a mosque in 1187, Christians of the different rites may celebrate their liturgies on their respective feasts of the Ascension inside the aedicule as well as within the sacred enclosure. It is said that the footprints of Jesus are still visible in the rock inside the small chapel.*

the city (for example, Nebuchadnezzar of Babylon in 587 B.C.; Titus of Rome in A.D. 70; Geoffrey de Bouillon, leader of the First Crusade, in 1099; and the Israeli Moshe Dayan in 1967). Because of its height and its strategic position over Jerusalem, Mt. Scopus is called in Arabic *Masharif*, which means "eminences," and *Har-ha-Tzophim*, the "mountain of scouts," in Hebrew.

The Mount of Olives is the height east of the Old City. Geographically as well as geologically, it is a part of the Mt. Scopus range, separated from it by a slight depression between the Augusta Victoria Hospital, considered to be on Mt. Scopus, and the Greek Orthodox Patriarch's residence on the site of the traditional Viri Galilaei ("men of Galilee," Acts 1:11) on the Mount of Olives. Mt. Olivet, as it is also called, is certainly the most beautiful of all the hills that surround Jerusalem. Ezekiel wrote that "the glory of the Lord rose from the city and took a stand on the mountain which is east of the city" (11:23). The Mount of Olives has always played an important role in the history of Jerusalem, especially from the biblical point of view. This was the scene of the sacrifice of the "red heifer," mentioned in Num. 19:1–22,[13] as well as the mountain from which Jesus ascended into heaven (Acts 1:6–12; cf. Luke 24:50–52).[14] In both Jewish and Christian traditions, the Mount of Olives is the mountain most associated with resurrections (Zech. 14:4–6), hence the

Plate 32 *Aerial view of the Mount of Olives, from above the Russian Garden of Gethsemani (onion-shaped domes in lower left). Between the Russian Church of the Ascension (tall steeple in center) and Gethsemani can also be seen the small mosque of the Ascension, the Discalced Carmelite Monastery, and the Church of the Pater Noster ("Our Father"). Lower down the slope is the little shrine of Dominus Flevit ("the Lord wept" [over Jerusalem]; see Luke 19:41–42). The Dead Sea, some 1291 feet below sea level, is visible above.*

Jewish cemetery situated on its western slope facing the Temple Mount, and the site of the former Christian Church of the Ascension, built by Pomenia in 387 but converted into a Muslim shrine since the conquest of Salah ed-Din in 1187.[15] The Mount of Olives was the place from which fire signals were sent up to announce the beginning of the New Year and other Jewish feasts (Mishnah *Rosh ha-Shanah* ii. 2).

The name Olivet points to the abundance of

Plate 33 *Greek Orthodox monastery of St. Onophrius, a great Egyptian Anchorite of the fourth or fifth centuries, near the traditional Akeldama. Jerome seems to have been the first to locate Akeldama here, though Eusebius sought the spot someplace to the north of Jerusalem. It lay directly opposite the Potsherd Gate at the southern tip of Ophel. Gehenna, identified with the valley shown here, was used as a burial ground, and it is said that excellent potter's clay could be found in this particular section of the hill across the Hinnom Valley.*

luxuriant olive trees that flourished on its western slope, as well as to the olive industry in the area of Gethsemani (meaning "olive press" in Hebrew), the garden of olive trees where, according to the longest and strongest tradition, Jesus spent the night in prayer before Judas the Sicarius and his band of conspirators arrested Jesus on the night before his trial, passion, and crucifixion (Mark 14:43–52; Matt. 26:47–56; Luke 22:47–53; John 18:1–14).

Opposite the southern flank of the Mount of Olives, across the modern Jerusalem-Jericho highway that leads down to the Pass of Maʿale-adummim is a rather small round hill known in Arabic as Ras el-ʿAmud. Pilgrims since the Crusader period of the twelfth and thirteenth centuries have called it the Mount of Scandal, for here Solomon was to have erected shrines in honor of the pagan divinities worshiped by his multiracial harem. Because of its rounded shape and windy area the local Arab population sometimes refers to this mount as Beten el-Hawa, the "Belly of the Winds." On its western side, facing the hill of Ophel, is nestled the old Arab village of Silwan, which takes it name from the nearby Pool of Siloam (Old Testament Shiloah; Isa. 8:6). Many of the villagers here have used for their homes the ancient tombs which have been there since the biblical period.[16]

A small oratory marks the alleged tomb of Isaiah on the property of the Franciscan Custody of the Holy Land, though there is no absolute evidence for the site.

Directly south of Jerusalem is another very large mountain, called Gebel el-Mukabber or "telescope mountain" in Arabic because it offers one of the most comprehensive panoramas of the Holy City from this direction. This mountain gradually slopes down towards where the Kidron and Hinnom valleys meet in the vicinity of the Spring of Rogel, modern Bir-ʿAyyub or "Well of Job." The lower slope of Gebel el-Mukabber opposite Mt. Zion is also known as the Mount of Evil Counsel,[17] traditional site of the villa of the high priest Caiaphas. However, Christian tradition points more specifically to the village of Abu-Thori, on the northern slope of Gebel el-Mukabber south of Mt. Zion. On the summit of Gebel el-Mukabber today is situated Government House, the headquarters of the United Nations in the Middle East.

Walking in a southeasterly direction from Abu-Thori along the slope of Gebel el-Mukabber towards Ein-Rogel, one arrives at the traditional location of the biblical potter's field (Matt. 27:7), a cemetery for the burial of foreigners, which the chief priests purchased with the betrayal money Judas returned to them. As a result of this shameful transaction, the field was renamed Akeldama (English Haceldama), the Field of Blood. A tradition based on the biblical account also points to Haceldama as the place where Judas later hanged himself. Save for the isolated monastery of St. Onophrius, this lower slope remains quite barren even today. The evil reputation of this field was probably inherited from the ancient child sacrifices to the Ammonite divinity Molek in Topheth practiced here by the Israelites, but condemned in Lev. 20:2 (see also 1 Sam. 15:23; 2 Kgs. 23:24).

As mentioned above, the large flat plateau in West Jerusalem, as it is known today, does not figure in this present study, for it is mentioned in neither Old nor New Testament records. It is today, as in antiquity, entirely different (geologically, geographically, and sociologically) from the eastern, more ancient, and most biblical part of Jerusalem. Some traditions, however, locate the tomb of Herod the Great's family on the side of the hill across the Hinnom Valley opposite Mt. Zion.[18]

The Valleys of the Holy City

THE CONTOURS OF JERUSALEM are such that the valleys within and around the city form an essential and distinctive geographical feature. The principal valleys that separate the Jerusalem promontory from the surrounding hills are the Kidron on the east and the Hinnom on the west and south. Within the city itself the Tyropoeon Valley separates the Lower, older part of Jerusalem from the Upper City, which was occupied much later.

In addition to the Tyropoeon, two smaller, much shallower valleys are located on the Jerusalem promontory itself, branching off, as it were, from the Tyropoeon Valley. These may be described as the "transversal" valleys of Jerusalem, rather imperceptibly dividing the city into four main quarters, according to the various heights discussed above. The first transversal valley originates in the southeastern part of the Tyropoeon and runs in a northwesterly direction, separating Mt. Zion in the south from Ghareb in the north. The Wadi es-Salahiye divides Mt. Moriah from the hill of Bethesda in the northeastern quarter of Jerusalem, running in a northwest-southeast course.

The Valley of the Rephaim, southwest of the city, plays a rather important role in the history of Jerusalem, but it did not form a part of the city itself until recently in the twentieth century. According to Josh. 15:8, this valley functioned as the border between the territories of Benjamin in the north and Judah in the south. In the tenth century B.C., it was the scene of David's great victory over the advancing armies of the Philistines (2 Sam. 5:17–40). One Christian tradition identifies this valley with the desert route taken by Philip the deacon on his way to preach the Good News at Gaza and Azotus and as far north as Caesarea. According to this tradition, the baptism of the eunuch of Candace (Acts 8:26–40) took place at Bettir[1] situated in this valley. Another Christian tradition points to Ein-Dirweh, on the Jerusalem-Hebron road, as the place of this event. Neither site can be established with any degree of certainty.

Most important of all the valleys in or around Jerusalem is the Kidron Valley. Though not the most

I will assemble all nations and bring them down to the Valley of Jehoshaphat.

Joel 4:2

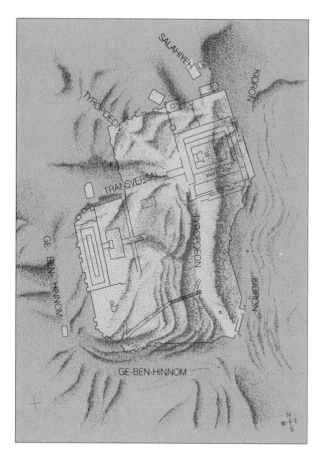

Figure 5 TOPOGRAPHY OF JERUSALEM: VALLEYS

Plate 34 *Kidron Valley or the Wadi en-Nar from the southeast, looking towards Jerusalem (above). The valley winds through the east Judaean desert for some twenty miles towards the Dead Sea.*

served as Jerusalem's burial ground from time immemorial.[2] According to Jewish, Christian, and Muslim traditions, the Last Judgment will take place here, so the Kidron Valley is also called the Valley of Jehoshaphat, from Hebrew *Yehoshaphet* (*Yahweh hashshophet*), meaning "Yahweh (God) is Judge." All three faiths honor deceased members of the family by interment in this valley, following the tradition that this is to be the first place where God will judge souls at the end of time. This name for the valley probably goes back only to about the fifth century A.D.

Most impressive of the tombs hewn out of the rocky cliffs of this valley are the four family sepulchres which date back to the Hellenistic period of the third and second centuries B.C.[3] History does not record whose sepulchres these actually were. The first (beginning in the south) is locally called in Arabic Qaber Jose Fira'on, the tomb of Pharaoh's wife, but is also known as the Pyramid of Zechariah (Zachary). According to Jewish interpretation, this cubical monolith is the tomb of the prophet Zechariah mentioned in 2 Chr. 24:20; but Christian tradition, dating back to the patristic exegesis of Matt. 23:34–35, identifies this tomb with Zachary, father of John the Baptizer, who was supposedly assassinated in the Temple between the altar and the Holy of Holies. Next is the so-called tomb of St. James the Less. Because of its shape the local population calls it Diwan Fira'on or the Pharaoh's Divan; but the Hebrew inscription on the cornice of the Doric architrave indicates that it belonged to the Jewish family of the Bnei Hezir, the "sons of Hezir," who are sometimes identified with the Hezir mentioned in 1 Chr. 24:15; Neh. 10:21. A sixth-century Christian tradition contends that the apostle James hid himself in this tomb from the time of Jesus' arrest until his resurrection. A fifteenth-century source adds that St. James the Less was buried in this tomb. According to the Copper Scroll from Qumran,[4] a treasure was supposedly buried beneath this tomb; excavations undertaken in 1960 exhumed no such treasure.

frequently mentioned in the Bible, it is very much an essential part of the city's history, particularly because of its depth, which helped in the defense of the city, and the location in it of Spring Gihon, which provided water for the Jebusite stronghold and the City of David.

The Kidron Valley separates the hill on which Jerusalem stands from the Mount of Olives east of the city. The name (Hebrew *Qidron*) is probably derived from the Semitic root *q-d-r* denoting something "dark" or "gloomy," as well as "to mourn," suggesting that the valley received its name from the many rock-hewn sepulchres in the area. The Kidron Valley may have

Ancient and modern tombs in the Kidron Valley below the Mount of Olives.

Plate 35 *(right) The Monolith of Siloam, thought by many to be among the most ancient tombs in the region, is located higher up the slope in Siloam village.*

✛ ────────────────────────────── ✛

Plate 36 *Four impressive tombs cut into the limestone hillside below Gethsemani: (from right) the Pyramid of Zechariah, perhaps resembling the tomb of Jesus; traditional tomb of St. James the Less; Absalom's Tomb; and (behind, not clearly visible) the multichambered tomb of Jehoshaphat. Along the western flank of the Mount of Olives (above) is a sizeable Jewish cemetery; originally an ancient necropolis, it contains several recent burials. The burial plot enclosed by the wall of the shrine of Dominus Flevit (upper left) belonged to a primitive Judaeo-Christian community.*

The tomb of Absalom is the most beautiful of the four monuments. Called the Pharaoh's Crown or Mitre (*Ṭanṭur Firaʿon*) in Arabic, it is a huge square monolith with Egyptian and Graeco-Roman architectural designs, crowned by a tall tiara, resembling the kind worn by the Pharaohs of Egypt. The Jews refer to it as Absalom's Pillar (cf. 2 Sam. 18:18). In memory of the disobedient Absalom it formerly was customary for Jews to cast stones against this monument. Behind this tomb is the traditional tomb of Jehoshaphat, carved into the rock of the hill, with an entrance on the left. Jehoshaphat was not buried here, but the sepulchre derives its popular name from the valley in which it is located. For many decades this funerary chamber served as a Genizah in which the worn-out scrolls of the Law were deposited. Like many other tombs in this area, it too served as a type of monastic cell during the fourth century A.D. for monks who wished to practice their special type of desert asceticism as close to Jerusalem as possible.

In the time of Jesus these were some of the most beautiful sepulchres in the vicinity of Jerusalem. They were whitewashed, like all other Jewish tombs in antiquity. Not only did the whitewash add to their beauty, but it made the tombs visible in the dark so Jewish passers-by would not become ritually contaminated by contact with the dead.[5] On at least one occasion Jesus excoriated the Pharisees and the scribes for their hypocrisy, calling them "whitewashed sepulchres that are beautiful on the outside, but their interior is filled with dead men's bones" (Matt. 23:27–28).

The Kidron Valley is not only the deepest but also the longest valley of Jerusalem. The accumulation of debris in the Kidron since ancient times measures some 50 to 100 feet; its real depth, therefore, is not easily perceptible now. Its length extends not only from the northernmost corner of the city down to the city's southern extremity at Ophel, but it continues its winding course down through the Judaean hills towards the Dead Sea for some twenty-one miles. In the vicinity of Jerusalem Kidron is only the beginning of the long depression through the Judaean desert called Wadi en-Nar, the Valley of Fire, where since the Byzantine period thousands of monks have built monasteries and lauras, some of which are still in use today.

The Kidron Valley is sometimes rendered by translators of the Bible as the brook Kidron, though it is really no more than a seasonal stream (wadi) flowing alongside Jerusalem down towards the Dead Sea. Its waters are no longer visible in the neighborhood of Jerusalem since they are now channeled through a conduit beneath the present road.

The Valley-of-the-Son-of-Hinnom borders Jerusalem on the west. Its full Hebrew name, Gey-Ben-Hinnom, probably identifies the original Jebusite owner of the property. The abbreviated name Gehenna undoubtedly deserved its evil reputation from the valley's location outside the bounds of the city, which served as a place of debris, fire, and smoke. Hence, Jesus' many references to Gehenna as the place of unquenchable fire, the pit into which evil men will be cast, and the place of weeping and the gnashing of teeth, where the bodies and souls of the wicked will be destroyed, make sense in this context.[6] The Valley of Hinnom was also a burial place in the Old Testament period; several Jewish tombs of the late First Temple period were discovered in 1975 during the widening of the stretch of the Jerusalem-Hebron road just below Mt. Zion. These rock-hewn tombs were undisturbed when opened, and contained many important finds including skeletons, pottery, and other artifacts,[7] which indicated that this place was used as a

Plate 37 *Whitewashed tomb in the Arab village of Kefar-Harris, a few miles south of Nablus in Samaria. Jewish and Islamic tradition associates this tomb with Joshua son of Nun.*

Plate 38 *"Valley of the Son of Hinnom," which borders Jerusalem on the west, southwest, and south. The modern road parallels the valley as it winds around Mt. Zion (right). The traditional site of Haceldama, the Field of Blood, is to the left. The fertile area below is near Ein-Rogel, where the three principal valleys of Jerusalem meet—the Kidron, the Tyropoeon, and the Hinnom.*

Jewish cemetery, probably by the refugees from Samaria who settled on the western spur of the Upper City during the Assyrian siege of Samaria from 725 to 721.[8] Not far from these tombs lay Birket es-Sultan, the Sultan's Pool, called Lacus Germanicus, the Lake of Germain, in the Crusader period; in the first century it was named the Serpent's Pool. Today the Valley of Hinnom is called in Arabic Wadi er-Rababeh, from the shepherds who played their rababeh, a one-stringed instrument resembling a fiddle, while keeping watch over their flocks along the slopes of this valley.

The Tyropoeon Valley is the most important valley within the city of Jerusalem. It bisects the Old City from north to south (running northwest to southeast), and thus separates the narrow Lower City on the east from the much larger and higher Upper City on the west. It is unlikely, as some think, that the Tyropoeon Valley was called Ge-hinnom in the sixth century B.C. during the time of Jeremiah. The site of the infamous sanctuary of Topheth, where Jeremiah accuses Jerusalemites of sacrificing infants to Molek, must be sought directly opposite the city in the south, on the traditional location of Haceldama. Also, in the light of recent archaeological discovery, the western hill had already been occupied and perhaps even fortified to some degree as early as the eighth century B.C., more than a century before Jeremiah. If the city were actually fortified at this point, then a gate in the city's wall here corresponding to the Gate of Hinnom must be taken for granted.

Within the Old City today, el-Wad or the Valley Street follows the contours of the ancient Tyropoeon, a name interpreted by Josephus to mean the "valley of the cheesemakers" (*BJ* v. 136, 140), though this philological interpretation we think can be reinterpreted. If the name is derived from the Hebrew root *t-r-ph*, meaning to "tear" or to "rend," then the Tyropoeon Valley is the one that "tore" or divided the city into two parts. However, we suggest that the Greek name Tyro-poion, which indeed means "cheesemakers" (an occupation or trade about which we know nothing in the ancient city) was an unconscious blending of philological assimilation

Plate 39 *The modern Arabic name of the Hinnon Valley, Wadi er-Rababeh, is adopted from the name of this oriental one-stringed musical instrument called a rababeh. Shepherds played this "fiddle" while pasturing their flocks along the hillsides of this valley.*

and conceptual accommodation of Hebrew *teraphim*, "idols." (The Greek diphthong "oi" [*oi*] was actually pronounced "i" as in "machine.") Many ancient roads, gates, and other sites took their names from their destinations or that which was close by. Hence, the valley of the *teraphim* was the valley that pointed in the direction of the idols at the end of it, namely the site of Topheth near the high place upon which Solomon had built shrines of pagan divinities for his non-Jewish wives. The Hebrew form in *teraphim* can be explained as a "plural of majesty" with special reference to the Ammonite Molek, derived from *melek*, signifying "king."[9] While the Jewish city grew, it is quite inconceivable that its population would have enclosed the heinous site of

Plate 40 *Jerusalem from the northwest, with the Tyropoeon Valley dividing the Holy City into two main parts. It runs southeastwards from the vicinity of the Damascus Gate in the present northern wall. The Lower City (left) embraces Bethesda, Moriah, and Ophel; the Upper City embraces the Church of the Holy Sepulchre on Ghareb and the place of the Cenacle and David's Tomb on Mt. Zion. The point where the Tyropoeon meets the Kidron and Hinnom ravines can also be detected south of the walls of the Old City.*

Topheth within the city walls. (This would be another reason for not identifying the Tyropoeon with the Gehinnom of Jeremiah, as shown above.) Finally, Greek *tyropoión* would have been less offensive to the sensitivities of the more orthodox Jews in Jerusalem than *teraphim.*

Wadi es-Salahiye, derived from *Salah,* the name of the great conqueror of Jerusalem Salah ed-Din (Saladin), is situated in the northeastern quarter of the city. Its natural course begins in the northwest in the region of the Tyropoeon Valley and leads southeastwards across the place of the Sheep Pool down towards where Birket Israïn once was, then drops rather abruptly into the Kidron Valley at St. Stephen's Gate. A slight trace of this valley can be detected in Tariq el-Mojahidin and the first part of the Via Dolorosa. Its contours are also noticeable following Bab el-Hutta Street from Herod's Gate down towards the open area of the Birket Israïn. In this natural depression, in the first centuries before and after Christ, were situated three huge reservoirs for collecting the rainwaters that ran down this decline: the Sheep Pool and the Pool of Israel in the east, and the double Strouthion Pool slightly towards the west. In the time of Jesus this part of Jerusalem was actually outside the ramparts of the city.

The so-called Transversal Valley is the designation of the east-west depression that originates in the Tyropoeon, following more or less the course of today's Chain Street (Tariq Bab es-Silsileh) and David Street, leading in the direction of the present Jaffa Gate. Most biblical scholars agree that these two streets also represent the line of the first north wall of Jerusalem, beginning at the Jaffa Gate and running in a fairly straight line towards the Gate of the Chain of the Haram esh-Sharif. The natural depression formed by this valley is more clearly discernible from a distance. The Transversal Valley is slightly deeper than the Salahiye in the northeastern section of the city. It neatly distinguishes the Hill of Ghareb from Mt. Zion. The ancient Tower Pool, the Amygdalon of Josephus (*BJ* v. 468) and identified with the Birket el-Batrak here, is located in this natural depression.

Plate 41 Northern ramparts of the Old City today, constructed by Suleiman the Magnificent in 1538–39. These walls, according to the most accepted theory today, follow the lines of the ancient third north wall of Jerusalem, described by the Jewish historian Flavius Josephus. Archaeological exca- vations at the Damascus Gate here have yielded material evidence of a first-century gate on this site, employed by Hadrian as the main northern portal of his Aelia Capitolina. The Hadrianic defenses followed those built by Agrippa I about a decade after Jesus' death and resurrection in A.D. 30.

CHAPTER **III** W̄ALLS OF THE HOLY CITY

The wall of the city had twelve courses of stones as its foundation, on which were written the names of the twelve apostles of the Lamb.

Rev. 21:14

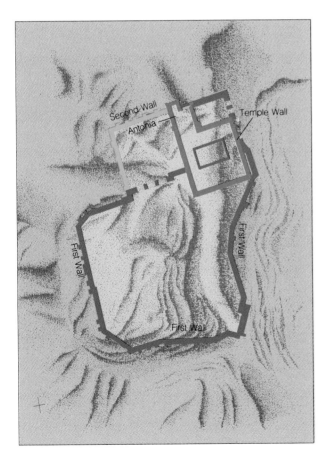

Figure 6   THE WALLS OF THE HOLY CITY

JERUSALEM was a veritable fortress in the time of Jesus. The first-century Herodian city was surrounded by massive ramparts that crowned the high rock on which it was built. The eschatological city is described as a royal diadem. "The wall was constructed of jasper; the city was of pure gold, crystal clear," wrote the author of the book of Revelation in the first century A.D. "The foundations of the city wall were ornate with precious stones" (Rev. 21:18–19).

Jerusalem could also boast of its famous gates. Its well-built entranceways were strategically placed—in time of peace, where its inhabitants, pilgrims, and merchants could live, worship, and buy and sell; in time of war, when the gates were closed and sentinels stationed on their lookout towers, to guard the people against attack. Each gate had its special name that reminded both inhabitants and visitors of Jerusalem's glorious history.

Two huge fortress towers protected the city in the northeast and the northwest. From here the entire countryside could be surveyed, thus insuring peace within the walls of Jerusalem. The Holy City was, in the fullest sense, the Lord's own vineyard, so lovingly did he care for it and protect it (Isa. 5:1–2; see Mark 12:1; Matt. 21:33).

There was an abundance of water in Jerusalem, so precious a commodity in a hot, dry climate on the border of the desert, but especially in time of siege. Indeed, Jerusalem knew very well what war really meant. In its long history it was always forced to defend itself and to build strong defense walls around itself.

The exact lines of the walls of Jerusalem are one of the thorniest problems confronting biblical scholars today. There exists practically no agreement among them. This is especially true regarding the position of the third wall of the city, built by Agrippa I and breached by Roman legions under Titus in A.D. 70. In that year Jerusalem fell, thus ending the Third Temple period, and along with it the celebrations and sacrifices in the Temple.

To study the course of the two walls of the Jerusalem of Jesus, we must first follow step-by-step the rather detailed description by Josephus:

> The oldest of the three walls was practically impregnable. This was due to the deep valleys and the high hill on which it was situated. In addition to this strategic position, the wall was strongly built. It was David and Solomon and their royal successors who took great pride in its construction. It began on the north, and it stretched from the Tower of Hippicus all the way to the colonnade and the adjoining Council Chamber, where it met the western wall of the temple portico. From the same tower it ran along the western ridge past a place called Bethso towards the Gate of the Essenes. It then turned south (eastwards) above the Spring of Siloam, whence it veered east directly towards Solomon's Pool. Then it extended alongside a certain area called Ophel, and ran straight up towards the eastern portico of the Temple. (*BJ* v. 142–45)

The first wall then would have appeared as shown in Fig. 6.

Josephus' description of the second wall reads: "The second wall began at the Garden Gate in the first wall. Its course enclosed the northern quarter only, as it crossed over towards Fortress Antonia" (*BJ* v. 146) The line of the second wall must therefore have been as shown in Fig. 6.

The first and second walls represent the geographical, social, and political growth of the city from David and Solomon in the tenth century down to the period of the Maccabees in the second century B.C. They also represent the walls of the Herodian city, which Jesus visited on so many occasions. It is interesting to note that the city expanded in the direction where it was most vulnerable or open to attack from the north. But the topography of the area around Jerusalem would not have allowed it otherwise. Jerusalem's main water supply was

just below Ophel, and it would have been difficult and expensive to fortify the surrounding hills. Had this been the case, Jerusalem would have been built in a valley rather than on a mountain top.

Plate 42 *Eastern slope of Mt. Zion as depicted in the Jerusalem Temple Model. Seen here are the city wall on top of Mt. Zion, characteristic houses, and stepped streets leading down to the City of David, where the Pool of Siloam, city gates, and Spring Gihon are located. Ancient steps are still visible near the shrine of St. Peter-in-Gallicantu.*

The First Wall

Your neck is like David's tower girt with battlements; A thousand bucklers hang upon it, all the shields of valiant men.

Cant. 4:4

Plate 43 *Relics of Hasmonaean wall and tower with a glacis (sloping buffer wall), which also functioned as the city wall during the time of Jesus, most probably Josephus' first wall along the eastern slope of Ophel. The tower was believed by R. A. S. Macalister to have belonged to the Davidic city and was called by him the Tower of David. Below are the remains of an Israelite house with well-preserved steps leading up to the entrance.*

THE FIRST WALL, said to have been built by David and Solomon, is the older of the two described by Josephus. This is not the exact wall which these kings of Israel had built, for the tenth-century battlements of the Jebusite fortress on this side of Ophel were considerably lower down the slope, as archaeological excavations have revealed.[1] But the city had always been defended on this side, from David's reign up to the rule of the Herodians in the first century A.D. During the intervening ten centuries, this eastern wall had to be rebuilt in some places and repaired in others. As the city expanded, a new wall was constructed to enclose and protect the developing quarters of Jerusalem around Ophel. Thus, the previous constructions, now in ruins, served as the foundations for subsequent structures, walls, and buildings. By the time of the Hasmonaean administration of Jerusalem in the Hellenistic period, Jerusalem's eastern rampart along Ophel was much higher up the hill, running along the Ophel ridge from its southeastern tip northwards towards the walls of the Temple Mount, not touching it but running parallel to the sacred enclosure.

It is not known whether the western ridge had also been surrounded by a wall during the preexilic period, but some kind of fortifications were essential, especially since the prophets of Judah awakened Jerusalem to the advancing Assyrian armies from the north in the seventh century B.C. The fugitives from Samaria began their settlement on Mt. Zion during this crucial period, as the recent discovery of the Jewish necropolis at the bottom of Mt. Zion testifies.[2] Moreover, archaeological evidence confirms Josephus' statement that a wall had indeed been built along the western ridge sometime during the postexilic period, certainly during the Hasmonaean dynasty in Jerusalem from the second century B.C. and on. There were also a northern and a southern wall, following the contours of the city from east to west.

The northern extension of the first wall from east to west joined two main landmarks of Jerusalem—the Temple in the east and Herod's palace (later the Praetorium) in the west. This wall also functioned as a bridge across the Tyropoeon Valley, linking the Lower

City with the Upper. In fact, its eastern section, that over the Tyropoeon, was a bridge constructed by the Hasmonaean rulers and subsequently repaired and embellished by Herod the Great. It was built near the Mishneh or "new quarter" of the lower town. The continuation of this wall towards the west was solidly built on rocky foundations, dictated by the topography of the area until it reached the royal palace of Herod the Great. If this wall were visible today, it might reveal a mixture of various types of masonry indicating rebuilding and repair from the time of Nehemiah up to the reign of Herod the Great. The patchwork would help determine the line, as well as distinguish and date the construction of this wall more precisely. Prof. N. Avigad has succeeded somewhat by his discovery of the so-called "broad wall" of Nehemiah in the Jewish Quarter of the Old City.[3] English archaeologists have dated material in the area of the Citadel to the Hasmonaean period.[4] However, the line of this wall can be discerned only from the general contours in this part of the Old City, beginning with the western wall of the Temple Mount and running in a westerly direction across the Tyropoeon up to the Citadel on the summit of Mt. Zion. This is the course of the Street of the Chain and David Street, beginning at the site of the former Islamic Madrasah et-Tankizie westwards towards David's Tower at Jaffa Gate.

The southern extension of the first wall from east to west is much more problematic, since very little remains of it today and the account in Josephus is not very precise. It began at the southeastern tip of Ophel, then stretched westwards up towards the southwestern corner of Mt. Zion. This would place its point of departure somewhere near Birket el-Hamra; its *terminus ad quem* would be just above the American School of Holy Land Studies, the former Bishop Gobat School on Mt. Zion. Despite excavations at various points in the intervening area, there is no general agreement among archaeologists as to the exact line of this wall.

In the light of archaeological discoveries, Josephus clearly is referring not only to two distinct building phases of the first wall of Jerusalem, but also to two different walls along this entire course. The first or early phase according to Josephus' interpretation belongs to

Plate 44 *Compound of the Citadel and Kishleh, which stand in the area of the three great towers built by Herod the Great, later the garrison of the Roman praetorian guard. The traditional Tower of David (Herod's Phasael) stands in the middle, immediately to the right of the Jaffa Gate pylon. The original Jaffa Gate (left of wide opening in wall) was built by the Turks for the visit of Kaiser Wilhelm II in 1898.*

the period of the Jebusite, Davidic, and Solomonic city up to the period of the Exile. This wall enclosed all of Ophel, the Temple Mount in the north, and the Mishneh Quarter above the Tyropoeon Valley. The second phase is much later. The enclosure on the summit of the western hill that formed the Upper City belongs to the postexilic period. The earliest evidence of a wall here is from the Hasmonaean period of the second century B.C. The two walls were joined (at exactly which point, when, and by whom is not certain) and constituted the first wall of the Herodian city which Jesus knew. Of the various city plans of first-century Jerusalem attempted,[5] we prefer that of the Jerusalem Bible as a basis for our own map.[6] Indeed, it is the plan accepted by the majority of Jerusalem scholars today, particularly in light of archaeological explorations of the last century or so. For all practical purposes, we can consider the line of this wall as fairly well established, despite the problems that may arise here and there.

According to Josephus, the first wall began at the Tower of Hippicus, of which, unfortunately, no remains have as yet appeared. However, we know in general

Plate 45 Jerusalem Temple Model suggesting location of Herod's three towers: Hippicus (left), point of departure of the first and third walls of first-century Jerusalem; Phasael; and Mariamne.

✝ ———————————————————— ✝

Plate 46 Silver tetradrachma picturing Antiochus IV Epiphanes, minted ca. 165 B.C. Antiochus encouraged the influence of the Jewish Hellenizers in Jerusalem, allowing them to build a Greek-styled gymnasium. He controlled tightly Jewish worship and encouraged the veneration of Greek deities, erecting an altar to the Olympian Zeus in the Holy City.

where this tower once stood. It was one of three magnificent towers built by Herod the Great in the northwestern corner of Jerusalem, overlooking the royal palace; Hippicus, like Phasael and Mariamne nearby, was constructed by the king for his own protection (*BJ* v. 161–62). This first north wall was strongly built; it began at Hippicus and extended eastwards towards the colonnade or *xystós*, incorporating the Council Chamber adjacent to the temple wall at this point. As noted above, the course of this wall is quite apparent today, for it followed a fairly direct west-east course from Jaffa Gate, along David Street and the Street of the Chain, up to Bab es-Silsileh of the Haram esh-Sharif. Once the principal streets of Roman, Byzantine, and Crusader Jerusalem, these streets today are a shopping thoroughfare. They also mark the course of the first north wall of the Herodian city, which had to be specially fortified because of its precarious position. As this wall collapsed in time of war and siege, its ruins formed a natural embankment, a strong foundation for future constructions. Thus, the houses and shops along these streets are noticeably constructed on a rise—not a natural contour of Jerusalem, but an artificial one built up through the centuries of remains of fallen walls, one on top of the other. Here and there remain traces of this wall, some huge blocks still in situ or relics of wall material strewn over the area, used and reused through the centuries. This is the wall which Josephus indicates was built by the successors of kings David and Solomon.

The first wall ran from Tower Hippicus to the Xystos, a covered colonnade in a gymnasium or other school of physical exercise where, especially during the rainy season, athletes could work out for sport and thus prepare themselves for the various athletic contests. The first Xystos or gymnasium in Jerusalem was built during the rule of the ungodly Antiochus IV Epiphanes, sometime between 175 and 164 B.C. It was the wretched Jason, brother of Onias, who bribed Antiochus to build a gymnasium in the Holy City in order that Jewish youths might be trained according to the fashions of the Greeks (2 Macc. 4:7–9; see also 1 Macc. 1:14).

The Jews in Jerusalem, after the second-century-B.C. Maccabean Revolt and in the days of Herod the Great, would not have tolerated such a worldly place or pagan institution in the Holy City, especially so close to the Temple. It was contrary to orthodox Jewish mores that a youth should expose his naked body to public view, lest his circumcision be revealed to the pagans and he himself should later hesitate to have his own male offspring circumcised. (This was required by Mosaic prescription, to distinguish him from non-Jews and as a special sign of the Covenant.) Orthodox Jewry of this period must have deeply resented that such a place of public exercise had been built adjacent to the Sanctuary.

But gymnastics were banned in Jerusalem by the time of Jesus, so the Xystos no longer served its original purpose. It functioned now as a porticoed walking place, built over the bridge that connected the Upper City with the Temple in the Lower. This must have been a beautiful promenade, called a *xystós drómos,* because of its smoothly polished pavement. Judging from the use of the term in the Roman period, *xystus* not only defined a gymnasium as such, but could be employed to describe a colonnaded terrace, especially the kind that embellished the homes and villas of the well-to-do. The Xystos above the bridge must have given exactly this impression to the Jerusalemites of the Herodian city.

Beneath the roofed colonnade on either side of the Xystos would have been shops and temporary stalls set up before the entrance into the Temple for changing money or purchasing various liturgical items for celebration of the feasts within the temple precincts. In addition to these stores, the Great Sanhedrin would have established one of their three Council Chambers in one of the more spacious halls of the Xystos immediately contiguous to the outer western wall of the Temple. According to Mishnah *Sanhedrin,* "There were three judicial courts [*batei-dinîn*]: one sat next to the entrance to the Temple Mount [*har-habayith*], a second sat by the gate of the Temple Court [*ha'azarah*], and a third sat in the Hall of the Hewn Stone [*lishkath-hagazith*]" (xi. 2). It is possible that in the Third Temple period the first of these three judicial courts was located in the Council Chamber on the Xystos, as Josephus indicates (*BJ* v. 144).[7] The less offensive Hebrew term *gazith* was applied (by assonance and conceptual accommodation) by the Jews to this meeting-place of the Sanhedrin, instead of the more odious Graeco-Roman Xystos, which revived

unpleasant memories of this place. The translators of the Septuagint rendered *gazith* by *xystós.*[8] So we would agree with E. Schürer that "the name by which it is called in the Mishnah, *Lishkath ha-Gazith,* probably means, not, as usually translated, 'Chamber of Hewn Stone,' but 'Chamber beside the Xystus.'"[9]

Because judgments usually took place at the gates of a city,[10] it would have been before the entrance into the sacred precincts that in the days of Jesus the Sanhedrin judged priests worthy or unworthy of entrance into the Temple (cf. Mishnah *Middoth* v. 4). The width of the area over Wilson's Arch here measures at least fifty feet, certainly ample room for such a court as well as for other transactions on the Xystos bridge. The buildings on either side of the present Chain Street are erected on foundations wide enough to have supported rather large public structures.

The Xystos bridge, in light of recent excavations, also served as an aqueduct, with the pipeline installed beneath the pavement of the causeway. It guaranteed a sufficient water supply inside the temple area for ritual libations and purifications.

We suggest the following ground plan for this area.

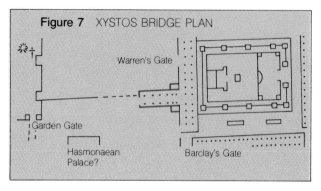

Having described the east-west segment of the first north wall of Jerusalem, Josephus then delineates the

western, southern, and eastern sections of these ramparts. The western portion began at the Tower of Hippicus and ran alongside the western ridge over (past?
across?) a place called Bethso towards the Gate of the
Essenes. The sixteenth-century battlements of Suleiman
the Magnificent follow the line of this wall, as archaeological excavations have revealed.[11]

Modern interpretations and archaeological discoveries have led to interesting conclusions regarding the
southwestern corner of Jerusalem in Jesus' days. Dominican priest-scholar Père L.-H. Vincent of the École Biblique in Jerusalem was correct in naming a gate discovered along the lines of the first wall in the southwestern
corner as the Dung Gate (Porte Sterquiline).[12] This
identification is even more certain today in the light of
Prof. Y. Yadin's work on the recently acquired Temple
Scroll and the investigations and interpretations of Fr.
B.-G. Pixner, O.S.B., of the Dormition Abbey on Mt.
Zion. Both scholars, as well as this author, have thoroughly reexamined the entire southwestern corner in
and outside the walls of Jerusalem.

On Mt. Zion the course of the first wall becomes
more apparent as one examines the contours of the slope
and the placement of the various buildings along the
upper ridge. Archaeological explorations have confirmed this. A careful study of the escarpment with its
unique installations along and on top of Mt. Zion also
help to identify the area and determine its purpose.

What is the meaning of Josephus' Bethso, and where
was it located? German scholar G. Dalman correctly
explained the name as a Hebrew word translated into
Greek.[13] *Bethso* is a grecized form of the Hebrew compound *beith-so'ah*, meaning "the house of excrement."
This was the latrine area of the Essenes who lived on Mt.
Zion but whose latrines were outside the walls of their
camp (*maḥaneh*). This location was in strict observance
of the Deuteronomic legislation regarding the cleanliness and scrupulous purity of the "camp"—their city,
quarter, or residential area (Deut. 23:10–15). No such
installations have as yet been discovered at Essenic
Qumran; however, the many ritual baths among the
ruins at this Dead Sea site witness to this practice. A
number of the cisterns at Khirbet Qumran must have
served as ritual baths or *mikvaoth*. On Mt. Zion in
Jerusalem there are also a number of such mikvaoth as
identified by Pixner; and this author noticed that at least
one had in it a typical Qumranic "step divider" which
was still quite intact. Most of these ritual baths were

found inside the walls of first-century Jerusalem, as at Qumran, but two were located immediately outside the wall, practically midway between the Gate of the Essenes and Bethso. Prof. Yadin locates the latrines of the Essenes someplace west of the present Jaffa Gate. We, however, are convinced that Bethso should be identified with the material examined in the American Institute of Holy Land Studies, just beneath the first wall of Jerusalem at this point. The material evidence here consists of rooms, pools, and canals, as well as plenty of soil which would have been necessary for sanitary purposes (cf. Deut. 23:13). Although the Temple Scroll gives a much larger figure for the distance between the city gates and Bethso—a number which is probably more symbolic than real—it is difficult to imagine that such an important facility would have been so far from the daily needs of the sect. Bethso must have been close enough to the Gate of the Essenes, and the ritual baths along the way would have served to keep Jerusalem pure and holy, so far as the Essenic community was concerned.

The exact location of the Gate of the Essenes has been established by the excavations of British archaeologist F. J. Bliss toward the end of the last century.[14] The material had been covered up, but B.-G. Pixner has recently uncovered the gate in the Protestant cemetery on Mt. Zion, just a few yards to the southeast of the grave of the famous Egyptologist, Sir W. R. F. Petrie. The gate here is clearly in line with the street leading into the city which Bliss uncovered at this juncture. It is also in line with the ancient roads leading southwards towards Bethlehem and Hebron, and southeastwards towards the Dead Sea, through the Wadi en-Nar, to the Dead Sea where Pliny and other ancient historians locate a settlement of the Essene community.[15]

Archaeological excavations have not yet been undertaken to identify the dwellings of the Essenes on Mt. Zion. However, numerous baths or cisterns have been exposed in the neighborhood, thus testifying to the existence of an Essenic community in the Upper City. The baths were used for ritual ablutions, but the cisterns could have served a double purpose. The fullers' quarter was here, and some cisterns were undoubtedly used for the bleaching of cloth, for it was the custom of the

Essenes to wear white garments, especially on holy days, such as Pentecost, the principal feast of the sect. Other cisterns here were used as collectors and reservoirs of rain water, essential for the mikvaoth.[16]

To continue with Josephus' description of the southern and southeastern sections of the first wall, the Jewish historian writes that the first wall veered southeast towards the Pool of Siloam and then continued east towards the Pool of Solomon. The line of this wall has been fairly well established. At various points Bliss unearthed segments of a wall following the contours of the terrain in this direction. With this evidence we can establish, to a certain degree, the course of Josephus' first southern wall descending into the Tyropoeon Valley towards the Lower City. It ran in the direction of the Pool of Siloam on the western slope of Ophel in the southeastern corner of the city. Siloam, the present Silwan, was situated in the Tyropoeon Valley itself, the pool being fed through Hezekiah's conduit originating at Spring Gihon on the eastern side of Ophel. There can be no doubt about the authenticity of this landmark, for the Spring of Gihon continues to send its fresh waters through Hezekiah's tunnel to the fountain of Siloam. According to our interpretation, therefore, the first wall in the southeastern part of the city would not have touched the Pool of Siloam, nor would its course have continued from the west to the east right over Siloam. Josephus' use of the Greek preposition hýper in this context simply means that Siloam was visible from the stretch of wall that was still on the Upper City as it descended towards the Tyropoeon Valley below. The wall skirted around the Siloam landmark, embracing Solomon's Pool nearby.

Solomon's Pool can be easily ascertained in this vicinity, though it is not altogether plain from the few historical references to it. An examination of the neighborhood, however, should convince the geographer, historian, and archaeologist that the present Birket el-Hamra is to be identified with the Pool of Solomon, as it was known by Josephus. Birket el-Hamra is a fairly large depression south of the Pool of Siloam. Prior to the rather elaborate hydraulic system of Hezekiah the Pool of Solomon was also fed by Spring Gihon. A conduit was built, most likely by Solomon,

Plate 48 *Southeastern corner of the Temple on the Jerusalem Temple Model. The Royal Stoa is situated on the top of the acropolis wall. The Huldah Gates can be seen piercing the southern outer foundation wall. In our judgment the eastern wall, as described by Josephus, would not have exactly touched the southeastern tip of the temple enclosure, but would have run along the ridge northwards, somehow joining the northeastern tower of Jerusalem's walls as described by Josephus. Steps, corresponding to those on the southwestern corner (Robinson's Arch), led from the Lower City to the temple storerooms (the present Solomon's Stables) at the southeastern corner of the temple precinct.*

along the eastern scarp of Ophel. A short segment of this tunnel, hewed out of the rock, is still visible here.

Having established this identification, one can continue following Josephus' first wall from the southeastern edge of the Ophel spur northwards, along the upper ridge of Ophel towards the southeastern corner of the temple platform. It did not touch it, as Josephus would have us believe; but this wall ran parallel to the temple enclosure along the ridge of the hill which contains an ancient Muslim cemetery still in use.

The first eastern wall of Jerusalem at the time of Jesus, therefore, could not have been identical with the Jebusite wall rebuilt by David and Solomon. Dame K. M. Kenyon excavated the eastern slope of Ophel and determined that the Jebusite-Davidic ramparts were much lower down the slope.[17] The fortifications along the ridge above, believed by Prof. R.A.S. Macalister to be Davidic, proved to be Hellenistic. They were constructed on much earlier material, much of it belonging to the Israelite period of the seventh century B.C. The Hellenistic or Hasmonaean ramparts encompassed the city on this side up to the time of the Roman destruction of Jerusalem. These were strong fortifications, as archaeological excavations indicate. Some can still be seen on the site. The tower which Macalister believed to be the Tower of David has now been shown to be of later

vintage. It is, in fact, a Hellenistic structure, probably belonging to a gate at this point in the wall. It is possible that the gate opened into the quarter of Jerusalem known by Josephus as Ophlas, where the common people, the poorer, more religiously conservative Jews lived. The Zealots would also have had their homes and quarters on Ophlas. This is where the Synagogue of the Freedmen (Acts 6:9) and the royal houses of the Adiabene family were located. The wall enclosing this part of Jerusalem would surely have been seen by Jesus on his many visits to Jerusalem.

We have observed, correcting Josephus' statement that the first wall touched the southeastern corner of the temple precinct, that it continued alongside the temple wall. This would mean that the eastern wall of the Temple, below Solomon's Portico, did not serve a double purpose—that of the outer precinct wall and the city wall at the same time. The Temple Mount was, in fact, a large acropolis independent of the city's ramparts on all sides. On it were the Temple proper, the Royal Portico, and the Fortress Antonia. It resembled, to a certain extent, the Athenian acropolis, though on a much more limited scale. The Temple Mount was an especially sacred area and therefore deserved to be richly embellished, its entire architectural design worthy of the God of Abraham, Isaac, and Jacob.

The Second Wall

FLAVIUS JOSEPHUS is very terse in describing the second north wall of Jerusalem. This wall served as the northern rampart of the city from the Hellenistic period of the second century B.C. until Jerusalem's fall in the first century A.D. The exact course of this wall cannot be ascertained, for Josephus' account is much too brief and there remains practically nothing in the Old City today that can certainly be identified with it.

According to the Jewish historian the second wall began at the Garden Gate in the first wall. From here it ran northwards, encompassing the populated area called the Mishneh, then turned eastwards where it joined the walls of the Fortress Antonia. Though the site of the Garden Gate cannot be definitely established, we think that its logical location would be at the junction of Suq el-Ḥuṣṣor and St. Mark Street, situated practically in the center of the Old City today. Its position here would have served excellent strategic purposes, for the towers on either side functioned as military lookouts to survey both the stretch of the first wall running westwards towards the three towers of Herod's military guard, as well as the south-north extension of the second wall, thus protecting the newer part of the city from enemy attacks from the north. Moreover, it is quite possible that some of the large masonry around the Bashura Gate once belonged to an ancient gate at this point. The Crusader arch of a gate, we believe, preserves the location of a city gate at this juncture. The Qahwe el-'Umdan (the Caffe of Pillars), a few yards to the north of the Crusader arch, marks the site of the Roman quadrivium where the four principal streets of Hadrian's Aelia Capitolina converged. The tetrapylon that stood here in the second century A.D. perpetuates the site not only of the ancient streets that met at this point, but also the city gate that served as an outlet of the main north-south street of first-century Jerusalem. This street together with its extension to the north during Hadrian's rebuilding of Jerusalem became the cardo maximus of his Aelia Capitolina, while the decumanus maximus, the east-west sidestreet, was formed partly by the Xystos causeway and the street leading westwards from it, and partly from a path that must have run along the northern side

The foundation of the city wall was ornate with precious stones of every sort.

Rev. 21:19a

Plate 49 *Masonry probably belonging to the second northern wall (running from south to north) built in the second century B.C., most likely upon earlier foundations. Because of this wall's size and strength it obviously served as the northern wall of Jerusalem during the time of Herod and Jesus. The huge ashlars seen here (later reused by Hadrian in the second century and Constantine in the early fourth) are part of Russian excavations in the Alexandrine Hospice on Dabagha Street in the heart of the Old City.*

of the first north wall, preserved in David Street today. The course of the second north wall is perpetuated in the line of Suq el-ʿAttarin and its northern extension, Suq Khan ez-Zeit, up to the traditional site of the Seventh Station of the Cross. It is important to remember that since very ancient times roads generally retained their previous directions, and sometimes even their names. Most of the principal streets in the Old City of Jerusalem today preserve the lines not only of former streets but also of ancient walls. Thus, the west-east stretch of the modern Via Dolorosa from the Seventh Station down to the Fifth Station on el-Wad Street perpetuates the course of the northern section of the second north wall of Herodian Jerusalem.

Some scholars are of the opinion that the large ashlars under the Hadrianic temenos wall of the temple of Venus, still visible in the Russian excavations in the Alexandrine Hospice on the corner of Suq Khan ez-Zeit and Dabagha Street, belonged to the second wall of Jerusalem, dating perhaps to the Hellenistic period. Much larger portions of the same type of blocks can be seen in the room behind the Zelatimo Bakery on Suq Khan ez-Zeit, just below the Ninth Station of the Cross. These are very impressive pieces of masonry, and it may be conjectured that they were used and reused, sometimes as parts of a city wall, as the foundations for Hadrianic structures here, and as the outer enclosure of Constantine's Church of the Holy Sepulchre. Archaeological excavations are practically impossible because Suq Khan ez-Zeit is still the principal street in the Old City, a characteristic oriental bazaar.

Another piece of masonry, sometimes identified as a part of the second north wall of first-century Jerusalem, lay deep beneath the chapel of St. Veronica at the Sixth Station of the Cross. If the second wall turned sharply eastwards at the Seventh Station, at the junctions where Tariq el-Khanqa and the classic stretch of the Via Dolorosa meet on Suq Khan ez-Zeit, there might be some concrete evidence of a wall along this line. But the actual age of this material beneath the Veronica Chapel of the Little Sisters of Charles de Foucauld cannot be ascertained. It is possible that the Byzantine builders of the first chapel on this site, dedicated in honor of St. Cosmas and Damian, simply employed the foundations

of the first-century wall for their own superstructure. In any event, most modern scholars position the second north wall of Jerusalem along the lines indicated above. From this point eastwards the wall extended, as Josephus reports, up to Fortress Antonia. But it is puzzling that, if Josephus names the builders of Jerusalem's first wall, he does not even suggest any authors of the second.[1] His summary description, moreover, is much too brief to delineate a wall with any degree of exactness, and it leaves many important questions unanswered, especially with regard to any gates and special towers that certainly must have been built into it. We must rely on the logic of strong Middle East traditions in this case.

Plate 50 *Detail of the same important wall amidst modern debris. This significant portion (notice the door sockets in the southern entranceway) corresponds to the central and, most likely, the principal portal of the Holy Sepulchre during the Byzantine period, as is seen on the Madaba Map. Authorities cannot establish whether this large opening served as a city gate in the first century.*

Plate 51 *Through the Damascus Gate the pilgrim can enter the Holy City and follow in an almost direct line the streets leading to his particular shrine—the Western or Wailing Wall of the Jews, the Muslim Dome of the Rock and Mosque el-Aqsa, or the Christian Basilica of the Holy Sepulchre.*

CHAPTER IV

THE GATES OF JERUSALEM

How awesome is this shrine! This is nothing else but an abode of God and that is the gateway to heaven!

Gen. 28:17

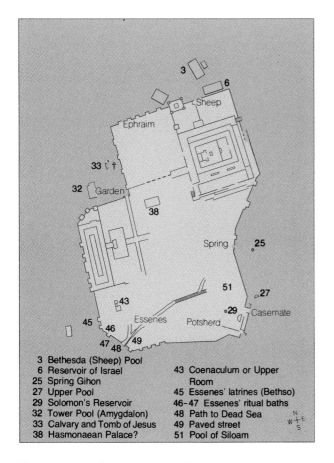

3 Bethesda (Sheep) Pool
6 Reservoir of Israel
25 Spring Gihon
27 Upper Pool
29 Solomon's Reservoir
32 Tower Pool (Amygdalon)
33 Calvary and Tomb of Jesus
38 Hasmonaean Palace?

43 Coenaculum or Upper Room
45 Essenes' latrines (Bethso)
46-47 Essenes' ritual baths
48 Path to Dead Sea
49 Paved street
51 Pool of Siloam

Figure 8 THE GATES OF JERUSALEM

AS ONE LOOKS AT the gates of Jerusalem today, he is impressed by their magnitude and beauty. They are massive defenses, artfully and skillfully constructed. However, the city gate in antiquity was not only the point of entry and exit, it was also the place where social, judicial, and economic affairs took place; it was the center of the city's activity, where the people would meet and exchange news, where courts of justice were set up, and the market where merchants sold their wares. But the gate was also the weakest point of the city's defenses, which an attacking enemy would try to breach in order to capture the city. For this reason ancient gates were usually flanked by strong towers on either side of the large stone halls and guardrooms inside the gates. Some gates had one or two narrower gates on either side of the main entranceway, which were used by pedestrians. The upper stories contained chambers that functioned as lookouts for guards or warriors. Early towns and cities had only a few gates, usually two or three. Later, as for example during the period of the Monarchy, cities had as many as seven gates.

Unfortunately, the Bible gives only a few, and only incidental, references to the gates of Jerusalem. Though a rather long list of their various names can be drawn up, frequently enough one gate had two or three different names, depending on the time of the original construction, later reconstruction, or position. Tradition also played an important role in this respect. The Fish Gate, for instance, where fish were sold, was also called the Gate of Ephraim, because it pointed to the territory of Ephraim in the north. The Sheep Gate, near which sheep were bought for the temple sacrifices, was also named the Gate of Benjamin, since it led directly to that portion of Canaan allotted to Jacob's younger son. This use of various names for the same gate is a common practice in the Middle East even today. The Damascus Gate in the northern wall, built by Suleiman the Magnificent *ca.* 1538–39, derives its name from the Christian tradition that St. Paul departed from Jerusalem for Damascus from this gate (Acts 9). However, the Arab population of Jerusalem called it the Gate of the Column, Bab el-ʿAmud, because a column stood just inside of it when the Arabs captured the Byzantine city in 638. (The column, placed here first by Emperor Hadrian in the second century A.D., indicated the distances from Jerusalem to other great cities of his empire.) Since the 1967 war, the Jewish people of Jerusalem have begun to call it the Gate of Shechem (or Shaʿar Shechem) because it leads to the northern district of Shechem on the West Bank. The Jaffa Gate also takes its name from its destination, the main port of Jerusalem on the Mediterranean Sea. But the Arabs know it as Bab el-Khalil, Gate of the Friend, with reference to Abraham, God's friend, who was interred at Hebron.

The New Testament does not explicitly name any of Jerusalem's gates except the Sheep Gate (John 5:2). But there may have been about seven gates during the time of Jesus: beginning in the north and moving clockwise, the Gate of Ephraim, the Sheep Gate, the Fountain Gate or the Gate of the Spring, the Water Gate, the Potsherd Gate, the Gate of the Essenes, sometimes called the Dung Gate, and the Garden Gate.

The God of your father blesses you with the blessings of the everlasting mountains, the delights of the eternal hills.

Gen. 49:25–26

Plate 52 *Material evidence of a first-century gate revealed by archaeological excavations at the Damascus Gate. The site was employed by Hadrian as the main northern portal of his Aelia Capitolina. The Hadrianic defenses followed those built by Agrippa I about a decade after Jesus' death and resurrection in A.D. 30.*

The Gate of Ephraim

THE GATE OF EPHRAIM opened towards the territory assigned to the clan of Ephraim in the mountain country to the north. It was always the most northerly of all the gates of Jerusalem, yet the gate did not always remain in the same position; as the city expanded from the Ophel spur to the present Old City, the northern gate also moved with the new walls, and it retained its former place name.

The first biblical reference to the Ephraim Gate is 2 Kgs. 14:13, which reports that Jehoash of Israel tore down a hundred cubits of the wall from the Gate of Ephraim to the Corner Gate. Jehoash ruled over the northern kingdom of Israel sometime between 837 and 800 B.C. But Jerusalem was a much smaller city during the earlier period of the divided monarchy of the First Temple period than it was eight centuries later in the Third Temple period. Because the extent of the northern quarter of Jerusalem at this time is open to debate, it is difficult to establish the exact line of the north wall and the precise spot of the Gate of Ephraim in the ninth century B.C. It must have been in the Tyropoeon Valley, in the vicinity of the present Fifth and Third Stations of the Cross at the maximum, or much farther south, probably near the southwestern corner of the Haram esh-Sharif. Our identification is based on the equation of the Gate of Ephraim with the Fish Gate.[1] From 2 Chr. 33:14 we learn that Manasseh (687–642) "built an outer wall for the city of David to the west of Gihon in the valley extending to the Fish Gate and encircling Ophel." This gate must have been near the preexilic Mishneh or New Quarter, as Zeph. 2:10 would indicate: "a cry will be heard from the Fish Gate; a wail from the New Quarter"; Zephaniah prophesied during the first part of Josiah's reign over Judah from 640 to 609 B.C.

This gate must surely have been the gate of the New Quarter which was to the west of the Temple in the postexilic period also, since the city expanded in a northwesterly direction. The postexilic chronicler Nehemiah calls this gate the "New City Gate" (Neh. 3:6). He writes that on the Feast of Tabernacles the people made booths in the open spaces of the Gate of Ephraim (in the north) and the Water Gate (in the south), thus indicating that the celebration took place throughout the Holy City (8:16). Nehemiah supplies another topographical reference when he describes the procession that took place on the city walls during the dedication feast in honor of their rebuilding. The second choir proceeded to the left along the top of the wall as far as the Broad Wall,[2] then past the Gate of Ephraim (identified with the New City Gate and the Fish Gate), up to the Tower of Hananel as far as the Sheep Gate (Neh. 12:38–39).

No other references to the Gate of Ephraim occur in biblical or extrabiblical literature. But we must assume that a gate actually pierced the northern wall of Jerusalem during the Hellenistic and Herodian periods. This gate perpetuated the name of the former gates facing this direction. Therefore, we can be quite sure that the Ephraim Gate was one of the gates through which Jesus must have passed on his many visits to Jerusalem.

The Sheep Gate

THE SHEEP GATE, near which sheep were bought and sold especially for the temple sacrifices, was located in the northeastern part of Jerusalem. It was an opening in the wall that stretched from the northeastern corner of the Fortress Antonia to the northeastern corner of the temple precincts, the Portico of Solomon. No traces of this wall have yet appeared, though various theories and plans have been offered regarding what this quarter of Jerusalem looked like during the time of Our Lord. The general location of the Sheep Gate, however, must be that of the sheep market held each Tuesday just below Burj el-Laqlaq in the northeastern corner of the city ramparts. Because the Near East even today is quite conservative, and many long traditions have been preserved, it must be in the neighborhood of the northeastern tower that we must locate the ancient Sheep Gate and the sheep market. The location of the Sheep Pool, which would have been nearby, has been clearly established.

When Jerusalem grew and developed towards the northeast, beyond the temple enclosure, walls were built to protect the inhabitants within this newer sector. For their convenience a gate was inserted into the wall at this point, facing northeastwards, towards the larger portion of the territory assigned to Benjamin. Hence, the gate was probably at first called the Gate of Benjamin; Sheep Gate was a more popular title.

The earliest biblical references to the Gate of Benjamin occur in the prophets Jeremiah (just before Nebuchadnezzar deported the Jewish people to Babylon in 587 B.C.) and Zechariah (sometime just before the dedication of the restored temple in 515 B.C.). Both Jeremiah and Zechariah speak of the Gate of Benjamin in the northeastern corner of Jerusalem. It is the upper gate through which the kings of Judah entered and left the city (Jer. 38:7), and the gate where Pashhur, priest of Jerusalem, had Jeremiah scourged and imprisoned (Jer. 17:19; 20:2; cf. 37:13–16).

Zechariah exalted the rebuilding of Jerusalem "from the Gate of Benjamin to the First Gate [identified, as we have seen above, with the Gate of Ephraim] to the Corner Gate [that is, towards the south where the first

Like a lamb led to the slaughter or a sheep before its shearers, he was silent and opened not his mouth.

Isa. 53:7

Plate 53 *Sheep market at the northeastern corner of the city. Today, as in antiquity, sheep are bought and sold near St. Stephen's Gate, so named from the Greek Orthodox belief that St. Stephen the Protomartyr was stoned outside this gate. At one time called the Sheep's Gate because of the weekly sheep market here, it is called by the Israelis the Lions' Gate from the four lions on the coat-of-arms of Sultan Beybars el-Bundugdari, founder of the Mameluke Dynasty, which is sculptured on the towers. The gate preserves the site of the Byzantine city gate as shown on the Madaba Map.*

and second walls met], and from the Tower of Hananel [in the northeast] to the King's wine presses [in the south]" (Zech. 14:10). This description is similar to that in Nehemiah.

Nehemiah also knew the Gate of Benjamin by its more popular name; for from the middle of the fifth century B.C. the gate was referred to as the Sheep Gate, where the sheep market and Sheep Pool were situated. This was the gate through which sacrificial lambs were led in the City of the Temple. According to Nehemiah, it was the high priest Eliashib and the priestly brethren who undertook the "task of rebuilding the Sheep Gate" (Neh. 3:1). Following Nehemiah's directions at the festivities of the dedication of the city wall, the Sheep Gate was the point towards which the second choir proceeded, followed by Nehemiah himself and the other half of the princes of the people (Neh. 12:39).

By the first century B.C. the Gate of Benjamin was officially called the Sheep Gate. This is the name by which it is known when Jesus visited Jerusalem sometime in the spring of A.D. 27 to celebrate the Feast of Pentecost.

English translations of John 5:2 are frequently enough mistranslations of the original Greek text: "Now in Jerusalem by the Sheep Pool there is a place with the Hebrew name Bethesda." But a more accurate translation should read, "Now in Jerusalem, by the Sheep [Gate], there is a pool with the Hebrew name Bethesda." The error is grammatical, most likely due to the Latin version of St. Jerome, or to his source, the Vetus Latina. In using the Latin *piscina probatica* Jerome took the Greek adjective *probatikè(i)*, "sheep," in the dative case, to modify *kolymbéthra* or "pool," which appears in the nominative. The dative adjective *probatikè(i)*, after the preposition *epí* ("by"), modifies an understood *pýlē(i)* or "gate." The name was construed so because of the popular usage of the adjective instead of the full name, as when one says the First National when he really means First National Bank.

We do not wish to preclude the existence of a Sheep Pool (which some authorities also call the Pool of Bethesda) in this neighborhood, however, for such a pool has been brought to light by the excavations on the property of the White Fathers near St. Anne's Church in northeast Jerusalem. The miracle of Jesus described in John 5:2–15 took place near this pool.

The Fountain Gate

THE FOUNTAIN GATE, or, more exactly, the Gate of the Spring, was named after Spring Gihon, and can be rather easily located. This gate must surely be one of the oldest, if not the oldest, gates in all Jerusalem. From earliest times it gave access to the source of water here, for water was indeed one of the principal reasons why Jerusalem was founded on this spur. The fortifications were to protect both the inhabitants and their precious source of life. It can be said that the history of Jerusalem closely parallels the history of Spring Gihon. This is the site of the early Jebusite stronghold, as the archaeological expeditions of Dame K. M. Kenyon in 1961–1967 have confirmed. The earliest wall and gate are dated according to the pottery sherds belonging to the Middle Bronze Age in Palestine, ca. 1800 B.C.,[1] long before David had captured Jebus around 995 B.C.

We know exactly where Spring Gihon is in Jerusalem today, for its waters are still flowing and providing much irrigation in the neighborhood of the village of Silwan. We are also confident in the authenticity of Hezekiah's tunnel, based on the important inscription found in it in 1880.[2] Thus, the position of the Gate of the Spring can also be established, the Fountain Gate that was here in the early periods of Jerusalem's history and its successor, the Gate of the Spring of the later periods up to the first century before and after Jesus. Approximately 350 years after the building of Hezekiah's conduit, Nehemiah also speaks of the Gate of the Spring in the vicinity of Gihon, with steps leading up from it to the City of David above. It was the gate restored by Shallum, who also repaired the wall of the Aqueduct Pool near the royal garden as far as the steps that lead down from the City of David (Neh. 3:15; 12:37).

The New Testament does not mention the Gate of the Spring by name, but it does speak of the Pool of Siloam, which was fed by the spring, at the opposite end of the tunnel. At this pool Jesus restored vision to the young man blind since the day of his birth (John 9:1–41). But the historic gate, excavated only recently, and the important spring to which it owes its origin prove that nearly five thousand years of Jerusalem's history occurred right here!

Mount my son Solomon upon my own mule and escort him down to Gihon. There Zadok the priest and Nathan the prophet are to anoint him king of Israel, and you shall blow the horn and cry, "Long live King Solomon!"

1 Kgs. 1:33–34

Plate 54 *Ruins of the Jebusite-Davidic gate tower on Ophel. The Gate of the Spring or Fountain Gate led to the Gihon Spring below. The large boulders (bottom) from which the oldest wall and gate of Jebusite Jerusalem were built were discovered by K. M. Kenyon on the eastern slope of Ophel. This excavation gives some idea of the course of the wall on this side of Ophel centuries before David's capture of the city.*

The "Casemate-wall" Gate

Then the king and all the soldiers left the city by night through the gate between the two walls which was near the king's garden.

2 Kgs. 25:4

Plate 55 *Near these ancient steps carved out of rock and traditionally identified with the City of David, a double wall with storage rooms was constructed as an extra defense measure crowning the southern part of the Ophel spur.*

THE "CASEMATE-WALL" GATE or "the gate between the two walls" must be identical with the Gate of the Waters. It was situated near the king's garden (2 Kgs. 25:4; Jer. 39:4; 52:7) at the far southeastern end of Jerusalem, where there was much water and where the Kidron, Tyropoeon, and Hinnom valleys met. The Casemate-wall Gate must have been a double gate, for it was built right into the two walls of the city at this juncture. It most likely contained a passageway flanked by twin towers into which were built guard rooms and storage chambers for military hardware. It was called the casemate-wall gate because it was an integral part of the double wall employed as an extrafortified defense system at this comparatively weak point in the topography of Jerusalem. Here the walls of the valleys are not really very steep, for the hills are rather roundish as they slope towards the spring of Rogel (Ein-Rogel) and even tend to become rather flat in some places, thus permitting an easy surprise attack. The wall and gate not only defended the inhabitants within the city, but also guarded the reservoirs that were dug in this area, as well as the Spring of Rogel, the "fuller's spring," in the Kidron Valley just a short distance southeast of Ophel.

Very probably because of the abundant water supply in this region the gate received its new name, the Gate of the Waters. The waters of Gihon fed the many reservoirs within and outside the city walls here. Water flowed from Gihon through Hezekiah's tunnel into the Pool of Siloam. It thereby naturally irrigated the royal garden close to Solomon's Pool, the present Birket el-Hamra at the southeastern end of the Tyropoeon Valley, though it was well inside the city walls in ancient times. This must help to clarify the rather ambiguous relationship between (1) the Gate of the Spring, the "Fountain Gate," (2) the Pool of Siloam, which led to the King's Garden, and (3) the Gate of the Waters on the east, as described by Nehemiah (3:15; 12:37).

Water originated from Gihon and flowed through a second aqueduct, a much older hydraulic system built along the eastern scarp of Ophel. Originally it veered southwestwards, as can be determined from some of its remains in the rocky scarp, and emptied into Solomon's

Pool before Hezekiah's tunnel was hewn out. After the construction of that conduit in 701, the waters of the older aqueduct were deviated to feed the "upper pool" in the Kidron Valley on the way to the fuller's field near Ein-Rogel (2 Kgs. 18:17; Isa. 7:3; 36:2).[1] Nothing of special archaeological interest remains of this upper pool near the Gate of the Waters. The keen observer, however, can detect a rather deep depression in the valley at this point, which is extremely fertile land, cultivated for the gardens and orchards of Silwan.

The New Testament authors do not mention an upper pool in first-century Jerusalem. Josephus, however, delineates the line of the first wall as first turning southwards above the Spring of Siloam, then again veering eastwards towards the Pool of Solomon. It is not altogether clear exactly what the Jewish historian intended to indicate as a landmark here. Apparently, there were two important reservoirs here in the first century A.D.: the first definitely known to Josephus as the Pool of Siloam (Birket el-Hamra) that collected the waters of the then much used Hezekiah's tunnel; the second, the upper pool, he knew as Solomon's Pool, because it was thought to have been built by that great king. On the basis of this explanation, we can clarify the biblical accounts concerning the Gate of the Waters and perhaps even identify the pools in the area that gave this appropriate name to the gate.

As mentioned, Casemate-wall Gate is the older name of this southern entrance into the city. We draw our conclusions from the references made to it in the preexilic editors of 1-2 Kings and of Jeremiah. Jer. 39:4; 52:7 relate how, when Nebuchadnezzar stormed Jerusalem, Judah's King Zedekiah and his warriors escaped during the night, leaving the city by the Royal Garden Road "through the gate between the two walls." This opening in the wall could perhaps even be identified with a type of postern gate in Jerusalem before the Exile, for such gates were not uncommon in ancient fortifications. They helped the city's defenders sally forth against the enemy in case of a surprise attack; and they were also useful should the king wish to escape if he realized that his city would fall anyway.

After the return of the exiles in 537 B.C., the gate was not only given a new name, but it seems to have become an even more important portal of Jerusalem. It was Pedaiah, son of Parosh, who repaired the Gate of the Waters on the east with its projecting towers (Neh. 3:26). It was at this portal, too, that Ezra the scribe stood in the open space of the gateway and read the book of the Law of Moses to all assembled there (Neh. 8:1-3). On the Feast of Tabernacles the people set up booths in the open places at the Gate of the Waters and the Gate of Ephraim. On the festival of the dedication of the newly restored walls, Nehemiah had the first great choir proceed along the top of the wall as far as the Gate of the Spring, at which point it ascended "by the steps of the City of David," then continued along the top of the wall until it reached the Gate of the Waters. From here the choir marched upwards towards the Temple where it joined the second choir "in the house of God" (Neh. 12:31-37).

In the time of Jesus, the Gate of the Waters would have been the more logical gateway for Jesus' triumphal entry into Jerusalem. The steps leading up to the city near the Gate of the Spring would have been far too difficult a climb for such a great procession, especially if Jesus were seated on a young colt, for the slope at this point is even today extremely steep. The entrance through the Gate of the Waters would have proved much more convenient, since the ascent at this point, following the lower steps of the City of David upwards and into the city itself, was much more gradual.

The Potsherd Gate

Go out toward the Valley of Ben-Hinnom, at the entrance of the Potsherd Gate; there proclaim the words which I will speak to you.

Jer. 19:2

Plate 56 *The present-day Dung Gate, though situated much higher up in the Tyropoeon Valley, recalls the need for a southernmost gate of Jerusalem since very ancient times. The sixteenth-century gate was widened for automobile traffic during the Jordanian administration of the city from 1948 to 1967.*

FROM ALMOST ANY POINT-OF-VIEW—topographical, strategic, historical, philological, biblical, and traditional—there should be no doubt that another gateway pierced the southeasternmost ramparts of Jerusalem from earliest time up to the present, although not always on exactly the same spot because of the continued northerly expansion and development of the city. The present Dung Gate (Bab el-Magharibeh, the Gate of the Westerners or Moroccans Gate—because it led into their quarter of the city) is just such a reminder.

In ancient times the gate in the southeast corner of the Lower City served as an outlet towards both the Spring of Rogel in the Kidron Valley and the high place of Topheth on the opposite slope across the Valley of Ben-Hinnom, which faced the City of David from the south. From this portal one could also walk through the Kidron Valley in a southeasterly direction towards the Dead Sea, a distance of about 22 miles. One could also take the ancient pathway slightly towards the southwest and join the main highway that led to Bethlehem, Hebron, and the other towns of Judah. From a topographical viewpoint this gate was very strategically positioned, and both the wall and the gate at this point were heavily fortified, as archaeological excavations have shown.

From 1894 to 1897 F.J. Bliss and A.C. Dickie traced practically the entire extent of the southern ramparts of first-century Jerusalem, from the upper hill on the west down towards the lower spur on the east.[1] Scholars still accept these plans, which quite clearly represent the line of the ancient first wall of Jerusalem. In 1927, J.W. Crowfoot undertook excavations in the Tyropoeon Valley,[2] where he discovered a massive wall and gateway that was, according to his calculations, certainly in use during the Maccabean period and onwards. Though neither the New Testament nor Flavius Josephus speaks of a gate at this juncture, the archaeological discoveries should indicate a gate here also during the first century before and after Jesus. Josephus, interestingly enough, traces the line of the first wall precisely in this direction. The sixth-century Madaba Map depicts a southern wall and southeastern gate of Jerusalem. It was not by chance, then, that ten centuries later Suleiman constructed a wall following a west-east course, from Mt. Zion down to Ophel, cutting off the city in such a way as to exclude the southern portion of Zion and the entire spur of Ophel, as did the wall of Hadrian. Thus, he did not follow a hypothetical line in the construction of his southern defenses; nor did he devise gates along these ramparts by personal choice. The Gate of the Moors (Moroccans), today's Dung Gate, was necessary in the busy Tyropoeon Valley, which divided the Upper City from the Lower. (Both the Tariq el-Wad, the Road of the Valley, and the Dung Gate are again much used in Jerusalem, especially since the capture of the Old City by the Israelis in 1967.) If, then, Suleiman the Magnificent did not erect a gate on the actual spot of the biblical Potsherd Gate, he certainly preserved the tradition and importance of a gate close by.

The Old Testament speaks of the Potsherd Gate in this area. Is it possible, therefore, to equate the preexilic Potsherd Gate (Sha'ar ha-Harsith) of Jeremiah (19:2) with the so-called Dung Gate (Sha'ar ha-'Ashpath or Sha'ar ha-'Ashpoth) of Nehemiah (2:13; 3:13) in postexilic Jerusalem? If so, then we know where this gate stood, and archaeological explorations can assist in arriving at such a conclusion. But if this identification cannot be made, we must try to solve two problems, one topographical, the other etymological.

The first question deals with an attempt to identify and justify the existence of two gates, the Casemate-wall Gate and the Potsherd-Dung Gate, probably just a short distance from each other in this strategic southeastern corner of the Lower City. The second problem in this research is by far the more complicated, dealing, on the one hand, with the significance of the Hebrew hapax legomenon harsith, "potsherd" (Jer. 19:2) and, on the other hand, with the root meaning of the terms 'ashpath (Neh. 2:13; 3:14; 12:31) and 'ashpoth (Neh. 3:13); it is clear that the two are derived from the same root, meaning "refuse." Without questioning the basic significance of harsith, it seems, scholars have translated the word as "potsherd." By the same token, they translated Nehemiah's 'ashpath as "dung." Apparently the translators of the Septuagint of Jeremiah in the third century B.C. were not familiar with the real meaning of harsith, which they interpreted to be a proper name and so sim-

ply transliterated the word as Charseith. The Vetus Latina (Old Latin) translation of Jeremiah gives Figlinae, an adjective meaning "of an earthen vessel," while Jerome's Latin Vulgate reads pro porta fictili, rendered as "before the earthen [vessel] gate." The Latin adjective fictilis is generally employed with reference to pottery, such as wine bottles, water jugs, etc.; the plural fictilia can either mean "clay vessels"[3] or, interestingly, "earthen figures of divinities."[4]

Could Jerome perhaps have been thinking of the latter use at Jer. 19:2, thereby associating the original meaning for the Tyropoeon Valley (Hebrew teraphim, "other" or "foreign gods") with the gate which pointed to the pagan shrines on the opposite hill across Ge-Hinnom? Indeed, it was because Solomon and the kings of Judah had built sanctuaries to Baal, Molek, and others and places for the heathen ritual of child sacrifice that the Lord had sent Jeremiah to purchase a potter's earthen vessel and go out towards the Valley of Ben-Hinnom, at the entrance of the Potsherd Gate to excoriate them. "It will no longer be called Topheth, or the Valley of Ben-Hinnom, but the place of Slaughter," wrote Jeremiah (Jer. 19:1–15), for this was indeed an evil place, a terrible reminder to all generations of the sins of their forefathers. If Jeremiah knew this, as is very possible, then his translation of the name of the gate in relation to the valley and the shrine is indeed interesting for analyzing these Old Testament place names.

Approximately a century and a half later, after the Babylonian Exile, the gate received a new name, according to our interpretation. Translations of Neh. 2:13; 3:13, 14, and 12:31 render Hebrew sha'ar-ha-'ashpoth as "the Dung Gate," which many commentaries explain as the gate through which the city's refuse was carried and dumped, and where the people threw away their broken pottery. Prof. B. Mazar rejects this interpretation, proposing that the Hebrew may mean "hearth" or that "the term ShPT [sic] may be derived from the archaic TPT conceived as a by-form of 'Tophet' as suggested by some scholars."[5] Could we conclude that the original name of the gate was the Gate of the Hearth, near the place of burning? It would be most interesting to know what the actual name of this gate was in the postexilic period.

It is possible, according to our interpretation, to

equate Jeremiah's Potsherd Gate with Nehemiah's Dung Gate on the same site. As shown above, gates in antiquity sometimes had several names. After fifty years of exile in Babylon where various deities were worshiped, the Jewish returnees did not forget the high place of Topheth in Jerusalem, for they knew well that their forefathers had performed similar rites to desecrate the Holy City. The book of Jeremiah, which they certainly knew well, would not allow them to forget the sins committed here less than a century before. And indirectly Nehemiah reminded them of the same guilt.

It is possible to detect in these passages from Jeremiah and Nehemiah an extremely cynical wordplay on the name or names of this particular gate. This wordplay is subtle, because it involves rather complicated roots with their sibilant sounds and special connotations. For instance, Jeremiah plays on the Hebrew roots ḥ-r-s and ḥ-r-ś, as well as ḥ-r-ṣ, which means "to cut, to mutilate, etc." The root ḥ-r-s, from which the Hebrew hapax legomenon ḥarsi(o)th or "potsherd" (Aramaic ḥarsutha') is formed, can also signify "scratch" or "lacerate" (ḥareś). It is akin to classical Arabic ḥarasha, "to scratch, provoke, or set people against each other." Hebrew ḥeres signifies something "rough" or "scraped," such as "common earthenware." Another word for an "earthen vessel" is ḥereś, as in Jer. 32:14 and Ps. 22:15. In this connection the forms ḥareś or ḥares plausibly can refer to a "sherd" or an "ostracon," which were sometimes used as votive offerings on which prayers or incantations were incised. It is possible, then, that sherds were picked up at the Potsherd Gate, written on, and brought to the pagan shrine of Molech on Topheth across the Hinnom Valley; Jer. 19:4–6, we think, can be read against such a background.

Ḥeres, moreover, is another word for the "sun" (Jgs. 14:18; Job 19:7), as well as for the "abode of the Amorites" (Jgs. 1:35), who by Ahab's reign (869–850 B.C.) may well have adopted the culture and some of the religious practices vis-a-vis Molek and Chemosh. Ḥeres, with the meaning "sun," is especially interesting. The Potsherd Gate, according to Jeremiah, was in the east (Jer. 19:2; cf. 18:2–15), the direction of the rising of the sun and the direction towards which ancient temples were oriented. The wordplay, therefore, contains a lesson for Jerusalem: the citizens of the Holy City should remember and so repent for their former sins of idolatry and infant-sacrifice as they think about or approach the Potsherd Gate, which faced the pagan shrine of Molek on Topheth in the east.

The play on words in Nehemiah can perhaps be construed in light of several roots involving the phonology and orthography of the gate's name 'ashpoth (Neh. 2:13; 3:14; 12:31) and shaphoth (Neh. 3:13), popularly and pejoratively called the Dung Gate in postexilic and even New Testament Jerusalem. The Aramaic noun 'ashaph (which occurs in Dan. 2:10, 27; 4:4, 7; 11:15) is derived from Hebrew 'ashshaph, "magician" or "conjurer." The word is probably a Babylonian loanword, like Assyrian āshipu (from Akkadian ishippu), signifying an "enchanter." Magicians, sorcerers, and the like, together with their arts and practices, were strictly prohibited in Israel, hence the pejorative use. (Though there is probably no connection with the ancient name, the Dung Gate is situated in the direction of the Mount of Evil Counsel, a designation of Crusader origin.) In any event, the Septuagint version renders the name of this gate as the Dung Gate (pýlē tēs koprías) and locates it in the vicinity of the Well of the Dragon, identified with nearby Ein-rogel, thus giving the second-century name of the gate also.

'Ashpath or 'ashpoth is also related to the root sh-ph-th ('ashpah), akin to Akkadian shupat, which denotes a fireplace[6] or, as in 1 Sam. 2:8 and Ps. 113:7, a dunghill. In this connection the gate could very easily have been referred to as the gate of ash heaps or dunghill gate, which the translators of the Septuagint most probably knew. Basically, sh-ph-th contains the idea of "giving, setting something upon (the fire)," etc., which we see in 2 Kgs. 4:38 and Ps. 22:16. Shephathayim, for instance, were places where things were set, put, or placed, such as stalls or folds for cattle (Ps. 68:14; Ezek. 40:43 to be compared with 24:3; Gen. 49:14; Jgs. 5:16), and can possibly be connected to such a place close to the Dung Gate. The radicals t-ph-th and ṭ-ph-th can be interpreted as by-forms, as pointed out above; thus, Topheth would point to the evil place south of Jerusalem opposite the Dung Gate. Perhaps there is also a wordplay between shaphath and shopheṭ, "to judge," suggesting God's vengeance upon Jerusalem's infidelity.

The Gate of the Essenes

Since the Lord, your God, journeys along within your camp to defend you and to put your enemies at your mercy, your camp must be holy; otherwise, if he sees anything indecent in your midst, he will leave your company.

Deut. 23:15

IN HIS DESCRIPTION of the first wall of Herodian Jerusalem Flavius Josephus mentions only one gate along its course—the Gate of the Essenes. For Josephus the Essene Gate may have been an important landmark here, for it is possible that the Jerusalem-born historian was once himself a novice or perhaps a member of this religious group.[1]

Although some questions still remain unanswered, the line of the southwestern and southern ramparts of the city at this time has long been fairly well established by the excavations of H. Maudslay in 1874 and by F.J. Bliss and A.C. Dickie for the Palestine Exploration Fund.[2]

The landmark Gate of the Essenes along these walls can also be traced. The present Zion Gate (Bab Nebi-Dahud) is its most probable successor, although much farther north. The southwestern gate on the Madaba Map is also oriented towards Zion—towards the site of the Cenacle and the traditional tomb of King David—though its actual location was probably a little more to the east where the present wall, directly in line with the former cardo maximus (the modern Suq el-Ḥuṣṣor, Suq el-ʿAttarin, and Suq Khan ez-Zeit), indicates the site of an ancient passageway, now blocked up. The actual gate of the Essenes was much farther south. Its location was determined by the explorations of Bliss and Dickie in the southeastern corner of the Anglican Cemetery on Mt. Zion. The threshold of this gate has again been revealed by the explorations of B.-G. Pixner, O.S.B., only within the last two years. Continuing southeastwards from this point and looking down the above-mentioned retaining wall, one can still see the stone blocks of what was probably the base of a Hasmonaean tower built into the wall near the Gate of the Essenes. From this tower the course of the first wall of Jerusalem was traced in an easterly direction, following the ridge of the limestone scarp of the western and southern sectors of Mt. Zion.

Near the Gate of the Essenes Bliss and Dickie also uncovered a well-paved street oriented in a northeasterly direction inside the city. A sewage pipe was built beneath this street in order to keep the quarter, which we identify as the *maḥaneh* or camp of the Essenes, pure

Plate 57 *Fr. B.-G. Pixner, O.S.B., indicates the site of the Gate of the Essenes on the southern ridge of Mt. Zion, marked by a slight depression in the Protestant Cemetery. This gate not only led out towards the community's gardens, latrines (Bethso), and ritual baths (miqvaoth), but was also oriented towards a road through the Kidron Valley (Wadi en-Nar) to the Dead Sea near Qumran.*

Plate 58 *The present Zion Gate, also known in Arabic as Bab Nebi-Daud or Prophet David's Gate, recalls the importance of a gate in the southwestern part of the city. Jerusalem's defense system in ancient times was farther south. The pock-marked gate, which remained closed during the division of the city from 1948 to 1967, was scarred during battles between Palestinians and Israelis for control of the Holy City.*

and holy, according to Deuteronomic legislation (Deut. 25:10–15).

The orientation of the street is also of interest to scholars. Even though now covered up, it leads across the hill of Zion and eventually joins the ancient steps on Zion's eastern slope, on the property of the Assumptionist Fathers of St. Peter-in-Gallicantu. The ancient stairs were excavated by the Assumptionists around 1887 and identified as the first-century B.C. and A.D. steps which led down from the Upper City to the Lower. It is possible that Jesus walked down these same steps towards Gethsemani on the night of Passover after his last Seder meal with his apostles. Although the Essenes who occupied this quarter did not participate in the temple sacrifices, they and their successors, many of whom must have become the first Judaeo-Christians, also used these steps to go down to the Temple.

Independently of Benedictine Fr. B.-G. Pixner's study of the area, we have concluded that the material evidence on Mt. Zion, studied in the light of biblical and extrabiblical texts, was not only the mahaneh of the

Essenes during the time of Jesus, but also the birthplace of this extremely orthodox Jewish sect in Jerusalem. Subsequent investigations of the same material and discussions with both Pixner and Prof. Y. Yadin convince us of the special importance of this area south of the sixteenth-century defenses.

Both the Essenes and the early Christians lived apart from the mainstream of first-century Judaism. The Essenes limited themselves, it would seem, to Mt. Zion and Qumran at the northwestern corner of the Dead Sea, although the latter could very well have been used as a base of operations for the sect's preaching and baptizing along the Jordan River. It would have been in such a context that John the Baptizer preached a baptism of repentance in the desert, and against this background that Jesus was baptized by his cousin John in the Jordan.

Before the founding of Christianity the Essene group, at least at Qumran, was rather large, to judge by the large cemeteries close to the site. The Essenes lived apart and rarely mixed with others. Their quarters were self-subsistent, lest anyone or anything defile the sanctity of their sacred mahaneh. If their special quarter on Mt. Zion were a walled-in settlement such as that at Qumran, it would be difficult to establish the line of a north-south wall bordering their eastern limit. It would be reasonable to conclude that their only ventures outside the camp would have been for visiting the Temple, joining their brethren in the desert, and working on their cultivated land just outside the southern city wall.

Within the area between today's southern ramparts and the course of the first wall of Herodian Jerusalem can be seen a number of fairly large pits or trenches. If studied in the context of an Essene community on Zion and compared with the baths and "cisterns" at Qumran, these can plausibly be identified with the *miqvaoth* or "ritual baths" of the Essenes at the Dead Sea site. As yet, no structures or remnants of any dwellings or other buildings have been excavated within this area and identified with an Essenic community here. However, if excavations are ever undertaken beneath the present Cenacle, we believe that they would be rewarding in this regard.

The material finds outside the line of the first-century wall along the rocky scarp of Mt. Zion, however, are very convincing that the Essenes lived around this quarter. In strict observance of Deut. 23:10–15, this was the area of their Bethso' or "latrines," their ritual baths, and their gardens. With respect to the purity of the quarter Deuteronomy prescribes:

> you shall keep yourselves from everything offensive. If one of you becomes unclean because of a nocturnal emission he shall go outside the camp, and not return until, toward evening, he has bathed in water; then, when the sun has set, he may come back into the camp. Outside the camp you shall have a place set aside to be used as a latrine. You shall also have a trowel in your equipment and with it, when you go outside to ease nature, you shall first dig a hole and afterwards cover up your excrement. Since the Lord, your God, journeys along within your camp to defend you and to put your enemies at your mercy, your camp must be holy; otherwise, if he sees anything indecent in your midst, he will leave your company (Deut. 23:10b–15).

Hence, the Bethso' and the ritual baths should be sought outside the walls of the city. In view of our examination of the entire southwestern area outside the city walls the most suitable candidate for the site of these latrines is that of the present American School of Holy Land Studies. The evidence fits: the cutting of the rocky scarp in such a way that would permit roofing, the water channels leading into the area, and the well-worn thresholds or doorsills, which had been observed by Bliss at the close of the last century.

The prescribed distance for these latrines differs: the measurement of 3,000 cubits specified in the Temple Scroll or even the shorter distance of 2,000 cubits men-

Plate 59 *Jewish miqvah or ritual bath outside the line of the southern wall of first-century Jerusalem, hewn out of the rock and neatly plastered with limestone. The step divider inside is identical with those at Khirbet Qumran on the northwestern shore of the Dead Sea.*

tioned in the War Scroll[3] would, if interpreted literally, be an extreme legislation which would be humanly difficult if not impossible to observe. The distance *within which* the latrines were supposed to be situated, as B.-G. Pixner suggests,[4] makes good sense. However, we think that it is more reasonable, given the geographical location of the Bethso' so close to the city walls, that the given numbers are representative not of any numerical value but should be construed in a figurative or symbolic sense, especially since the ancient Hebrews do not seem to have taken any special interest in mathematics.[5] Thus, the measurement of either 3,000 or 2,000 cubits (roughly the distance of one English mile) should denote neither a terminus ad quem nor a terminus in quo, but rather a reasonable distance away from the camp so as to keep it holy and yet be humanly convenient.

Within the area between the Bethso' and the Gate of the Essenes must have been a number of miqvaoth or ritual baths for purification before entering the quarter. However, only two such baths remain outside the line of the ancient city wall; they can be seen in the Anglican cemetery just beneath the ruins of the Hasmonaean tower. Their measurements correspond to those given in the Mishnah.[6] The most interesting feature which we ob-

Plate 61 *Hasidic Jew of the orthodox Mea Shearim quarter in West Jerusalem, dressed in a black suit with a prayer shawl, the Tallith, and tassels draped over his shoulders. On his head he wears the characteristic fur hat (Yiddish Shet-raimel) of eastern European Jewry. In his hands he holds the ceremonial bouquet of the Feast of Tabernacles ritual, tech-nically called the Four Species (ʾarbaʿ minim): a citron (ethrog), a branch of the date palm (lulab), three springs of myrtle (hadissim), and two stems of the willow tree (ʿaraboth), bound together as a sign of unity, cooperation, and brotherhood.*

Plate 60 *Hasmonaean tower (second century B.C.), just above the Jewish ritual baths. Considered one of the more unique relics of the wall of Jerusalem during the time of Herod and Jesus in the first centuries before and after Christ, it was constructed of neatly dressed ashlars.*

served is that one includes the characteristic step divider of miqvaoth that is so common in the ritual baths at Khirbet Qumran. Unfortunately, the other ritual baths, both inside and outside of the quarter, no longer display such dividers. They must have disappeared after the Es-senes abandoned their camp on Mt. Zion and the cis-terns were transformed into ordinary water catchers. But there can scarcely be any doubt concerning the function of these rock-hewn shafts during the first centuries before and after Jesus. The ritually unclean would walk down along one side of the stairs, perform their ablutions in-side the bath, and then ascend along the other side, which was considered clean.

The material evidence on the site supports our con-tention that the Essenes actually dwelled in this quarter of Mt. Zion. This was the birthplace of the sect, as it would be the birthplace of Christianity in A.D. 30.

Scholars are by no means in agreement with regard to

the etymology of the name Essene (Greek *Essénoi*). Most likely, members of the sect did not call themselves by this name. Some earlier authorities have suggested that the title is derived from either Greek *hósioi*, the "holy ones," or *ísoi*, "individualists." Some other au-thorities offer a list of Hebrew and Aramaic words such as *sanuʿa*, "modest"; *ʿashin*, "powerful"; *ʾasyaʾ*, "physician"; *haziaʾ*, "seer"; *seha*, "to bathe," because of the sect's frequent ritual ablutions; *ʿasah*, "to do," in the sense of observing the Law; *hazan*, a "watcher," which connotes a "worshiper"; and *hashaʾim*, the "silent ones." Now scholars tend to see in the name the Aramaic root *hasan*, equivalent to Hebrew *hasid*, signifying the "pious ones." It is rendered *eulabés* in Greek, a compound of *eu* and *lambánein* meaning "to take well hold (of something), to be circumspect or discreet," hence "pious" or "devout."

As mentioned, the Essenes originated in Jerusalem where, because of the complicated political situation and the corrupt priesthood, they preferred to live by themselves in order to practice a rigorous asceticism based primarily on the Law. They most likely stem directly from the Hasidean Jews who had abandoned the politics of the Maccabees in order to follow as strictly as possible the doctrine of the Teacher of Righteousness, a teacher of the Zadokite line. (Whether this teacher was an individual, a group of individuals forming a type of institution, or perhaps a personification of the Law is not certain.) The Hasideans were also divided among themselves into the Pharisees, who took a rather liberal approach towards the Law, and the Essenes, a splinter group, which lived according to the most rigid exegesis of the Law. This rigorous observance of the Law and studied asceticism was for some impossible to maintain in the City of the Temple, so some of the Essenes then moved into the desert at the northwestern corner of the Dead Sea, forming their own community at Qumran.[7]

The peculiar nature of the sect suggests another etymological explanation for the name of the Essenes. Since the majority, or at least a significant number, of the members were priests, it may be suggested that they either called themselves or were referred to as Essenes after Hebrew *ḥoshen*, meaning a "breastpiece" or a "sacred pouch," such as described in Exodus (28:26; 39:8), which contained the Urim and Thummim (Exod. 28:30; Lev. 8:8; Deut. 33:8; 1 Sam. 28:6), cultic objects which the high priest used to consult Yahweh. (It is possible that their priests wore a symbolic "breastpiece," a simple apronlike garment over their shoulders and breast, something like a modern scapular, to remind them of their profession of faith in Yahweh and his Law and also to distinguish themselves from all others.) This etymology may explain the remarks in Luke's account of a large-scale conversion in Jerusalem: "There were many priests among those who embraced the faith" (Acts 6:7). These priests, we believe, were the Essenic covenanters whose quarter was on Mt. Zion.

Finally, we suggest that the name "Essene" is derived from the word *ṣiyon* (Sion or Zion), especially because of this sect's strong attachment to and strict observance of the Mosaic Law in the city of *Sion*. It is also possible, then, that the name of the southwestern spur of Jerusalem perpetuates the name of the Essene (*ha-siyonim*) sect that established itself here.

Plate 62 *Cave 4 of Khirbet Qumran in the Wadi Qumran at the northwestern corner of the Dead Sea. This cave produced about four hundred Dead Sea Scroll manuscripts. Cave 4, along with the now collapsed Cave 5 on its right, was very close to the Essenes' monastery complex and easily could have served as a genizah or depository for worn-out scrolls, or as a hiding place for the Essenes' sacred library before the Roman attack on the site.*

The Garden Gate

THE UNIDENTIFIED AUTHOR of the comforting letter to the early Hebrew Christians must have had a definite location in mind when he compared Jesus' crucifixion to the high priest's burning the carcasses of animals slaughtered to provide blood for the temple sin offerings. He would have had in mind the traditional place of execution outside the northwestern gate of the city, certainly a well-known site.

The northwestern portal, which played such an important role in the history of primitive Christianity in Jerusalem, was the Garden Gate. Its location today would be practically in the heart of the Old City, in the quarter known as el-Bashurah, the former site of Hadrian's quadrivium and tetrapylon. During the late first and early second centuries A.D., before the building of Aelia Capitolina, the first Christians must have passed through this gate often on their way to both Golgotha and Jesus' tomb nearby. It would have been through this gate that the Roman soldiers had led Jesus on his way to Calvary, and perhaps here that Simon of Cyrene was pressed into helping Jesus carry his cross.

Recently, Israeli archaeologists, digging in the Jewish Quarter a short distance south of el-Bashurah, uncovered a fairly large section of a paved street in use during the Byzantine period, as illustrated on the Madaba Map. This pavement must surely have followed the course of a road oriented in this direction even in the preceding century (or centuries), since its terminus ad quem was a gate at the junction of the first and second walls. In the second century, during Hadrian's Aelia Capitolina, the street led directly towards the quadrivium, where four roads met. This juncture was also adorned by a tetrapylon, an elaborate edifice with four gates, which embellished the heart of the city. El-Bashurah is the most logical place where the north-south cardo maximus (Suq el-'Attarin and Suq el-Hussor) bisected the east-west decumanus (David Street and Tariq Bab es-Silsileh) to form the quadrivium. It is quite possible that the present Qahwe el-'Umdan, the Coffeehouse of the Columns, preserves the location.

The discovery of this ancient pavement further confirms that the grid of the Old City's streets today is

Therefore Jesus died outside the gate, to sanctify the people by his blood.

Heb. 13:12

Plate 63 *El-Bashurah junction near the Qahwe el-'Umdan, site of the Roman quadrivium and the impressive tetrapylon of Hadrian's Aelia Capitolina. The Herodian Garden Gate (Gennath), built on the site of the Old Testament Corner Gate, was also located here, most probably at the time of the building of the second north wall of Jerusalem.*

Plate 64 Pavement of Byzantine street preserving the direction of Hadrian's cardo maximus. Jesus followed more or less identical lines on his way to the Garden Gate, through which he was led towards Golgotha.

practically in direct line with the principal streets of ancient Jerusalem, especially those of the first centuries before and after Christ. In rebuilding Jerusalem according to typical Roman street planning, Emperor Hadrian apparently followed the lines of the principal existing roads, which he also beautified, for they probably had not been paved before. In this way, Hadrian preserved, we are convinced, two important features of first-century Jerusalem: (a) the authentic direction of Jesus' way of the cross—at least the south-to-north stretch, and (b) the site of the Gennath or Garden Gate through which Jesus passed on his way to Calvary.

The Garden Gate must have been an important landmark for Josephus in his description of the second wall of the Holy City (*BJ* v. 146). Briefly, it began at the gate called Gennath (the grecized form of Aramaic *ginna'* [Hebrew *gan*], "garden") and ran in a northerly direction where at a certain point it veered eastwards and then joined the Antonia. It is possible to trace the earlier history of this gate in the light of biblical texts, for a gate in this general vicinity must have pierced the northern defenses perhaps as early as the ninth century B.C. The Garden Gate took the place of the former Corner Gate in this neighborhood, but not on the exact spot.

King Joash of Israel (801–786) tore down four hundred cubits of the city's fortifications from the Gate of Ephraim to the Corner Gate (2 Kgs. 14:13–2 Chr. 25:23). King Uzziah of Judah (783–742) repaired them, building towers "at the Corner Gate, at the Valley Gate [in the Tyropoeon], and at the Angle [the extreme southeast corner of Ophel]" and fortifying them (2 Chr. 26:9). Jeremiah, who prophesied just before the Exile in the sixth century, is perhaps more explicit with regard to its location:

The days are coming, says the Lord, when the city shall be rebuilt as the Lord's, from the Tower of Hananel [in the northeastern corner] to the Corner Gate [at the northwestern end]. The measuring line

shall be stretched from there straight to the hill Ghareb [which we identify with the northwestern hill of Jerusalem] and then turn to Goah [a place unidentified, but we think that it points to the southeastern corner of the slope of Ghareb, between the central and transversal valleys[1]]. The whole valley of corpses and ashes [Israeli archaeologists exhumed tombs of the First Temple period a little farther to the southeast, just opposite the Western Wall], all the slopes toward the Kidron Valley, as far as the corner of the Horse Gate at the east, shall be holy to the Lord (Jer. 31:38–40).

After the Captivity in Babylon, Zechariah (*ca.* 518) prophesied that Jerusalem

shall remain exalted in its place. From the Gate of Benjamin [in the northeastern corner, also the site of the Sheep Gate], to the place of the First Gate [the Gate of Ephraim or Fish Gate, probably one of the oldest names of the northern gate in Jerusalem], to the Corner Gate; and from the Tower of Hananel [in the northeast] to the king's wine presses [probably in the southeast in the Kidron Valley], they shall occupy her (Zech. 14:10–11).

In the light of these texts, the topography of Jerusalem described in them, and the landmarks mentioned at various points, the general location of the Old Testament-period Corner Gate can be determined fairly certainly. The Corner Gate, according to our interpretation, received its name because of its position in the northwest

Plate 65 *Ruins of the great tetrapylon at Palmyra, 144 miles northeast of Damascus in the Syrian Desert. This splendid four-gated monument originally consisted of four massive pedestals, each supporting lofty Corinthian-styled granite columns upon which rested a richly ornamented entablature and roof. The tetrapylon of Hadrianic Jerusalem must have been quite similar.*

corner of the city's ancient defenses. It opened towards the Hill of Ghareb, whereas the Gate of Ephraim along the same wall faced directly north, towards the territory assigned to Ephraim.

The gate must have been known as the Corner Gate for some time, especially when the second wall was built from it, thus forming a corner, to enclose the newly developing Mishneh quarter. For historical and strategic reasons, we would locate this quarter in the upper portion of the central valley alongside the Temple Mount, rather than on the eastern slopes of Mt. Zion where, because of the much higher elevation of the hill above it, the city would have been very easily exposed to assault. Eventually another wall, the first wall of Josephus, was extended westwards from this gate in order to encompass the occupied area of Mt. Zion. It is known that a wall was constructed on the top of Mt. Zion during the Hasmonaean period. Thus, the juncture between the first east-west rampart and the second north-south de-

fenses is where the ancient Corner Gate must have been located. Later on it was popularly referred to as the Garden Gate. Why?

The area to the northwest of the city's defense system had not been enclosed by a city wall until about a decade after the crucifixion of Jesus, when the so-called third north wall, whose course the present sixteenth-century battlements follow,[2] was constructed by Herod Agrippa I (A.D. 41–44).[3] Prior to the building of the wall this was an open area. It was the site of an Iron Age limestone quarry, followed by a rubbish dump. By the end of the second century B.C. the dump was transformed into a type of garden, an orchard perhaps, wherein the Jews interred their dead in the rocky walls of the previous quarry. This was also the site of Golgotha and the future burial place of Jesus in a garden tomb close by. We picture this not as a completely desolate spot but as a fairly wooded area, which must have been popularly known as a garden in the first century. It was to this garden that the northwestern gate of the city opened, hence its new name. Although it is not so named in the Scriptures it was clearly remembered by Josephus.

"And now we have set foot within your gates, O Jerusalem—Jerusalem, built as a city with compact unity!" (Ps. 122:2–3).

Plate 66 *Water means life in the Middle East. These plants in the Judaean desert east of Jerusalem, along the ancient Roman road to Jericho, blossom only during the first part of the March rainy season. They are followed by green scrub which covers the hillsides until the beginning of the dry season in mid-May.*

CHAPTER V WATERS OF JERUSALEM

"If anyone thirsts, let him come to me. . . . From within him rivers of living water shall flow."

John 7:37–38

Plate 67 *The palm tree signals the presence of water in the parched lands of the Middle East. As the Arab saying goes, "the palm tree always spreads its branches towards the sun, but its roots reach deep for water."*

TO THE ANCIENT, water literally meant life. It promised survival; it gave hope. Indeed, from the great Anatolian Plateau in Asia Minor (modern Turkey), through the countries of the Middle East, the land is parched and dry for at least half of the year. Cities and towns are like pockets scattered here and there, sometimes hundreds of miles apart, or along the few good rivers. The history of the Fertile Crescent is the history of the cities, towns, and villages along the Levantine coast down into Egypt. This was the great caravan route and military highway, which fostered economic growth and prosperity or brought war and devastation. A city's water supply was as vital to its survival as its defense system.

Jerusalem was situated along this route. Traders and generals from Egypt passed through the Palestine corridor on their way to Mesopotamia and Asia Minor: from the east, merchants and soldiers crossed en route to Egypt. Thus, Jerusalem, traditionally the city of peace, rarely knew the meaning of the word. The city was born on a small hill next to a tiny spring of water. In war time, the hill served as a natural fortress, a vantage point from which its defenders could shield the water supply below, and gain the upper hand over their attackers. So, in spite of the obstacles, Jerusalem flourished. As its population increased, the city expanded as did the need for water. This chapter deals with Jerusalem's water supply, the beginning of its history at Spring Gihon, and the concerns for water at the time of Jesus.

LEGEND

1. Sheep (Probatic) Pool, sometimes also called the Pool of Bethesda, meaning the Place of Mercy.
2. Strouthion (Swallows) Pool, probably from the Hebrew/Canaanite Ashtoreth (Astarte).
3. Pool of Israel, said to be one of the pools that supplied water for the Temple.
4. Tower (Amygdalon, "Almond") Pool, so named because it was in the neighborhood of the three towers built by Herod the Great.
5. Aqueduct which conveyed water from Ein-'arrub south of Bethlehem. Pontius Pilate, procurator of Judaea from A.D. 26 to 36, repaired the Herodian aqueduct with money taken from the Temple treasury.
6. Spring Gihon, the birthplace of Jebus and Jerusalem.
7. Hezekiah's Tunnel, hewn out of the solid limestone rock sometime around 701 B.C. to bring water into the city itself during the siege of Sennacherib, king of Assyria.
8. Pool of Siloam (Shiloah, "sender"), scene of the miracle of the man born blind. The village of Silwan on the opposite slope of Ophel derives its name from this biblical reservoir.
9. Possible location for the biblical Upper Pool dating back to about the tenth and ninth centuries B.C. It cannot be clearly detected today.
10. Birket el-Hamra, equated with the Pool of Solomon. The identification is very probable.
11. Serpent Pool, mentioned by Josephus. It was restored during the Crusader period and named Lacus Germanus after St. Germain (?) and again in the sixteenth century by Suleiman the Magnificent, after whom it is still called the Sultan's Pool (Birket es-Sultan).
12. Ritual baths (*miqvaoth*), identified with the Essenic community that lived on Mt. Zion.

Figure 9 THE WATERS OF JERUSALEM

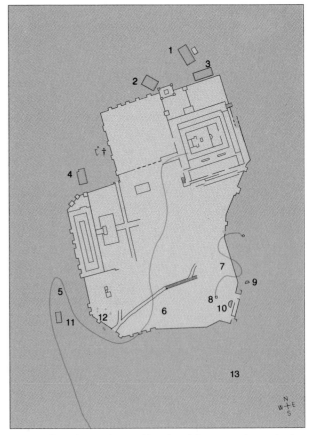

13. Ein-Rogel, a spring and landmark between the territories of Judah in the south and Benjamin in the north.

Spring Gihon

THE HISTORY OF JERUSALEM is literally that of the Spring Gihon, so vital to the city's life has been this water supply. Located in the Kidron Valley, the spring gushes forth (Hebrew *giaḥ*) from a natural cave several times a day. The growth of the city, the plan of its gates and defenses, and its political and military vicissitudes have been intimately related to this spring in virtually every period of the city's existence.

The Canaanite tribe of Jebusites established its dwellings in the neighborhood of Gihon. When the scattered Israelite clans settled in Canaan, David foresaw that to unite them he needed a centrally located capital, and so he chose Jerusalem for this purpose, capturing the Jebusite stronghold through Gihon. From then on the history of Jerusalem really parallels the history of Gihon. It was here that Solomon was anointed king over Israel (1 Kgs. 1:33–35). If only indirectly, the spring even figured into the Roman attack of A.D. 70, for Titus realized that he could not attack Jerusalem from any of the points in the south, the east, or the west. He chose to come down upon the city from the ominous north. How reminiscent this was of Isaiah's and Jeremiah's repeated warning that the enemy would come down upon the people from the north.[1]

No doubt, Hezekiah's subterranean aqueduct had very much to do with such a strategy also, especially in the later periods when it was virtually impossible to cut off Jerusalem's water supply at this particular point. Hezekiah brought the water into the very heart of Jerusalem by means of one of the most ingenious engineering accomplishments of hydraulic systems of ancient times. In length it was second to none in Palestine. Its 1758 feet far surpassed the tunnels of Megiddo (210 feet) and Hazor (90 feet). The biblical records in 2 Kgs. 20:20 and 2 Chr. 32:30 are anticlimatic in comparison with the dramatic account scratched on the walls by the tunnelers themselves when they had finished the laborious task of constructing this vital artery of Jerusalem's water supply. The ancient graffito expresses the joy of the two teams of workers, beginning at the opposite ends of what remains one of the most authentic biblical sites in all of Jerusalem.

With joy you will draw water at the fountain of salvation!

Isa. 12:3

Plate 68 *Spring Gihon, looking towards the eastern entrance of Hezekiah's tunnel near the conduit through which David captured Jebus. Waters still flow from this source, supplying the villages of Ophel and Siloam; the spring's overflow helps to irrigate the fertile region of the Kidron Valley.*

This is the story of the boring through: while [the tunnellers lifted] the pick each towards his fellow and while three cubits [yet remained] to be bored [through, there was heard] the voice of a man calling his fellow, for there was a split in the rock on the right hand and on [the left hand]. And on the day of the boring through, the tunnellers struck, each in the direction of his fellows, pick against pick. And the water started to flow from the sources of the pool, twelve hundred cubits. A hundred cubits was the height of the rock above the head of the tunnellers.[2]

Today, Spring Gihon is called St. Mary's Spring (Ein Sitti Miryam) by the local Arab population of Silwan village located opposite the Spring, just outside the walls of the Old City. The Christians of the Crusader period identified this spring as the one where Mary, the mother of Jesus, came to fetch water, and also in which she washed her infant son's swaddling clothes.[3] The tradition, however, is completely unfounded.

Spring Gihon is also known by the local Arabs as the Spring of the Mother of Steps (Ein Umm ed-Daraj). Steps cut into the rock do indeed lead down into the

Plate 69 *Siloam Inscription, discovered by Arab schoolboys playing in Hezekiah's tunnel in 1880. This inscription, which underscores the accounts in 2 Kgs. 20:20 and 2 Chr. 32:24, is now in the Classical Museum in Istanbul, where it was taken during the Ottoman Turkish rule over Palestine. (Classical Museum, Istanbul)*

cavernlike entrance where the source of water actually is, and the lowest steps are probably authentic. Outside the spring is another course of steps, leading upwards towards where the walls and gates of ancient Jerusalem once stood. These steps are modern, built only within the last ten years or so, but indirectly they can serve as a reminder of "the steps at the Gate of the Spring leading up into the City of David" that existed here in the Old Testament period (Neh. 12:37).[4]

In continued observance of the spring's life-giving significance, modern Jews maintain the ritual of the Tashliḥ, the throwing of bread crumbs into the waters of Gihon on the feast of Rosh ha-Shanah, the Jewish New Year.

Plate 70 *Waters of Siloam. The inscription commemorating the completion of Hezekiah's tunnel was discovered about 10 yards inside the exit. It is still customary for women to fetch water from Siloam, and the village youth come to swim in its refreshing waters.*

Reservoirs

FROM ITS ORIGIN at the Spring Gihon, the life-giving water is conveyed through Hezekiah's tunnel to the Pool of Siloam, located on the western slope of Ophel at a point safely within the fortified bounds of the city.

The pool is as sacred as it is historical. On the first morning of the Feast of Tabernacles (Sukkoth), the great pilgrim festival of thanksgiving for the autumn vintage harvest, both priests and pilgrims marched to the Pool of Siloam to draw water in a golden pitcher for the temple libations performed throughout the seven-day festival.[1] It is in response to this observance, according to John, that Jesus proclaimed on the last day of the feast, "If anyone thirst, let him come to me; let him drink who believes in me. Scripture has it: 'From within him rivers of living water shall flow'" (John 7:37).

As the hind longs for running waters,
so my soul longs for you, O God!

Ps. 42:2

Judging from the Johannine sequence, it must have been on the following day that Jesus came upon in the vicinity of the Pool of Siloam a man blind since birth, to whom he said, "I am the light of the world." Jesus anointed the man's eyes with clay and sent him to wash in the pool, whereupon his sight was restored (John 9:1–41). In memory of this miracle Empress Eudocia (A.D. 444–460) constructed upon the ruins of the Hadrianic Nympheium on a hill just above the pool a chapel called the Church of our Savior the Giver of Light. The chapel, which was destroyed by Persian soldiers under Chosroes in 614, was replaced by a mosque. Excavations by F.J. Bliss and A.C. Dickie between 1894 and 1897 have authenticated the site;[2] however, the place has been neglected and little remains visible except a Roman column inserted in the wall at the entrance to the pool and some scattered fragments of column bases in the pool itself.

The importance of the Pool of Siloam as an historical landmark is underscored by Josephus' frequent references to it in his work on the Jewish Wars.[3] Most important is his discussion concerning the topography of Jerusalem and the important material along its walls in the fifth book of his *Jewish Wars*; here he describes the first wall of Jerusalem of the time of Jesus as running from the Gate of the Essenes southwards (actually, southeastwards) above the Spring of Siloam (v. 145).

Jerusalem grew as a city towards the north and west. As the city expanded, water became more in demand, particularly in areas far removed from its original natural water supply, for there were no other springs in this direction. In fact, Jerusalem's particular location on the border between the desert and the sown sometimes put it in an acute situation. In the late Second Temple period, when the population of Jerusalem numbered about 35,000, its dependence on water developed into much greater proportions than ever before, so large had the city grown by this time. Private water collectors were not sufficient. It became imperative to provide other types of hydraulic systems; most of these can still be identified, and some are still in use.

John 5:2 mentions an important reservoir in the vicinity of the Sheep Pool in the northeastern sector outside the walls of Jerusalem. Josephus speaks of yet three other pools, though there must have been more. He mentions the Pool of the Serpent (*BJ* v. 108), traditionally identified with the Birket es-Sultan or the Sultan's Pool, for it was Suleiman the Magnificent who restored it in the Wadi er-Rababeh, the biblical Valley of Hinnom, just below the southwestern corner of the city wall. Josephus also mentions the Amygdalon or Tower Pool just outside the first north wall (*BJ* v. 468; cf. 115). Though the Greek noun *amýgdalon* means "almond," the reservoir actually derived its name from the Hebrew or Aramaic word for tower, *migdal*, precisely because of its proximity to the three great towers built by Herod the Great as part of his palace-fortress in the northwestern part of the city. This Tower Pool is to be identified with the present Birket Hammam el-Batrak, the Pool of the Patriarch's Bath, a large reservoir between the modern Jaffa Gate and the Greek Orthodox Church of St. John the Baptizer, on Christian Quarter Street (Haret en-Nasara) inside the Old City. Originally, this reservoir measured some 279 feet long and about 135 feet wide; it is visible now only from some of the rooftops in the area. The Tower Pool is mentioned by Josephus as the scene where very fierce fighting resumed over Jerusalem in this area between the Jewish defenders of the Holy City and the Tenth Roman Legio Fretensis.[4]

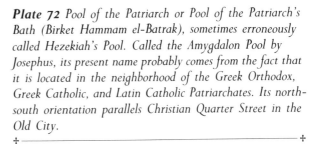

Plate 72 *Pool of the Patriarch or Pool of the Patriarch's Bath (Birket Hammam el-Batrak), sometimes erroneously called Hezekiah's Pool. Called the Amygdalon Pool by Josephus, its present name probably comes from the fact that it is located in the neighborhood of the Greek Orthodox, Greek Catholic, and Latin Catholic Patriarchates. Its north-south orientation parallels Christian Quarter Street in the Old City.*

Plate 73 *Strouthion Pool, beneath the Convent of the Sisters of Sion in the northeastern quarter of the Old City. The pool was carved out of the rock and was open to the sky until the destruction of the city in A.D. 70; it was covered over by huge limestone slabs to form the public square of Hadrian's Aelia Capitolina.*

The third large pool recorded by Josephus is the famous Strouthion Pool, located below the northwestern corner of Fortress Baris, which was later rebuilt and renamed Antonia by Herod the Great (*BJ* i. 75, 118; *Ant.* xv. 403–9). This was a fairly large double pool, hewn out of the rock at this point exclusively to supply water for the Baris Antonia fortress. From Josephus we learn how the Fifth Roman Legion was able to breach the northern walls of the fortress by undermining the ground right up to the earthworks of the fortress itself.

The Strouthion Pool of the first century was open to the sky, as strongly supported by the description in Josephus and confirmed by archaeology. The pool can be visited beneath the second-century-A.D. Hadrianic pavement in the basement of the Convent of the Sisters of Sion. There is no doubt that the reservoir is a Herodian construction, and that the pavement above it is clearly Hadrianic.[5] The pool is 176 feet long and 46 feet wide. It still functions as a reservoir.

It is difficult to explain why Josephus, the only ancient author to mention this pool by name (*BJ* v. 467), calls it the Strouthion, which in Greek signifies a small bird such as a sparrow.[6] Perhaps this, as in the case of the Tyropoeon Valley, is an example of the blending of phonological assimilation and conceptual accommodation to explain the meaning of the word, and perhaps even to give an insight into the history of the place before the pool was hewn out of the rock. According to our interpretation, *strouthíon* stands for Astarte, the fertility goddess called Ashtharah or Ashthoreth in the

Plate 74 *Site of the huge Sheep (Probatic) Pool, also referred to as the Pool of Bethesda, excavated by the White Fathers of St. Anne's Church in the northeastern quarter of the Old City.*
The Basilica of St. Anne is one of the finest examples of Palestinian Crusader-Gothic architecture in the country. On the northern side (left foreground) is the excavated area of the Graeco-Roman Asclepieion. Reconstruction of the five-

porticoed shrine is difficult if not impossible. The ruins in the right foreground formed a part of the apse of a Byzantine church constructed directly over the large double Sheep Pool, the Byzantine Moutier de la Probatique (the Monastery of the Probatique [Pool]). The large water basins here probably served for baptisms.

Old Testament.[7] Clearly, there is a similarity, especially since all of the major consonants can be linguistically explained (*STRouThion = aSTaRTe*). The word is almost a homonym. Obviously, according to the biblical record, the Canaanite fertility cult of Astarte was practiced in Jerusalem, and the proximity of this place to Bethesda makes the explanation all the more plausible since Astarte was the divine consort of the Phoenician god of healing, Eshmun. Her cult must have been practiced in this area, the name Josephus preserves for us in the form of *strouthíon*.

The Birket Israïn, or the Pool of Israel, ran alongside the northern wall of the Haram esh-Sharif; but it has recently been filled in and transformed into a parking lot for traffic entering the city through St. Stephen's Gate. The date of this pool, according to some scholars, can-

not be ascertained. However, Canon J. Wilkinson seems to suggest that it could have been built here around the first half of the third century B.C., when the population of Jerusalem began to expand to the north of the temple enclosure. When the city grew and the need for water increased, larger reservoirs were hewn out of the rocky slope of Bethesda hill north of Birket Israïn. Thus, the latter served no purpose, except perhaps to catch some of the overflow from the other pools.[8]

Père Benoit, however, maintains the opposite view.[9] He believes that the pool is a Herodian construction of the first century B.C. Indeed, the need for water was great in this new, developing part of the city under Herod the Great, and the Pool of Israel was well located to receive the water coming down from the upper part of the Tyropoeon through a small valley that was here in ancient times. The pool was 363 feet long and 126 feet wide, and its depth measured a clear 20 feet. Like most ancient pools, it too had a series of steps leading down into it. It is reported that Capt. C. Warren discovered two subterranean vaulted chambers below this great reservoir, one over the other. An opening beneath this pool, on the north side of the Haram, allowed any superfluous water to flow away.[10] This device probably served as a type of decanter. The pool could very well have served as a source of water for the various temple libations, excepting the Feast of Tabernacles on which water was brought from the Pool of Siloam.

Birket Hammam Sitti Miryam, the Pool of St. Mary's Bath, after which St. Stephen's Gate was also named (Bab Sittna Miryam), is situated outside the present city walls. Its construction is also difficult to date. Perhaps this comparatively small water collector was built here to receive the drain-off from the Sheep Pool. The pool is still visible in the Muslim cemetery outside St. Stephen's Gate, but it serves no modern purpose.

The Sheep Pool, sometimes called the Pool of Bethesda[11] or the Probatic Pool[12] after the Greek word for sheep, próbaton, was an extremely large double reservoir, the largest of the water catchers in the northeastern part of the new city. Its discovery began in 1871, when ancient ruins appeared as the White Fathers were building the Greek Catholic Seminary on the property of the Crusader Church of St. Anne. Intermittent excavations were carried out by the White Fathers with the assistance of the Dominicans of the Ecole Biblique. In 1928 Père L.-H. Vincent published a summary of these efforts. Systematic archaeological explorations were resumed in 1956 by White Fathers Blondel and Pocher, under the direction of Père Rouzée, O.P., also of the French Dominican school. Two important discoveries emerged from these excavations: the Sheep Pool and a complex installation identified with a shrine dedicated to a healing divinity. Both areas are important for a better understanding of John 5:2–15, which describes the healing of a paralytic here.

Excavations on the site of the biblical Sheep Pool revealed one huge irregular trapezoidal cistern, divided into two parts by a rather broad wall about 20 feet wide, running from east to west. The entire reservoir measured approximately 160 feet square: 135 feet on the north; 148.5 on the east; 142.5 on the west and 196.5 on the south. The southern pool was the larger of the two. The depth of this hydraulic installation was some 45 feet, and indications remain that steps led down to the bottom. Located in the vicinity of the ancient sheep market and the biblical Sheep Gate to which it pointed, the Sheep Pool naturally received its name from these two landmarks.

The excavators have established that this pool certainly antedates the foundation of Aelia Capitolina by almost three and a half centuries. They have suggested that it was the high priest Simon II, the son of Onias (Jochanan), who built it sometime between 219 and 196 B.C., for there appears to be an allusion to its construction in Ben Sirach (Ecclus.) 50:1–3. Referring to the reign of Simon (220–195 B.C.), v. 3 reads, "In his time the reservoir was dug, the pool with the vastness of the seas." Scholars usually point to the twin pools on the property of St. Anne's church as the possible location of this reservoir.[13] Aristeas Judaeus, writing in the first century B.C. to a certain Philocrates, mentions the many underground reservoirs in the temple area. It is not altogether certain whether Aristeas is alluding to the great pools outside the temple enclosure or to the subterranean cisterns beneath the temple esplanade itself.[14] We think that it is to the latter, though it may be argued that Aristeas is describing all of the reservoirs related to the Temple, particularly because of the great need of water for animal sacrifices and the like on the Jewish festival days.

In any event, there should be no doubt concerning the existence of the Sheep Pool on the slopes of Bethesda during the time of Jesus. Archaeology confirms it. Also, one of the longest Christian traditions identifies this as the scene of Jesus' healing of the sick man who had waited thirty-eight years for someone to help him step into the waters. As early as the Byzantine period, an impressive basilica was built over and between these two pools, though its builder is not known.[15] The structures in this area can be identified on the famous Byzantine Madaba Map, according to Fr. R.T. O'Callaghan, S.J.[16] The red-roofed edifice on this map would be the church dedicated either to Christ the

Plate 76 *Byzantine foundations of the Moutier de la Probatique. Surrounding the area of the caves and pits must have stood the porticoes mentioned by John. We can envision a square or rectangular enclosure formed of four walls, while a fifth portico located inside the sanctuary was actually the little temple or shrine in which stood the statue of the god Asclepius. It was probably built over the main grotto in this area, the scene of special cures or "miracles," while the others, along with some of the buildings or rooms adjacent to the sanctuary, functioned as the places of incubation and shrines dedicated to such divinities as Telesphoros and the goddess Hygeia, both related to the healing cult as practiced at the great sanctuaries of Asclepius at Pergamum, Epidaurus, and Memphis.*

Plate 77 *(right, middle) Votive gift to Asclepius presented by Ponpeia Loucilia.*

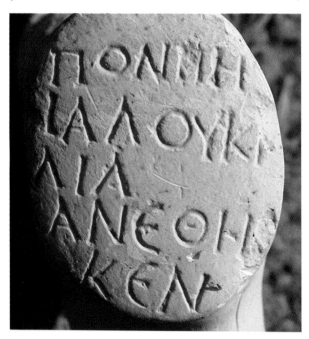

Plate 75 *Greek inscription indicating that Ponpeia Loucilia had presented this thanksgiving offering. The original ex voto is in the Louvre Museum, Paris.*

Plate 78 *Terra-cotta figurine of woman dressing herself after having been cured by the healing waters of Asclepius. She indicates the place of her ailment and cure by holding her left breast in her right hand.*

Healer or to the Virgin Mary who, according to a long tradition, was born in this quarter of Jerusalem close to the Temple. The round golden-domed building adjacent to the church probably served as the baptistery. Judging from its location on the sixth-century map, it seems to have been constructed on the site honoring the miracle performed by Jesus.

The archaeological explorations undertaken by the White Fathers have exposed further evidence for the existence of a healing-cult shrine in this special area. To the right of the Sheep Pool the excavators discovered a rather complex hydraulic installation of vaulted underground chambers cut out of the rock. These were grouped together within a rather limited area around a more important natural grotto. Some of these caverns were decorated with paintings and mosaics, but it is not clear exactly what they represented. Steps led down into these grottos. In addition to the basins found in them, a water tunnel and a series of canals were also uncovered.[17] This ensemble has been dated to the Roman period, but it was later reused in the time of Hadrian's Aelia Capitolina, and identified as an Asclepieion, a shrine dedicated to the god Asclepios (Latin Aesculapius), the tutelary god of medicine and healing in the Graeco-Roman world; Asclepios is also to be equated with Serapis, the ancient Egyptian god of the underworld. This identification was confirmed by the discovery of a number of interesting ex voto offerings from the period of Hadrian, deposited here by pilgrims who had obtained the favor they had prayed for from the divine thaumaturge. Within each cavern of the Hadrianic period were found small pools or baths, employed in the Asclepian ritual of incubation underground, for Asclepios was also a chthonic divinity like Serapis. Both the incubation rite, which was a central feature of the cure, and the ablutions in the pools were essential, for the waters were believed to possess medicinal qualities. Miracles were said to take place at the sanctuaries of Asclepios. Some, it is believed, were genuine, while others could be explained by either auto-suggestion in dreams or dances, or by therapeutic methods such as baths, diets, and various kinds of exercises. The sanctuary was indeed a sanatorium where believers in Asclepios' miraculous powers came to be healed.

In gratitude for their cures the worshipers placed some of the ex voto offerings that have been recovered in excavations. These have helped in identification of both the site and the type of cure sought. They are indeed similar to those found at the famous Asclepieia of Epidaurus in southern Greece and Pergamum in western Asia Minor, as also more recently at Memphis in Lower Egypt.[18] The cures and favors represented include: 1. a terra-cotta statuette of a young woman with her right hand over her left breast, indicating the place where she had been healed; 2. an ex voto of a foot with the Greek inscription of the donor, "Pompeia Lucilia dedicated [me]"; 3. a white marble bas-relief which depicts a woman in the ritual bath inside a cavern (another possible explanation is that the woman is in the state of incubation); 4. two small boats carved out of rock, offered in thanksgiving to Asclepios for the protection received from the dangers of the sea; and, of particular interest, 5. two fragments of a small shrine of Asclepios: the bottom part depicts the sacred serpent that assisted the god in the cures, while the upper part features sheaves of wheat, associated with the death-life ritual of chthonian divinities, as on the famous Chore relief of Eleusis.[19] Unhappily, the middle section and a part of the right side are lost, but we can conclude that they represented a figure of Asclepios with perhaps a grateful devotee kneeling beside him. In view of this material evidence, it is clear that the cult of Asclepios (Roman Aesculapius) was practiced here in the time of Hadrian's gentile Aelia Capitolina.[20]

To whom was this sanctuary-sanatorium dedicated during the Herodian period, when Jesus visited Jerusalem? There are two possibilities, especially since this area certainly was devoted to a healing cult, as mentioned by the evangelist John. The shrine was either that of (a) the Semitic Eshmun or Shedrapha or (b) the Hellenistic Asclepios, known as Serapis in Egypt. In Aramaic the site was simply referred to as Beth-hesda', the Place (or, more literally, "house") of Mercy, as also with reference to the name of the northeastern hill and quarter of Jerusalem.

Foreign divinities had been introduced by the rulers of Jerusalem and welcomed by its more liberal-minded inhabitants as early as Solomon (961–922 B.C.). By the

Plate 79 Two fragments which apparently belong to a small shrine (or shrines) of Asclepius used as an ex voto in fulfillment of a vow made to the divinity for a favor granted to the worshiper. One can easily see the serpent, perhaps coiled around the staff of Asclepius, the symbol of the god, and the grains of wheat generally associated with chthonic divinities as a sign of the fruitfulness of the earth.

time of Manasseh, the impious king of Judah (687–642 B.C.), the worship of the healing god Eshmun of Sidon (meaning "he who restores the heat [*esh, "fire of life," according to Damascius)[21]or of the Syro-Phoenician god Shedrapha (interpreted by J. Starcky as the "genius-healer"[22]), must have been common in Jerusalem, and it is possible that the sanctuary of the thaumaturge was located here. This area was chosen, we think, not only because it lay a convenient, if not proper, distance from the Temple of Yahweh, but also because the rain waters collected in the wadi here were believed to have curative properties. The pagan tradition of a healing cult was perpetuated here until the capture of Jerusalem by the Greek armies of Alexander the Great around 331 B.C.[23] and by the Romans under Pompey in 63 B.C. Thus it is quite possible that only the Semitic name, not the divine qualities or attributes of the divinity worshiped on the site, now changed. In other words, the Semitic shrine of Eshmun or Shedrapha was now known as that of Asclepios (Aesculapius).

The more orthodox and pious Jews, however, disgraced and ashamed of such a profanation of Jerusalem, the city of Yàhweh, would have refrained from calling this place by its pagan name, and would have euphemistically referred to it simply as Bethesda, the place or house of mercy, where their pagan neighbors worshiped and prayed for miracles. Thus the historical and religious background of Bethesda and consequently that of John 5:2–9 is the story of a pagan sanctuary which, according to our interpretation, was an Asclepieion. Archaeology confirms this identification for the Hadrianic period in Jerusalem; history and the Scriptures help us understand the nature of the place in the Old and New Testament periods. The story goes back to the second century B.C. and is based on the account given in 1 Macc. 1:1–63, which should be read and studied in conjunction with Josephus *Ant.* xii. 237–256.

In Jerusalem, prior to the accession of Antiochus IV Epiphanes to the throne of the Syrian Seleucid Dynasty, some Jews of the rich class and the sacerdotal aristocracy were literally breakers of the law and seducers of the people. They were strongly opposed to orthodox Judaism and desired to embrace a thoroughly Hellenistic way of life. By abandoning traditional Jewish religious and cultural practices, these Hellenizers antagonized the more orthodox majority, and various factions arose in the city. To restore peace, if even with a strong force, Antiochus resolved to suppress Judaism, so he authorized the pagan religion of the Hellenistic Gentiles. This pleased the Hellenizing Jewish group; but it all but annihilated the orthodox, for whoever refused to worship the pagan divinities or to live completely like a Gentile was put to death. In more ways than one the city of the Temple became the abode of strangers, of false gods and foreign customs. At the request of the Jews, Antiochus had a gymnasium built in the city. He invaded the Temple, desecrated the Holy of Holies, and carried off its many treasures. Sacrifices were now offered to the Olympian Zeus in the Temple, and the Sabbath was profaned. The scrolls of the Law were torn up and burnt. By royal decree Jerusalem became a city of pagan altars, temples, and shrines, among which must have been a sanctuary-sanitorium dedicated to Asclepios and a shrine to Ashtoreth (Astarte) nearby.

This situation in Jerusalem lasted until 165 B.C., when Judas Maccabaeus purified the Temple and rededicated it to Yahweh on the twenty-fifth day of the month of Kislew (December), commemorated by the Feast of the Dedication of the Temple or Hanukkah.[24] However, even after the Jews renewed their devotion to Yahweh, many Gentiles continued to live in the Holy City with the Jews. After Pompey's conquest of Palestine the people were permitted to practice their pagan cultus. The sanctuary of the Graeco-Roman Aesculapius with its five porticoes and pools for cures still stood outside the city walls in the vicinity of the Sheep Gate and sheep market. Archaeological excavations on this site have failed to bring to light any remains of a five-porticoed shrine. The more probable explanation is that this shrine, because of its position in the northeastern sector of the city, had already been destroyed by Titus' armies. Then, too, the Hadrianic monument on this site must have been quite different in design from its first-century predecessor. Finally, when in the early Byzantine period the Christian majority in Jerusalem began building churches and shrines throughout the Holy City, the material of the pagan shrine of Aesculapius was reused to build a Christian church on the site of Jesus' healing of the paralytic here.

In John's Gospel we read that the five porticoes of the shrine were crowded with sick people—blind, lame, and variously disabled. Some believers in Aesculapius' healing powers waited there a very long time, like the sick man mentioned in John 5:5, who hoped for thirty-eight years that someone would help him into one of the baths in the sanctuary.

It is difficult, if not now impossible, to draw an exact plan of the shrine described in John. Quite certainly, we think, it did not look like those designs which equate the two large basins of the Sheep Pool with the Asclepieion of Bethesda.[25] The reference to five porticoes could depict a pentagonal shrine of Aesculapius adjacent either to the Sheep Pool or to a square colonnaded enclosure around a central, probably circular and domed, aedicule, also adorned with columns, in which was enshrined a statue of the god of medicine and healings. According to our reconstruction, the five ambulatories would have been open on all of the sides. Walking alongside one of these porticoes Jesus saw the paralytic and cured him, for he had come there to teach by example that he alone was the true source of life and the healer of the sick.

Some reliable texts of John 5:7, which St. Jerome followed in his Latin Vulgate, insert an adjectival clause to describe and explain, from a Christian point of view, the miraculous cures that were supposed to have happened during the pre-Christian era. The many invalids lay beneath the porticoes, "waiting for the movement of the water" (A D W Θ p^{66}, etc.), "for at a certain season an angel of the Lord went down into the pool and troubled the water; whosoever then stepped in after the troubling of the water was made whole of whatsoever disease he had" (A Ψ Θ L p$^{66, 75}$). One possible explanation for the "stirring up" of the water at a certain time of the year would be that towards the end of a particular heavy rainy season (during the winter months in Palestine), when the large Sheep Pool had been filled up, its surplus could have easily been channeled from it into the basins inside the Asclepieion. The channels mentioned above (p. 81, note 17) help to support this view, though much relevant material evidence probably was destroyed in building the Byzantine structures on the site. The pagans attributed their cures here to the god of medicine; the Christians later credited them to the Angel of the Lord. The biblical text, however, clearly indicates that it was Jesus himself, the Lord.

Plate 80 *A pipe of the Upper Aqueduct, as it curves along the slope of Mt. Zion a few yards above the modern road.*

The Aqueducts

DURING THE Graeco-Roman period aqueducts were quite common, and there are excellent traces of such ancient hydraulic systems in various parts of the Holy Land today. Aqueducts supplied water for the storage cisterns of the Alexandreion (Qarn Sartabeh, "Fortress of the Slayer"), Jericho, Qumran, Masada, the Herodion, Samaria-Sebaste, and Caesarea on the seacoast. Jerusalem was by no means an exception. Indeed, the Holy City was gifted with two such water conveyors, both bringing water from the south. If the north forebode danger and possible death, the south promised life and survival.

Spring Gihon and the winter rains that provided water for the reservoirs proved to be an insufficient source of water for the rapidly growing Jerusalem of Herod the Great. Gihon, a small though very rich spring, provided enough water for the southern portion of the Lower City. The winter rains from November to April supplied the pools and cisterns excellently located in the wadis in the other quarters of Jerusalem. But Jerusalem could not rely on these exclusively during Herod's reign. Water was needed as much in the home for domestic purposes as it was in the Temple for the various ritual ablutions, animal sacrifices, and ceremonial libations, as well as for the ordinary cleaning of the huge temple courts.

New sources of water were essential; but, as can be seen from the geography and topography of Jerusalem, the only other good spring in the immediate surroundings was Ein-'Rogel (Bir-'Ayyub or the "Well of Job") in the Kidron Valley. This spring, which marked the boundary of Judah and Benjamin, lies about 345 feet below the esplanade of the Temple, and it measures about 123 feet deep, depending on the amount of rainfall. It was never incorporated into the city by walls, and would have been virtually inaccessible in wartime.

Water, therefore, was sought in the higher hill country south of Jerusalem, from which direction it was difficult to storm the city's defenses. The mountainous Judaean terrain south of Jerusalem was on a higher altitude than the city itself (over 2220 feet above sea level). The hills in the vicinity of Ein-'arrub, on the watershed

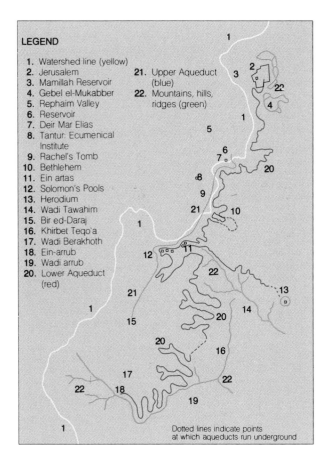

LEGEND

1. Watershed line (yellow)
2. Jerusalem
3. Mamillah Reservoir
4. Gebel el-Mukabber
5. Rephaim Valley
6. Reservoir
7. Deir Mar Elias
8. Tantur: Ecumenical Institute
9. Rachel's Tomb
10. Bethlehem
11. Ein artas
12. Solomon's Pools
13. Herodium
14. Wadi Tawahim
15. Bir ed-Daraj
16. Khirbet Teqo'a
17. Wadi Berakhoth
18. Ein-arrub
19. Wadi arrub
20. Lower Aqueduct (red)
21. Upper Aqueduct (blue)
22. Mountains, hills, ridges (green)

Dotted lines indicate points at which aqueducts run underground

Figure 10 AQUEDUCTS

He made streams flow from the crag and brought waters forth in rivers.

Ps. 78:16

route about 15 miles south, were approximately 2490 feet above sea level. The neighborhood of Ein ed-Daraj and the so-called Pools of Solomon (near the springs known as Ein-Saleh and Ein-Artas), situated on the same route 12 miles south, was slightly lower, approximately 2400 feet. Water could, therefore, be easily enough conveyed from these distances through an ingenious system of aqueducts, with which the Hellenistic and Roman rulers of Palestine were quite familiar.

Jerusalem had two aqueducts that supplied water from the south, commonly referred to as the lower and upper aqueducts. The course of each is easily traceable, but scholars differ regarding their builders and the dates of their construction. The lower aqueduct, for instance, is thought to have been built by Solomon or perhaps some king of Judah not mentioned by name in the Bible. Yet there seems to have been no pressing need for an extra source of water at this early period. Spring Gihon, Solomon's Pool, Hezekiah's conduit, and the Siloam Pool, not to mention the private cisterns that were replenished during the rainy season, would have sufficed, because the city was rather small, limited mostly to the lower, eastern slopes of the Jerusalem promontory.

With regard to the upper aqueduct, however, scholars are on much safer ground in attempting to establish the builder and the period of the aqueduct's construction and restoration. The workmanship of this channel is clearly Roman. It was evidently executed under skillful technicians during the reign of Herod the Great (37–4 B.C.) and completed by Pontius Pilate's craftsmen sometime during his governorship of Judaea between A.D. 26 and 36.

It is possible but not probable that Herod the Great, in order to supplement the local water reserve in the rapidly expanding city, had a fresh supply of spring water brought in to fill his newly-built reservoirs as well as to replenish the existing pools. Most authorities attribute the construction of the upper aqueduct to Idumaean rulers of Jerusalem. Josephus assigns its construction to Pontius Pilate, however, accusing him of appropriating the temple treasury (*korbōnás*) for the construction of the Jerusalem aqueduct from a distance of 400 stadia (*BJ* ii. 169–177; *Ant.* xviii. 55–69).[1] It may be argued, however, that this action was justifiable because the

Plate 81 General view of the Roman aqueduct in Bethlehem along the Jerusalem-Hebron highway. Notice how the large blocks serve as foundations for the houses built above this historic hydraulic system.

Plate 82 Detail of one of the pipes. Each block was made of hard limestone, then carved in such a way that one pipe would fit exactly into another.

Jerusalem municipality had neglected its duty to keep the aqueduct in good repair.[2]

This important water channel was in constant need of care and repairs during the seventeen long centuries that it served the growing Jerusalem community—from the first century of Herod and the Herodian kings through the subsequent Roman, Byzantine, early Arab, and Crusader periods, until the Saracenic Sultans in the seventeenth century.

As early as the second century, the Roman Legio Decima Fretensis restored the upper aqueduct for Hadrian's Aelia Capitolina. Almost a century later, the same Roman legion repaired it during the reign of Septimius Severus (193–211); among the nine names of Roman centurions inscribed on the channel's drums was that of Julius Clemens who served as the tribune and legate under Septimius Severus.[3] Père F.-M. Abel, O.P., says that both aqueducts, the lower as well as the upper, were used during the later Roman and Byzantine period.[4]

What was the course of these aqueducts? The line of the lower system began at Ein-Arrub, 15 miles south of Jerusalem. The water from this powerful spring, channeled with the waters of nearby Bir-Kufin and Ein-Kuweiziba, was conveyed through a channel, which in some places was made of rocks covered with plaster, while in other sections it was hewn out of the limestone terrain, following a very tortuous route through the twisting valleys alongside the clusters of hills in this area. From its source at Ein-Arrub this aqueduct turned eastwards towards Tekoa, whence it followed a northerly direction to Ein-Artas, then veered westwards towards Eitam and the so-called Pools of Solomon. From here it passed through Bethlehem. It then followed the contours of the southwestern slopes of Gebel Mukabber in the direction of the Hinnom Valley, from which point it moved along the slope of Mt. Zion, crossed the Tyropoeon Valley, and finally terminated on the Temple Mount (at the present site of el-Kas just north of the el-Aqsa Mosque). The distance is only 15 miles, but the aqueduct itself winds and twists, as can still be seen today, for some 50 miles!

The rough workmanship of this aqueduct naturally suggests an earlier builder than the finer construction of the upper-level water system. It can perhaps be assigned to the end of the second or beginning of the first century B.C., towards the close of the Second Temple period. Jerusalem was now a much larger city, due partly to the Jews' having reestablished themselves in the city after the Maccabean victory of 165 B.C., and partly to the increased numbers of Gentiles who made Jerusalem their permanent residence during the Hellenistic period.

The course of the upper aqueduct was shorter (12 miles) and straighter. The copious spring at Bir ed-Daraj,[5] its source on the Jerusalem-Hebron highway, the newer subterranean conduit conveyed the waters in a rather straight northerly direction, curving slightly northeastwards for only a short measure at Eitam, where it touched Ein-Saleh near Solomon's Pool. As it straightened again, the channel then appeared above ground, by-passing Bethlehem and continuing towards Tantur, Deir Mar Elias, and Ramat-Rachel in the direction of Jerusalem. It disappears in the Beqa'a (in the vicinity of the modern Jerusalem railway station) southwest of the city, but it is logical to assume that it joined the older aqueduct somewhere in this neighborhood.

The execution of this hydraulic system is more precise than that of the older lower channel. The underground sections display much finer tunneling through the hard rock, while the stretches above ground, the stone siphon pipes, display more sophisticated methods of engineering. The latter were made of gigantic blocks of stone fitted tighly together and cemented with lead and limestone mortar. Sections of this aqueduct are still visible above ground near Bethlehem and the traditional Tomb of Rachel on the Jerusalem-Hebron road.

The elaborate measures taken to obtain, convey, and protect Jerusalem's vital supply of water, and the impact of that essential commodity on the religious, economic, and political history of the city are underscored by the language used by Jesus to proclaim his mission. "If anyone thirsts," he cried out on the Feast of Tabernacles, "let him come to me; let him drink who believes in me!" (John 7:37).

Plate 83 *Aerial view of Jerusalem, from the northwest.*

CHAPTER **VI**

Fortress Jerusalem

Walk about Jerusalem, make the round; count her towers. Consider her ramparts, examine her castles.

Ps. 48:13–14

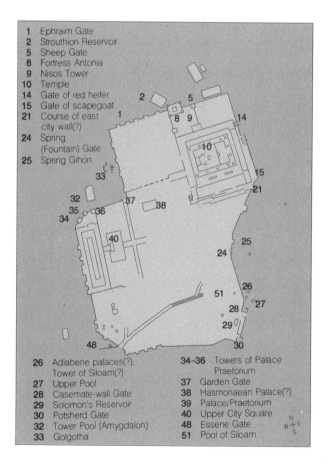

1	Ephraim Gate
2	Strouthion Reservoir
5	Sheep Gate
8	Fortress Antonia
9	Nisos Tower
10	Temple
14	Gate of red heifer
15	Gate of scapegoat
21	Course of east city wall(?)
24	Spring (Fountain) Gate
25	Spring Gihon

26	Adiabene palaces(?), Tower of Siloam(?)	**34–36**	Towers of Palace Praetorium
27	Upper Pool	**37**	Garden Gate
28	Casemate-wall Gate	**38**	Hasmonaean Palace(?)
29	Solomon's Reservoir	**39**	Palace/Praetorium
30	Potsherd Gate	**40**	Upper City Square
32	Tower Pool (Amygdalon)	**48**	Essene Gate
33	Golgotha	**51**	Pool of Siloam

Figure 11 FORTRESS JERUSALEM

ISAIAH AND JEREMIAH repeatedly warned the citizens of Jerusalem against the ominous north. "For there comes a smoke from the north without a straggler in the ranks," Isaiah forebode (Isa. 14:31). Just over a century later, Jeremiah alerted the people of Jerusalem with the cry, "Listen! a noise! it comes closer, a great uproar from the northern land: to turn the cities of Judah into a desert haunt of jackals" (Jer. 10:22). Throughout the centuries the north signaled danger for Jerusalem because Palestine was not much more than a corridor, an international highway, for armies marching southwards: the Greek generals and the Emperors of Rome, the monarchs of Assyria, Babylon, and Persia, the Seleucid rulers of Syria, all advanced their troops towards Jerusalem. The city's water supply and walls were not sufficient by themselves for the security and survival of its inhabitants. Therefore, to look out for and hold back the invaders from the north the rulers of Jerusalem built strong fortresses.

From its earliest days Jerusalem's citizens not only built a strong northern defense system, the walls of Jerusalem, but they also strategically positioned watchtowers and fortresses to warn and protect themselves from the inevitable danger. In the days when Jesus would visit the City of the Temple, fortified as it was by Herod the Great, his eyes would have marveled at the two magnificent palace-fortresses in the northern parts of the Holy City. Herod, who embellished his city, would not expose Jerusalem to be attacked and plundered as easily as it had been in the past.

In the northeast, Herod built the mighty Fortress Antonia, surveying the Sacred City from just above the temple area. In the newer northwestern part of the city, he erected his royal residence, at the same time a palace and a fortress, with its courts and towers designed not only to guard his own household but also to oversee the modern Hellenistic quarter on Mt. Zion.[1] Herod must have felt perfectly secure in the city he had beautified and fortified for his own pleasure and safety.

Today, virtually nothing remains of these particular buildings. Archaeologists search among the debris beneath the present structures, while artists try to recapture Herod's former pride and glory. Scholars continue to debate where these splendid buildings stood and to imagine what these edifices must have looked like.

Plate 84 *Artist's representation of the Fortress Antonia according to the Jerusalem Temple Model, giving some idea of the northern and western porticoes of the Temple, which were contiguous with Antonia. The first tower (right foreground),* which would have been built over the secret passageway beneath the Tadi Gate of the Temple, was much larger than the other three towers seen here.

Fortress Antonia

QUITE CERTAINLY some kind of tower or lookout post existed on the rocky eminence that rises just a short distance from the Temple in the northwestern part of the Ophel-Moriah spur. The height of this rocky platform is approximately 75 feet, and its flat top measures around 369 feet from east to west. From such a tower the structures below and, indeed, the entire countryside for miles could be surveyed, forewarning Jerusalem's inhabitants in case of imminent danger. The city's gates then would have been shut and bolted immediately, and the defending army would have positioned itself in strategic places on the battlements and in the towers, all ready against the enemy's assault.

Judging from the history of Jerusalem, there can scarcely be any doubt concerning the importance of this particular high point in the city. Its history must surely go much farther back into the distant past than might at first be suspected. For instance, records show that the Tower of Hananel, mentioned first by Jeremiah *ca.* 587 (Jer. 31:38), stood on this site. For Jeremiah, this was to be the starting point of the new Jerusalem. "'The days are coming,' says the Lord, 'when the city shall be rebuilt as the Lord's from the Tower of Hananel to the Corner Gate. The measuring line shall be stretched from there straight to the hill of Gareb [that is, westwards] and then turn towards Goah'" (Jer. 31:38–39).

It is not known exactly why this tower was named Hananel ("God is gracious"). Perhaps this was either because it served as Jerusalem's stronghold in the north, thus protecting both the city and the Temple below from complete obliteration and thereby showing God's graciousness. Or, perhaps this name was given because on top of this platform or nearby had stood some of the pagan Canaanite high places and sanctuaries to whose cult many of the kings of Judah had been attracted; but in the days of Jeremiah, the cult places were destroyed, so complete dedication to Yahweh was rendered him by all of his people. Later, both the hill and the district to the north of Hananel would be called Bethesda, the place of mercy.

One may very well ask at this point if it is possible to identify this site with some biblical reference prior to

O you who are to remind the Lord, take no rest, and give no rest to him, until he reestablishes Jerusalem and makes of it the pride of the earth!

Isa. 62:6c–7

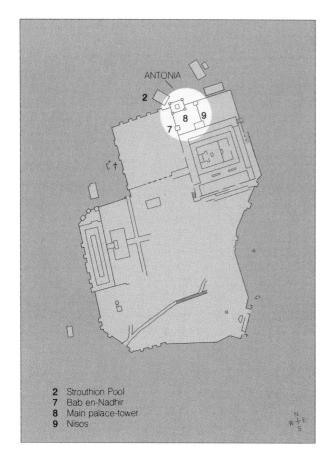

2 Strouthion Pool
7 Bab en-Nadhir
8 Main palace-tower
9 Nisos

Figure 12 FORTRESS ANTONIA

Plate 85 Muslim Omariyyeh School, on the Turonian limestone elevation in the northwest corner of the Moriah spur. This corner of the Haram was not one large, level plateau, but originally a rocky hill dominating the southern portion of the present Islamic sanctuary, the former Temple Mount. The school is founded upon the solid rocky platform that was once the foundation of the palace proper of Fortress Antonia and its many predecessors. The main palace tower stood on this platform, while the large open space in front of it (the present northwestern area of the esplanade) formed a part of Antonia's courtyards and barracks.

Jeremiah in the sixth century B.C. We think that this is possible in light of the study of the topography and history of the upper portions of the Ophel-Moriah hill and a reexamination of the biblical passages themselves.

Considering the topography and history of the area, the promontory that forms the northwest corner of the Ophel-Moriah spur was much too high and conspicuous to have been ignored, especially from a military point of view. It was very close to the threshing floor which David had purchased from Araunah[1] the Jebusite on which he would erect the altar that Yahweh had ordered (2 Sam. 24:16–25). David would have instinctively sought to fortify this elevation, which was the natural defense for the holy place, and would eventually become his own fortress and stronghold (Hebrew *meṣudah*). In the early tenth century B.C., then, this would have been the logical location of Jerusalem's citadel. David did not need to rebuild the walls of the Jebusite fortress city because he did not capture it by storm. Thus, the old Jebusite fortifications were still standing throughout his reign. The walls which he is said to have built would have been much higher up the eastern hill, enclosing the area newly settled by the Israelites under David. The Jebusites would have remained below, living side by side with the Israelites who built their homes in the neighborhood of Yahweh's altar. This explanation offers another insight into the meaning of 2 Sam. 5:9, which reads: "David then dwelt in the stronghold, which was called the City of David; he built up the area from Millo to the palace." From this vantage point, now his dwelling-place, it was easy for David to keep watch over

the newly developed quarter, its people, and its altar.

With its increased population Jerusalem was a larger city now. The Jebusites remained undisturbed in their quarter of the town, as suggested by the presence of both Araunah and David (2 Sam. 24:16–25; 1 Chr. 21:15–30). In light of this, we would distinguish here between the Jerusalem of the Jebusites (called specifically "Jebus" in Jgs. 19:10–11; 1 Chr. 11:4–5) and the Jerusalem of the Israelites (named the "City of David" in 2 Sam. 5:7, 9, considered a gloss; 6:10, 12, 16; and mentioned frequently in 1–2 Kings as the burial place of the kings of Judah; see also 1 Kgs. 3:1; 8:1; 9:24; Isa. 22:9). Under David's strong administration, both Israelites and Jebusites must have lived together in relative peace and security.

In 1 Kgs. 9:15 begins the "account of the forced labor King Solomon levied in order to build the Temple of the Lord, his palace, the Millo, the wall of Jerusalem." If Millo is taken to be the stronghold situated on the platform (1 Kgs. 1:15), the highest point of the northwestern part of the Ophel-Moriah spur, and this is identified with the palace-fortress in which David lived, then we can also suggest a location for Solomon's palace and define the biblical Millo. We are of the opinion that it is possible etymologically and syntactically to equate the two. The Hebrew text of 1 Kgs. 9:15, which states the reason for the levying of the tax on the people, may be translated "to build the Temple of the Lord, his palace, Millo, the wall of Jerusalem" (New American Bible). We propose that *we-* be construed as an epexegetical *we-*, meaning "namely," especially since the idea of totality is conveyed not by conjunctions but by the nouns. Thus, Solomon imposed taxes on his citizens "to build the Temple of the Lord, his palace, namely the terrace, and the walls of Jerusalem."[2] (To our knowledge there is no specific biblical text indicating that David's fortress and Solomon's palace were in the former Jebusite city [identified by Kenyon with the southern spur of Ophel[3]] or that it lay somewhere south of the altar or Temple.)

Many scholars have speculated on the meaning of the word "Millo." Kenyon suggests that the original translators of the Old Testament did not understand what was meant, simply transcribing the Hebrew original, which is from a Semitic root meaning "filling in." The stone-filled terraces discovered in her 1961–1967 excavations "could very justly be described as *Millo*."[4] However, such a derivation would make it difficult to understand the purpose of the tautology expressed in the translations and interpretations, such as "filling in the Millo," or "building up the Millo" in the sense of filling (something) up.

The suggestion that Millo be derived from Assyrian *mulû*, hence *tamlû* meaning a "terrace," which is etymologically related to Hebrew *m-l-'*,[5] is, in our estimation, correct and offers a plausible explanation of 1 Kgs. 9:15 and parallel passages.[6] Thus, this word described originally a "platform," or, more precisely, the platform or terrace of a temple or palace. In Mesopotamia such a platform was usually made of baked bricks,[7] but it could also point to the higher spur of Moriah, especially when this rocky elevation was cut and dressed, first by David for his own stronghold, then by Solomon for the palace.

In view of these etymological and topographical explanations, this platform must have functioned as the foundation subsequently also for the palaces of the kings of Judah, from Rehoboam's accession in 922 B.C. to the close of Zedekiah's reign in 587, when the Babylonian captivity began. Sometime during this period, we suggest, this spur was also referred to as the Tower of Hananel, since Hebrew *migdal* can signify either a tower or a fortress. Thus, this site was a landmark of very special importance for some four hundred years. It would certainly have been remembered by the Jewish returnees from Babylon in 537 B.C. After the Exile, Zechariah alludes to this site when he writes that Jerusalem will

remain exalted in its restoration "from the Tower of Hananel [the northernmost point of the city's defenses] to the king's wine presses [the southernmost part of Jerusalem]" (Zech. 14:10). Later, Nehemiah refers to it as "the fortress" (*birah*) of the Temple (Neh. 2:8). Hanani and Hananiah were stationed on it (7:2). The Tower of Hananel should be identified with the tower located between the Sheep Gate to the east and the Fish Gate to the west (Neh. 3:2).

During the Hasmonaean rule over Jerusalem and Judaea in the second century B.C., the sons of the Maccabees made this spot the site of their fortress-citadel, the Birah or "capital."[8] Around 167 B.C. the Seleucids of Syria destroyed the Birah, but Antiochus IV Epiphanes rebuilt it (*Ant.* xii. 362–64, 369, 405–6). The Syrians were now in an excellent strategic position to control both the temple area and the city proper from this vantage point (*BJ* i. 39). But when in 165 B.C. the Maccabees under Judas Maccabaeus regained control of Jerusalem after their victory over Lysias (1 Macc. 4:26–35), the Temple was purified and rededicated, and the city restored to its former position of honor (1 Macc. 4:36–60; 2 Macc. 10:1–8). Again some thirty years later, when the Hasmonaean party won Jerusalem *ca.* 134 B.C., John Hyrcanus I (135–105 B.C.) rebuilt the Birah and called it, in Greek, Baris (*Ant.* xviii. 91). In sum, the Maccabean Birah, Seleucid Akra, and the Hasmonaean Baris should all be considered as situated on the same site and so virtually one and the same fortress.[9]

That fortress Baris was also known as the Akra in the first century B.C. is explicit in Josephus' account of Pompey's conquest of Jerusalem in 63 B.C. (*BJ* i. 137–39). It is plausible that the same fortress stood intact until the reign of Herod the Great over Judaea (37 to 4 B.C.) However, in his vast building program Herod rebuilt the citadel of Baris and renamed it Antonia after his Roman friend and patron, Marcus Antonius (*BJ* i. 75, 118; cf. *Ant.* xviii. 92). This reconstruction would have been early in Herod's reign, no doubt before Antony's humiliating defeat in the battle of Actium in 31 B.C. Herod also lived in the Antonia during the first years of his administration, between 35 and 23.

Located in the northwestern corner of the Lower City

and overlooking the temple area (*Ant.* xx. 110), Fortress Antonia was situated at the angle where the northern and western porticoes of the Temple met (*BJ* v. 238). Indeed, the walls of the Antonia were contiguous with those of the northern portico of the Temple. From this location it commanded a strong military position unparalleled in that part of Jerusalem.

Josephus gives a rather detailed, though not always clear, description of the Antonia (*BJ* v. 238-247). He defines it as a fortress (*phroúrion*) with the over-all appearance of a large tower (*pyrgoeidés*), with four other towers (*pýrgois*) at each of the four corners of the entire military installation. It looked like a city, Josephus says, because of all its special facilities, and it resembled a palace, because it was so impressive. Indeed, this special landmark was the product of Herod the Great's genius as a builder, architect, and artist.

The principal tower of the Antonia was built on a rocky spur fifty cubits (*ca.* seventy-five feet) high. The tower itself measured forty cubits (sixty feet) high. This was the royal residence until the palace-fortress on the western or upper city was completed. In front of this gigantic structure ran a wall three cubits (*ca.* four feet) high. The interior of the entire complex was like a palace: spacious, with all sorts of palatial accommodations and even military facilities; it was adorned with many porticoes, its own baths, and wide courtyards for the troops.

On the evidence of Josephus (*BJ* v. 242-44), the great tower was surrounded by four other towers: three of these measured 50 cubits (75 feet) high, but the tower on the southeast, which looked directly into the temple precincts, was 70 cubits (*ca.* 105 feet) tall. This tower had stairs on both sides; one set led into the temple area, the other into the Antonia fortress. When the Roman procurators governed Palestine from A.D. 6, a cohort of about 1,000 Roman soldiers was permanently stationed in Antonia, and a brigade (*manipulus*) of between 120 and 200 men was positioned at this southeastern tower. According to Josephus, this tower and the southern wall of the Antonia were contiguous with the northern wall to the Temple. On the principal Jewish festival days when literally thousands of pilgrims thronged to Jerusalem, crowding the narrow streets of the city and filling the temple esplanade, the procurator's armed soldiers took up positions on the roofs of the fortress and the temple porticoes to watch the crowds below. Guards occupied the city, the Temple, and the fortress, keeping a watchful eye on the pilgrims as well as on their own comrades, in the event that either trickery or violence should break out into rioting. In this way the Romans were determined to keep peace and order in the city at practically all costs.

To judge from Josephus' description, Antonia was a very large and truly magnificent fortress. It was worthy to stand so near to the Temple; in fact, a very large portion of it occupied the same platform as the Temple itself, and was very probably encompassed by the same walls. Josephus describes the masonry of these walls: the rock on which Antonia stood was covered with smoothly dressed blocks of stone from the base up to the very top. This stonework not only embellished the fortress and the Temple Mount, but it also functioned as a deterrent which caused the intruder to slip off should he attempt to scale the ramparts. Herodian masonry is still visible in many sections of the wall today. More segments have come to light since the 1967 war, as Israeli archaeologists, under the direction of Prof. B. Mazar, have attempted to explore as much of the area around the Haram esh-Sharif as possible in order to determine scientifically the extent of the Herodian enclosure (cf. *BJ* v. 244). However, relatively nothing was discovered of either the Antonia or the Temple as such. Subsequent armies, such as that of Emperor Hadrian, had leveled off most of the material in order to rebuild a new Roman Jerusalem. Since the excavations have closed, it is unlikely that new material will be brought to light concerning these monuments.

Serious topographical questions remain concerning the exact location and extent of this fortress. For instance, where did the tallest of the five towers stand in the days of Herod and of Jesus' visits to Jerusalem? Where were the four other towers which Josephus describes? Where was the wall "in front of the structure of the tower" (*BJ* v. 240)? How large were the buildings, and how spacious were the courtyards for the cohorts, especially if at least 1,000 troops were stationed here? Finally, does the title Antonia in conjunction with the

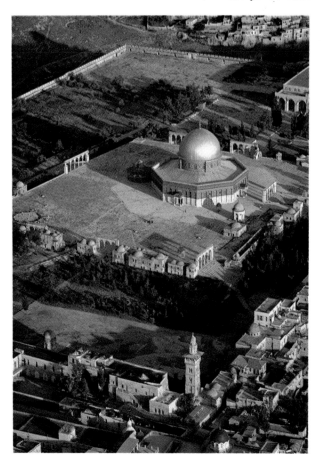

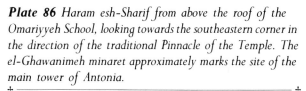

words for fortress (*phroúrion*) and tower(s) (*pýrgos, pýrgoi*) as employed by Josephus imply two separate entities or only one large palace-fortress complex?

During the past 150 years or so, scholars have proposed theories and drawn sketches of the Antonia, in order to answer these questions or to shed light on Josephus' account. One now completely outdated and certainly unfounded plan is that drawn up by J. Ferguson, who in his study on the Jewish temples and other buildings in the Haram esh-Sharif represents what might be called the extreme southern theory. According to Ferguson the north wall of Antonia would have begun only a short distance northeast of the Dome of the Rock, extending westwards about 450 feet, then veering slightly southeastwards towards the present Chain Street (Tariq Bab es-Silsileh), where it turned directly westwards, incorporating the entire area (north and south) over Wilson's Arch. Consequently, according to this plan, the temple building proper would have been much farther to the southeast than it should be, for it does not take into consideration the strong tradition regarding

the history and sanctity of the Dome of the Rock, nor does its area correspond to the measurements given by ancient writers such as Josephus or the Mishnah and "Temple Scroll."

The exponents of the extreme northern theory maintain that Antonia was built not only on the rocky promontory in the northwest corner dominating the Haram—today the site of the Arab el-Omariyyeh School, Turkish barracks prior to 1917—but also covering an extensive area to the northwest and northeast of this point. According to Père L.-H. Vincent, O.P., Sr. Marie-Aline of the Sisters of Sion, Prof. M. Avi-Yonah[10] (though it is reported that he has changed his opinion), and some others (mostly of the Israeli school),[11] Fortress Antonia stood virtually where the Convent of the Sisters of Sion and the Franciscan Biblical Institute now stand.

In light of the archaeological investigations beneath the Convent of the Sisters of Sion on the traditional Via Dolorosa (Tariq el-Alam), Père Vincent and Sr. M.-Aline interpret the pavement uncovered on this site to be of Herodian vintage and therefore conclude that this was the site of the Herodian Antonia, which they also equate with Pilate's Praetorium. This they claim was the scene of Jesus' trial and death sentence by Pilate. The Apostle Paul's rescue by the Roman officer from the Jewish mob gathered in the northern esplanade of the Temple (Acts 21:34) would likewise have occurred here. But neither Vincent nor Aline satisfactorily explains how Paul could have so easily been brought into the fortress, especially if it were on the other side of the rocky promontory. They imagine a massive fort covering an immense area built in the valley between two rather high points, the promontory itself and the hill of Bethesda. Furthermore, they explain the striated street, traced in this pavement and running from east to west directly through the center of this huge military installation, as a public thoroughfare; this led through a series of

Plate 87 *Pavement beneath the Convent of the Sisters of Sion. Solidly dated to the second century A.D., when it served as the public city square in the northeastern corner of* Hadrian's Aelia Capitolina, it is erroneously equated with the lithóstrōtos (Pavement) of John 19:13.

vaulted archways, one of which they identify as that of the Ecce Homo. The first two of these explanations clearly violate the principles of sound military tactics. The third is historically and biblically anachronistic. The pavement referred to is Hadrianic, approximately a century after the trial and condemnation of Jesus, which would have taken place near the Praetorium in the northwestern part of the city.

In response to his colleagues, Père P. Benoit, O.P., has recently reexamined the excavated material on the site in the light of the ancient sources. The large cistern below the pavement, an essential discovery in relation to the date of the material above, is clearly Herodian, the Strouthion Pool (*BJ* v. 467).[12] This double pool, situated in the valley between the hill of Bethesda and the Antonia, supplied water for the fortress. It was made

up of five gradations and was quite large.[13] This reservoir was open to the sky from the time of its construction until the Roman legions employed it in breaching the ramparts of Antonia. In describing the tense preparation for an assault on Jerusalem from the north by means of this water catcher, Josephus relates how the Roman soldiers under Titus labored continuously for seventeen days in building the four siege ramps against the northern walls of the city and erecting the battering-rams that would be hauled up on the ramps to breach the city's battlements (*BJ* v. 466–68).[14] The Fifteenth Legion worked strenuously against the northwestern wall opposite the monument of John Hyrcanus (*BJ* v. 468),[15] while the Tenth Legion, about forty feet away from them to the north, was setting up its siege ramps in the vicinity of the Tower Pool (Amygdalon). The Fifth and

Plate 88 *Alleged Greek "B" on second-century pavement. There has been more imagination than scientific fact in the explanations given regarding this figure and its relationship to the flagellation and the crowning of Jesus by the Roman soldiers.*

the Twelfth Legions were positioned about twenty-five feet apart in the valley just below Fortress Antonia (*BJ* v. 238, 246). Josephus clearly states that the Fifth Legion erected its siege ramp "over against [i.e., right through] the middle of the pool called Strouthion" so they could thus begin the break through the walls of the fortress above them. This operation clearly demonstrates that, although the Strouthion was contiguous with the northwestern angle of the Fortress Antonia, it was in no way a covered water reservoir beneath the courtyard of the fortress itself. In fact, there is no evidence of any ancient pool hewn out of this rocky platform on which the present Muslim school stands.

Benoit demonstrated that this pavement and the arch above it is clearly Hadrianic and not Herodian. This date is arrived at by an examination of three important elements on the site, all contemporaneous: 1) the inside vaulting above the reservoir, 2) the pavement itself, and 3) the arch. The vaulting was intended, obviously, to cover the open pool in order to support the pavement above it. The pavement belonged to the Roman forum or public square that Hadrian built in the northeastern quarter of his Aelia Capitolina. There is sufficient archaeological evidence to prove that the arch that adorned the square was erected at the same time. This arch, in our opinion, did not function as the northeast entrance into Hadrianic Jerusalem; rather, it was a triumphal arch built in the public square to commemorate his victory over Jerusalem, similar to those Hadrian had seen in the fora at Rome. This is apparent from the abundance of both smooth and striated flagstones which Rev. Bellarmino Bagatti, O.F.M., found east of the arch on the property of the Franciscan Biblical Institute, which would further indicate that the arch was inside Aelia and did not function as a city gate.

Pilgrims and tourists visiting the ancient relics beneath the Convent of the Sisters of Sion are shown the pavement and the game boards scratched into it. The pavement is explained to them as the "*lithóstrōtos*" (Greek, "pavement"), mentioned in the Passion narrative according to St. John (19:13). It is further explained that this pavement belonged to the courtyard of the Antonia, the Praetorium where Jesus was supposedly condemned to death.[16] The game board is the one with which the Roman soldiers entertained themselves, playing the Graeco-Roman game *basilikós*, the game of the "king."[17] Pilgrims are led to believe that here Jesus was flogged and mocked by the Roman soldiers, and treated as though he were a king, arrayed in a purple cloak and crowned with thorns. However, Père Benoit has shown that this pavement with its striations and game inscriptions belonged to a period at least one hundred years after Jesus' crucifixion. In addition, it is difficult for us to decipher an actual Greek "B" or even a spear incised in one of the stone blocks, although some kind of crown and a "star of David" appear rather clearly. We suggest, therefore, that this was some other game, perhaps similar to those in the paved floor of the synagogue at Capernaum or the many types of games visible in the public square at Philippi.

As we have seen, abundant biblical and extrabiblical evidence supports the view that the rocky platform in the northwest corner just outside the Haram esh-Sharif esplanade has played a very important role in the religious and civic life of Jerusalem—from David and Solomon to the present. It is this prominent spur and not the valley below it to the north that demands attention in any reconstruction of the Antonia.

Josephus employs two technical terms in his description of Herod the Great's royal fortress: one is Greek *pýrgos*, signifying a tower as such, though it may also be predicated of any fortification, castle, or fort; the other is Greek *phroúrion*, denoting a watchpost, a garrisoned fort, or a citadel. *Pýrgos* is equivalent to the Hebrew word for tower, *migdal*, as seen with reference to the Amygdalon Pool.[18] *Phroúrion*, however, can be rendered into Hebrew by either *mibṣar*, if, as in Num. 32:71, it defines an ordinary fortress that is cut off and made inaccessible to the general public, or by *meṣudah*, if it describes a stronghold or citadel as such, usually situated on a mountain, as in Jer. 48:41; 51:30.[19] We shall distinguish between *pýrgos* as pointing to a specific tower, and *phroúrion* as designating the entire royal fortress compound. With regard to the latter, Josephus uses Greek *anástēma*, translated by H.St.J. Thackeray as "the tower (of Antonia)" (LCL, *BJ* v. 240),[20] whereas the term in general denotes a height, high ground, a prominence, an erection, or a building. (The nineteenth-century Codex Laurentianus, however, reads *diástēma*, which defines an "extension" or "dimension," as in Aristotle *Physica* 209ª.4.)

Another extreme position, also outmoded and quite unfounded, is that of W. S. Caldecott.[21] Caldecott keeps the principal structures delineated by Josephus grouped together over the northwestern rock, but he extends the courtyards much too far to the east as well as to the north, so as to incorporate the Pool of Israel, thus creating an open area north of both the wall and the five fortress-towers of Antonia.

Bagatti would also extend the area of Antonia in this direction. He offers the following plan of the Temple Mount, including both the Temple of Yahweh and the Antonia Fortress of Herod.[22]

Some scholars argue that a plan of Antonia that de-

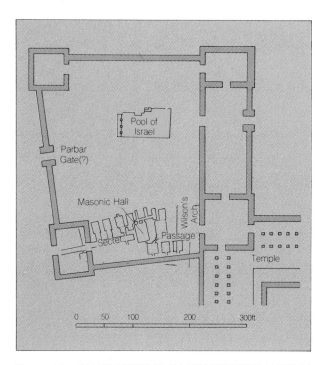

Figure 13   CALDECOTT'S PLAN OF FORTRESS ANTONIA

Figure 14   BAGATTI'S PLAN OF FORTRESS ANTONIA

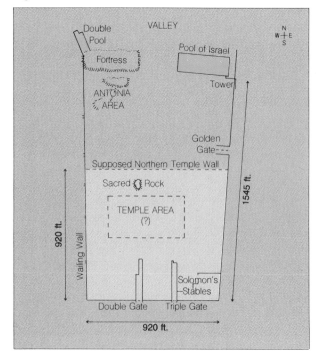

lineates its area southwards over and beyond the rocky promontory on which the present Omariyyeh School stands cannot be accepted because there is no archaeological evidence. Such a plan would have embraced a very ample area, beginning with a line just south of the Golden Gate and extending directly westwards towards Bab el-Hadid on the other side of the Haram enclosure. Thus there would have been two gates in the southern part of the Antonia complex: one in the southeast corner, where the Golden Gate now stands, and one in the southwestern angle, where Bab el-Hadid pierces the western wall of the Haram, assuming that the present gates indicate where ancient gates once stood. But those who object contend that such a plan militates against the evidence of Josephus and point out that Herodian masonry has been detected in the northeastern part of the Haram, along the Pool of Israel.[23] But this masonry belonged either to the Antonia (which we doubt) or to the general area of the Temple Mount, but excluding the sacred precincts of the Temple, because the Sheep Gate must have been located someplace along the northeastern wall of the entire enclosure.

Josephus lists six gates around the temple precinct: four on the west and two on the south. He does not identify any gates piercing the northern or eastern temple enclosure. Mishnah *Middoth*, however, names five gates: the Kiphonos Gate on the west, the two Huldah Gates on the south, the Shushan Gate on the east, and the Tadi Gate on the north. With regard to this last gate, the Mishnah states that it "served no purpose" (*Middoth* i. 3), suggesting that the Tadi Gate was not used at all, either by the general public or by the priests or the Roman soldiers stationed in the Fortress Antonia nearby.

Josephus speaks of the Antonia, with its tall towers and spacious courtyards, as northwest of the Temple; he does not describe its having occupied the whole area up to the northeast and east walls of the enclosure. We suggest that the northeastern part of the present Haram was neither included in the Antonia complex, nor did it form any part of the Temple's Court of the Gentiles. This must have been an open area, a free zone, probably used as a gathering-place for those who had just bought sheep and just before they entered the sacred precinct of the Temple. But it was somehow surrounded by a northern wall (it is difficult to establish the exact line of this wall, unless it is to be identified with the Herodian masonry found in the vicinity of the Pool of Israel), which could tentatively be equated with the "ancient enclosure" (*archaío*[i] *períbolo*[i], which in this passage really points to a city wall) to which the third wall described by Josephus was joined (*BJ* v. 147). Furthermore, the Herodian masonry found at this juncture could be a restoration and embellishment of the older ramparts to match the magnificent walls of both the great temple enclosure and Antonia.

As mentioned, the Sheep Gate cut through this northern wall, though exactly where is difficult to determine. Perhaps some of its remains—the corner of which must have been a tower gate—can still be seen opposite King Feisal's Gate of the Haram esh-Sharif along Tariq el-Mojahidin (also known as Tariq Bab Sitti Miryam), about midway between the Convent of the Sisters of Sion and St. Stephen's Gate. Some scholars[24] interpret this ancient material to have belonged to the northeastern tower of Antonia; but we have shown that the fortress was not located in the valley here. The ancient relics on this particular site formed a part of the Mojahidin Mosque of the last few centuries.

Thus, on the evidence of Josephus and our own examination of the site, the Antonia occupied a much larger section of the northwest corner of the Haram than had been previously accepted, though a number of modern scholars would disagree (see note 23). Briefly, our reconstruction of Fortress Antonia includes the following two large areas: 1) the platform which serves as the foundation of the Omariyyeh School, and 2) the northwestern section of the Haram esh-Sharif forming an almost square area, from the school eastwards to Bab el-'Atem, then south to the *aqwas* or pillar arches directly opposite Bab el-Jannah, the Gate of Paradise or the northern gate of the Dome of the Rock; from here the line would then turn westwards towards a point which we shall fix later, in the western wall between Bab el-Hadid and Bab en-Nadhir, then northwards to the Omariyyeh School.

In light of our study concerning the site, the tallest of the five towers described by Josephus would have been situated on this platform, thus forming an integral part

of the royal residence and fortress. One of the three
smaller towers would have stood at the extreme northwestern corner, also on this platform, in such a position
as to be able to protect the Strouthion Pool in the depression just below it. The two other smaller towers
would have been strategically erected along the northern
and western ramparts of the entire fortress compound—
one along the northern wall east of the Antonia, most
likely where the present Bab el-ʿAtem is located, whence
it could guard the large reservoirs in the Bethesda quarter, and one in the vicinity of the offices of the Supreme
Muslim Council, probably on the site of the gate called
Bab en-Nadhir, the "Gate of the Consecrated One" or
the "Gate of the Herald." The tower here guarded the
quarter of Jerusalem that developed in the northern part
of the Tyropoeon Valley, and the gate at this point must
be the scene recorded in Acts 21:35-40. The fourth
tower, the tallest, was in the southeastern corner of the
fortress area, from where it dominated the entire Temple
Mount. More specifically, this high tower would have
been over the entrance that leads to the subterranean
passages, now used as cisterns, north of the Dome of the
Rock, and in almost direct line with Bab el-ʿAtem,
perhaps the former Sheep Gate, whose successor it must
have been.

The underground passage can be equated with the
ancient Niṣoṣ which led from the inner courts of the
Temple to the northern gate. It is related to the ancient
Tadi Gate and the Moqed, the Chamber of the Hearth,
where the priests on duty warmed themselves during the
night. The tower in this vicinity should be identical to
that which Herod the Great had built for himself over
the subterranean, secret passageway leading from the
Antonia into the court of the Temple at the eastern
gate. Josephus does not mention a gate on the eastern
side of the temple enclosure; the Greek phrase *pròs tèn
anatolikèn thýran* (*Ant.* xv. 424)[25] must refer to the east
gate of the Antonia military compound.

Why did Herod erect this tower? Josephus adds that it
was constructed specifically that the king might use the
subterranean access beneath it to protect himself in the
tower should the people revolt against him (*Ant.* xv.
424). Also, since during Herod's reign the high priest's
vestments and all of his accessories were stored in the

Antonia (*Ant.* xviii. 90-95), they could be brought
guarded from the fortress into the temple area through
this passage.

The steps that Josephus describes (*BJ* v. 243) in his
account of the tower, in which the Roman garrison was
stationed, are likely the scene of St. Paul's arrest and his
dispute with the Jewish people (Acts 21:27-40). Near
the end of the seven-day period of purification, some
Jews from Asia recognized Paul in the temple courts and
began to incite the people, accusing him of heresy and of
profanation of the sanctuary by bringing Gentiles into
the Temple. They dragged Paul outside the Temple and
closed the gates. A riot erupted through all Jerusalem
until quelled by the Roman military commander with his
troops. Paul was arrested, bound with chains, and led
away to the army headquarters. When they arrived at
the steps, he received permission to address the people.
Tradition places the scene at the stairs in the temple
court leading up into the Fortress Antonia. However,
this identification cannot be certain, since it is not a
question of the difference of terminology between Luke
and Josephus. Rather, it is the chronology of events as
Luke relates them that would provide some clue to indicate whether Roman soldiers dragged Paul through the
temple courts (though the Jews had previously closed the
temple gates) or along the outer temple enclosure, along
the western side of it, until they reached the steps leading into the Antonia. If the former is true, presuming
that the gates were kept shut by the infuriated mob, then
this tower would be the scene described by Luke. If not,
however, it is virtually impossible to say exactly where
this tumultuous event occurred, for Josephus does not
mention a set of stairs leading from the city into the
Antonia. Nevertheless, there would still have to have
been some entrance from the city (from the side of the
Tyropoeon Valley) up to the west gate of the fortress.
One possible suggestion would be, depending on the
gate through which the Jews dragged Paul into the city,
that the Roman soldiers led him to the gate beneath one
of the smaller towers that stood over the western wall of
Fortress Antonia. According to our interpretation, this
would have been the gate where the present Bab en-
Nadhir opens into the Haram esh-Sharif, for this was the
closer of the two gates from the Temple into the city, as

Josephus depicts them (*Ant.* xv. 410). Moreover, this gate would have been near to one of the two lower gates from the Temple into the city.

With respect to the terminology, there is no real distinction between Luke's *anabathmoús* and Josephus' *katabáseis* in this connection. Both words are of Classical Greek origin, attested to as early as Herodotus in the fifth century B.C.[26] *Anábasis* points to a flight of steps going up, as would be expected in the Lukan narrative; *katábasis* is just the opposite, indicating a way down, a descent, which is precisely the meaning of the term as employed by Josephus (*BJ* v. 243). Moreover, Luke uses *parembolé* with reference to Antonia. It is a military term meaning "barracks," an encampment of soldiers or soldiers' quarters in general. This military usage is rather late; it is chiefly found in the works of Polybius (second century B.C.). Josephus consistently uses *phroúrion* (which best corresponds to the Hebrew *meṣudah*), a much older word appearing as early as the sixth century B.C., in Aeschylus.[27] On the other hand, Luke employs *parembolé* as practically synonymous with *phroúrion;* the subtle distinction is that *phroúrion* points to the entire Fortress Antonia whereas *parembolé* spells out more precisely the military headquarters and encampment attached to it.

The other possibility for the scene of Paul's arrest, imprisonment, and subsequent trial is the Praetorium on the other side of the city, but this seems quite unlikely, especially because the Greek word employed by Luke (*parembolé*) would have been much more precise, at least from a topographical point of view.

Authorities are still divided with regard to the scene of Jesus' trial and condemnation,[28] his scourging and crowning with thorns, and the place where he received his crossbeam. The Arabic Omariyyeh School, the former site of Antonia, is the scene of the traditional First Station of the Cross in the Old City of Jerusalem today. However, this tradition is an exclusively post-Crusader identification of Antonia with the Praetorium of Pontius Pilate.[29]

Herod's Palace and Pilate's Praetorium

Your neck is like David's tower girt with battlements; a thousand bucklers hang upon it, all the shields of valiant men.

Cant. 4:4

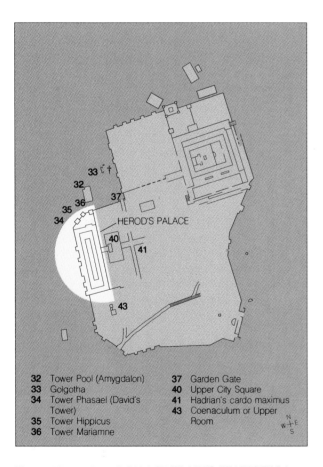

32	Tower Pool (Amygdalon)	**37**	Garden Gate
33	Golgotha	**40**	Upper City Square
34	Tower Phasael (David's Tower)	**41**	Hadrian's cardo maximus
35	Tower Hippicus	**43**	Coenaculum or Upper Room
36	Tower Mariamne		

Figure 15 HEROD'S PALACE/PILATE'S PRAETORIUM

PRIOR TO THE CRUSADER PERIOD the scene of Jesus' trial and condemnation before Pilate's Praetorium was almost consistently sought in the vicinity of the traditional Tower of David on Mt. Zion.[1] However, some early pilgrim accounts have also placed it in the neighborhood of the Church of St. Sophia, on the east slope of Zion just above the Tyropoeon Valley.[2] The Praetorium, the former palace (*aylé*) of Herod the Great and the subsequent residence of the Roman procurators in Jerusalem, was known to be on Mt. Zion, in the vicinity of the present Jaffa Gate. Today, this is the area called the Citadel or el-Qala'a in Arabic, also known as David's Tower, a Byzantine identification apparently based on Josephus' identification of the upper hill with the stronghold or City of David (although this is not explicit in Josephus).[3] This tradition was perpetuated by the early Christians, probably based on Peter's first *kerygma* (proclamation of the "good news") on the Feast of Pentecost in A.D. 30, recorded by Luke in Acts 2:14–36.[4] Acts 2:29 reads, "Brothers, I can speak confidently to you about our father David. He died and was buried and his grave is in our midst to this day." But according to the Scriptures, David was buried in the City of David, which in the tenth century B.C. occupied only the eastern or lower section of Jerusalem. Occupation of the Upper City did not begin until sometime during the seventh century B.C.[5] However, it is not the intent here to search for David's tomb; rather, it is of special interest to the readers of the Bible to know where Herod's palace and the Praetorium of Pilate (John 18–19) stood in the first centuries before and after Christ. Where was Jesus tried and sentenced to death? What route did he take to Golgotha?

Prof. G. Dalman was the first modern scholar to adopt the pre-Crusader and Crusader tradition regarding the location of Herod's palace and Pilate's Praetorium in the vicinity of David's Tower on Mt. Zion.[6] Père P. Benoit has revived interest in this location of the Praetorium on the upper hill.[7] In general, we agree with this identification; in particular, however, we propose a more precise location of the Praetorium, the barracks of

Plate 89 *Aerial view of the Upper City, looking north-wards. In the foreground stands the Dormition Church and Abbey of the Benedictine Monks. The small minaret indicates the traditional site of David's Tomb (on the ground floor) and the Upper Room above it. The southwest corner of the Old City's walls overlook the Hinnom Valley on the west.*

Plate 90 *Aerial view of the Citadel or David's Tower (center), looking towards the northeast. The Hasmonaean wall is on the right of the tower, and the Roman wall is on its left.*

Plate 91 Temple Model showing Herod's palace. The artist imagines the Caesareum and Agrippeum, the two large halls of the palace, as separate structures, whereas we would hold that they were a part of one large palace, but located in different parts of the structure. Towers Phasael and Mariamne are clearly visible; Hippicus stands behind Mariamne.

the praetorian guard, the Roman forum or upper "city square," and the "way of the cross." Our position is founded on 1) the evidence of John's Gospel, the testimony of Josephus and other ancient sources, and 2) the material evidence of archaeological investigations.[8] It is important to investigate in detail each of the sites.

Pilate's Praetorium was the former palace of Herod the Great. Josephus indicates that Herod's palace defies all description. It must, therefore, have been a truly magnificent structure, worthy of his genius and political aspirations. In many respects Herod the Great can be compared to other great leaders of antiquity, such as Pharaoh Ramses II of Egypt, King Solomon of Israel, the statesman Pericles of Athens, and Emperor Hadrian of Rome. These men were not only outstanding leaders, but also great builders with a genius for architectural form and composition.

There should be no doubt, according to Josephus' account, that Herod's palace (*aylé*) stood on the upper hill, in the new quarter on the northwestern part of Mt. Zion. It was constructed by Herod here for two reasons: first, for his own protection and pleasure; and, secondly, for the defense of the city against an advancing army from the northwest. Like the Antonia on the east, Herod's palace on the west also had its great towers, splendid apartments, and spacious courtyards, yet on a much larger scale.

In the north Herod's palace was protected by three great towers, strategically positioned quite close to each other, and built into the old Hasmonaean wall of the second century B.C. But unlike the smaller masonry of the old wall, the white stone blocks of the palace and towers were marvelous and wonderful to behold (*BJ* v. 174).[9] Each block measured 20 cubits in length (over 30 feet), 10 cubits wide (about 15 feet), and 5 cubits deep

(approximately 8 feet). Each tower was built and named in honor of some person close to Herod. Hippicus, for instance, which stood in the northwest, was named after a friend of the king, though historical records provide no more information about him. Phasael, which dominated the northeast angle, was named after Herod's own brother; he later took his own life when taken prisoner by the Parthians (*BJ* i. 271). Mariamne, the third tower, apparently stood at a close distance east of Phasael, and Josephus describes it as the most beautiful of the three (*BJ* v. 171). The king named it after his queen, the daughter of Simon the high priest (*BJ* i. 509, 573, 588). Herod later would have Mariamne assassinated (*BJ* v. 588).

The exact locations of towers Hippicus and Mariamne are not known, but the site of Phasael has been established. Tower Hippicus, according to George Adam Smith,[10] probably stood where the northwest tower of the citadel now stands. It would be an important discovery for archaeologists and topographers of Jerusalem to locate at least the base of this tower, for Hippicus served as the point of departure for the first and third walls of Jerusalem, just before its destruction by the Romans (*BJ* v. 144, 146–47). From Josephus' description, however, it is possible to glean some idea of what this tower must have looked like (*BJ* ii. 439; v. 134, 144, 147, 161, 163–65, 284, 304; vii. 1). It stood 80 cubits (over 120 feet) high and was divided into three parts: a square base made of solid masonry, over which

Plate 92 Tower Phasael, popularly called David's Tower, in the Citadel today. The Hasmonaean wall into which the Herodian towers were built, according to Josephus, can be seen to the right of the base of Phasael. The lower level of the tower is clearly Herodian; the upper level is Ottoman Turkish. The buildings on the left are Mameluke on a Roman wall.

was a reservoir to receive the rainwaters of the winter season; over this reservoir was a room with two chambers (Greek *distegos* can also point to a two-storied structure) which was crowned by beautiful turrets and battlements.

It would appear that Mariamne stood a short distance to the south of Tower Phasael, probably where the present police station is located in the northeast corner of Kishleh. Mariamne, which Josephus indicates stood over 55 cubits (83 feet) high, very probably dominated the royal palace itself, on its eastern flank where it could also look down on the upper forum and residential area.

Phasael was by far the tallest of the three towers. Its base was excavated by C.N. Johns, who also discovered Hasmonaean and early Hellenistic masonry on the site.[11] The identification of Phasael has been fairly accurately determined by mathematical calculation, though it is erroneously equated with the Tower of David. The figures given by Josephus are in round numbers, as was standard Semitic usage. A square of 40 cubits would be approximately 60 feet on all four sides, whereas the tower in the citadel ascribed to be Phasael measures 70 feet in length by 50 feet wide, and its height is calculated to be 66 feet. Yet there is no other candidate for Phasael in this area, and the Herodian masonry in situ, if it does not actually confirm the site, is at least tempting.

What did Tower Phasael look like? Based on Josephus, it resembled the Pharos of Alexandria (*BJ* v. 169; cf. iv. 613). Above Phasael's gigantic base Herod's engineers constructed another huge tower that brought the entire structure to a height of 90 cubits (135 feet). A beautiful portico ran along the base of this second tower. In it were luxurious appartments, including a Roman bath (Latin *balneum* or *thermae*). Around the summit of the tower ran a parapet with projecting defenses. Here again, as with Fortress Antonia, Herod's defense system was as practical as it was spectacular.

But the splendor of Mt. Zion in Herod's day was not limited to these three towers. Josephus reports that words cannot adequately describe the royal palace (*aylé*) itself, to which the towers were contiguous (*BJ* v. 176). It lay inside the city, south of the towers and ramparts along the northern ridge of Mt. Zion, enclosed by a wall also along the western ridge. A wall 30 cubits (over 45 feet) high, decorated with ornamented turrets at equal distances, encircled the whole palace compound, which was itself constructed on an artificial platform that served as its foundation. Archaeologists have brought to light sections of both the enclosing city wall and some palace foundations.

This city wall began at Tower Hippicus and ran along the western ridge of Mt. Zion, the exact course of the present Ottoman Turkish battlements. But the thickness of the Herodian enclosure was double that of the Turkish wall. During the 1968 and 1969 excavations R. Amiran and A. Eitan exhumed part of the foundation platform near the Citadel. This huge stonework measured some 9 to 12 feet high. In 1971 D. Bahat and M. Broshi excavated large areas in the Armenian garden and brought to light more sections of this platform beneath the Turkish wall on the west and south. Thus, we now have a fairly good idea of the northern, western, and southern limits of Herod's royal palace. It is not yet known how far the palace extended eastwards, though various suggestions have been proposed.

It has been suggested, for instance, that the entire

palace covered an area of some 900 feet from west to east.[12] However, in our estimation the palace would not have extended so far eastwards. There must have been enough room east of the palace for the upper city square and the sumptuous residences of the Hellenizing Jews who lived on Mt. Zion in the first centuries before and after Christ. Josephus does not even hint as to how large Herod's palace really was; it would be scientifically unwise to present mathematical figures when there is no literary or archaeological evidence.

In view of the lack of such evidence at present, we suggest that the eastern limits of the foundation platform ran along a north-south course following the line of today's Street of the Armenian Patriarchate. Canon J. Wilkinson rather convincingly shows that this is a line of an ancient street, for "the grid layout of a city goes back to the time of its foundation."[13] This is very plausible here, so it is logical that there existed some kind of an open space—a street or a lane—between Herod's palace on the west, which had a wall around it, and on the east, where the upper public square and wealthy residential quarter of the Hellenized Jews were located.[14] A similar phenomenon can be observed in the formation of the east-west course of the Street of the Chain (Bab es-Silsileh) and David Street in the direction of Jaffa Gate, which most scholars agree was the line of the Herodian first northern wall. It is almost a commonplace in Near Eastern topography and archaeology that the site of a city gate usually follows a previously existing gate; thus, too, the lines of a city wall invariably follow the course of preexisting fortifications. It is also true in the history of the Holy Land that an important building today usually occupies the site of a former principal edifice. From a literary and archaeological viewpoint, therefore, the site of Herod's palace, which later functioned as the Praetorium, is clearly established: it was built on the large foundations discovered in the Citadel and the Armenian garden on Mt. Zion.

If Josephus has bequeathed a rather detailed description of three palace towers, he offers no more than a glimpse into the royal residence itself, constructed on this immense foundation platform. He indicates that the entire palace was enclosed by a wall 30 cubits high. Within it were rooms for hundreds of Herod's guests and two large, magnificently ornamented banquet halls, one called the Caesareum after Emperor Caesar Augustus and the other the Agrippeum after Vipsanius Agrippa (BJ i. 402; Ant. xv. 318). The roofs of all the buildings inside of the palace compound were made of long beams with brilliant decorations. The hundreds of apartments were very elegantly furnished with a variety of accessories in silver and gold. Courtyards and gardens featured various kinds of plants and trees, as well as covered promenades bordered by canals and lovely pools, decorated with fancy water spouts. (The general appearance of Herod's palace might be compared with Villa d'Este at Tivoli outside Rome.) Josephus adds that there were also many dovecotes. Yet although Josephus could not find enough superlatives to describe Herod's palace, neither could he forget how the conspirators within its walls ravaged it by fire in the battle of Jerusalem (BJ v. 182–83).

Today literally nothing from these elegant palace furnishings has been recovered by archaeological excavations. But the history of the intervening centuries testifies to the importance of the site.

Herod the Great died in 4 B.C. From A.D. 6 until the fall of Jerusalem, Judaea was administered by Roman procurators whose headquarters (praetorium) was at Caesarea on the seacoast. On the great Jewish festivals the procurators and their armies would come up to Jerusalem as peacekeeping forces, lest demonstrations and riots break out against Roman rule. The procurator himself took up residence in the royal palace (aylé), which from this time was technically called the Praetorium.[15] The regular army stationed in Jerusalem was also reinforced by the troops from Caesarea. Soldiers were garrisoned throughout the city, but especially in the Antonia, which dominated the temple area, and in the praetorian barracks (on the site of Herod's three great towers) which overlooked the Praetorium itself. Thus, the Greek word for palace, aylé, now encompassed Latin praetorium, the headquarters or residence of the procurators in a subjugated province.

It is abundantly clear that Jesus was not sentenced inside the Praetorium. The Jews who brought Jesus to Pilate would not enter into the Praetorium because they could not legally. They had to avoid ritual impurity if

Plate 93 *Viale delle Cento Fontane, the Avenue of the Hundred Fountains, in Villa d'Este, about 21 miles east of Rome. This is perhaps one of the finest more recent examples of how the Herodian promenade must have looked as described by Josephus. (Valerie Schultz, Loyola University of Chicago)*

they were to eat the Passover meal that evening, as is clear from John 18:28 and Jewish Law.[16] Moreover, the Praetorium had been heavily guarded by the Roman soldiers around it, and also, given the description by Josephus, there would not have been enough room within the courtyards for the large crowds that had thronged towards the Praetorium in protest. Furthermore, prosecutions and sentences according to Roman law took place in public,[17] and the Praetorium was hardly accessible to the ordinary man.

Nor would Jesus' public trial and condemnation have taken place on the site of the present Citadel.[18] This was the scene of Herod's three towers, Hippicus, Phasael, and Mariamne, which compound was converted into a Roman garrison. These three towers were built into the old Hasmonaean wall—the first north wall delineated by Josephus—which in Jesus' day formed the northwestern limits of Herodian Jerusalem. The city which Jesus knew was south of this wall and the towers. To the north was an open area, outside the city, which we would identify with Ghareb (Jer. 31:39). Here were located the Tower Pool (Amygdalon), a Jewish necropolis, and, nearby, Golgotha, the scene of crucifixions. The garrison of the praetorian guard in the west was no more accessible to the general public than the Antonia in the east.

Under Roman law prosecutions were public events that usually took place in the forum or "marketplace," actually the public "city square," a piazza or plaza. Josephus affirms that there was just such a large city square in the Upper City, specifically called the upper city square and located next to the royal palace, the future Praetorium (*BJ* ii. 305–6, 315–17). It was a spacious open area where large multitudes could gather. During his administration as procurator of Judaea from A.D. 26 to 36, Pilate was involved in two sacrilegious scandals against the Jews in Jerusalem. The first concerned the procurator's setting up of the images of the Roman emperor in Jerusalem; this scandal is of concern

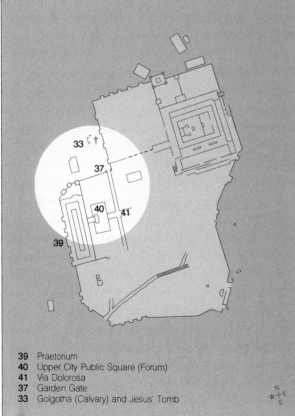

39 Praetorium
40 Upper City Public Square (Forum)
41 Via Dolorosa
37 Garden Gate
33 Golgotha (Calvary) and Jesus' Tomb

Figure 16   JESUS' TRIAL, CONDEMNATION, AND ROUTE TO GOLGOTHA

here because the equation between the procurators' residence and the royal palace is mentioned by the Jewish philosopher Philo who records this event (*Legatio ad Caium* vi. 175.23).[19] The second scandal is more to the point. Pilate incited another riot by the Jews when he appropriated the sacred temple treasury for the construction of the Jerusalem aqueduct (*BJ* ii. 175–77; *Ant.* xviii. 60–62). Josephus describes huge crowds (multitudes in the "ten of thousands"—a round number indicating an extremely large mob) gathering before Pilate's judgment seat (Latin *sella curulis*) on the speaker's platform (Greek *béma*) set up in front of the Praetorium. The only place near the Praetorium where such large mobs could gather was precisely the upper square mentioned by Josephus. It was somehow adjacent, though not contiguous, to the Praetorium.

Sometime during his brief term as procurator A.D. 64 to 66, the brutal Gessius Florus came up to Jerusalem from Caesarea and established his residence in the praetorian palace.[20] Immediately he had his judgment seat set up in front of the palace to judge all of the Jews who had insulted him. He sentenced them to be scourged in the public square and crucified outside the walls of the city as was customary. The parallels with the trial of Jesus are striking. There should be little doubt, in the light of the above accounts, that the large public square was close to the Praetorium. This public square would certainly not have been north of the city, as we have shown above, nor would it have been south of the praetorium, for this quarter, we believe, belonged to the Essene community of Jerusalem. Thus, given the topographical indications (and some mathematical calculations) and the important extrabiblical references, the large open square would have been east of the Praetorium. It is only logical to assume that Herod's palace and the procurators' Praetorium also faced east. Therefore, the only candidate, in our view, in the Upper City is the Armenian Orthodox compound of St. James' Cathedral. This cathedral is built, in view of the above data, on or near the site of Jesus' trial and sentencing. Briefly the Street of the Armenian Orthodox Patriarchate today divides two ancient historical sites: the Praetorium, on the west, and the forum or agora on the east.

Plate 94 *Artist's conception (Jerusalem Temple Model) of the gate leading from the public city square into the Praetorium. The bema, however, would not have been the steps leading up to the procurator's residence, but a special platform in the city square, as at Corinth and Rome.*

After Jesus' arrest in the Garden of Gethsemani and after the preliminary trials before the Sanhedrin, the high priest and other prominent Jews came up to the Praetorium to present Jesus before Pilate. Pilate had to come out (*éxō*) of the Praetorium to address the crowd that had gathered in the forum, as he had to on at least two previous occasions when rioting threatened. Pilate then walked up on the speaker's platform (*béma* or *tribunale*) on which the magistrate's seat (*sella curulis*) had been placed. From this raised platform he questioned the Jews concerning their accusation against Jesus (John 18:29–30). Finding no just charge, he reentered the Praetorium and then had Jesus summoned into it so he could personally interrogate him (John 18:33–38). After this cross-examination Pilate went back out onto the rostrum to announce that he could not find Jesus guilty.

It is not altogether clear from the evangelists' accounts whether Jesus was scourged in public in the city square just before his crucifixion, as was usually the case,[21] or whether he was led away by the Romans and flogged in the courtyard of the praetorian barracks annexed to the procurator's residence. The Johannine and Lukan accounts favor the interpretation that Jesus was led away to be scourged, but according to Matthew and

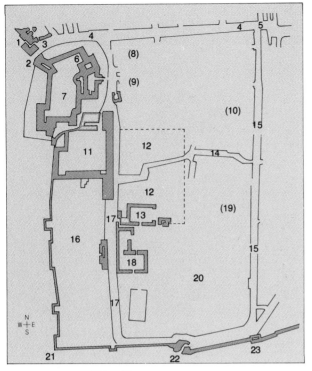

Figure 17   CITADEL

1. Original Jaffa Gate or Bab el-Khalil, the Gate of the Friend. For the Arabs it takes its name from its destination, Hebron (Arabic *Khalil*), where Abraham is interred; for the Jews it points to Jerusalem's main port city, Jaffa.

2. Wide opening in the Jaffa Gate, made in 1898 in honor of Kaiser Wilhelm II's entry into Jerusalem. It was also used on General Allenby's triumphal entry in 1917.

3. Omar Ibn el-Khattab Square, named after the Arab Caliph who captured Jerusalem for Islam in A.D. 638.

4. David Street, leading towards the center of the Old City. It, like its continuation, the Street of the Chain (Tariq Bab es-Silsileh), followed the course of Josephus' "first wall" in the north. Some scholars believe that this is the line of Jesus' way to Calvary.

5. Site of the Hadrianic quadrivium and tetrapylon, known today as el-Bashurah. It marks the site of the Old Testament Corner Gate and the New Testament Garden Gate. In our opinion, Jesus passed through this gate on his way to Golgotha. This could also be the scene of Simon of Cyrene's helping Jesus carry his cross and the meeting of the weeping women of Jerusalem, as recorded in the New Testament.

6. Tower Phasael, one of the three towers built by Herod the Great north of his palace. Its base, along with a large section of the Hasmonaean wall (Josephus' first north wall) and a segment of the Roman wall, is still visible in the Citadel (see page 103).

7. Citadel; (el-Qala'ah). This fortresslike structure dates back to the Crusader and Turkish periods, but archae-

ological explorations have revealed more ancient material in the area. The flagellation and crowning with thorns may have taken place here. Some scholars have erroneously equated the Citadel with the palace/Praetorium.

8. Site of the Maronite Convent.

9. Site of Christ Church and pilgrims' hospice adjacent to it.

10. Site of the Syrian Orthodox church and monastery of St. Mark. This very ancient group of Christians in Jerusalem believe that this is also the site of the Upper Room in the house of John Mark.

11. Police barracks (el-Kishli). The Roman praetorian guard very likely had its garrison here. This could also have been the courtyard where Jesus was scourged and mocked by the Roman soldiers. The site was later occupied by the Tenth Roman Legio Fretensis.

12. Upper city square, the Greek agora and Roman forum. It is not possible to delineate the exact extent of this important meeting place and market. The trial and condemnation of Jesus and also the Ecce Homo scene would have taken place here. This is where Jesus received his crossbeam and began his walk towards Calvary.

13. St. James' Cathedral of the Armenian Orthodox. We would identify this site with the First Station of the Cross; Pilate's judgment seat (*sella curulis*) on the speaker's platform (bema) could have been here.

14. St. James' Street, identified on some maps as the Street of the Armenians, marking the line of an important ancient street leading from the Praetorium into the public square, thence into the upper part of the city.

15. Probably one of the most ancient streets in Jerusalem, marking the southern extension of Hadrian's *cardo maximus*. Recently archaeologists discovered large sections of a Byzantine paved street following the same course.

16. Armenian Orthodox Seminary, on the former site of the Praetorium. Archaeological excavations have brought to light some very large sections of the foundation platform on which the structure stood.

17. Armenian Orthodox Patriarchate Road, another sign of an Herodian road. It separated the king's palace from the upper city square.

18. Armenian Orthodox Convent and Library. It is likely that the upper city square extended this far south.

19. Site of the Church of St. George.

20. Armenian Quarter, anciently occupied by the Hellenizing Jews of the Upper City.

21. Southwest corner of the sixteenth-century walls built by Suleiman the Magnificent. They indicated the extent of Jerusalem in the south from Hadrianic times onwards.

22. Zion Gate or the Gate of Prophet David (Arabic, Bab en-Nebi Daud), marking the line of the street shown on the Madaba Map, leading towards Holy Sion the Mother of All Churches.

23. Original gate that served as the southern end of the Roman cardo maximus and the Byzantine colonnaded street. Presently walled up, it is in direct line with the Damascus Gate in the north.

Plate 95 *Aerial view of Jerusalem, looking eastwards. From the Citadel (center) can be discerned David Street and the Street of the Chain leading directly eastwards towards the Haram esh-Sharif. Visible within the southwestern corner of the walled city is the Armenian Orthodox quarter, which in the first century A.D. comprised the palace of Herod the Great,* *and later the Praetorium. The Way of the Cross can be traced from St. James' Cathedral, along the street leading eastwards towards Suq el-Ḥuṣṣor, then northwards towards the Garden Gate (located to the right of the Lutheran Church of the Holy Redeemer), towards the Holy Sepulchre.*

Mark, the scourging preceded the crucifixion in keeping with Roman practice. Matthew and Mark agree that the Roman soldiers took Jesus and led him inside the Praetorium (Matt. 27:27; Mark 15:16). It is unlikely that they or their redactors would have actually had the procurator's residence in mind, but were referring to the praetorian barracks adjacent to the officers' apartments. It should be remembered from Josephus' description that the sites of the royal residence and the three great towers formed one huge compound. Thus, when the Roman procurators took over the king's residence, the Herodian *aylé* was converted into the residence and headquarters of the Roman governors, while the fortress area was transformed into a separate military installation for the praetorian guard.

That Jesus was scourged in the praetorian barracks is also to be deduced from the Johannine account: "Pilate went out [of the Praetorium] a second time and said to the crowd: 'Observe what I do. I am going to bring him out [of the praetorian barracks] to you to make you realize that I find no case (against him).' When Jesus came out wearing the crown of thorns and the purple cloak, Pilate said to them, 'Look at the man!'" (19:4–5).[22]

After the physical torture and psychological humiliation the soldiers brought Jesus back into the public square so that Pilate could show him to the mobs, but they clamored for his death. The death sentence was publicly pronounced in the city square. The crowds were thus satisfied and the condemned was given his crossbeam to carry to the place of execution.

As has been established, at least indirectly, Jesus was not condemned in the Antonia, as a post-Crusader tradition and some scholars maintain. Hence, the tra-

Plate 96 *Byzantine pavement, formerly thought to be that of Hadrian's second-century Aelia Capitolina. We have little doubt that this was one of the principal streets of first-century Jerusalem, the course taken by Jesus to Golgotha.*

ditional Way of the Cross from east to west cannot be original. Vis-a-vis the identification of Pilate's Praetorium with the present site of the Citadel and/or the Kishleh compound, the site of the trial and condemnation of Jesus and the point of departure of the Via Dolorosa, according to some scholars,[23] militates against biblical, historical, and archaeological data. As already demonstrated, the biblical Praetorium once occupied the site of the modern Armenian Orthodox Seminary south of Kishleh and the Citadel, which formed an integral part of the praetorian barracks. We know that the northern first wall of Herodian Jerusalem ran along the course of the present David Street and the Street of the Chain. Anything northwest of this line would have been outside of the city proper. The material within this line, south of David Street, would have been first-century buildings and streets. The west-east direction of David Street as the suggested route of the Way of the Cross, therefore, lacks support and cannot be accepted.

In retracing Jesus' steps to Calvary we must begin with the location of the upper city square, the present property of the Armenian Orthodox Cathedral of St.

James and the adjoining Armenian quarter. This must have been the scene of the First Station of the Cross, where Pilate condemned Jesus to crucifixion.

Jesus and the two others condemned to death with him had their upper crossbeams (*patibula*) fastened upon their shoulders in the public square. From there the Roman soldiers followed by the crowds paraded through the narrow streets of Jerusalem. There are no biblical indications of the exact route. Of the many maps of ancient Jerusalem, Wilkinson's grid of Hadrianic Jerusalem is perhaps the most dependable for reconstructing this route because it offers an insight into the street plan of Herodian Jerusalem. By comparing this grid with a detailed map of the Old City today, it is possible to determine both the general site of the public city square and the course of the main streets leading from it to the other parts of the city.[24] The city square can be easily enough discerned in the neighborhood of St. James' Cathedral and the surrounding Armenian compound. St. James' Road and el-Arman Street preserve the direction of the principal west-east street from the Praetorium eastwards through the city square to the main north-south street (the present Suq el-Ḥuṣṣor) and the Street of the Jews (Mundalîn), down through Western Wall Street towards the Lower City. Whether or not the procession followed the course that led to the Lower City where the more anti-Roman population was concentrated cannot be established, though it is tempting to think that it did. However, the streets must have been crowded with Jewish pilgrims for Passover, making it unlikely that the Romans would have taken such a comparatively long course.

Thus, the original Via Dolorosa would have followed the course of the modern Street of the Armenians eastwards until it reached Suq el-Ḥuṣṣor. At this juncture it turned left and followed a northern course along Suq el-Ḥuṣṣor. This, according to Wilkinson, preserves the line of a very ancient street, indeed—the southern segment of the second-century cardo maximus of Hadrian's Aelia Capitolina, which followed the course of its first-century predecessor, Herodian Jerusalem.

CHAPTER **VII** # THE CITY OF THE TEMPLE

His parents used to go every year to Jerusalem
for the feast of Passover.

Luke 2:41

✝ ——————————————————————————— ✝

Plate 97 Temple Mount, the present Haram esh-Sharif,
from the northeast (above the former site of Antonia). The
wall on the east (left) had two gates: the northern gate, now
called the Golden Gate, through which the priests led the red
heifer to its sacrifice on the Mount of Olives; and the
southern gate through which the scapegoat was driven into
the wilderness on the Day of Atonement. These two gates
pierced the eastern wall of the Jewish temple enclosure,
Solomon's Portico. The Royal Stoa or Basilica stood along the
southern wall where the Mosque el-Aqsa stands today. If one
were to draw a line from the Golden Gate westwards towards
the building of the Supreme Muslim Council in Jerusalem, he
would receive some idea of both the square area of the Jewish
temple (south of this line) and the compound of the Antonia
Fortress (in the northwestern corner of the Haram, north of
this line). The gate on the west, Bab en-Nadhir, just below
the offices of the Islamic council, is where we would locate
the scene of Acts 21:30–22:29. Note the paved paths
leading to the northern gates of the Haram: that on the
right leads to Bab el-ʿAtem, the Gate of Darkness; the path
on the left, towards Bab el-Hutta, the Repentance Gate;
these walks might indicate the eastern limits of the Antonia
compound, and point in the direction of the biblical Sheep
Gate. Birket Israïn, the Pool of Israel, now filled up, is in the
lower left.

TEMPLES AND SACRED SHRINES dedicated to various divinities have been discovered on almost every archaeological site in the Middle East. Egypt, for instance, abounded in temples—both in the cities of the living on the east bank of the Nile as at Memphis, Amarna, Luxor, and Aswan, and in the cities of the dead on the west bank of the river, where archaeologists have brought to light magnificent mortuary temples at Giza and Saqqarah in Lower Egypt, and at Medinet Habu, the Rameseum, and Deir el-Bahri, in Upper Egypt. Ancient Mesopotamia was also famous for its many sanctuaries and high places, the ziggurats upon which religious fertility cults were practiced from Nineveh, Ashur, and Nimrud in the north, through Babylon and Kish, and down towards Lagash, Obeid, and Ur of the Chaldees, supposedly where Abraham was born.

Archaeological excavations have also uncovered numerous temples in Syria, Phoenicia, and Canaan—later known as Israel in the Old Testament period, then called Palestine in New Testament times. In many cases the city was named after its special divinity, as particularly along the Levantine coast, such as Baalbek (the Valley of Baal) in Lebanon, Bethlehem (the House of [the goddess] Lahami), and Jerusalem (the Foundation of [the god] Salem). Indeed, it was sometimes difficult, if not impossible, to clearly distinguish between the religious, political, and social life of the people in the ancient Middle East, for everyday life centered around the cult of the particular divinity whose shrine dominated the city, with palaces, administrative buildings, and houses clustered around it. The great religious festivals were as much holy days as they were civic and social events relating to the king, who in some cases was identified with the deity, and whose subjects shared in the liturgical rituals and celebration in his honor.

Ancient Near Eastern literature and archaeological explorations have expanded and enriched our knowledge of these ancient theocratic city-states. But the god and the religion of the ancient Hebrews was different. Monotheism left its permanent stamp on Middle Eastern society, as is evident in the practice of Judaism, the belief in the Israelites' El (Elohim) or Yahweh, upon Christianity, and also upon Islam, which requires of its followers complete submission to the will of Allah, etymologically and theologically identified with the El of the ancient Hebrews.

If, therefore, in ancient times each city or city-state had its own divinity and a temple dedicated to it, Jerusalem was the City of the Temple par excellence. From the tenth century B.C. until the almost complete devastation of the city by the Romans in A.D. 70, Jerusalem was the spiritual, cultural, and civic center of the Jews in Palestine and throughout the Diaspora. Three times a year pilgrims from all over the country and its neighboring states came up to Jerusalem to celebrate the great feasts of Passover, Pentecost, and Tabernacles. The focus of their minds and hearts, the center of all liturgical celebrations, was the City of the Temple.

Plate 98 Nine-branch candleholder at Western Wall, in celebration of the Feast of Hanukkah (Dedication), which commemorates the recovery, purification, and rededication of the Temple of Zerubbabel by Judas Maccabaeus in 165 B.C.

The Temple Site

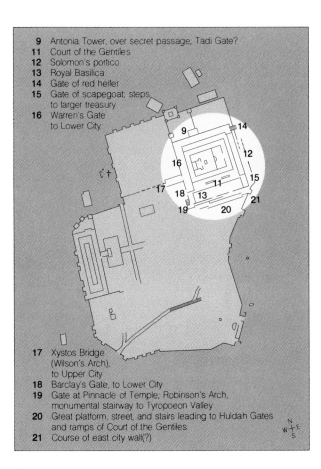

Figure 18 TEMPLE OF YAHWEH

Who can ascend the mountain of the Lord? Or who may stand in his holy place? He whose hands are sinless, whose heart is clean.

Ps. 24: 3–4

JERUSALEM'S HISTORY in the course of just over a thousand years is intimately bound up with the three great temples of Yahweh built on the Lord's holy mountain.

The first temple was built by Solomon, who reigned over Israel *ca.* 961–922 B.C. Solomon inherited land from his father King David, who had purchased property from Araunah the Jebusite to build an altar to Yahweh. But the Lord spoke to David: "It is your son whom I will put on your throne in your place who shall build a temple in my honor" (1 Kgs. 5:19). Thus, after the death of his father, Solomon commenced the building of the great Jerusalem sanctuary, which took seven years. ("The foundations of the Lord's temple were laid in the month of Zib in the fourth year, and it was completed in all particulars, exactly according to plan, in the month of Bul, the eighth month, in the eleventh year"; 1 Kgs. 6:37–38.) The Solomonic structure stood for some 363 years before it was destroyed by the Babylonians under Nebuchadnezzar in 587 B.C.

The second temple was built by Zerubbabel, after the return of the Hebrews from exile in Babylon. If the description of the Solomonic structure is rather detailed (1 Kgs. 6:1–8:13), there exists no exact information concerning the building of the second temple. The few general references in the Old Testament do not provide the information necessary to reconstruct it (Ezra 3:1–13; 5:1–17; Hag. 1:1–2:9). Begun in 537 B.C., the program was interrupted for a while because of objections from Israel's neighbors. Work was resumed *ca.* 520, the second year of King Darius of Persia, and the Temple was completed and dedicated in 515. It was erected on the same site as the Temple of Solomon and stood practically intact until disassembled by Herod the Great for the building of the third temple.

Herod's temple was begun *ca.* 20 B.C. and was solemnly dedicated ten years later, but construction actually was not completed until just a few years before its total destruction by the Romans in A.D. 70. The largest and most magnificent of the Temples of Yahweh in the Holy City, it was built on a scale previously unimagined.

In addition to three major accounts—Josephus (*BJ* v.

Plate 99 *Bronze coins minted by Herod the Great.*

184–237; *Ant.* xv. 380–475), Mishnah *Middoth* i–iv, and the recently published Temple Scroll from Qumran[1]—a number of other ancient literary sources provide some description of the Jerusalem temple. These references include Strabo (*Geography* vii. 281; xvi. 28–40; cf. xvi. 2.34), Tacitus (*Historia* iv. 4), Dio Cassius (*History of Rome* xxxvii. 15–17; xlix. 22; lxvi. 4–12). Pliny the Elder (*Naturalis Historia* v. 14), and Polybius (*Histories* xvi. 4), as well as the early seventh-century Christian Paschalion (also known as the Chronicon Paschale).[2] Moreover, pilgrims, artists, and scholars throughout the centuries often have attempted to picture the Temple in their diaries, pictorial maps and plans, and various treatises,[3] some as early as the fourth and sixth centuries A.D. Many modern scholars have published the results of their investigations.[4] But these texts, literary documents, and even the scientific examinations of the site itself have all been challenged.

In view of the abundant literary and material evidence available, some kind of temple plan should be possible which essentially agrees with the most ancient source. As Prof. Y. Yadin asserts, enough biblical and extrabiblical descriptions of the Jerusalem temple are now available to enable reproduction of the sanctuary to almost the minutest detail.[5] But it is not the intent of the present work to do so. The primary concern here is with the site itself.

Even if an exact model can be recreated, the precise location of the shrine, according to some scholars, is still a matter of discussion and can only be ascertained by thorough archaeological exploration of the area. Such a project is as unlikely as it is unrealistic, given not only the unstable political situation in the Middle East today, but especially the sanctity of the Haram esh-Sharif in Islamic tradition.

Dame K.M. Kenyon contends that "There can be no real doubt as to the site of Solomon's Temple, for there is no significant break in the chain that links it with the site of the Haram esh-Sharif or the Dome of the Rock."[6] This magnificent shrine, certainly one of the most beautiful sanctuaries in the world today, is the masterpiece of the Omayyad Caliph Abdul Malek Ibn Marwan (685–705). It commemorates the transporting of Muhammed from the "farther" (*el-Aqsa*) temple in

Jerusalem through the seven heavens up to the presence of Allah (Surah xvii; cf. xxxvii). The original building on this site was completed in 691, approximately seventy-two years after the Hegirah (the year of Muhammed's flight from Mecca to Medina in A.D. 622), the event that marks the year "1" of the Islamic calendar. The original structure has undergone a number of restorations and repairs to make it the beautiful shrine that it is today. It had even been converted into a Christian sanctuary, the Crusaders' Templum Domini (Temple of the Lord), for almost nine decades from 1099, when Geoffrey de Bouillon took the Holy City for the Latin Kingdom of Jerusalem, until 1187, when Jerusalem was forced to capitulate to Salah ed-Din (Saladin) on October 2, ninety days after the fall of the Horns of Hattin on July 4.[7]

Prior to 691—the period from the fall of Jerusalem in A.D. 70 to the surrender of the city to the orthodox Caliph Omar Ibn el-Khattab, after whom the plaza inside Jaffa Gate is named—knowledge of the Temple Mount is based largely on early Christian sources, which include the Itineraries of Christian pilgrims and a few other documents, neatly collated in Padre D. Baldi's *Enchiridion Locorum Sanctorum.*[8] Jewish sources concerning this period stem mainly from references to the Temple by Jews living in the Diaspora.[9]

The Itinerarium of the so-called Pilgrim of Bordeaux, dated to A.D. 333, gives some idea of how the temple area looked after Hadrian's Aelia Capitolina was converted into a Christian city, when in 313 Flavious Valerius Constantinus I (Constantine the Great; 288–337) proclaimed religious toleration and Christian property rights were restored by the Edict of Milan.

In the East, interest in the Holy Places was very much revived. Many beautiful churches and shrines were built and dedicated in memory of the various events of Jesus'

Plate 100 *Mosque of Abraham (el-Haram el-Ibrahimi) at Hebron. This is undoubtedly the finest example of what the outer precinct wall (peribolis) of the Herodian temple in Jerusalem must have looked like, but on a much larger scale. This view from the southwest shows the extent of the southern and western walls which encompass the sacred area. The broad steps in the foreground are modern. The crenelation on top of the wall, as well as the two minarets, belongs to the Islamic period. The structure projecting from the northern part of the western wall dates to the Crusader period. However, the lower and upper courses of masonry, the wall itself, are clearly Herodian and are exactly like those of the Jerusalem outer temple wall. Some of these blocks measure a yard and a half thick and more than twenty-one feet long. No mortar was employed to keep them in place, so finely were they cut and dressed to embellish this sacred enclosure. The upper course of square pilasters is composed of smaller blocks, also neatly fitted together.*

life. But not all of these sites are authentic. The account of the Pilgrim of Bordeaux mentions various features of Hadrian's *quadra,* the square esplanade of the Temple, in relation to a Solomonic structure believed to have stood here in his day. For instance, he mentions the altar where the postexilic prophet Zechariah was supposed to have been assassinated (2 Chr. 24:20–23, alluded to by Matt. 23:35; Luke 11:51), and the pinnacle of the Temple where Satan was supposed to have tempted Jesus (Matt. 4:5; Luke 4:9). Judging from the Bordeaux Pilgrim's account, the two statues of Hadrian and Antoninus Pius which were erected here by the Romans were still standing not far from the "sacred rock," the *lapis pertusus* or "perforated rock" which Jewish pilgrims visited to lament the destruction of the Temple.

However, if the Christians themselves did not build any shrine on this site, the temple site was never really forgotten. For several centuries the Temple Mount seems to have been very barren; but the sanctity of the place itself could not have been obliterated from the minds and hearts of Christians and Jews, whose thoughts and aspirations were always directed towards the House of the Lord. If, then, in the seventh century Muslims built their sacred shrine and principal mosque on the

temple site, it was only because they too revered this holy place.[10]

In particular, the Dome of the Rock in the Haram esh-Sharif ("Noble Sanctuary") indicates the site of the sacred Temple of Jerusalem. No modern scholar doubts that the Muslim Haram in general preserves the site of the Jewish sanctuary (*hekal*), but a number debate the actual site of the Temple within the sacred precincts. Two schools of thought have arisen with regard to the location of the Debir, the Holy of Holies, and the site of the altar of holocausts.

At present there is no certain way of knowing how much land Solomon's temple and the rebuilt temple of Zerubbabel occupied in pre- and postexilic Jerusalem. As archaeological excavations in the area of the Dome of the Rock are most unlikely in the near future, scholarly debates and suggestions must suffice. But a fairly accurate understanding of the extent of the Herodian temple compound is available. Herodian masonry has been identified definitely on three sides of the Haram and identical masonry reportedly was brought to light along the fourth or northern extension of the compound.[11] The entire east-west line of the southern wall is known; much of it has been exposed and measured. A very large

Plate 101 Sacred rock in the Dome of the Rock. According to Jewish tradition this was the site of Abraham's intended sacrifice of his son Isaac. Muslims believe that Muhammed the Messenger of God ascended into the Seventh Heaven from this rock. During the Crusader period, when the shrine was converted into the Templum Domini (Temple of the Lord), this rock served as the foundation of the Christian altar. The altar of the Jewish temple was situated on this rock, and the Holy of Holies stood a little farther west, most probably where the beautiful fifteenth-century Sebil Qayit-Bai now stands. The cave beneath the sacred rock is known as the Bir el-Arwah, the Well of Souls. According to one Islamic tradition, Allah's throne will be placed on this rock at judgment day, and Muhammed supposedly said that one prayer here was worth a thousand said elsewhere.

portion of the Western Wall (*Kotel ha-ma'arabi*), the Wailing Wall, is discernible. Some segments clearly identified as of Herodian construction have been identified along the eastern side of the Islamic enclosure. If it is true that Herodian masonry has been detected in the vicinity of the Pool of Israel outside the northeastern corner, then the area built up by Herod the Great to form the entire Temple Mount can be ascertained as more an artificial acropolis surrounded by a wall than an ordinary mount as such.

Various measurements of the walls have been made, though they do not always agree. F.J. Hollis, for instance, gives the following figures: 1041 feet for the northern wall, 950 feet for the southern, 1556 for the eastern, and 1596 for the entire western wall.[12] Measurements according to N. Avigad are as follows: 315 meters (945 feet) on the north; 280 meters (840 feet) on the south; 470 meters (1410 feet) on the east; and 485 meters (1455 feet) on the west. The height of the Herodian Western Wall in the vicinity of Wilson's Arch, excluding the upper Arab, Crusader, and Turkish accretions, measures some 90 feet (30 meters), according to the calculations of Sir C. Warren, who dug deep shafts at strategic points along the wall.

Excavations along the same wall between 1965 and 1967 by Kenyon and after 1967 by B. Mazar confirmed that both the Herodian southwestern and southeastern

corners of the Temple measured approximately 129 feet. Indeed, most of the huge ashlars used in the construction of this enormous enclosure measured from 3 to 9 feet in length and more than 3 feet high. One is more than 36 feet long, and the heaviest monoliths weigh about 100 tons.[13] No wonder, then, that one of Jesus' disciples exclaimed, "Teacher, look at the huge blocks of stone and the enormous buildings!" (Mark 13:1). And Josephus, if sometimes prone to hyperbole, surely does not exaggerate his description of the Temple.

With respect to the area enclosed within the temenos, the outer enclosure of the sacred precinct, most scholars maintain that the entire esplanade of the Haram esh-Sharif, which measures some 174,200 square yards (145,600 square meters), equals the area of the Herodian temple area. This vast area would have embraced the Temple proper with its courtyards surrounded by the four porticoes described in the ancient sources, including the Royal Stoa on the south. These scholars are the maximalists, whose modern advocates are Benoit,[14] Mazar, Avi-Yonah, Kenyon, and Wilkinson.[15] We neither accept this position in its entirety, nor do we completely espouse that of the minimalists, represented by B. Bagatti, O.F.M., and E. Vogt, S.J.[16], who followed Josephus and Mishnah *Middoth*,[17] maintaining that the Temple was square—*tetrágonos* or four-cornered. Each of the four sides measured one stadion

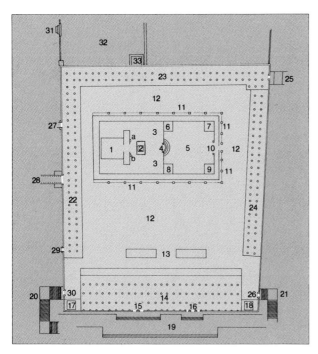

Figure 19   FLOOR PLAN OF TEMPLE BEFORE A.D. 70

1. "Holy of Holies," the Debir of the Temple.
   a.,b. Boaz, (Yakin), the two bronze pillars (1 Kgs. 7:15–22)
2. Altar of Whole-burnt Sacrifices (Holocausts).
3. Inner Court of the Priests and the Israelites.
4. Nikanor Gate and the Steps on which the priests blew the trumpets.
5. Court of the Women, with the shofar-shaped treasuries attached to the columns within this court.
6. Room for the Lepers.
7. Room for storing wood.
8. Room for storing oil.
9. Room of the Nazirites.
10. Main entrance into the forecourt (Ulam) leading into the principal parts of the temple complex. ("Beautiful Gate?")
11. Balustrade (Soreg) with Greek and Latin inscriptions forbidding Gentiles to the sanctuary under penalty of death.
12. Court of the Gentiles.
13. Entrance (right) and exit (left) ramps leading into the Temple area through the Huldah Gates in the Southern Wall of the enclosure.
14. Royal Basilica (Greek *stoá*, "portico"; Hebrew ḥanuyoth, "shops").
15. Double Huldah Gate (used for exiting from the temple area).
16. Triple Huldah Gate (used as an entrance into the temple court).

17. Place of the trumpeting (our Pinnacle of the Temple).
18. Traditional Pinnacle of the Temple above the great storageroom (*gazophylákion*), as contrasted with the treasuries and storerooms within the Temple proper.
19. Large platform and street in front of the Huldah Gates.
20. Monumental staircase leading down into the Tyropoeon Valley.
21. Large staircase leading from the Lower City towards the temple treasury (18), where the faithful could deposit their gifts.
22. Western portico of the Temple; it had four gates.
23. Northern portico of the Temple, contiguous with the portico of the Antonia in the northwestern part of the acropolis. The Tadi Gate was located here.
24. Porch of Solomon or the eastern portico of the Temple, said to be the oldest of the four porticoes surrounding the Temple Mount. It had two gates.
25. Gate and ramp through which the priests led the red heifer for sacrificing on the Mount of Olives. The Golden Gate occupies this site today.
26. Gate through which the scapegoat was driven into the desert on the Day of Atonement (*Yom ha-Kippurim*).
27. Temple gate leading into the Lower City (*proásteion*, "suburb"); identified with Warren's Gate.
28. Gate of the Arch, according to our identification (instead of the Coponius Gate). It led towards the Upper City across Wilson's Arch, and is called today the Gate of the Chain. The Xystos was here.
29. Another temple gate leading into the Lower City.
30. Southwesternmost Temple gate in the vicinity of our Pinnacle of the Temple (the place of the trumpeting) built above the great staircase supported by Robinson's Arch. It led down into the Tyropoeon Valley.
31. Gate leading into the main courtyard of the Antonia Fortress, identified by us with the Bab en-Nadhir. We locate Acts 21:27–40 here; see in particular verses 30, and 34–37.
32. Courtyard of the Antonia, now occupying the northwestern section of the Haram esh-Sharif.
33. Great tower of Fortress Antonia, built over the secret passageway from the Temple to the fortress.

✝ ————————————————————————————— ✝

(607 feet), according to Josephus (*Ant.* xv. 399), and 500 cubits or 750 feet according to the Mishnah (*Middoth* ii. 1).[18]

Why this discrepancy between these two important Jewish sources? Josephus wrote *Wars* and *Antiquities* after the fall of Jerusalem, *ca.* A.D. 75 and 95 respectively, hence he was an eyewitness to the site of the Temple and to the siege of Jerusalem during which the sanctuary was destroyed. Moreover, as a member of the priestly family of Jerusalem and, according to Yigael Yadin, probably a former member of the Essene brotherhood,[19] Josephus must surely have known the Temple very intimately. However, the Jewish historian penned his *Wars* and *Antiquities* from five to twenty-five years after leaving Jerusalem, most probably in Rome, and therefore was writing from memory, which recalls images and descriptions much more facilely than precise mathematical calculations. Describing the length as a stadion—perhaps as a round number to denote a fairly long unit of measurement—Josephus was simply trying to convey in somewhat superlative terms not exact measurements but the Temple's beauty and magnificence.

By contrast, Tractate *Middoth* was compiled and written about a century after Josephus, but it is believed that the authors did in fact survey the Temple themselves and so recorded the data. The reliability of the compilers of the Mishnah rests on the data which they provided in light of Jewish interpretations based on their sources.

The point of agreement between Josephus and the compilers of the Mishnah is most striking in that both sources delineate the temple area as a perfect square, though the exact measurements differ considerably. It is impossible to reconcile the mathematical calculations unless, as Bagatti suggests, one examines the earliest codices of Josephus to find, perhaps, a missing statement or reference to a "stadia and a half" which would correspond, more or less, to these measurements.

To determine the square area that composed the huge platform on which the Temple itself and the other buildings stood, Bagatti proposes that Avigad's figure of 280 meters, the length of the southern Herodian wall, be tested with regard to the Muslim Haram. Beginning at the southeastern corner, the traditional Pinnacle of the Temple, he moves northwards for a distance of 280 meters to a point in the eastern wall where the original line of the rampart ends and whence another wall, projecting about 2 meters from the former, begins its northerly course towards the northeastern corner of the Haram. This important junction in the wall appears only a few meters south of the Golden Gate, thus excluding it from the temple area, as conforms with Josephus' description of the eastern temenos of the Herodian temple. Moreover, according to Bagatti, Herodian masonry ceases to appear at this point. A glance at the topography of the Islamic enclosure, along an east-west line from Bagatti's point in the east wall across the Haram to the opposite wall on the west, clearly reveals a depression along this line where trees now grow, indicating the absence of solid rock at this level.[20] Much filling must have taken place here, most likely by the seventh-century builders of the Muslim sanctuary.

Following this east-west direction, then, one arrives in the neighborhood of the Iron Gate (Bab el-Hadid) of the Haram, or, more precisely, at the gate adjacent to the offices of the Supreme Muslim Council, Bab en-Nadhir. The distance between these two points measures 280 meters (*ca.* 850 feet). There is evidence of courses of Herodian masonry along the northern portion of the western wall. In view of this data Bagatti has successfully identified the square temple outer enclosure as delineated by Josephus and the Mishnah.[21]

In Bagatti's opinion the dull, rugged rock below the resplendent Dome of the Rock did not receive its sacred character until the seventh century A.D. It is true that for political reasons, initiated by Caliph Abdel Malek, the builder of the original shrine from 687 to 691, Muslims then attached a special religious significance to the rock in Jerusalem in opposition to the Ka'aba, the black cuboidal structure believed to be the house of Abraham in Mecca. According to Islamic tradition, it was from the sacred rock in Jerusalem that Muhammed made his famous *mi'raj*, his ascent to God through the seven heavens. But according to Bagatti, no particular significance was attributed to this rock during the Old and New Testament periods, nor was it venerated by either Jewish or Christian pilgrims from the time of the destruction of the Temple to the early Islamic period.

In *ca.* A.D. 438 Barsauma and his pilgrim group found Jews gathered together in veneration of their Temple, although he does not specify the place where they prayed. Bagatti interprets the statement "at the gates which lead to Siloam"[22] to refer to the entrance of the Huldah Gates, which were indeed the gates in the southern wall leading down towards the Pool of Siloam. These gates can still be detected in the Haram enclosure, but the Double Gate may be visited beneath the el-Aqsa Mosque. For Bagatti the Temple was situated someplace between the Mosque and the Dome of the

Plate 102 Bronze coin of Emperor Hadrian (A.D. 131–138), struck in Jerusalem. He rebuilt the city completely according to Roman city planning (using the quadrata or square, especially with respect to the arrangement of the street grid of a Roman city), and renamed the city after himself, Aelia Capitolina. The coin shows the Temple of Jupiter in Jerusalem.

Rock, the latter a bit farther to the north of the temple building proper. Thus, the rock does not enter into his reconstruction of the Temple.

However, M. Avi-Yonah objects that it is quite unlikely that the Jews would have prayed on the Temple Mount, as they do not pray there today:[23] it is still less likely that they would have prayed on the sacred rock itself, since it indicated the site of either the Holy of Holies or the altar of holocausts in the center of the Temple Mount. The fourth-century Pilgrim of Bordeaux states that this rock was not far from the statues erected by Hadrian in the quadra, but this does not preclude that Jews were already praying at the Western Wall as early as the fourth century. Furthermore, they would not have prayed at a place that had already been desecrated.

Bagatti, who positions the Temple between the Dome of the Rock and the el-Aqsa Mosque, explains that scholars have attached so much importance to the sacred rock only because the Muslims first regarded it as holy. Only later did Jewish and Christian pilgrims associate the Islamic monument with the Temple of Yahweh. But this interpretation militates against the longest and strongest traditions regarding the sacred character of the Dome of the Rock itself. We concur with this traditional identification of the site.

Much scholarly discussion continues as to whether the rock itself served as the foundation of the Holy of Holies or as the site of the altar of whole-burnt sacrifices, which stood in front of the Temple but within the court of the priests. Cogent arguments may be offered on both sides.

Scholars who would place the sacred Debir, the Holy of Holies, on the rock itself must necessarily shift the Temple much farther to the east, leaving much more room on the west—in back of the Temple—than is indicated in the ancient sources. Those who locate the Holy of Holies on or near the fifteenth-century Sebil of Qaitbai situate the altar on top of the sacred rock, as the legitimate successor of David's altar (2 Sam. 24:25; 1 Kgs. 8:22, 64; 9:25; 2 Kgs. 16:14–15). This localization of structures in relation to the measurements of the

Plate 103 Fragment of inscription restricting Gentiles from temple area proper under penalty of death.

altar agrees substantially with both the sources and the strong religious tradition regarding the site. Our analysis of the ancient texts in light of our own examination of the site convinces us that the sacred rock is the site of the altar of sacrifices; the area to the west is where the Holy of Holies once stood. The temple courts and the four porticoes around them formed a square area, as the oldest sources show.

Therefore, any reconstruction of the Herodian temple, which Jesus knew so well, must be based essentially on the ancient literary sources available, and in light of the material evidence found on the site. Secondary sources are also helpful, but they may not be based on sound literary and archaeological evidence.[24]

Plate 104 *Southwestern corner of the Haram and earlier Israeli excavations along the western and southern walls of the temple site. This southwest corner, a short distance to the right of the el-Fakhriyeh minaret, may be identified with the biblical Pinnacle of the Temple. Robinson's Arch is the projection in the western wall below el-Fakhriyeh. Three types of masonry can be observed along the western wall: the lowest course is Herodian; the middle, part Arab and part Crusader; the top, Turkish. The silver dome of Mosque el-Aqsa is seen above the southern wall, along which ran the Royal Basilica of the Herodian enclosure. Beneath it is a Crusader structure built directly against the Double Huldah Gate, which led into the Court of the Gentiles (above). In the foreground are mostly remains of Omayyad palaces.*

The Porticoes

THE BEAUTIFUL COLONNADES which crowned the Jewish high place were the famous porticoes of the Temple, mentioned in both sacred and secular literature. The portico on the east, the Porch of Solomon, was the oldest; the Royal Stoa on the south was the largest and the most famous.

The eastern colonnade was called the Porch of Solomon because it supposedly dated to the tenth century B.C. The prophet Ezra called it "the Street of the House of the Lord," using Hebrew *reḥob* in the strict sense (Ezra 10:9). But it is quite unlikely that in the Herodian reconstruction of the Temple any traces of the ancient Solomonic wall actually remained. Many centuries of destruction, repair, and reconstruction, as well as the complete rebuilding of the Temple by Herod the Great, would have concealed any preexisting blocks.

Solomon's Portico was the oldest of the four courts surrounding the Temple.[1] It was quite certainly the scene of many New Testament events. Jesus and his disciples must have met here quite frequently, for this was where the rabbis and their students would gather to read and discuss the Scriptures. It would be here that Mary and Joseph found their twelve-year-old son sitting among the learned teachers of the Law (Luke 2:41–52). Here, too, Jesus would later speak of his own resurrection in figurative tones reflecting the as yet uncompleted Temple (John 2:13–22). It would also have been on this ancient porch that he called himself the Son of God, for which the Jews sought to stone him (John 10:22–39). Peter cured a cripple at the Beautiful Gate—most probably the site of the sixteenth-century Golden Gate in the eastern rampart of the Old City—and he delivered his second discourse on the "Good News" in the Portico of Solomon (Acts 3:1–4:4). This was also where by mutual agreement the earliest Judaeo-Christians met daily to pray and discuss their new theology with the Apostles (Acts 2:46a; 5:12b).

By viewing the descriptions of these scenes by Luke and John in relation to the picture which Josephus presents, one may envision their taking place in a portico of stately white columns supporting an expansive roof of cedar wood. In pleasant weather the rabbis would have held their academic sessions in the courtyards or beneath

For to his angels he has given command about you,
that they guard you in all your ways.
Upon their hands they shall bear you up,
lest you dash your foot against a stone.

Ps. 91:11–12

Plate 105 *Temple Portico as envisioned by the artist of the Jerusalem Temple Model. The four porticoes surrounding the temple area built by Herod the Great not only embellished the sacred precinct of the Jerusalem temple, but also served as a place where the Law was explained and discussed by the various rabbinic schools.*

this colonnade. Paul would have studied Law here at the feet of Gamaliel (Acts 22:3; 5:34–39).

The colonnade on the south side of the temple area was popularly called the Royal Stoa (Greek *stoá*, a colonnade or a place enclosed by pillars) because popular tradition placed it on the site of Solomon's royal palace. This identification, however, can no longer be accepted.[2] Furthermore, although the present el-Aqsa Mosque follows a basilica-type layout, there should be no historical connection between it and the Royal Basilica built by Herod the Great on this site.

Both G. Dalman and B. Mazar, who have investigated the site, agree that the Royal Stoa can be equated with Hebrew *hanuyoth*, "shops." The faithful Jewish pilgrims from the various parts of Palestine and the Diaspora would have exchanged their money here, to purchase whatever was needed for the celebrations within the temple enclosure itself. For strict religious reasons, these pious worshipers would not have used the civil coins bearing the imperial portrait, but would have exchanged them for the Jerusalem coinage. This was in observance (by extension) of the Mosaic injunction "you will not carve idols for yourselves in the shape of anything in the sky above or on the earth below" (Exod. 20:4). Mazar reports some 1500 coins of Jerusalem mintage discovered in the vicinity of the Huldah Gates along the southern wall of the Haram, but few coins of foreign provenance were discovered in the Herodian level.

During the time of Jesus at least three different kinds of currency were used in Palestine: the official imperial money issued by the Roman procurators, the provincial coins minted in such cities as Tyre and Antioch-on-the-Orontes, and the local Jewish currency, probably minted in the larger cities of the country. Except for the silver Tyrian shekel, which was used in the census tax for the upkeep of the Jerusalem temple,[3] the standard Jerusalem coins were used by the Jews specifically for sacral purposes, especially in the temple area on the great Jewish festivals. In the New Testament period, the official moneychangers (*kollybistaí*, Matt. 21:12; Mark 11:15; John 2:15; but see *kermatistaí*, John 2:14) would set up their stalls and counters for this traffic in money, not only at the city's gates but also at the gates of the

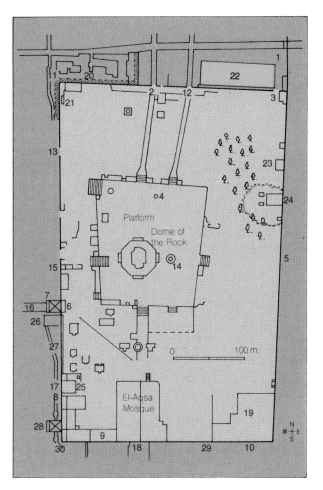

Figure 20 HARAM ESH-SHARIF

1. St. Stephen's Gate
2. Bab el-'Atem
3. Bab el-Asbat
4. Dome of the Small Rock
5. Moslem Cemetery
6. Bab es-Silsileh (Gate of the Chain)
7. Wilson's Arch (below)
8. Bab el-Maghariba
9. Women's Mosque
10. Single Gate
11. Minaret
12. Bab el-Hutta
13. Bab en-Nadhir
14. Dome of the Chain
15. Bab el-Mat-hara (Ablution Gate)
16. Street of the Chain
17. Barclay's Gate (below)
18. Double Gate
19. Solomon's Stables
20. Scarp of Antonia
21. Bab el-Ghawanima
22. Pool of Israel
23. Throne of Solomon
24. Golden Gate
25. El-Buraq Mosque
26. School of Tingiz
27. Wailing Wall
28. Robinson's Arch
29. Triple Gate
30. Pinnacle of the Temple

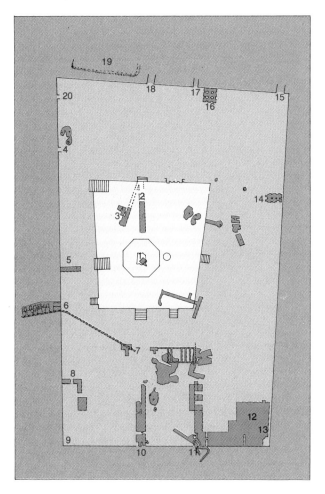

Figure 21 SUBTERRANEAN PASSAGES
OF THE HARAM ESH-SHARIF

1. Cave beneath the Dome of the Rock, named Bir el-Arwah, in which, according to Islamic tradition, souls gather for prayer twice weekly.
2. Underground passage leading to the Tadi Gate in the northern wall of the Temple.
3. Maze of subterranean halls, possibly the Chamber of the Hearth and the ritual baths of the priests (on duty).
4. Bad en-Nadhir, also called the Gate of the Watchman. This gate led into Antonia during the Herodian period.
5. Bab el-Mat-hara, Ablution Gate, identified as one of the Temple Gates (near Warren's Gate).
6. Bab es-Silsileh or Chain Gate, which we identify as the Gate of the Bridge; erroneously, we think, called the Coponius Gate (above Wilson Arch).
7. Aqueduct leading to the ablution fountain called el-Kas, the Cup.
8. Barclay's Gate, which led from the Temple to the Lower City; beneath Bab el-Maghariba.

9. Robinson's Arch, the spring of the arch which supported the platform just before the southwest gate of the Temple.
10. Double Huldah Gate (exit?).
11. Triple Huldah Gate (entrance?).
12. Solomon's Stables, which we identify with the gazo-phylákion or larger temple treasury.
13. Gate, now blocked, used for the release of the scapegoat on the Day of Atonement.
14. Golden Gate, used by the priests to lead the red heifer for sacrifice on Mt. Olivet.
15. Bab el-Asbat, the Gate of the Tribes, in the northeast corner of the Haram.
16. Large two-story reservoir connected with the Reservoir of Israel outside the Haram.
17. Bab el-Hutta or Repentance Gate (near ancient Sheep Gate?).
18. Bab el-'Atem, the Gate of Darkness (near ancient Sheep Gate?).
19. Rocky platform on which stands the Omariyyeh School, the former site of the palace-tower proper of Fortress Antonia.
20. Bab el-Ghawanima, a family name, perhaps preserving the site of another gate which lead into the Antonia compound.

Temple and even inside the Royal Portico on the Temple Mount.

The Royal Stoa was also a favorite gathering place for pilgrims, tourists, and traders, for it was not a religious structure per se. It served the same purpose as the great basilica in the imperial fora in Rome, the Stoa of Atticus in the public square in Athens, and the Roman stoa in Sebaste in Samaria during a later period. Everybody mixed here, either for business or to exchange religious and political news and views. Judging from the various biblical accounts of Jesus in Jerusalem, he must have had many discussions in this portico, as well as in the others around the sacred precincts of the Temple.

Josephus' rather complete description of the southern side of the Temple Mount makes it comparatively easy to reconstruct the biblical scenes here (*Ant.* xv. 411–16). There were four rows of columns, counting the pilasters attached to the stone wall, which formed three

Plate 106 *An Aqwas facing directly south towards the el-Aqsa Mosque. The ablution fountain called el-Kas, the Cup, stands between the pillared arches and the mosque. An ancient water pipe led to this important Sebil. Fr. B. Bagatti and his followers would situate the Herodian Temple someplace between the Dome of the Rock and the el-Aqsa Mosque.*

aisles beneath the roofed colonnade. This triple ambulatory ran from east to west, from the Kidron Valley to the Tyropoeon. The two side aisles were 30 feet wide and one stadion (607 feet) long, and they were 50 feet high. The central ambulatory, however, was one and a half times as wide, and its height was double that of the side aisles. The ceilings of these colonnades were richly embellished with woodcarvings representing various kinds of figures. The entire structure was built of highly polished stone, and visitors who had not seen it before were simply amazed by its grandeur and beauty. Jewish pilgrims and Gentile visitors had easy access to the Royal Portico, for the southern outer wall of the temple court also had gates in the middle leading to the portico itself above the wall. From beneath or from above it was a building unparalleled by any other under the sun, says Josephus, and the entire foundation on which it was built was so high that one would easily become dizzy from just looking down, though he would not be able to see the valleys below (*Ant.* xv. 412).

Apparently, the biblical Pinnacle of the Temple was some rather high point of either the Temple itself or a part of the temple enclosure. It is mentioned only in the New Testament, in the Matthaean and Lukan accounts of Satan's taking Jesus to Jerusalem and tempting him (Matt. 4:4–5; cf. Ps. 91:11; Deut. 6:16; see Luke 4:9, which follows Matthew here). Whether or not this encounter actually took place is an issue for the biblical exegete,[4] but that there was such a corner, structure, or high place we do not think reasonable to doubt.

Tradition locates the Pinnacle of the Temple at the southeastern corner of the outer temple wall. Much Herodian masonry at this juncture of the Haram esh-Sharif is quite discernible today. Modern guides are usually quite quick to point it out to pilgrims and tourists in Jerusalem. But this identification is based on a rather late tradition. The only real foundation for it is that this happened to be the highest point of the exposed wall until recent excavations brought to light a parallel height at the southwestern corner of the Haram. It is important to note that the early Christian pilgrim accounts sometimes confused or were not altogether clear with respect to the location of the "cradle of Jesus" (Mahed ʿIsa) in relation to the biblical Pinnacle.[5] Sometimes the "cradle" was sought at the southeastern corner or sometimes in the southwest. In general, however, some of these accounts can be interpreted to point to some kind of shrine, called the cradle of Jesus, in the southwestern area of the Haram.[6]

Moreover, G. Dalman suggested in the last century that the Pinnacle of the Temple be identified with the southwestern corner of the present-day Haram. In light of his recent excavations at the western and southern walls of the Temple Mount, B. Mazar now concurs. This corner dominated Jerusalem—the occupied quarters in the south on Ophel, the newer quarters looking towards the southwest on Mt. Zion, and the newest sections on the Hill of Ghareb in the northwest. This was the corner of the sacred temenos which was best seen from almost every part of Jerusalem. It was the best known, for it was from this high point that the trumpet was blown ushering in the New Year; moreover, it was also from this corner that the Sabbath repose was announced weekly. In 1970 Israeli archaeologists discovered a huge limestone block that toppled from the top of this corner nineteen hundred years earlier, during the destruction of the Temple in A.D. 70. The Hebrew inscription engraved on this rock identified the site: "This is the place of the trumpet-blowing."[7] By contrast, it would have made no sense to blow the trumpet from the southeastern juncture, below which there was hardly, if any, settlement in the vicinity. Thus, it is reasonable to identify

Plate 108 Limestone block excavated at the southwestern corner of the Temple Mount. The Hebrew inscription refers to "the place of the trumpeting," perhaps the biblical Pinnacle of the Temple from which the shofar was sounded. (Israel Exploration Society)

Plate 107 Southeastern corner of the Haram esh-Sharif, traditionally identified with the Pinnacle of the Temple (Matt. 4:5; Luke 4:9) [we suggest that the southwestern corner would be the more suitable location; see p. 126]. At least four types of masonry are identifiable. The projecting wall from the southeastern corner belongs to the Byzantine period. Large segments of the southern and eastern walls of the enclosure are Herodian. The master course, the largest section of Herodian wall, is visible midway between the top of the Byzantine wall and the point where the Herodian material terminates on top. The window in the eastern wall is in the vicinity of the gate that led into the temple storeroom (gazophylákion), now known as Solomon's Stables. A large staircase led from the Lower City up to this entrance, corresponding to Robinson's Arch on the western side. The rather rough stones, north of the Herodian masonry along the eastern rampart, are Hasmonaean, and have been equated with the Syrian Akra. The upper strata with the crenelated battlements belong to the sixteenth-century walls built by Suleiman the Magnificent. Particularly noteworthy in this first-century wall is the artistically sloping corner, moving inward from bottom to top.

the famous pinnacle or wing of the Herodian temple with the southwestern corner of the Temple Mount.

Josephus gives some rather interesting details with regard to the western and northern colonnades or cloister walks of the temple enclosure. Both of these porticoes consisted of a double row of columns, which were monoliths, supposedly of pure white marble (but most likely of the white meleke limestone quarried in Jerusalem). Each column measured 37 feet high. A protective roof of rich cedar wood was built over them to protect the many visitors to the Temple from the elements. Because these porticoes were so striking just as they were built, there was no need for additional sculptured or painted ornamentations as with the Royal Portico in the south. The width of these two promenades—that on the west stretching from the Pinnacle of the Temple to the Antonia in the north, and that in the north running from west to east, parallel to the northern wall of the temple enclosure proper—was approximately 49 feet. The length of both temple cloisters, embracing the Antonia, measured some 1360 yards. The esplanade of the open temple court added to their attractiveness. It was made of beautiful *opus sectile*, a pavement of variously colored slabs of polished stone composed in a definite pattern.[8]

Today, nothing remains along any of the walls within the Haram that would recall the splendor of the four colonnades that once graced this holy site. What happened to this material? The Romans destroyed it, not leaving a stone upon a stone, as Jesus had predicted (Matt. 24:2). It is quite possible, though perhaps impossible to prove, that many of the Corinthian capitals still evident in the streets or buildings in Jerusalem once belonged to the temple area. A number of these capitals and even some columns were brought to light in the recent excavations beneath the Temple Mount. Many of these architectural relics must surely have originated in the Jewish occupation of the Mountain of the Lord. (For instance, Josephus numbered 162 Corinthian columns in the Royal Stoa only.) Where are they now?

In the Middle East, as in Greece and Rome, ample concrete archaeological evidence shows that various kinds of building materials were used and reused, even in the very early years of Israel's occupation of Canaan. Since much of this material can no longer be found on the site, it must be sought in other places, though frequently close by, such as in the Dome of the Rock or in some of the Christian churches (some of which date back to the early Byzantine period). All too frequently ancient sites were used as quarries for subsequent builders and engineers commissioned by their rulers. In the second century A.D., for example, Hadrian employed skilled stonecutters to hew out large blocks from the southern portion of the Ophel-Moriah spur in the area of David's tomb. Byzantine monarchs followed suit, cutting

out huge blocks of stone from just below the southern wall of the Temple as both the Kenyon and Mazar excavations have shown.[9] Quarrying was not only a very arduous process but also an expensive one. Hence, why should new blocks for columns and capitals be cut and adorned if so much of this material was already available? One needs only to study the material in and around Jerusalem to try to reconstruct for himself the splendor and the glory that was once the Temple Mount.

Plate 109 *First-century steps leading to the Double Huldah Gate in the southern wall of the Temple, shown prior to their recent restoration. The lower course of masonry is clearly Herodian. The ornate lintel is visible between the Crusader projection (left) and the Turkish wall (right), built along the lines of the original Herodian course.*

The Temple Gates

Lift up, O Gates, your lintels; reach up, you ancient portals, that the King of Glory may come in!

Ps. 24:7

Plate 110 *Interior of the Double Huldah Gate, looking south. The column and Herodian masonry are original. This ancient material is located in the el-Aqsa el-Qadimeh, below the present el-Aqsa Mosque.*

ON THE TESTIMONY of Josephus and the Mishnah, and in view of the recent archaeological discoveries, it is possible here to examine the nature and purpose of the entrances to the sacred area as they must have looked in the Herodian structure during Jesus' visits to the City of the Temple.

Unhappily, however, the two literary sources are by no means in accord with each other, either concerning the number of gates of the temple compound or their position. Moreover, it is not possible completely to reconcile these sources, although attempts can be made. But the two can be interpreted to complement each other, both as to the nature of the gates and their position in the temple wall. Briefly, Josephus mentions six gates: four gates on the west side and two along the southern wall (*Ant.* xv. 410–11). There is no indication that Josephus knew of a northern and eastern gate. Mishnah *Middoth* lists five gates: two on the south, corresponding to those identified by Josephus, only one on the west (Josephus says that there were four), and one on the northern and eastern sides of the outer walls (i. 1, 3).

In more detail, the two sources provide the following important information regarding the entrances to the temple precinct. According to Josephus, the four gates on the western flank were as follows. The first gate led across the Xystos bridge over the Tyropoeon Valley, from the temple courts to the royal palace. Two gates positioned in the lower courses of the western wall opened into the lower part of the city, the central portion of the Tyropoeon Valley, just below the temple acropolis. The fourth gate led down to the southern quarter of the Lower City, known in the first century as Ophlas, the Greek rendition of the Old Testament Ophel. From this last gate, situated in the southwestern portion of the wall, a monumental stairway led down to the Tyropoeon Valley, with a corresponding flight of steps on the other side of the valley, leading to the Upper City on Mt. Zion. There were two gates in the middle of the southern wall, on top of which stood the Royal Stoa, identified as the Huldah Gates (*Ant.* xv. 411; cf. Mishnah *Middoth* i. 3).[1] At this point in his account Josephus rather abruptly breaks with his descrip-

Plate 111 Triple Gate in the southern wall (blocked), used by Jews and Gentiles as the main southern entrance to the Temple Mount. Inside both the Double and the Triple Gates were ramps leading upwards towards the main court of the Temple (see Fig. 19).

tion of the gates and immediately proceeds to describe the temple courts and the temple building proper. Perhaps he had intended to do so, but there is no literary evidence.

As for the Mishnah, it indicates that the outer wall of the temple quadrangle had five gates. The two Huldah Gates were located on the south, for the coming in and the leaving of the temple area. The Triple Gate, whose successors are visible today in the later accretions to the wall, served as the entrance to the temple compound. The Double Gate functioned as the exit. Parts of this gate in the outer wall can still be seen today; large portions can be admired beneath the present el-Aqsa Mosque, built over the original el-Aqsa el-Qadimeh of the seventh century. The so-called Kiphonos Gate was located along the western wall. It is identical with the gate mentioned by Josephus, leading across the Tyropoeon Valley to Herod's palace on the western hill of Jerusalem. The Tadi Gate on the northern wall was not used, at least not by the ordinary visitor to the Temple Mount. But the Shushan Gate, which pierced the eastern wall of the Temple at the northern end of the Porch of Solomon, was the gateway through which the high priest and his sacerdotal entourage marched from the Temple Mount across the Kidron Valley to the Mount of Olives for the sacrifice of the red heifer (Num. 19:1–10).

The position of the Huldah Gates has been quite clearly established not only in the light of their successors, now blocked, in the sixteenth-century battlements of Suleiman the Magnificent, but also by the recent excavations beneath them. Both Josephus and the Mishnah agree that, looking from a point south of this outer wall towards the southern façade of the temple acropolis, the first set of gates, the Triple Gate and the Double Gate to the left of it, led by means of a ramp or series of steps into the Royal Basilica above this wall.

Mishnaic *Middoth* gives the names of these gates and their specific functions. They were called the Huldah Gates after the seventh-century Jewish prophetess Huldah (mentioned in 2 Kgs. 22:14–20; cf. 2 Chr. 34:22–28), whom King Josiah of Judah consulted to determine the authenticity of the law discovered in the Temple. The larger of the two gates, the Triple Gate, served as the entrance "for the coming in" to the Temple, whereas the smaller gate functioned as the exit, "for the going out," since more people were supposedly anxious to enter and stay in the Holy Place than in a hurry to leave it.

One of Mazar's most interesting archaeological discoveries at the southern wall was the monumental staircase leading up to the Huldah Gates. This discovery is unusual, especially because there is no literary reference to such a stairway outside the Huldah Gates. Beyond the southern wall of the Triple Gate one can still observe a portion of the doorpost, which must date back to the Herodian construction of the entrance. But much more ancient material survives left of the Double Gate, namely the threshold, a part of the lintel and practically the entire vestibule, with a central pillar and four decorated arches. These are preserved in the Muslim el-Aqsa el-Qadimeh below the present mosque.

These gates evoke many memories of Jesus' visits to the temple area. The Triple Gate would be the terminus of Jesus' messianic entry into Jerusalem, having entered the City of David through one of the gates in the southeastern corner. After dismounting outside the temple

Mount, the Gate of Shushan and the gate leading into the larger temple treasury in the southwestern corner of the temple esplanade. Why the compilers of the Mishnah would not have mentioned these important entrances into the temple area is not clear. Perhaps this information was lost or had not come down to them by the time this source was being written down in its present form. Surely, the original compilers must have been aware of four gates on the western side of the temple enclosure, just as they knew of the Huldah Gates in the southern wall. It simply would have been logical to have more than one entrance on the west side, since this side faced the majority of Jerusalem's population in the first centuries before and after Jesus.

Therefore, it appears sound to follow Josephus' description rather than the Mishnah. If the two sources do not agree with regard to the number of gates here, both at least mention the important gate that linked the Temple Mount with the king's palace on the other side of the Tyropoeon Valley. It was called the Gate of Kiphonos (*BJ* ii. 117–18). The bridge that spanned the valley between these two points is known as Wilson's Arch, after C. Wilson, director of the British survey who discovered it shortly after the middle of the last century. The bridge is still in situ below the Chain Gate (Bab es-Silsileh), known as the Porta Speciosa during the Crusader period, and the direct successor of the first-century gate.

Instead of following the traditional identification of this gate with the name of the Roman procurator Coponius (A.D. 6–9), we suggest that it was originally called the Gate of the Arch, the plural of Aramaic *kipha'*, "arch" or "vault." This must have been the popular, perhaps the accepted name of this gate during the first century, naturally drawn from the arch to which it pointed from the temple esplanade. By the time the Mishnah was finally compiled, *ca.* A.D. 200, the Jewish

gates, Jesus entered the Triple Gate, going up the ramp into the temple area, where he found the money-changers and venders. Had they limited their business to the Royal Stoa itself, there probably would not have been such an outburst. But, by gradually moving their tables outside the portico and close to the sacred precinct, these "hypocrites" turned their own Father's house into a "den of thieves."

With regard to the gates in the north, east, and west, there is no agreement between Josephus and the Mishnah. Where Josephus is silent about a gate in the northern wall, there the Mishnah places the Tadi Gate. Josephus does not speak of a gate in the eastern wall, but the Mishnah mentions the Shushan Gate. The Mishnah speaks of only one gate in the western wall, but Josephus names four gates, as seen above.

Thus, it is rather difficult to reconcile the accounts of Josephus and the Mishnah, especially because there is material evidence of four gates along the western wall, and at least two on the eastern side of the Temple

compilers simply knew the name of this gate in its Aramaicised version—*Kiphonos*, transliterated from Latin *Coponius* or Greek *Kōpōnios*. Later commentators must have equated this with Coponius, the first Roman procurator to rule over Judaea and Samaria.

It is difficult to imagine that a gate of so sacred a place would have been named after a pagan ruler, particularly since the second meeting place of the Sanhedrin, who judged the worthiness of priests to enter the temple precinct, was located here (hence its name "Priests' Gate").[2] When the territory of Archelaus had been reduced to a Roman province in the restless Near East, Caesar Augustus commissioned Coponius, a senator of the equestrian order, to govern Palestine with plenary authority, including capital punishment (*BJ* ii. 117). If for some reason the gate was named after this Coponius, one could detect a derisive play on the Greek word for sparrow, *képhos*, and Hebrew *kaphas*, meaning "to deal unfairly" with others. Furthermore, if *képhos* equals *képphos*, as is clear from the comedian Aristophanes (*Pax* 1067), the connotation is a pejorative reference to a feather-brained person. Another insight into this name is derived from the Greek spelling *Kauponios* (from *kápēlos*), which designates a "retail dealer," a "huckster," or a "tavernkeeper." Thus, the adjective *kapēlikós* (whence Latin *cauponius*, from *caupere* or *copere*, an "innkeeper") metaphorically describes one who is knavish or deceitful.[3]

Excavations at the southwestern corner of the Temple Mount have remarkably confirmed the location of Josephus' fourth gate in the western wall. He writes that the last of these gates led to the other quarter of Jerusalem, and that many steps led from it down into the Tyropoeon Valley (*Ant.* xv. 410).[4] In the last century E. Robinson identified the spring of an arch, which he believed to have belonged to a bridge connecting the temple area with the Upper City. This spring is even now popularly known as Robinson's Arch. During the 1969–1970 excavations beneath this protrusion in the western wall, Mazar brought to light the supporting base of this arch, along with many stone slabs which were indeed relics of the monumental staircase mentioned by Josephus. The stairs led upwards to the gate above, in the vicinity of the New Testament Pinnacle of the Temple, and to the Royal Stoa. No other supporting bases

Plate 113 *A recently discovered flight of steps leading towards the street along the western wall below Robinson's Arch. The spring of the Herodian arch can be seen above the excavated area, in which were found some of the huge blocks of the arch that collapsed into the shops below during the Roman destruction of Jerusalem.*

✛ ———————————————————— ✛

Plate 114 *Southwestern corner of the Temple Mount, as depicted by the Jerusalem Temple Model. Note the monumental stairs leading to the Royal Basilica along the southern wall. The large curved structure below the southern wall is the Hippodrome, though we question its location here.*

Plate 115 *Panorama showing the oldest and most sacred sanctuaries in Jerusalem, the Muslim Haram esh-Sharif (Noble Enclosure) and the Jewish Western (Wailing) Wall. The original wall (the first courses of Herodian masonry below the Arab, Crusader, and Turkish additions) is from the Third Temple period. The golden dome marks the site of the altar of holocausts. The silver dome belongs to the el-Aqsa Mosque (over the Double Huldah Gate). Note the grill separating men and women, as customary also in the biblical period.*

were found in the area between this base and the western hill opposite the Temple Mount.

Josephus does not name the two gates in the western wall that opened into the Lower City, the suburb in the Tyropoeon Valley just below the temple acropolis.[5] These two gates allowed easy access to the Temple Mount for the Jews who lived in the neighborhood of the Mishneh, the second or newer quarter of first-century Jerusalem. Given the depth of the Tyropoeon Valley and the height of the Herodian temple wall in this area, there must have been stairs or ramps leading up to these gates, but they would not have been as monumental as those leading to the gate at the southwestern corner or to the Huldah Gates in the southern wall. Of these two gates, that in the north, between the gate leading into the Antonia and the Gate of the Arch, can be identified with Warren's Gate. It was discovered in 1870 by C. Warren, who dug deep shafts into the centuries-old debris that had accumulated in the Tyropoeon Valley along the western wall of the Temple Mount.[6] Its modern successor is Bab el-Mat-hara or Mutawadda, the Ablutions Gate.

The lower gate in the southern portion of the western wall, between the Gate of the Arch and Robinson's Arch, is known today as Barclay's Gate, identified by the British architect Barclay as one of the four gates mentioned by Josephus that led into the temple area. It is situated about 246 feet from the southwestern corner of the Haram, and lies about 48 feet below the present level of the ground. It can also be observed in the subterranean Mosque of el-Buraq which, according to Islamic tradition, is related to Prophet Muhammed's night journey from Mecca to Jerusalem. Hence, the gate is sometimes referred to as the Gate of the Prophet. The upper part of this gate, though almost completely altered since the building of the Dome of the Rock, can be seen immediately to the left of the ramp leading to the Gate of the Moors (Bab Harat el-Maghariba), the direct successor of the ancient gate mentioned by Josephus, which opens into the Haram esh-Sharif at this point.

At this juncture one may very well ask if there really were gates positioned along the northern and eastern walls leading into the sacred area of the Temple. We feel that it is possible somehow to reconcile the specific identifications of the Mishnah, which mentions a northern gate (*Middoth* i. 3), with allusions to certain gates in this area by Josephus (*Ant.* xv. 424). There seems to be substantial evidence in both sources, as well as in the Haram esh-Sharif itself, to identify and equate the Mishnaic Tadi Gate with the gate leading into the secret passageway below the tower built by Herod in the northern wall that was actually contiguous with the Fortress of Antonia. Thus, the northern temple gate was located just above or very close to the northwestern *aqwas* or

Plate 116 *Golden Gate, from inside the Haram esh-Sharif looking directly eastwards toward Mt. Scopus and the Mount of Olives. In many respects its architectural design resembles that of the Double Huldah Gate (see p. 130). The Ottoman Turks walled up the gate in 1538, but explanations differ: some historians say it was blocked to prevent the Messiah's coming to Jerusalem; others cite the reference to the closed gate in Ezek. 44:1 –3. According to Islamic tradition the pillars that divide the passageway into two parts are gifts to King Solomon from the Queen of Sheba.*

pillar-arches north of the Dome of the Rock, which lead in the direction of the present Bab el-ʿAtem, the Gate of Darkness, one of the northern gates of the Haram.

The Tadi Gate, therefore, would not have been seen by all pilgrims and visitors to the Temple Mount. Tractate *Middoth*, in fact, clearly states that it was not used at all. But the Roman soldiers posted along the northern wall of the temple courts, as well as the priests and Levites stationed in the Temple itself, must surely have known of its existence. The soldiers must have used it in order to take up their positions on the wall to protect both the fortress and the sanctuary, and the Jewish priests were allowed access to the Antonia where their precious sacred vestments were stored for safekeeping.[7]

North of the Dome of the Rock, writes G. Cornfeld, lies a straight passageway covered by a vaulted stone roof. Its length is about 120 feet from north to south. Some scholars associate it with the secret passage named Niṣoṣ which led from the inner temple court to the northern gate called the Tadi Gate in the Mishnah. However, close by, west of this passage, is a cluster of underground chambers which some authorities relate to the purification baths of the priests and the Chamber of the Hearth, also mentioned in the Mishnah. Possibly, then, this passage on the left functioned as the lower level of the ritual bath, whereas the principal tunnel led to it from the Chamber of the Hearth.[8] According to some accounts, this was the most ancient of all of the gates of the Temple, which makes further sense in view of our placing David and Solomon's palace in the northwestern corner of the Temple Mount, rather than in the south as generally believed. This gate would have provided easy access for the king from his palace to the Temple proper.

In further support of the above, some material evidence on the site helps to strengthen the relationship between the ancient Tadi Gate, the Niṣoṣ, and the

Moqed on the one hand, and the Bab el-ʿAtem and the two subterranean corridors beneath the northern platform of the Dome of the Rock on the other. Tractate *Middoth*, for example, describes all of the temple gates as having lintels with the exception of the Tadi Gate, which had two stone slabs leaning against each other to form a type of pointed arch (ii. 3). This we can verify on the site. By extension in place and time, Bab el-ʿAtem, (the Gate of Darkness), known today as the Feisal Gate, preserves the direction of the ancient passageways beneath the platform (called in antiquity the Niṣoṣ and the Moqed), just as Bab el-Hutta, the Gate of Repentance, perpetuates the site of the biblical Sheep Gate. Bab el-ʿAtem, moreover, would point to the dark underground passages, which anciently were lit by oil lamps, hence the meaning of the two Hebrew terms: *moqed*, from *yaqad*, means "burning," while *niṣoṣ*, from *naṣaṣ*, signifies "shining." The Chamber of the Hearth, located north of the Temple proper, was just such a place. Thus, identifying these sites with the existing underground material would also provide support to delineate the northern temple area along this line, thus describing and completing the general temple enclosure as a square (*tetrágōnos*), as depicted by Josephus (*Ant.* xv. 399) and measured by the Mishnah (*Middoth* ii. 1).

Josephus mentions no gates on the eastern side of the Temple. But the Mishnah explicitly names the Gate of Susa (Shushan) along this stretch of the sacred *per’bolos* (*Middoth* i. 3). There were, in fact, two gates, the Susa Gate in the north and an unnamed gate in the south

Plate 117 *The meeting of Sts. Joachim and Annah at the Golden Gate of the Temple. This late nineteenth-century fresco can be seen in the Grotto of Elijah, a cavelike chapel of the Laura of St. John Koziba, deep in the Wadi el-Qelt on the way to Jericho.*

leading into the temple treasury, called the *gazophylákion* in John 8:20.

The Susa Gate received its name from the relief of the famous Persian city portrayed on its lintel, in grateful commemoration of the permission which King Cyrus of Persia gave to the Jews to rebuild their sacred shrine after their return from exile in the sixth century B.C. This gate should be located on the site of the now-closed Golden Gate, Bab ed-Daheriyeh (from a misinterpretation of Greek *hōraía,* "beautiful" [Acts 3:1–2], and the Latin *aurea,* "golden"), just a few yards south of the Kursi Suleiman, the Arabic version of Solomon's Throne. Bagatti, following Josephus, excludes an eastern gate from his study of the temple enclosure on this side, explaining that the jog or architectural shift just a few yards south of the Golden Gate delineates the length of the eastern wall beginning at the southeastern corner.[9] However, it is important to position an eastern gate at this point. The Mishnah plainly indicates that through it the high priest passed on his way to the Mount of Olives for the sacrifice of the red heifer (Num. 19:2–13). It opened onto the ramp called in the Mishnah the *kebesh ha-parah,* the causeway of the red heifer.[10] Furthermore, according to our own measurements of the temple square,[11] we include the Golden Gate as an essential feature, the descendant of the Gate of Susa on the eastern side of the temenos wall. (We tentatively suggest that the shift mentioned by Bagatti probably marks the extent of Solomon's Portico above it, though it is difficult to say exactly how long

this ancient colonnade really was.) Thus, the wall on the east included a gate in the northeastern corner which also helps to determine the area and the description of the Jerusalem temple as square.

In his rebuilding of the ramparts of Jerusalem in the sixteenth century, Suleiman the Magnificent blocked the Byzantine and Crusader gate on this site, for, according to Islamic tradition, it would be opened only when the *Nasi* or "prince," identified with the Son of Man mentioned in Ezek. 44:1–3, appears in the Holy City at the end of time. The Byzantine gate here was built or restored by Empress Eudocia, daughter of Theodosius II and wife of Emperor Valentinian, when she visited Jerusalem in the mid-fifth century. A fifth-century tradition locates Peter's curing of the lame man at the Beautiful Gate (Acts 3:1–10). A sixth-century Christian tradition, based on the second-century apocryphal gospel known as the Proto-Evangelium of St. James,[12] describes the meeting of Joachim and Anna at this gate, a scene vividly depicted in an nineteenth-century fresco in the grotto of Elias in the desert laura of St. John and George Koziba, deep in the Wadi el-Qelt between Jerusalem and Jericho. In 615 the Byzantine Emperor Heraclius recovered the relic of the "True Cross" of Jesus from the Persians and, carrying it in solemn procession, entered the Holy City through this gate. Pilgrims in the eighth century believed that this was the same gate which Jesus used on the occasion of his triumphal entry into Jerusalem, though we have suggested one of the Huldah Gates in the south wall for this biblical event. The Golden Gate was restored by the Crusaders in the twelfth and thirteenth centuries, but has been closed since the sixteenth century. Both the interior and exterior of this gate, the interior resembling that of the Double Gate beneath the el-Aqsa Mosque, make it one of the most impressive of the eight gates of the Old City of Jerusalem today. Its history, as we have outlined it above, makes it equally important.

The second gate led from the northeastern corner of the Lower City up towards the temple treasury situated beneath the southeastern corner of the temple esplanade. It is not mentioned by name in any literary source, but the presence of a gate at this particular point may be deduced from archaeological investigation of the site. It served practically the same function as its counterpart at the southwestern corner (Robinson's Arch), the monumental stairway mentioned by Josephus and confirmed by recent excavations.

Whereas the southwestern stairs and gate led to the Place of the Trumpeting and the Royal Stoa which opened to the Court of the Gentiles, the staircase built into the southeastern corner of the temple citadel led first towards the temple storeroom, known as the Chamber of Utensils (*lishkat-ha-kelim*),[13] then up towards the southeastern end of the Royal Stoa or southern part of the Porch of Solomon along the eastern wall.

One need only study the masonry of the southern portion of the eastern wall of the Haram esh-Sharif to detect two different types of stonework: Herodian blocks are clearly discernible for about 32 yards from the corner of the wall until they reach an entirely different kind of stonework to be identified with the eastern *perĭbolos* of the Hellenistic period, and not, as has been hypothesized, with the foundations of the Syrian Akra.[14] The ashlars that form this stretch of wall are quite impressive, though they do not measure up to the high quality workmanship of the Herodian blocks that surround the entire sacred acropolis. In the Herodian stonework along the southern portion of the eastern wall one can also observe the remnants of the spring of an ancient arch, corresponding to Robinson's Arch on the west. It is to the right, and below, the window that opens into the so-called Solomon's Stables. This arch must have been a part of the stairway leading from the Lower City up to the acropolis of the Temple on the east side. It is possible to identify it with the *kebesh ha-śa'ir*, the "ramp of the scapegoat" (Lev. 16:20–22) mentioned in the Mishnah (*Shekalim* iv. 2; *Yoma* iv. 2). Further archaeological examinations and explorations are needed to locate the base that supported the pillar of this arch. However, the material evidence outside and inside the wall points to such a gate at this particular juncture in the eastern wall.

As noted above, the latter ramp and gate also led from the Lower City into the temple area via the temple storerooms, which can be identified with a temple treasury located beneath the Haram esplanade where Solomon's Stables are to be found. Various kinds of temple treasuries were attached to sanctuaries in the ancient world (cf. 1 Kgs. 7:51; 1 Chr. 28:11–13; 2 Chr. 5:1; Josh. 6:19, 24; Dan. 1:2; Neh. 10:38; 12:44; 13:12; Matt. 13:52; Mark 12:41; Luke 21:1, and John 8:20).[15] These were rooms or chambers in which sacred vessels and various kinds of gifts to the shrine were stored for safekeeping, at least temporarily. The Jerusalem temple had many such chambers or treasuries for the donations of money and other kinds of gifts, such as personal offerings of the people or the spoils of war, which were brought to the Temple and stored in appropriate places.

The appropriate Hebrew word for such a treasury is *lishkah*, etymologically related to Greek *léschē*, which signifies a public building, a council chamber, or simply a place for lounging around. Literally, *lishkah* means a room (usually connected with a shrine), a hall, chamber, cell, or compartment. In connection with the Jerusalem temple, the term describes the Chamber of Secrets (*lishkat ha-sha'im*), also known as the Hall of Secret Donations wherein devout Jews would deposit their gifts for support of the poor, and the Chamber of Utensils (*lishkat ha-kelim*) where anyone could place various articles for temple repairs or to be sold in case of a surplus. Both the Chamber of Secrets and the Chamber of Utensils differ from the thirteen horn-shaped collection boxes, called *shopharoth*, which were around the temple walls (or perhaps attached to the columns) in the Court of the Women.[16] The Greek term for these shophar-shaped treasuries is *gazophylák(e)ion*, partially derived from Persian *gaza* meaning a "king's treasury."[17] But *gazophylákion* can also be used in the sense of Hebrew *lishkah*. Josephus, who employs the plural form *gazophylákia*, says that the Romans, once the Temple itself was on fire, did not spare any of the other buildings, including the treasury chambers connected with it, in which were stored large amounts of money, huge piles of clothes, and many other valuable items.

Such a large chamber or hall in the temple area may easily be equated with the vast area beneath the southeastern platform of the Haram esh-Sharif. Below this platform one can still admire the vaulted hallways, almost 30 feet high, resting on eighty-eight piers of Herodian workmanship. Alterations have been carried out in this area through the centuries, but especially during the Latin Kingdom of Jerusalem, when the Knights Tem-

plars tethered their horses here, hence the popular designation Solomon's Stables. Used as a huge storehouse,
the *lishkah* or *gazophylákion* of the late biblical period,
this would have been the scene in which Jesus on the
Feast of Tabernacles spoke to the Pharisees, telling them
that he was "the light of the world" (John 8:12).

To conclude, there can be no doubt that the splendid
Islamic Haram esh-Sharif eloquently perpetuates in
stone the memory of the Jewish Temple of Yahweh, so
sacred in Judaism, Christianity, and Islam. It is the
property of the Islamic world today, the third most holy
site in Islam, and the special prerogative of Muslims to
protect it and preserve its sanctity.

In Judaism this area always has been venerated, and
the focus of all aspirations—"next year in Jerusalem!"

For Christians throughout the world, the Temple was
the place where God dwelled in a special way, with
which Jesus identified himself: "Destroy this temple and
in three days I will raise it up" (John 2:19).

Plate 118 Interior of Solomon's Stables beneath the southeastern corner of the Haram esh-Sharif, which may be
equated with the large temple treasury (gazophylákion) or
storerooms. The pillars are composed of large Herodian blocks
used to extend and support the temple esplanade above.
Huge wooden beams were placed in the square holes seen
above the arches, upon which the stone slabs of the pavement
rested. The entire area measures 598 square yards.

Plate 119 Fresco "Last Supper" (1495 –1497) of the Florentine artist Leonardo da Vinci. It is located in the old Dominican Convent adjacent to the Church of Santa Maria delle Grazie in Milan, Italy. The artist pictures the group partially reclining, as was the Jewish custom since the Hellenistic period. From left: Bartholomew, Jacob, Andrew, Judas, Peter, John, Jesus, Thomas, James the Greater, Philip, Matthew, Thaddaeus, Simon. (Department of Antiquities, Milan)

CHAPTER **VIII** # The Upper Room

I have greatly desired to eat this Passover with you before I suffer.

Luke 22:15

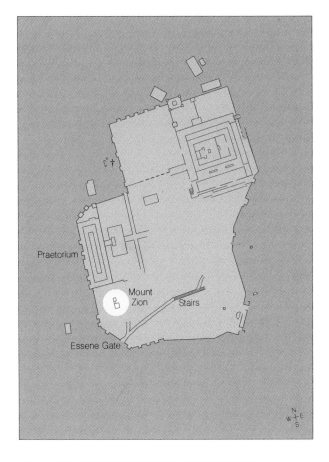

Figure 22   COENACULUM OR UPPER ROOM

SINCE THE FIRST DAYS of Christianity the southwestern corner of Mt. Zion has been remembered and venerated as the birthplace of Christ's Church. Here he shared his last Passover meal, the Jewish Seder, with his chosen twelve disciples, instituting the Eucharist and ordaining the apostles as his priests. Here on Mt. Zion the promised Paraclete, the Holy Spirit sent by Jesus, descended upon the group assembled in the Upper Room, initiating Christ's disciples into a new, specially ecclesial way of life. He incorporated them into his Church, the visible, tangible Kingdom of God on earth. What had been taught and promised during the preparatory years of Jesus' ministry through Galilee and Judaea was now fulfilled. Christianity, the "new way," became a reality to persevere.

The earliest Christians were "Zionists," not in the national and political sense understood today, but in a fuller sense, not only religious but also geographical and topographical. The longest and strongest traditions point to Mt. Zion as the place where the Upper Room of the Last Supper was located; and all arrows of tradition focus on Mt. Zion as where, most probably, in the same Upper Room, the Holy Spirit descended upon Christ's apostles, thus giving birth to his Church.

The long tradition in this particular case corroborates historicity. The events that took place here can be demonstrated in light of sound biblical exegesis and archaeological investigations. Even if complete excavations have not been undertaken in this area, sufficient material evidence shows that the primitive church had its modest origins in the vicinity of the imposing shrines that dominate Mt. Zion, particularly its southern half, which lies outside the sixteenth-century city walls.

Jews settled on the upper, western hill of Jerusalem as early as the latter part of the eighth century B.C.[1] In

Plate 120 *Aerial view of Mt. Zion, showing the Dormition Abbey in front of the sixteenth-century southern wall of Jerusalem. The small minaret marks the site of the Cenacle or Upper Room and the alleged Tomb of David inside the same building.*

✦————————————————————————✦

Plate 121 *Probable ancient Roman wall, the lowest course on the right, indicates the scene of the Passover and Pentecost events on Mt. Zion in A.D. 30. This important wall can easily be seen in the former cloister of the Franciscan Convent: the lower windows on the right look into the two rooms, formerly one large chamber, of the traditional burial place of King David; the vaulted windows above indicate the Upper Room of the Crusader period, later transformed into a mosque called Nebi Daud (Prophet David). The minaret, built by the Muslim Dajani family of Jerusalem, is a post-Crusader structure.*

Plate 122 *Minaret and former mosque (Nebi Daud) indicating the site of Jesus' last Seder meal on the Feast of Passover and the scene of the descent of the Holy Spirit upon the Apostles on Pentecost.*

✦————————————————————————✦

the course of time a Jewish community grew and expanded in this quarter, and by the first centuries before and after Christ it had developed into one of the largest and most affluent Jewish quarters of Herodian Jerusalem, no doubt rivaling those of Alexandria and Rome. Ironically, a mixed Jewish population inhabited Mt. Zion during those first centuries—both those espousing an up-to-date Hellenistic way of life and those living out the letter of the Law according to the most rigid interpretations of ancient Judaism.

The Hellenistic Jews had their Graeco-Roman-styled homes in the northern portion of the western hill, roughly corresponding to the present Armenian Quarter, save for that part where Herod's palace and the upper city square were located. It stretched eastward beyond Suq el-Ḥuṣṣor and the Street of the Jews into the now rebuilt Jewish Quarter of the Old City, and from David Street, the line of the "first wall" in the north, towards the present southern wall of the Old City, and even to the south of it, as archaeological explorations have shown.[2]

The most conservative Jews lived in the southern half of Mt. Zion. B.-G. Pixner, O.S.B., of the Dormition

Plate 123 *Interior of the Upper Room. Although the room may date back only to the Crusader period, in the light of a long and strong tradition now corroborated by archaeological research, there can be no doubt as to the historicity and holiness of this place for Christians.*

Abbey has demonstrated ample evidence on the site that it was an Essenic community with its major "camp" or "quarter" here.[3] It was the Essenes' profound love for Zion, the Holy City of the Temple, that first brought them here, and it is possibly due to them that the western hill is called Mt. Zion. The Essenes' Apostrophe to Zion sings a psalm in its honor: "It is pleasant to praise you, O Zion, for you are cherished throughout the world. I remember you often for your blessings; and I bless you with all my heart!"[4] As ultraliteral interpreters of Mosaic Law, they wished to separate themselves from all other Jews, whom they disregarded either for their loose interpretations of Judaism or for their devious allegiance to pagan rulers. Here in their own quarter they could live in accord with the strictest observance of the ancient Law with little or no interference. Their *maḥaneh*, as well as can be geographically measured, would have incorporated the area within the first wall of the city, as outlined by F. J. Bliss, on the southern portion of Mt. Zion. Today this is the scene of the Benedictine Church and Abbey of the Dormition, the Greek Orthodox Seminary, and the Anglican Cemetery. The little chapel of the Franciscan Fathers, called Ad Coenaculum, and the Crusader structures of the Upper Room, beneath which tradition locates the cenotaph of King David, are also to be found in this neighborhood. These are inside the small mosque named in Arabic Nebi Daud or Prophet David, undoubtedly the most important landmark on the site. Here Jesus celebrated the Passover Seder meal, and here the Christian Church was born on the Feast of Pentecost. It must have been here, the regular meeting place of the Judaeo-Christians, that the Jerusalem Council was held some twenty years later, around A.D. 50 (Acts 15:1–29; Galatians 2:10).

It is not possible to reconstruct exactly what the Upper Room looked like in the first century A.D. It must have been a very simple dining hall in keeping with the simple life of the Essenes. Certainly it was different from those depicted in frescoes by the famous Florentine artists Domenico Ghirlandaio (*ca.* 1480) and Leonardo da Vinci (*ca.* 1496). Nevertheless, the site is much more solidly established in writing and in stone than would at first be imagined.

The strong memory of the important events attached to this place has persevered from A.D. 30 until modern times.[5] The fourteenth-century Gothic-styled room, the best surviving relic of the magnificent Crusader church that dominated the site during the period of the Latin Kingdom of Jerusalem, assists in retracing the long history of the place. The present room of the Last Supper, the Coenaculum, is partly a reconstruction of the Crusader chapel, which the Latins were compelled to abandon in 1187, when Salah ed-Din's warriors forced the Crusaders to capitulate, and it is partly a later Islamic transformation into a mosque in memory of Prophet David, hence the name of the mosque and quarter, Nebi Daud.[6] Thus, by surrendering to Salah ed-Din (Saladin) Jerusalem was spared from total destruction by the overpowering forces of Islam. However, in 1219 practically nothing remained of the magnificent Crusader basilica called Sancta Maria in Sion, to which the Coenaculum was incorporated, when the Damascene Sultan ordered it razed. Nevertheless, the memory of the site had been fixed in the minds and hearts of the Christians, so that as compromises were made and tensions somewhat eased between the followers of Jesus and those of Muhammed, Pope Clement VI (1342–1352) was in a reasonable diplomatic position to negotiate with the Muslims and thus entrust Palestine to the Franciscan Fathers, thus naming them the official Guardians of the Holy Land, the Custodia Terrae Sanctae. The Franciscans immediately carried out repairs and restorations on the little room of the Last Supper, so the chapel was once again available for Christian worship.

By 1523, however, which coincided with the newly-converted Iñigo of Loyola's pilgrimage to the Holy Land, pressures on the Christians began to mount again, and the small room of the Coenaculum was converted into an Islamic mosque, remaining so until the present century. The architectural designs in the hall still display Christian and Islamic features: the pillars and the vaulting of the ceiling are clearly Crusader artwork; the *miḥrab* or prayer niche, indicating the direction (*qibleh*) of Mecca, is obviously an Islamic addition.

In 1551 the sons of St. Francis were expelled from Mt. Zion, but the recollections of so holy a site persevered. After 1917, the year the British commander, Gen. E.H. Allenby, liberated Jerusalem, conditions for all three monotheistic religions in Palestine changed, when the Palestinian State was placed under the British Mandate from 1920 until May 14, 1948 when Israel proclaimed itself an independent state. In 1936 the Franciscans were permitted to return to Mt. Zion, where they now have a convent and a small chapel referred to as Ad Coenaculum, built practically contiguous to the historical site of the Crusader Upper Room. Neither Christians nor Muslims are allowed to hold religious services in this sacred place; the Jews venerate the so-called Tomb of David in the room just below. The Latins hold liturgical celebrations in the Franciscan chapel or in the Church of the Dormition close by.

Through the intervention of Emperor Wilhelm II, who visited Palestine in 1898 while it was part of the vast Ottoman Turkish Empire, the present Benedictine Church of the Dormition and its adjoining abbey were built over much of the area covered by the Crusader church of Santa Maria in Sion and its Byzantine predecessor, the church of the Hagia Sion. The present structure of the Dormition was built in 1910. Kaiser Wilhelm II gave this much disputed property to the Archepiscopal See of Cologne. In 1957 the Dormition was elevated to the rank of basilica.

The two predecessors of the present structure maintain an unbroken chain of churches that links the site with the sixth, fourth, and even earlier centuries of

Plate 124 *Tomb of King David on Mt. Zion, venerated by Orthodox Jews who follow a Christian tradition locating it there rather than in the Lower City (as specified in 1 Kgs. 2:10). The niche behind the cenotaph is perhaps part of the ancient Roman wall of what must have been an early Judaeo-Christian synagogue-church.*

Christianity. In 1099, when the Crusaders under Geoffrey de Bouillon of Lorraine liberated Jerusalem from Islam during the First Crusade (1096–1099) and declared the Holy City the capital of their Latin Kingdom, the Latins restored the previous churches which had lain in ruins on Mt. Zion. They employed as much as possible of the material from the former buildings for their Romanesque reconstruction of the church on the site of the Upper Room.

It can be assumed that much of the material used by the Crusaders in building the Sancta Maria in Sion came from the great Byzantine basilica of Hagia Sion, the "Mother of All Churches." The Church of Holy Sion was constructed on this site sometime during the first part of the fourth century, before A.D. 350. It can be identified clearly on both the Madaba Map and the fourth-century mosaic of Jerusalem in the apse of the church of St. Pudentiana in Rome. On both maps

Bar-Kokhba during the years 132 to 135, the fourth-century ecclesiastical writer Epiphanius penned the following important lines regarding the small church on Mt. Zion: Hadrian

> found the city completely leveled to the ground and God's temple treaded down, except for a few houses and the church of God, which was quite small. To it the disciples returned after the Savior's ascension from the Mount of Olives. They went up to the Upper Room, for it had been built there—that is, in the part of the city called Sion, which part was exempted from destruction, as also were some of the dwellings around Sion and seven synagogues, the only ones which existed in Sion, like monks' cells. One of these survived until the time of Bishop Maximos and King Constantine. It was like a tent in a vineyard, to quote the Scriptures. (*De Mensuris et Ponderibus* 14)[8]

Apparently, Epiphanius is relying on older sources and ancient traditions[9] stemming from the New Testament accounts (Matt. 28:17–29; Mark 14:12–25; Luke 22:7–38; 24:33–43; John 13:2–18; 20:19–29; Acts 1:12–26; 2:1–47). For example, St. Cyril (*ca.* 313–386), Bishop of Jerusalem, wrote *ca.* 348 that on the Feast of Pentecost the Holy Spirit descended from heaven "in the upper church of the apostles" in Jerusalem (*Catechesis* 16.4).[10] An earlier Palestinian clergyman, Eusebius of Caesarea (265–340), said that the Gospel, the Law of Christ, spread through Christ and his apostles to all the nations from Mt. Sion in Jerusalem, where Jesus stayed a long time and taught his disciples many things (*Demonstratio Evangelica* i. 4).[11] These accounts are in all likelihood eyewitness reports of the material evidence on Sion during the third to the fourth centuries. The place of the Lord's Supper and that of the Pentecost event were combined. No other candidate for this spot has such a long chain of unbroken tradition and place of pilgrimage.[12]

The strongest literary evidence, based on Acts (1:13–14; 2:46; cf. also 2:42–47; 4:32–37; 5:12–16), illustrates that the earliest communal meetings of Jesus' disciples who gathered together on Mt. Zion for prayer and the Eucharistic Agape (love feast) were held in private homes which later became churches (in the modern

Plate 126 *Jerusalem cartouche of the Madaba Map showing detail of the Church of the Holy Sepulchre. Note the steps and three large portals leading into the atrium or forecourt of the Constantinian structure, as it appeared about two and a half centuries after its original construction. The large red-roofed building is the Constantinian Martyrion, the site of the former Hadrianic basilica. The golden dome, the Anastasis, marks the spot of Jesus' burial and resurrection.*

the church dominates Mt. Zion, and the detailed artwork reveals its ancient splendor. Its importance, moreover, during the Byzantine period is demonstrated on the Madaba Map by a rather wide street leading from the square next to the Church of the Holy Sepulchre directly towards the large basilica on Mt. Zion. This street has been uncovered during the recent archaeological excavations in the Armenian cemetery by the Israeli scholar M. Broshi.[7] Its most impressive relics can still be viewed south of the present walls of the Old City, leading southwards towards the Dormition Abbey.

On the St. Pudentiana mosaic, next to the Church of Holy Sion, on the right, the south side of the church, can also be seen the wing, which was probably a separate chapel attached to the church, either incorporating or built over the small first-century house or church, which survived the destructions of Jerusalem by Titus and Hadrian. In his report on the Jewish revolt, led by Simon

Plate 127 According to the Assyrian Orthodox Church in Jerusalem, one of the oldest communities in the Holy City, the location of St. John Mark's house is to be identified with the church and buildings on their property. It was to this convent that Muhammed ed-Dib brought and sold the Dead Sea Scrolls to the Assyrian Patriarch Mar Athanasius Shemuel in 1947.

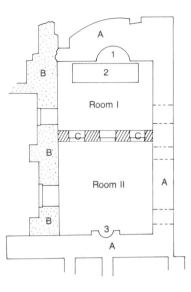

Figure 23 Lower structures or foundations of the Upper Room above David's Tomb on Mt. Zion (Adapted from Plan of J. Pinkerfeld)

A. Original (late) Roman wall built of strong ashlars. Its north, east, and west lines are still in a good state of preservation, but only the eastern wall is preserved in its entirety. The east–west extension of the north and south walls cannot be determined to ascertain thereby the size of the room (I–II) of the Roman period.

B. West wall, belonging to the Arab Mameluke period 1250–1517).

C. Late Turkish wall, which divided the chamber into two sizeable rooms (I–II).

1. Original apse of the structure (synagogue? church?) built into the Roman wall. It is oriented slightly to the northwest, rather than the northeast as Pinkerfeld maintains.

2. Crusader cenotaph of David (David's Tomb), constructed on a pavement of the same period. Below it Pinkerfeld found a mosaic floor of the Roman or Byzantine period, and beneath this decorated pavement still another floor, the stone pavement which belonged to the original Roman building (along with Wall A and the apse in Room I).

3. Muslims' prayer niche (*miḥrab*) facing in the direction of Mecca, built into the original Roman wall during the Arab period.

Room I, originally forming one large hall, presently containing the cenotaph or tomb of King David. It was probably intended as the Jewish place of prayer during the Turkish period.

Room II, with its prayer niche in the southern wall, we think designed to be a mosque, along with the minaret outside, during the Turkish period.

sense). Quite certain evidence of this development is available at such sites as Dura-Europas,[13] Ephesus, Philippi, and Rome.[14] Evidence of such a conversion of a home into a church is present at Nazareth.[15] Even more certainly, the earliest Christians, the first-century Judaeo-Christians, held their meetings and continued their apostolic work on Mt. Zion.

Only a stone wall marks the site of this primitive church. Hidden beneath this wall lay the ruins of the original foundations of the Church of Holy Sion, as archaeological investigations supported by tradition and literary evidence show. Some explorations have been carried out beneath the Upper Room in the place known today as David's Tomb. In 1951, when J. Pinkerfeld examined the area,[16] he identified masonry that belonged to the later Roman period. It was made up of rather large ashlars still in their original position. The dating of the building coincides with the restorations undertaken by Bishop Makarios of Jerusalem ca. 335, before the reign of Julian the Apostate (361–363). The building was identified as a pre-Byzantine synagogue such as those at Dura-Europas on the Euphrates River in Syria and Eshtamoa, a small village southeast of Hebron. The only discrepancy we detect in this report is that the niche described by Pinkerfeld is not oriented directly northeast towards the Temple Mount, but directly northwest. Synagogues in the Holy Land were oriented towards Jerusalem; those in Jerusalem were oriented towards the Temple itself. However, the general style of the building does not preclude its specific use as a synagogue on Mt. Zion. Pinkerfeld's plan shows the following information.

Moreover, judging from the floor levels of the structure, the buildings must be much older than first supposed. The site, therefore, is much more important than first believed, for at first it had been considered only to be the site of the Lord's Supper and the Pentecost event; now it can be established as the place of the Upper Room, the earliest Christian meeting place and church on Mt. Zion. The material evidence on the site shows that beneath the marble slabs of the Turkish period lies a Crusader plastered floor, which in turn covers a mosaic of either the early Byzantine or late Roman period. This mosaic covered a stone pavement, probably also a mosaic, which belonged to the original first-century building. According to Pixner, who recently has reexamined the area thoroughly, the steps leading up from the Church of St. Peter-in-Gallicantu, on the eastern slope of Mt. Zion, led up towards a point identified as the most likely spot for a doorway or a vestibule of an ancient house. This door would have opened towards a platform leading up to a house whose level would correspond to a second story upper room. The site, therefore, must be secure, for it has been the only candidate for the Cenacle (Coenaculum or dining hall) from primitive Christianity until today.

Why did Jesus celebrate his last Passover meal in this quarter of Jerusalem; and why did the Pentecost event, seven weeks later, take place here? These questions are all the more intriguing if the history of the area is examined in light of further historical arguments based on archaeological examinations of other sites in the vicinity of the Dormition Abbey and the Franciscan Ad Coenaculum.

In view of Bagatti and Pixner's research, it is historically sound to assert that a community of Essenes lived in this quarter of Jerusalem. The most up-to-date evidence to support this view is the Qumran Temple Scroll. Of utmost importance are the Halakhic rules concerning the rubrics of cleanliness and purification according to the strict legislation contained in Deuteronomy. This section deals with the purity of the quarter where the eschatological community lived, necessitated by the presence of the Ark of the Covenant.

With respect to the presence of a community of Essenes residing in Jerusalem in the first centuries before and after Jesus, numerous references to this rigid Jewish sect are found in the writings of Philo Judaeus,[17] Flavius Josephus (BJ ii. 120–161; Ant. xviii. 18–22), Pliny the Elder (Naturalis Historia v. 17, 73), and Hippolytus.[18] These sources as well as the New Testament reveal that Herod did indeed esteem the Essenes. The Evangelist Mark certainly gives the impression that even Herod Antipas, tetrarch of Galilee, held John the Baptizer in high regard (Mark 6:20). Some scholars hold that John was in all likelihood himself a follower if not a member of the Essenes (at least at some time),[19] just as Y. Yadin believes that Josephus had also been an Essene but later abandoned the sect.[20] Interestingly, the Essenic

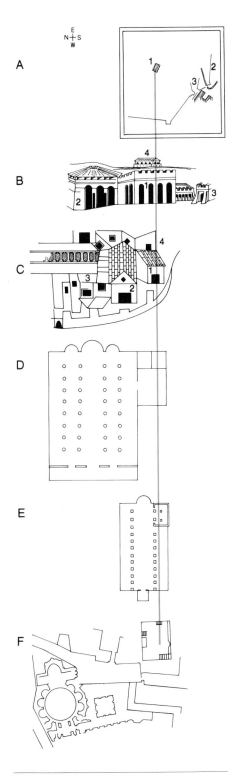

Figure 24   HISTORY OF THE COENACULUM OR UPPER ROOM

A Essene Quarter in the southern end of Mt. Zion, probably dating to the second half of the second century B.C. (1) Site of the Cenacle or Upper Room (of the house of John Mark) where Jesus celebrated his last Passover Seder, and where, later the Pentecost event took place. (2) Southern "first wall" of the city, according to Josephus. (3) Gate of the Essenes.

B Fourth-century pictorial (map) of Jerusalem in the Church of St. Pudentiana in Rome. (1) Cenacle, used as a palaeo-Judaeo-Christian church-synagogue from around A.D. 50/70 to 135. (This was probably a synagogue during the reign of Julian the Apostate [361–363].) Eusebius of Caesarea (265–340), the Bordeaux Pilgrim (333) and Epiphanius (392) are some of our earliest witnesses that the site was associated with the biblical events of the Last Supper (washing of the feet and Judas' betrayal) and the Pentecost event. (2) Great church of Hagia Sion, Holy Sion the Mother of All Churches, built by John II around 417. (3) Southern city gate of Jerusalem; Hadrian did not incorporate this area into his Aelia Capitolina (135). (4) Church of the Eleona built by Constantine the Great on the Mount of Olives.

C Byzantine sixth-century mosaic Madaba Map, depicting (1) the Cenacle attached to (2) the church of Holy Sion; (3) an ancient Byzantine street which was recently discovered in this direction; (4) another ancient street of the Byzantine period recently uncovered leading towards the south gate of the city (see Endpaper, no. 6).

D Floor plan of the Cenacle and the Hagia Sion, after M. Geisler, O.S.B. The Upper Room is situated directly above the alleged Tomb of King David (see Endpaper).

E Floor plan of the Crusader building, according to Geisler. According to Saewulf (1102) it was destroyed by the Saracens under Hakim (1009) and rebuilt by the Latin Kingdom of Jerusalem, though on a much smaller scale. Scholars are not sure whether the Upper Room had been incorporated into the Crusaders' Holy Sion Church or not.

F Present site of the Cenacle. Some of the original Roman period wall can still be seen in the courtyard outside the small building housing David's Tomb on the ground level and the Cenacle above it. The large Church of the Dormition was built by Kaiser Wilhem II for the Latin Catholics in Jerusalem.

maḥaneh was just south of Herod the Great's palace on Mt. Zion.

Historically, it is possible to show that the very first Judaeo-Christian community in Jerusalem sprang from a first-century Essenic (Hasidic?) sect whose dwellings were on Mt. Zion, probably the houses referred to by Epiphanius. Certainly not the entire community on Mt. Zion converted to Christianity on Pentecost, A.D. 30, but only a splinter group, who not only were moved by the events described in Acts, but who also sincerely believed that the Law and the Prophets were being fulfilled in Jesus of Nazareth.

The "devout Jews of every nation" settled in Jerusalem at the time of Pentecost in A.D. 30 would have included the Essenes. These orthodox believers interpreted the Scriptures literally, and so were eager to accept Jesus and predicate Messianism to him. Because John the Baptizer, a first cousin of Jesus, was probably an Essene, it is possible that Jesus, too, could have been in some way associated with the sect. Some of his family went up to Nazareth to live, while some, like James, remained in Jerusalem. Both branches had their roots on Mt. Zion, however. Father Pixner believes that a reconciliation took place between the two branches during the crucifixion on Calvary. Jesus' words on the cross, "Son, behold your mother; woman, behold your son," can be so interpreted.[21]

The unbroken historical chain regarding the history of the founding of Christianity on this site is solid. Despite the catastrophes of A.D. 70 and 134 as well as the later destructions of Jerusalem or the expulsion of Christians from the City of Jesus, Christian tradition is persistent. In the fullest sense of the word Hagia Sion, the Mother of All Churches, is here, and there cannot be any other candidate. All of the arrows of scholarly research point to this holy place.

Plate 128 Christian pilgrims carrying a replica of the cross into the Church of the Holy Sepulchre.

Plate 129 Aerial view of the Church of the Holy Sepulchre. The large dome marks the site of the original Constantinian Anastasis; the smaller dome is the apse of the Greek Orthodox Katholikon. Two mosques flank the basilica: the el-Khanqa Mosque (below) and the Mosque of Omar (above). Partially visible are the Russian Hospice and the Lutheran Church of the Redeemer (upper left).

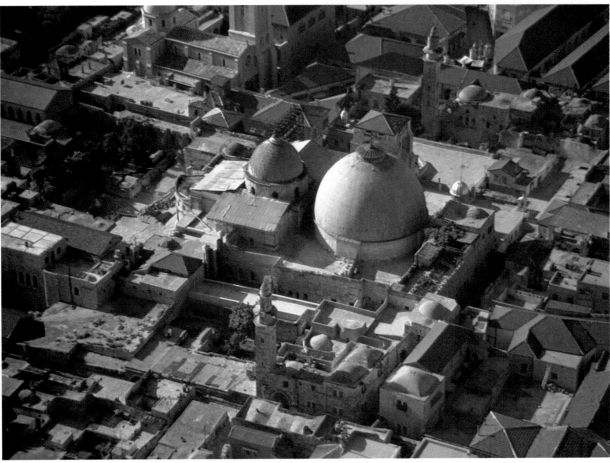

CHAPTER IX JESUS' CROSS AND TOMB

Therefore Jesus died outside the gate, to sanctify the people by his own blood. Let us go to him outside the camp, bearing the insults which he bore.

Heb. 13:12–13

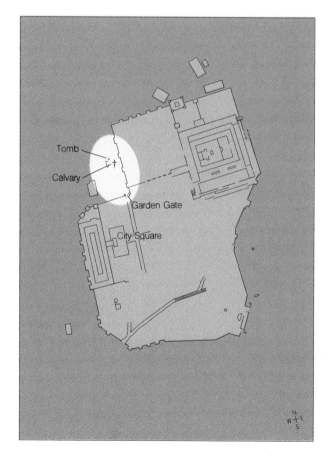

Figure 25 CALVARY AND JESUS' TOMB

Church of the Holy Sepulchre

JERUSALEM is the home of the most celebrated church in Christendom, the Basilica of the Holy Sepulchre. This most venerated monument embraces both Calvary where Jesus was crucified and the tomb of Joseph of Arimathea wherein he was interred. The present Crusader structure was dedicated on July 15, 1149, fifty years to the date after Geoffrey de Bouillon's victory over the Holy City in 1099. Tradition, history, and archaeology all support the authenticity of this site.

In the process of restoring the twelfth-century Romanesque basilica to the way it looked in the period of the Latin Kingdom of Jerusalem, more and more ancient material is gradually coming to light. Much concrete historical evidence lay concealed for centuries, and many a scholar or visitor to Jerusalem had questioned the authenticity of the site. Now there can be no doubt concerning the sites of Golgotha and Jesus' "garden tomb."

The church as it stands today embraces much earlier evidence, from the early Byzantine period, from Hadrian's Aelia Capitolina, and from the first centuries before and after Christ. There is also archaeological evidence with regard to the site's history before its use as a place of crucifixion and a Jewish cemetery.

The Crusader church contains abundant material from the rebuilding and restorations undertaken by Constantine Monomachos in 1048. Earlier, in 1009, Sultan Hakim had systematically destroyed much of the previous church. In fact, considerable damage was done to the grotto-like tomb of Jesus, according to various historical records concerning the early eleventh-century devastations of Jerusalem's holy places, many of which dated back to the Byzantine period.

Plate 130 *Detail of the fourth-century mosaic of the apse in the church of St. Pudentiana in Rome. The principal buildings illustrated here are the Rotunda or Anastasis ("Resurrection") with its dome open to the sky at this early date, the Basilica or Martyrion (Place of Witness) on its right (mostly behind the mound of Calvary), and the Baptistery or Baptisterion on its left. This latter structure may have been the Diakonikon, an annex of a Byzantine church where the necessary supplies for the altar and liturgy were kept.*

On May 4, 614 Chosroes Parvis led the Persian attack on Jerusalem. He did not completely demolish the Church of the Holy Sepulchre, though he did set it in flames. The fourth-century Constantinian edifice was still standing thanks to the excellent restorations directed by the Greek Patriarch Modestos, former abbot of St. Theodosius Monastery in the Judaean desert southeast of Jerusalem. Modestos carried out his repairs sometime around 628, the year that Emperor Heraclius jubilantly carried the relic of the True Cross into Jerusalem after it had been seized by the Persian Chosroes.

A fairly good idea of what Constantine's buildings looked like is available not only from the lengthy eyewitness documentation of Eusebius of Caesarea in his Life of Constantine,[1] but also from a number of ancient depictions of the edifice. The famed mosaic in the church of St. Pudentiana in Rome depicts the important churches of Jerusalem built during the fourth-century reign of Constantine. The mosaic contains the following early Byzantine structures: the Baptistery adjacent to the Anastasis or the rotunda of the Holy Sepulchre, the magnificent golden-domed Anastasis itself, the large Martyrion of the Constantinian ecclesial basilica behind the mound of Calvary, the great church of Holy Sion with the wing of the Cenacle immediately at its right, and, in the distance, the church of the Eleona on the Mount of Olives. The cross naturally dominates the scene: Calvary was incorporated within the Constantinian structures, though it stood within a garden or courtyard between the Anastasis and the Martyrion within the Constantinian enclosure.[2] During the Crusader period most of the small shrines within the compound were enclosed within the single church known today. Thus, the Crusader Church of the Holy Sepulchre, especially the western part around Calvary and the Tomb of Jesus, incorporates structures dating back to the earliest years of Christianity in Jerusalem, contemporaneous with the Cenacle on Mt. Zion.

Further evidence of this fact is clearly distinguishable on the famous sixth-century Madaba Map. The dominant cartouche on this oldest map of the Holy Land features a detailed plan of Byzantine Jerusalem. The layout of the Holy City is clearly that of Hadrian's *urbs quadrata,* Aelia Capitolina. Many public buildings, both ecclesiastical and civil, can be identified with a high degree of certainty, but the principal Christian attraction on this map is clearly the Basilica of the Holy Sepulchre.

To approach the church from the north one enters the city through the Gate of the Column (Bab el-ʿAmud, more popularly known as the Damascus Gate) and proceeds southwards along the principal north-south street, the former cardo maximus of Aelia Capitolina. The street is clearly identifiable by the porticoes or colonnades on either side. A few columns can still be seen along the north-south main thoroughfare of the Old City. Later, shops were built into these porticoes, just as in a number of other cities such as Samaria-Sebaste north of Nablus. As one follows the ancient cardo, or Suq Khan ez-Zeit as it is known today, he arrives at the entrance of the enclosure of the Holy Sepulchre building complex. Three steps lead up to the triple-portaled façade, beyond which is the red-roofed Byzantine Martyrion and the golden dome of the Anastasis.

Most of this material can still be viewed today. The huge main portal of the façade is visible in the room behind the Zelatimo Bakery in Suq Khan ez-Zeit, just below the traditional Ninth Station of the Cross. The southern entrance of the façade can be admired in the Russian Hospice of Alexandrova on the southeastern corner of Dabagha Street, opposite the Lutheran Church of the Holy Redeemer (*Erlöserkirche*). The Constantinian basilica, the Martyrion, lay beneath the present portion of the church now called the Katholikon of the Greek Orthodox sanctuary. A. Ekonomopoulos brought to light the Constantinian apse under the recent pavement of this Katholikon in his 1968 excavations of the site, enabling him to determine the orientation of the

Constantinian structure. It followed the lines of the Hadrianic public basilica built in the northwest public square of Aelia Capitolina.[3] To the left of the church (looking west on the Madaba Map) is the Byzantine baptistery with a pavement, a type of forecourt, in front. This material can be seen from the rooftops of St. James' Chapel and the Romanesque belfry adjacent to the Crusader façade of the Basilica of the Holy Sepulchre.

Furthermore, an excellent idea of the interior of the Anastasis can be seen from "pictures" of the aedicule over the tomb of Jesus. The silver pilgrim flasks, the *ampullae* of Bobbio and of Monza of the Byzantine period, have sketches of the *aediculum* of the Holy Sepulchre stamped on them. They eloquently illustrate the descriptions which Eusebius of Caesarea bequeathed in his Life of Constantine. They also complement the accounts which the fourth-century pilgrims, the Pilgrim of Bordeaux (333) and the nun Aegeria (*ca.* 380), wrote in their diaries, at least two centuries before the Madaba Map was made. These flasks also supplement the topographic and toponymic data in the writings of such ecclesiastical authors as Origen (185–254) and Epiphanius (315–403). Origen, for instance, who visited Palestine in the third century, explained the toponymy of Calvary thus: "Because of the place of the skull we heard that the Hebrews have a tradition that Adam lies buried there" (*Commentarium in Mt. libr.* 10–17).[4] Epiphanius, a native Palestinian, wrote that "when Jesus was crucified here . . . he wet the bones of our first ancestor with his blood. . . " (*Panarion seu Adversus LXXX haereses* lxvi. 5).[5]

In the fourth century A.D. the Christian east was a battleground of debate and conflict. Anxious to preserve the public order and Christian discipline, Constantine in 325 summoned to Nicaea in Asia Minor the Fathers of the Church to decide on matters pertaining to Christian belief and practice, and thereby to attempt to restore peace and order in the empire. It was on this providential occasion that the Patriarch of Jerusalem, Bishop Makarios (312–334), appealed to the Emperor to erect shrines over some of the most sacred places of Christendom in the Holy Land, particularly in Jerusalem, on the Mount of Olives, and in nearby Bethlehem. Palestinian monasticism had begun to

flourish, and many zealous souls attached themselves to the Holy Places, both to protect and preserve them, as also to provide places of worship for the many pilgrims. Makarios possessed such accurate information that even his rival bishops supported his appeal to Constantine at Nicaea. The precious information he possessed was handed on to him in Jerusalem from bishop to bishop, believably from the first bishop of Jerusalem, St. James the Younger, martyred in Jerusalem in A.D. 62.

Thus, it was the precision of the intensive Christian tradition that pointed directly to the Venus Temple in the public square of the second century as the place where the Holy Sepulchre was to be located; the statue of Jupiter, also set up by Hadrian in the same square, indicated the site of Golgotha.

The primitive Judaeo-Christian and Gentile-Christian communities in Jerusalem could not possibly have forgotten or lost sight of these extremely important holy places. They frequently visited them, as long as it was possible for them to do so, until Hadrian reconstructed the city a century after Jesus' death. It is possible that many Gentile-Christians remained in the city, though they could not openly profess or practice Christianity. Would Hadrian, then, also have wished to obliterate from their memory associations of these places, particularly by prohibiting their visiting them? Père Charles Coüasnon, O.P., does not think there was actually any anti-Christian gesture by the emperor here. The topography of the area around Calvary and the tomb of Jesus demanded the leveling of some sections and the construction of special earthworks for the large public square and the beautiful temple of Venus. Some authorities hold that Hadrian also built his *capitolium* here.

The Christian community of the second century must surely have been aware of all the new building activity in progress in their city. In this way the information regarding the sacred sites in Jerusalem was kept alive within Christian circles and thus passed on from one generation to another. For instance, Jerome wrote that from the reign of Hadrian until that of Constantine, a period of approximately 180 years, a statue of Jupiter stood on the rock where the cross of Jesus was once fixed, and a marble statue of Venus marked the site where Jesus was buried (*Epistola* 58).[6]

In the early fourth century, when Constantine's mother Queen Helena came on a pilgrimage to Jerusalem, a very different kind of building activity was going on: its special objective was to preserve, protect, and embellish the holy places in Jerusalem. The former city square had been quite an unlikely area in which to look for the site of Christ's crucifixion and his burial place nearby. The quarter must have been cluttered by many different kinds of buildings. Also, it was within the city walls, within the third rampart built in the north of Jerusalem by Agrippa I between A.D. 39 and 41, whereas the biblical account states that Jesus was crucified and buried, according to Jewish Law, outside the walls of the city. "But the Jerusalem tradition," writes Coüasnon, "had established a site so difficult to admit, that it must have taken all the weight of an extremely strongly-rooted tradition to make such an improbability acceptable."[7]

Thus, the place of the crucifixion and the site of the Holy Sepulchre have been certainly established, both by a long and very strong tradition and by excellent scholarly investigations in the neighborhood. The following sections will examine these two sites and how they probably looked in A.D. 30.

They have pierced my hands and my feet; I can count all my bones. They look on and gloat over me; they divide my garments among them, and for my vesture they cast lots.

Ps. 22:16b–18

Plate 131 *Grotto of St. Helena beneath the southeastern corner of the Church of the Holy Sepulchre. Only the side walls of this grotto belong to an early date. The general construction of the crypt is that of the early twelfth century. Archaeological explorations seem to indicate that the Constantinian edifice had no crypt. Christian tradition mentions this grotto as the place in which St. Helena, empress mother of Constantine I the Great, found the wood of the cross on which Jesus was crucified.*

Calvary

ALL FOUR EVANGELISTS interpret Golgotha to signify "the place of the skull" (Mark 15:22; Matt. 27:33; Luke 23:33; John 19:17b). But this interpretation of the name is open to question.

Frequently the ancients, as do the peoples of the Middle East still today, employed orographic terminology to describe and thus to identify a place. In first-century Aramaic, Gabbatha defines the Upper City of Jerusalem, the southwestern spur of Mt. Zion which actually does look like a "back," thus describing a rather flat height, which that hill in Jerusalem actually was. Did Golgotha, then, resemble a skull? The Latin translators of the Gospels rendered Aramaic *Gulgultha* as *Calvaria*, which in Latin means "skull." However, the popular stories about Adam having been buried here or that skulls were strewn all over the site are unfounded.

In our view, the name *Gulgultha* originates from the Semitic root *galal*, meaning "to roll away," hence *galgal* means a "wheel." In this case the word pointed to the roundish hillock of Golgotha and perhaps even to the many rolling stones of the Jewish necropolis close by, which we know existed outside the walls of first-century Jerusalem in this area.

In Ezra 5:8 and 6:4, which are written in Aramaic, the term *'eben gelal* connotes a "cut stone," very likely referring to the quarries and stonecutters in the neighborhood of Jerusalem. According to Coüasnon, it is certain that a quarry existed in this area during the Iron Age II period (600–330 B.C.)[1] The rebuilding of the Temple took place at this time, following the return of the Jewish exiles to Jerusalem. Ezra 5–6 contains interesting historical data with respect to the reconstruction of the Temple—in relation to a quarry where the stone was cut for the sacred structure, and in relation to the subsequent name of this area in the first century. In our view the stone blocks for the Temple could have been hewn out of this Iron Age quarry, for the date of the quarry and the rebuilding of the Temple correspond to the reign of King Darius I of Persia (521–486 B.C.).

The cut or untrimmed stone mentioned in Ezra 5:8; 6:4 appears in no other biblical or extrabiblical litera-ture. Thus, by popular usage the name Golgotha was probably transferred to the site of the Iron Age quarry, because it was well known that here the stone blocks were cut and dressed, and from here they were rolled down, with wooden wheels fixed around them, from the quarry site on Ghareb towards the construction site in the neighborhood of the Temple. The stone for the building of the second temple of Jerusalem could have been carved from the quarry where five centuries later Jesus, who identified himself with the Temple of Yahweh, was crucified, buried, and rose from the dead.

In the light of this interpretation, it is possible to glean further insight into the statement in the liturgical Great Hallel that "the stone which the builders rejected has become the cornerstone" (Ps. 118:22). Scholars are not in complete agreement as to the date of the composition of this thanksgiving psalm. It is probably preexilic in origin, but with later insertions or additions. Thus, it is possible that the phrase referring to the "stone rejected by the builders" is a postexilic proverbial saying inserted into the psalm. The postexilic quarriers, hewing stone out of the Iron Age quarry on Ghareb, had probably intended to square off a certain huge block for the Temple, perhaps for the cornerstone itself. It is possible that once the area around this mass of stone had been cut and cleared, the workmen set their minds on cutting and dressing this huge block. Perhaps, too, during this cutting process it cracked and was, therefore, rejected by the builders. Such a fissure is still visible in the rock of Calvary today, but guides explain it in terms of the earthquake that supposedly shook the earth when Jesus died on the cross (Matt. 27:51).

Coüasnon's thorough study of the area shows that the traditional mound of Golgotha was actually an isolated vertical block about 30 feet high, standing alone in the corner of an ancient limestone quarry.[2] He suggests that this could have been the *nephesh* or "monument" of a Hellenistic sepulchre. This may be so; however, by the third and second centuries B.C., this cube-shaped limestone block would already have been covered over with much debris from the preceding centuries, and, therefore, would have been a hillock of some sort, used for crucifixions since the time of Alexander Jannaeus in the second century B.C. In the course of four or five cen-

Figure 26   HISTORY OF CALVARY AND JESUS' TOMB

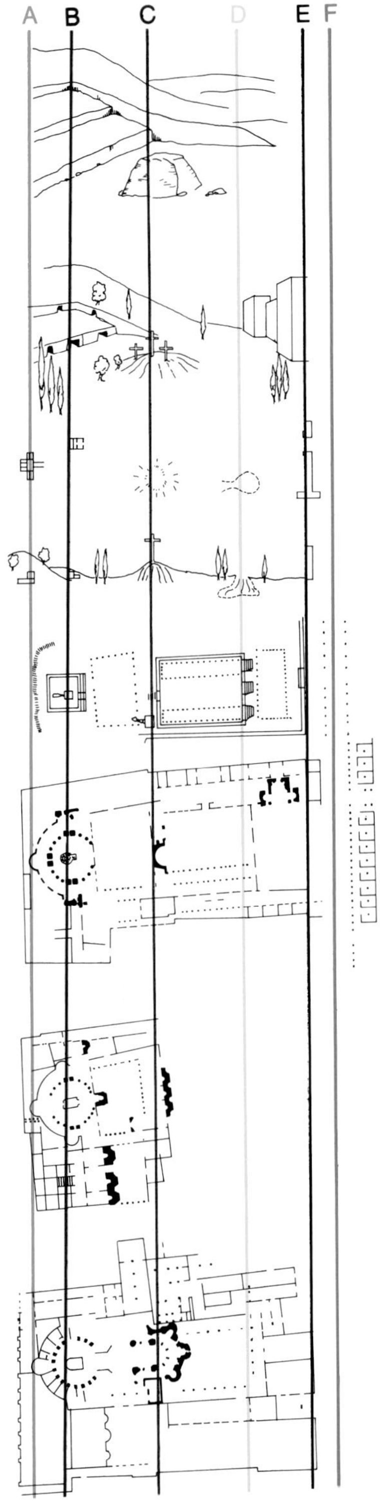

A: Jewish Tombs
B: Jesus' Tomb.
C: Golgotha (Calvary).
D: Pit or Crypt.
E: Second Wall.
F: Street (Cardo; Suq Khan ez-Zeit).

1 Iron Age quarry in the northwestern part of Jerusalem, but outside of the city walls. Date: *ca.* 600 to 330 B.C. Note the steplike quarrying and the block (C) left isolated at the quarry site.

2 In course of time this area outside the city ramparts served as a rubbish dump during the third and second centuries B.C. By the first century, it also functioned as a Jewish necropolis (among the olive groves) and a place of public execution.

3 "Aerial" view of the northwest corner of the city during the time of Jesus until the sector was incorporated into the city of Herod Agrippa's "third wall."

4 Scene at the time of Jesus' crucifixion, death, burial, and resurrection in A.D. 30.

5 Roman emperor P. Aelius Hadrianus, after the Jewish revolt of A.D. 132, transformed Jerusalem into a Roman city (*quadrata*). He filled in the area over which he built a public city square (*agora, forum*), and erected a temple of Venus (Aphrodite) on the site.

6 Constantine the Great, after the Council of Nicaea in 325, followed Jerusalem Bishop Makarios' knowledge about the holy sites and had large structures built on them: a rotunda, the Anastasis, and basilica called the Martyrion. Note the colonnaded street (F) as depicted on the Madaba Map.

7 Constantine Monomachos restored the buildings on the site after Hakim's systematic destruction of the Holy Sepulchre in 1009. Though Constantine Monomachos' eleventh-century structure was on a much smaller scale, many parts of it are still visible in the basilica today.

8 Crusaders' Basilica of the Holy Sepulchre, built on a much larger scale. It also incorporated a monastery complex whose remains can still be observed on the rooftops in the vicinity of the Holy Sepulchre. This twelfth- and thirteenth-century building, save for the additions just mentioned, is undergoing intensive reconstruction today.

Plate 132 *Bare rock of Golgotha facing eastwards towards Jerusalem. This very sacred relic was cleared by the Greek Orthodox Church in Jerusalem during the excavations behind the present site of Calvary.*

oriental practice of crucifixion, which the Persians had invented in the sixth century B.C. and spread to the Egyptians and the Phoenicians (Herodotus *History* ix. 20). Crucifixion functioned as a savage penalty for criminals and as a terrifying deterrent to others. It was used in the Greek colonies, but not in Greece proper, and was extensively practiced by the Romans, but could not be inflicted on Roman citizens. In Palestine even before the Romans it was the manner of capital punishment employed by the Seleucid ruler Antiochus IV Epiphanes (175–164 B.C.), who crucified all Jews who did not comply with his edict of Hellenization (1 Macc. 1:12, 44–50).[3] The Hasmonaean Alexander Jannaeus (103–76 B.C.) sentenced his opponents among the Pharisee party to death by crucifixion (*BJ* i. 87; *Ant.* xiii. 380). Under the Romans many Jewish prisoners were crucified (Josephus *Vita* 420). It was the mound of Golgotha just outside of the walls of Jerusalem where this severe mode of punishment took place. Practiced in the Mediterranean area since the sixth century B.C., it was not abolished until the fourth century A.D., when in 337 Constantine the Great suppressed it out of respect for Christ's death on the cross.

After flagellation, the Romans forced the condemned to carry the horizontal crossbeam to the site of execution, where the upper stake had already been fixed in the ground. This stake, embedded in the rocky mound, was high enough for all the passersby to see the victim and to read the placard stating the reason for his death sentence. This hillock during the time of Jesus would have been large enough for three, or perhaps four, crosses.

The site of the rocky mound on which Jesus' cross once stood is fixed in tradition and has been corroborated by thorough academic research. Through all the generations, it is with confidence that Christian pilgrims and scholars can point to this rock in the Church of the Holy Sepulchre as the authentic site of Jesus' crucifixion. There can be no other candidate for this biblical event.[4]

turies, after the quarry had ceased to serve its purpose, the neighborhood apparently had been used as a rubbish dump, hence the build-up of debris. (Note that Aramaic *galal* can also be used in a pejorative sense to denote something morally degrading like ordure or excrement, which in Judaism caused ritual uncleanness.) Also, by the second and first centuries B.C., this quarter of Ghareb had various kinds of trees planted in it, and so a part of it at least was transformed into a kind of orchard or garden, to which the Garden Gate, the Gate of Gennath mentioned by Josephus (*BJ* v. 146), now pointed. Tombs in this garden were also hewn out in the walls of the former quarry.

The Romans, like the Carthaginians, adopted the

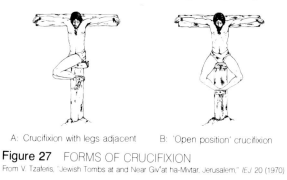

A: Crucifixion with legs adjacent   B: 'Open position' crucifixion

Figure 27   FORMS OF CRUCIFIXION
From V. Tzaferis, "Jewish Tombs at and Near Giv'at ha-Mivtar, Jerusalem," *IEJ* 20 (1970)

The Garden Tomb

ACCORDING TO ALL FOUR EVANGELISTS, after Jesus had been taken down from the cross Joseph of the town of Arimathea offered to bury him in his own rock-hewn tomb close by. If the site of Golgotha is certain in light of ancient tradition, archaeological research, and modern scholarship, the site of the garden tomb in which Jesus was interred and from which he rose from the dead can be equally sure.

The writers of the Gospels portray Joseph as a good and righteous man, a wealthy person from the town of Arimathea, identified with either er-Ram, about five miles north of Jerusalem, or Rentis, slightly farther to the northwest. Joseph of Arimathea was a member of the Jewish Council or Sanhedrin. As such he was in a good position to approach Pilate for the necessary permission to take the body of Jesus down from the cross and to give it a proper burial. Under his direction the body was hastily embalmed (for the Sabbath was about to begin), then wrapped in a linen shroud, and placed in Joseph's new tomb in the garden just outside the Garden Gate in the northwest corner of the city (John 19:38). There can be no doubt that the garden and Jewish necropolis were very close to the mound of Calvary, the site of crucifixions.

Death was a very common occurrence in antiquity, much more so than now. Families were large; infant mortality was high; and only some people lived to a fairly old age. Sickness, plagues of various types, malnutrition—especially in time of famine, tribal feuds, and national warfare—contributed to early deaths. Because of this heavy toll it was a religious and even civil obligation for other relatives and friends in some way or another to share in the interment of the deceased.

Abundant material evidence in various parts of the Middle East shows that since prehistoric times proper interment was the rule of the day, often very strictly enforced. Examples are numerous, for archaeologists are particularly interested in burial grounds for the rich insights gleaned from them with regard to social and religious life. Tombs provide a wealth of information, not only with respect to man's beliefs in some tangible existence in a life hereafter, but also because the many

In the place where he had been crucified there was a garden, and in the garden a new tomb in which no one had ever been buried.

John 19:41

Plate 134 *Garden Tomb near the site of Gordon's Calvary outside the north wall of Jerusalem today, considered by some religious groups as the tomb of Jesus.*

+ ———————————————————— +

Plate 133 *(opposite) Site of Calvary in the Church of the Holy Sepulchre. The marker beneath the small altar is believed to be the spot where Jesus was crucified.*

household or military artifacts which accompanied burials aid archaeologists and scholars to understand daily life and customs.

Examples of ancient Palestinian burial grounds are abundant. During the Patriarchal period, corresponding to the Middle Bronze Age (2100–1600 B.C.) in Palestine, family burial plots were not uncommon. The graves discovered in them were of various types, depending on the locality, not to mention the social and economic status of the family. Sepulchres were subterranean chambers excavated on a rocky hillside, or towerlike monuments above the ground, as generally the case of the more affluent families and wealthy tribes. The poor, however, buried their departed in natural caves if they lived in the hill country, or in graves dug into the ground if the land or soil conditions were conducive to digging trenchlike sepulchres in the earth.

Proper burial of a person was extremely important, essentially for religious reasons. This custom is the background of Sophocles' classic Antigone. Modern Jews in Jerusalem who come to visit the graves of the deceased, for instance on the Mount of Olives, place small stones on the slabs of the tombs as a sign of their sharing in the burial of the departed members of the family or of a friend.

Burial customs in the New Testament period differed only a little from those of preceding generations in Palestine or neighboring countries. For example, Luke mentions the washing of the deceased (Acts 9:37), and Mark briefly describes the anointing of the corpse (16:1). Jesus' body was wrapped in linen cloths (John 19:40; Mark 15:46; Matt. 27:59; Luke 23:53); however, it was not embalmed in the technical sense, as by mummification in Egypt. It was contrary to Israelite beliefs that a corpse be embalmed in the manner of the ancient Egyptians. Acts reports that a group of "young men came forward, wrapped up the body [of Ananias], and carried it out for burial" (5:6). This clearly parallels the role played by Joseph of Arimathea and Nicodemus who, together with Mary and some women, prepared Jesus' body for interment (Mark 15:42–47; Matt. 27:57–61; Luke 23:50–56; John 19:38–42).

A formal, outward expression of grief accompanied burial. Loud ritual lamentation, weeping, and shrieking

Plate 135 *Site of Golgotha (Calvary) and the first-century Jewish necropolis nearby, outside the city walls of Jerusalem during the time of Jesus' death, burial, and resurrection. Behind the nineteenth-century cenotaph which was built over the tomb of Jesus can be seen these Jewish kokhim or sepulchral niches carved in the rocky bank of the ancient quarry. Some of these tombs are shaft graves cut downwards into the limestone floor of the area, while others were niches hewn out of the rock above. The huge blocks on the left belong to the Constantinian foundations of the huge rotunda (Anastasis) which they supported. There exists no foundation for the tradition that one of these burial chambers is the tomb of Joseph of Arimathea.*

accompanied by other gestures of mourning, which sometimes bordered on hysteria, are still quite characteristic of some parts of the eastern Mediterranean world, and were prescribed funeral rites in biblical times (2 Sam. 14:2; 1 Kgs. 14:13; Job 27:15; Jer. 16:4, 6; Mark 5:21–43; Matt. 9:18–26; Luke 7:11–13; John 11:31–33). The body of the deceased was carried by relatives and friends on a bier (Luke 7:12,14) to a common burial plot (Matt. 27:7), always located outside the city walls (Lev. 21:1; Num. 6:6; 19:13). Because of the hot climate, and because embalming was either forbidden, as in the case of Jews and of Muslims today, or unknown, or too expensive, interment usually took place almost immediately, usually on the day of the person's death.

A period of mourning was prescribed after all funerals. In Old Testament times it lasted seven days (Gen. 50:10; 1 Sam. 31:13; 1 Chr. 10:12; Jdt. 16:29; Ecclus. 22:12). This was strictly a time of prayer and fasting, which could only be interrupted by a funeral feast or banquet (Jer. 16:7). Family and friends visited the graves of the deceased quite frequently during this period, especially during the first three days, which were known as "days of weeping." It was believed that the

Plate 136 Nineteenth-century cenotaph marking the spot of Jesus' Holy Sepulchre, beneath the huge dome that preserves the outlines of the original Constantinian rotunda. The ancient columns that were once imbedded in cemented pillars by the British to prevent the structure from collapsing are being replaced according to their original design. Artists have restored the capitals of the columns, sometimes employing ancient methods. The nineteenth-century cenotaph is supposed to imitate the original tomb of Jesus: a small door leads into a rather tiny vestibule, while an even smaller door opens into the funerary chamber where one can pray over the marble slab upon which Jesus' body, wrapped in a shroud, supposedly was laid. To the left of the shrine were discovered remains of Hadrian's public square, as well as the original limestone floor of the quarry.

✝————————————————————✝

spirit of the dead still hovered over the tomb, seeking an opportunity to reenter the body. The soul was believed to have left the body permanently on the fourth day. The last four days were called "days of lamentation," after which time decomposition of the corpse was believed to have set in and, therefore, it would have been impossible for the soul to return. This belief helps explain the report that the women visited Jesus' tomb three

days after his burial, on "the first day of the week" (Matt. 28:1; Mark 16:1–2; Luke 24:1; John 20:1).

The place of burial was outside the first and second north walls of Jerusalem, as delineated by Josephus. The third wall, along whose lines the present north wall of the Old City is constructed, was built by Agrippa about a decade after Christ's crucifixion, sometime around A.D. 39 or 41. The neighborhood of Ghareb in the time of Jesus, therefore, was not encompassed by walls, so that Golgotha and the Jewish necropolis close by were obviously in an open area outside the walls. One can also picture a road leading from the Garden Gate northwards, while some kind of footpath led in the direction of Calvary and the Jewish burial place within the nearby garden. Outside this area, most likely to the north and west, must have been some small houses in the open place, very likely those of the poor who could not afford housing inside the crowded city walls. Mourners at the graves, which must have been a rather common scene in ancient times as it is today in some parts of the Middle East, perpetuated the ancient practice of visiting and honoring the dead. This was very much a part of the daily lifestyle. Even when the northwestern sector of Jerusalem was incorporated into the city by Agrippa, the early Christians continued to visit Jesus' tomb and the site of his crucifixion close by.

In view of the long history of the Church of the Holy Sepulchre, in view of the strong traditions regarding the sites of Golgotha and the tomb of Jesus inside this church, both now beautifully corroborated by intensive archaeological investigations and academic research, there should be no doubt that Christians throughout the centuries have kept alive in memory and in stone the exact places of their Founder's crucifixion, burial, and resurrection in the City of Jesus to this very day.

Plate 137 *Following the traditional route from the Mount of Olives, a Palm Sunday procession of the Latin Rite enters* *Jerusalem through St. Stephen's Gate.*

EPILOGUE: HOLY WEEK, A.D. 30

Now is the Son of Man glorified, and God is glorified in him.

John 13:31

Plate 138 *Akanthos ("thorn") plants in full bloom in Jerusalem on Good Friday. The leaves and thorns of this species (Notobasis syriaca) were used by Roman soldiers to plait a "victory crown" upon Jesus' head in imitation of the crowns worn by victorious Roman emperors (see Plate 150).*

IT WAS SPRINGTIME in the year A.D. 30. Feeling that he had completed his ministry and preaching concerning the Kingdom of Heaven in Galilee, Jesus intended to go up to Jerusalem for the Feast of Passover and Unleavened Bread. He was aware that "his hour" was approaching. Thousands of Jews from all over the country and the Diaspora were also going up to the City of the Temple. There they would celebrate the ancient festival, in which shepherds sacrificed their lambs and farmers offered their first sheaves of barley in gratitude for the generous blessings the Lord had bestowed upon his people. This they would do in remembrance also of their forefathers' redemption from Egypt.

We do not know the exact route Jesus and his disciples traveled from Galilee to Judaea. They could have walked the Roman road from Scythopolis (Old Testament Beth-shan) and traversed the hill country along the border of Samaria, heading directly southwards towards Jerusalem. Or they could have taken the road along the Jordan Valley southwards towards Jericho and then turned westwards to begin the ascent to Jerusalem along the ancient Roman road. The journey would have taken about three days. Jesus was prepared for what would happen on this last pilgrimage to Jerusalem. The Jews "were on the lookout for Jesus, various people in the vicinity of the Temple saying to each other, 'What do you think? Is he likely to come for the feast?' (The chief priests and the Pharisees had given orders that anyone who knew where he was should report it so they could apprehend him)" (John 11:56–57).

Jesus reached Bethany, a small village on the southeastern side of the Mount of Olives, apparently coinciding with the beginning of the Sabbath rest. He stayed in Bethany at the home of his friend Lazarus and his two sisters Martha and Mary. A banquet was given in his honor, and many friends came to visit. Meanwhile, the Jews in Jerusalem learned that Jesus indeed had decided to come to Jerusalem to celebrate Passover, and that he was staying in Bethany. The following day would be crucial to all concerned: to Jesus and his apostles, to his followers who anticipated his triumphal entry as the Messianic King, and to those who already had set the scene for his arrest.

Jesus then left Bethany for Bethphage on top of Mt. Olivet. A young colt was provided for him to ride in triumph. In this manner Jesus captured the attention of the crowds concerning his kingship: first, by fulfillment of a prophecy quite familiar to his followers; second, by recognition of a divinely appointed Messiah, which role Jesus accepted as his own.

According to Matthew, Jesus' triumphal entry into the city was to fulfill the promise Zechariah made centuries before: "Rejoice heartily, O daughter of Zion, shout for joy, O daughter Jerusalem! See, your king shall come to you; a just savior is he, meek, and riding on an ass, on a colt, the foal of an ass" (Zech. 9:9), a beast of burden. Now the heavenly Father was bringing this prophecy to fulfillment.

In contrast to the pomp of ancient kings in their moments of triumph, Jesus of Nazareth rode on a donkey, the ordinary beast of burden in the ancient Middle East. The leaders of the people must have been quite amused by this ridiculous spectacle. Here was a man proclaimed a king, yet seated on a beast that was the symbol of the outcast—a fitting vehicle for one riding into the jaws of death. They could not have taken this scene less seriously. If Jesus had entered the city with regal pomp, the people might have taken him as the political Messiah expected to liberate them from the Roman yoke. But the circumstances Jesus had chosen validated his claim that his kingdom was really not of this world. There was no suggestion that this pauper monarch actually rivalled Caesar; yet, when Jesus did appear before Pilate that week, the charges against him were sedition: Jesus was both anti-Caesar and anti-Rome, even a rival to Pilate.

Jesus rode slowly along the Jericho-Jerusalem road to the summit of the Mount of Olives, where he saw for the first time a magnificent panorama of Jerusalem: the magnificent Temple, royal palaces, public buildings,

towers, and strong walls surrounding the city like a sanctuary. We would identify this spot with the residence of the Greek Orthodox Patriarch of Jerusalem, traditionally known as Viri Galilaei or "Men of Galilee." Here Jesus wept over the city, and said: " 'If only you had known the path to peace this day; but you have completely lost it from view! Days will come upon you when your enemies encircle you with a rampart, hem you in, and press you hard from every side. They will wipe you out, you and your children within your walls, and leave not a stone on a stone within you, because you failed to recognize the time of your visitation' " (Luke 19:41–44).

Nevertheless, the jubilant procession continued slowly towards the Kidron Valley below. The white-washed sepulchres of the Hellenistic period were on their left; to the right, crowning the ridge of Ophel, they could see the walls of David's City—not, of course, the walls which David had constructed, but those of the Hasmonaean and Herodian periods enclosing the lower or popular quarter of the city, repaired by Herod the Great in the first century. The throngs followed Jesus through the Kidron perhaps as far as the Gate of the Waters (the Casemate-wall Gate of the Old Testament period), situated at the southern end of the Ophel spur. At this juncture Jesus and his followers entered the City of David. Again, loud cries of joy and triumph filled the streets as he rode up towards the Mountain of the Lord. "Hosanna to the Son of David! Blessed is he who comes in the name of the Lord! Hosanna in the highest!" (Matt. 21:9). The entire city must have been moved by this scene: some people kept inquiring who this was, while others shouted out with joy: "This is the prophet Jesus from Nazareth in Galilee" (Matt. 21:11).

This event would have occurred on Sunday, the third day before the Passover celebrations began. Jesus would not have felt safe to move freely about the city, for he was being watched very closely. At night he with his chosen twelve would spend the night outside the city walls, in an olive grove at the foot of Mt. Olivet. Judas the Sicarius no doubt had already made the necessary arrangements with the chief priests and leaders for Jesus' arrest in this garden. Little time remained now, and the festival would begin shortly.

Biblical scholars do not always agree on the sequence of events or the dating of Jesus' final days in Jerusalem. The more conservative maintain the traditionalist view as more accurate. There are, indeed, plausible arguments for this long venerated tradition.

However, in light of numerous ancient sources, especially the Dead Sea Scrolls, some scholars propose an alternative dating of the events of Holy Week in A.D. 30. The family relationship between Jesus and his cousin John the Baptizer, perhaps somehow or at sometime associated with the Essenic sect; the fact that Jesus cele-

brated his last Passover supper in the Essenes' quarter on Mt. Zion; and the fact that Pentecost was the most important feast in the Essenes' eschatological community; plus the numerous parallels between the New Testament and the Qumran scrolls—all are evidences of a relationship Jesus had with this sect, though he himself would not have been an Essene. Therefore, we espouse the more recent theories regarding the dating of the events of Jesus' last days.

The "normative" Jews of Jesus' day followed a lunar calendar. The Passover festival was observed according

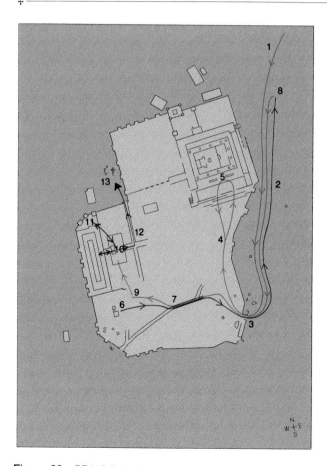

Figure 28   PRINCIPAL SEQUENCE OF EVENTS OF HOLY
WEEK, A.D. 30

1. *Palm Sunday:* the possible route of Jesus' triumphal entry into Jerusalem.
2. Hellenistic tombs (whitewashed) in the Kidron Valley.
3. Casemate-wall Gate: entrance into the City of David.
4. City of David on Ophel. Jesus enters the Temple compound through the Triple Huldah Gate.
5. Jesus in the Yahweh temple of Jerusalem. He exits through the Double Huldah Gate leading down into the City of David.
6. *Tuesday:* Jesus eats his last Passover meal with his apostles in the Upper Room (Coenaculum) in the Essene Quarter on Mt. Zion.
7. Jesus and his apostles walk down the ancient steps towards the Lower City, through the Kidron Valley.
8. Garden of Gethsemani at the foot of Mt. Olivet; Jesus' agony in the garden and the arrest by Judas and his band of Jews and Roman soldiers. They lead him along the same route through the Kidron.
9. *Wednesday-Thursday:* Jesus is brought to the palace of the high priest Caiphas. He is tried there and kept in custody until the arrival of Pontius Pilate and his Roman legion from Caesarea.
10. *Friday:* Jesus is brought before Pontius Pilate in the Upper City public square. Pilate interrogates him.
11. Scene of the scourging and crowning with thorns. Jesus is then brought back into the public square ("Ecce Homo!"), then sentenced to capital punishment by crucifixion. He receives his crossbeam.
12. Crossbeam fastened to his shoulders, Jesus and the two other condemned criminals are paraded through the streets of the City.
13. Golgotha, where Jesus was crucified and died. He was interred in a garden tomb close by.

to the vernal equinox, and the other Jewish feasts were determined by the moon's relation to the solar year. Months were twenty-nine or thirty days. Jesus, however, would have followed the solar calendar used by the Essenes and determined the seasons and the feasts according to the sun. Therefore, Jesus would have celebrated the combined feasts of Passover and Unleavened Bread following the solar calendar, which remained fixed. The fourteenth day of the month of Nisan (March–April) on which Passover began was always celebrated on a Wednesday. Thus, his Seder or Passover meal would have fallen a few days earlier than for ordinary Judaism. The Seder was celebrated after sunset on the evening before the Feast, on the third day of the week (Tuesday), while the fourth day (Wednesday) was a festive occasion for the Essenic community.

For the Jews Passover commemorated God's special providence over his people by delivering them from slavery in a foreign land. As is evident in the New Testament, the Seder was indeed a very sacred event for all Jews, even for the primitive Judaeo-Christians who still felt a strong attachment to the Mosaic teaching. Jesus also must have shared these sentiments on this night, a night described in the Seder ritual as "different from all other nights"; but for him it was also the awaited time when he would share the paschal lamb with his chosen ones in a magnificent eucharistic and priestly setting. The Last Supper was celebrated in the context of an eschatological celebration or meal. It denoted the end time of his special mission on earth; but much more so, it looked forward to his second coming, the Parousia, which played a vital role in his own missionary activity and the theology of the early Christian church. Thus, whereas the Jewish Seder looked back in gratitude for what Yahweh had accomplished for his people in Egypt and during their sojourn in the desert, for Jesus and his followers this solemn meal was celebrated in anticipation of even greater rewards and blessings, both on earth and in the Kingdom of Heaven. Thus, the Christian Eucharist is essentially different from the Hebrew Passover meal, though the meals have many parallels in structure.

In view of our topographical study of the site of the Upper Room there really cannot be any doubt that this

Plate 139 *"Then he poured water into a basin, and began to wash the disciples' feet." Washing of the feet is observed on Holy Thursday, according to the Armenian Orthodox tradition, in the Cathedral of St. James on Mt. Zion.*

solemn feast took place on Mt. Zion, in the neighborhood of the present Church of the Dormition and the Franciscan chapel Ad Coenaculum.

After the meal Jesus and the eleven—Judas had already left the Upper Room to do what he had previously conspired—began their solemn walk towards the Garden of Gethsemani. They walked down from the Upper City's Essenic quarter, using the steps that are still visible beside the Chapel of Peter-in-Gallicantu on the eastern slope of Mt. Zion. They continued towards the City of David on Ophel, the Lower City, that is the oldest part of Jerusalem. Most probably they left the city through the same gate through which they had entered in triumphal procession just a few days before. The valley was lighted only by the full moon as the group walked through this rather steep ravine, passing along the city ramparts on the left and the whitewashed Hellenistic tombs on the right. They reached Gethsemani, the olive orchard with its olive press close by. Here Jesus often had spent the nights on his visits to Jerusalem. This night he would spend in watchfulness and prayer, a vigil of anxiety and anguish, for his hour had now begun.

The exact location where his "agony in the garden" took place cannot be ascertained. The traditional site across the Brook Kidron at the foot of Mt. Olivet is quite

Plate 140 *" 'Now I am going to him who sent me.' When he had spoken these words, he went forth with his disciples across the Kidron Valley." Ancient steps lead down from the Upper Room on Mt. Zion to the City of David.*

Plate 141 *"Then Jesus went with them to a place called Gethsemane, and he said to his disciples, 'Sit here, while I go yonder and pray.'" Ancient olive trees still grow in the traditional Garden of Gethsemani across the Kidron Valley on the slope of Mt. Olivet.*

plausible, venerated even in the earliest Christian pilgrim accounts. Such monuments as the Basilica of the Agony (also called the Church of All Nations) and the Russian Church of St. Mary Magdalene above it, give further witness to the authenticity of this sacred place. Here Judas and the Jews, accompanied by a band of Roman soldiers, apprehended Jesus while his disciples fled out of fear.

This was a special night even for the "normative" Jews, who did not celebrate the Passover feast on this day because they were primarily interested in Jesus' arrest. They would keep him in custody until formal charges and a public trial could be held. The preparations involved conspiracies and false charges needed to prosecute him according to the law of the state.

Christian tradition, in the light of history and archaeology, has not firmly established the sites of the events of Jesus' trial. However, according to the Armenian Orthodox Church, the palace of the high priest Caiphas, where the initial proceedings before the Sanhedrin were held, stands on Mt. Zion not far from the Dormition Abbey; the high priest's palace would have been but outside the Essene quarter. The ninth-century *Life of Constantine* mentions that Queen Helena had a sanctuary built on the site of Caiphas' house, dedicated to Peter in memory of his repentance after having betrayed Christ in the courtyard here (Mark 14:53-65; Matt. 26:57-68; Luke 22:54-71; John 18:13-24).

Although the events were probably telescoped by the biblical writers, the interval between Jesus' arrest in Gethsemani and the formal public trial before the Roman procurator must have been two days, the fourth and fifth days of that week (Wednesday and Thursday). The Jews had to wait for Pontius Pilate's arrival from Caesarea on the seacoast, for the Roman governors customarily came up to Jerusalem with their legions at Passover to watch the crowds and suppress any eventual rebellion.

When Pilate arrived on the fifth day of the week, he sensed discontent among his subjects, but he was not to learn its exact nature and ramifications until the next day. Having completed the mock trials, the conspirators decided to bring Jesus for trial before the Roman magistrate on the sixth day (Friday), since by then Pilate would have established himself in the Praetorium. Determined to formalize their decision to have him condemned to capital punishment, "at daybreak they brought Jesus from Caiaphas to the Praetorium. They did not enter the Praetorium themselves, for they had to avoid ritual impurity if they were to eat the Passover supper" (John 18:28). This was a full day of preparations for the festive meal: the markets were crowded with pilgrims buying unleavened bread and bitter herbs, and the one-year-old paschal lambs were brought to be slaughtered as evening set in, all in accordance with the Mosaic prescriptions (Exod. 12:1–28). Not much time remained for the anxious crowd to have Jesus tried and executed before the important evening celebration.

The situation had both religious and political overtones, and Pilate could afford no more public demonstrations during his procuratorship. (His term would end in A.D. 36, when the Syrian legate Vitellius had him summoned to Emperor Tiberius in Rome for having attacked the Samaritans during a religious ceremony on Mt. Gerizim.) Nor did Pilate really want to confront the Jews on this occasion.

So Jesus, the "King of the Jews," faced Pilate, the official delegate of the Emperor of Rome. Pilate was suspicious of the accusations brought against Jesus and questioned their sincerity, for he knew how much the Jews detested him and Caesar. In particular, the charge that Jesus was a "King" was of much concern to the procurator. Then Jesus replied to Pilate's questioning by clearly distinguishing between political and religious kingship, making it abundantly clear that his kingship was not of an earthly nature, obtained by military campaigns and victory; rather, it was a spiritual kingdom, firmly established on justice and truth.

Luke writes that Pilate reported to the chief priests and the crowds that he could find no case against the man. They retorted that Jesus had stirred up the people throughout Judaea, from Galilee to Jerusalem itself. Upon learning that Jesus was a Galilean, and therefore under Herod's jurisdiction, Pilate sent him to Herod, who also happened to be in Jerusalem at this time (Luke 23:4–7).

But John presents a different picture. Pilate hesitated to condemn Jesus outright, and was anxious to release him. He reminded the assembled Jews of his custom of releasing to them a prisoner at Passover time. But the mob chose freedom for the insurrectionist Barabbas rather than Jesus. Hoping to arouse pity among the crowd, Pilate ordered his soldiers to scourge Jesus. They wove a victory crown of acanthus leaves and thorns and fixed it on his head, and threw around his shoulders a cloak of royal purple, taunting him with cries of "All hail, king of the Jews." Returning Jesus to the crowd, Pilate said to them, "Look at the man!" But the chief priests and temple guards shouted, "Crucify him! Crucify him!" Pilate said, "Take him away and crucify him yourselves, for I find no case against him." Again the Jews responded, "According to our law he must die because he has made himself God's son." This made Pilate more afraid than ever, and he returned to the Praetorium to question Jesus. But Jesus would not answer. "Do you not know that I have the power to release you and the power to crucify you?" asked Pilate. Jesus answered: "You would have no power over me whatever unless it were given you from above. That is why he who handed me over to you is guilty of the greater sin." Pilate was eager to release Jesus, but the Jews shouted, "If you free this man you are no 'Friend of Caesar.' Anyone who makes himself a king becomes Caesar's rival." Hearing this, Pilate brought Jesus outside and took a seat on a judge's bench at the place called the Stone Pavement (*lithóstrotos*; Hebrew *Gabbatha*). He said to the Jews, "Look at your king!" but they shouted, "Away with him! Crucify him!" "What!" Pilate exclaimed, "Shall I crucify your king?" The chief priests replied, "We have no king but Caesar." So Pilate was compelled to hand Jesus over to be crucified (John 18:38b–19:16).

This trial took place in the public square of the Upper City, which we identify with the compound of the Armenian Orthodox Patriarchate, very probably close to the Cathedral of St. James. Pilate's Praetorium, formerly the palace of Herod the Great, has been established archaeologically as built on the property where the Armenian Orthodox Seminary now stands. The barracks and courtyard of the procurator's praetorian guard we identify with the present Citadel and Kishleh compound, the Israeli police post inside the Old City walls;

Plate 142 *"Pilate brought Jesus out and sat down on the judgment seat at a place called the Pavement. . . . He said to the Jews, 'Here is your king!' . . . Then he handed him over to them to be crucified." This detail of an ancient Roman sarcophagus shows Jesus standing before Pilate seated on his judgment chair. (Pontifical Archives, St. Priscilla Catacombs, Rome)*

Plate 143 *"They compelled a passerby, Simon of Cyrene, who was coming in from the country, to carry his cross." The Latin Rite, led by Franciscan fathers, guides pilgrims along the traditional Via Dolorosa every Friday at 3 p.m.*

here Pilate ordered the Roman soldiers to scourge Jesus before he finally sentenced him to death. The speakers' platform (*béma*) on which was placed Pilate's judgment seat (*sella curulis*) would also have been located in the present compound of St. James' Cathedral of the Armenian Orthodox Church. This would also be where Jesus and the two other condemned criminals received their crossbeams (*patibulum*), and here began the sorrowful way of the cross through the streets of Jerusalem. It was the custom to parade condemned criminals in order to teach others a lesson. This route, according to our interpretation, can also be traced in the streets of the Armenian Quarter today—St. James' Street (or the Street of the Armenians) veering eastwards as far as the junction of Suq el-Ḥuṣṣor, the former cardo maximus of Emperor Hadrian's Aelia Capitolina, then turning at a right angle northwards towards the ancient Garden Gate (Gennath), preserved at the junction where the four principal streets of the Old City meet: David Street from the west, Chain Street from the east, Suq el-ʿAttarin (the southern portion of Suq Khan ez-Zeit leading southwards from the Damascus Gate), and Suq el-Ḥuṣṣor from the south.

The Good Friday procession would then have continued northwards up to a certain point where it veered in a northwesterly direction towards Golgotha. There the crucifixion took place on a hillock just outside the walls of Jerusalem, on one of the main roads leading out of the city.

John writes: "Jesus was led away, and carrying the cross by himself, went out to what is called the Place of the Skull (Hebrew *Golgotha*). There they crucified him, and two others with him: one on either side, Jesus in the middle. Pilate had an inscription placed on the cross which read,

JESUS THE NAZOREAN
KING OF THE JEWS

This inscription, in Hebrew, Latin, and Greek, was read by many of the Jews, since the place where Jesus was crucified was near the city" (John 19:16b–19). The actual site of the crucifixion is established: the rock of Calvary is clearly visible in the Church of the Holy Sepulchre.

From about the sixth hour to the ninth (noon to

Plate 144 *"There they crucified him and the criminals, one on the right and one on the left." Clad in a prisoner's uniform, Jesus on this stylized crucifix in the shrine at the Dachau concentration camp is a stark reminder of the ordeals of crucifixion.*

Plate 145 *"Very early on the first day of the week they went to the tomb when the sun had risen." The Greek Orthodox community celebrates the kindling of the Easter fire in the Church of the Holy Sepulchre.*

Plate 146 *"The angel said to the women, 'Do not be afraid; for I know that you seek Jesus who was crucified. He is not here, for he has risen, as he said.'" The risen Lord Jesus is depicted on a Crusader capital in the Church of the Annunciation at Nazareth.*

mid-afternoon) Jesus hung on the cross. It was customary to leave the crucified sometimes for several days. The victim died of excruciating pain, of hunger and thirst, and often from asphyxiation. Jesus' death within hours probably came as a surprise to the Roman soldiers who stood nearby. But his death did not mean defeat. It signified triumph: a short-lived triumph for those who had him put to death; a perpetual triumph for those who would pick up his cross and follow him.

By mid-afternoon most of the crowd must have dispersed. It was necessary now to prepare for the festivities of Passover and Unleavened Bread. Jesus' family and friends would not allow his body to hang on the cross, so they secured Pilate's permission to take him down and bury him. Joseph, from the town of Arimathea, a respected member of the council and a friend of Jesus, offered to provide a proper burial. Nicodemus, another friend of Jesus, also came to assist in the funeral rite. When evening came they prepared Jesus' body for

interment in a new garden tomb close by, which Joseph had had carved out of the rock for himself. There the group buried Jesus. In it he lay for three days (Jews reckon a part of a day as comprising a full period of time), from the sixth day, through the Sabbath, until the first day of the week.

On the first day of the week, which Christians identify as the Lord's Day, Jesus rose from the dead. There were no witnesses at the tomb; no one saw his body rise from the slab on which it was lain; no one saw the tombstone roll away; and no one actually witnessed how he triumphantly walked out of the grave. But just as certain as the actual site of this glorious event of A.D. 30, Jesus' presence is still very much felt and witnessed in his followers, the Church, which is indeed his Temple. As he had predicted, if anyone were to destroy this Temple, he would rebuild it in three days. And this Jesus actually did!

Plate 147 The triumphant Jesus. Detail from mosaic in the Church of St. Pudentiana, Rome. "Destroy this Temple and in three days I will build it up again." (John 2:19) (Richard Duslack, Loyola University of Chicago)

OUTLINE HISTORY OF JERUSALEM

1. *Prebiblical Epochs* (20,000–1,000 B.C.)

A. Stone Ages: Evidence of human occupation in the Jerusalem region.

20,000–12,000 = Palaeolithic or Old Stone Age
12,000–6,000 = Mesolithic or Middle Stone Age
6,000–4,000 = Neolithic or New Stone Age

B. Bronze Age: Immigration of a Semitic people known as the Canaanites during the Early Bronze Age. Around 2300 the Canaanites were followed by another Semitic group called the Amorites. The Jebusites inhabited Jebus, also known as Jerusalem, from around 1800 B.C. to just before the arrival of the Israelites, about 1000 B.C., and apparently cohabited Jerusalem with them, at least during the Davidic period: the Jebusites occupied the Ophel spur, while the Israelites began a new settlement higher up, near the threshing floor which David purchased from Araunah the Jebusite for the purpose of erecting an altar there (2 Sam. 24:16).

Ca. 2500 = Jerusalem (*Uru-sa-lim*) mentioned for the first time in recorded history in the recently discovered tablets at Tell Mardikh (Ebla).

Ca. 1900 = Jerusalem (*Urusalim*) mentioned in the Egyptian Execration Texts (cf. *ANET*, p. 329) as one of the cities of the land of Canaan.

2. *Patriarchal Period to Period of the Judges:*

1850 = Abraham welcomed by Melchizedek, king of Salem (Jerusalem?) (Gen. 14). In Gen. 22 Abraham was to sacrifice his son Isaac on Mt. Moriah, which tradition identifies with the Temple Mount in Jerusalem.

1375 = Jerusalem (*Urusalimu*), named in the cuneiform Amarna correspondence (during the reign of either Amen-hotep III or Amen-hotep IV [Ikhnaton]). Jerusalem was ruled by a satellite king named Abdu-Heba, perhaps a Hittite or Horite name of the period. The Habiru (Hebrews?) were described as a growing threat to the occupants of the land during the early fourteenth century B.C.

Ca. 1234 = Flight of the Israelite tribes from Egypt after the death of Pharaoh Ramses II and the accession of Mer-ne-Ptah (cf. *ANET*, p. 378). The Exodus began under Moses. The conquest of Canaan was undertaken by Joshua.

Ca. 1200 = Period of the Judges, between the Israelite settlement in Canaan and the establishment of the United Monarchy under Saul (*ca.* 1000 B.C.).

3. *Kingdom* (1040–922 B.C.)

1040–1010 = Saul ben Kish accepted as king of the Israelite united tribes (1 Sam. 11:12–15). He established his capital at Gibeah, a few miles north of Jerusalem.

1009–961 = David anointed king (2 Sam. 2:1–7) and proclaimed king of Israel (2 Sam. 5:1–5). Ca. 1000 B.C. he captured the Jebusite fortress on Ophel (2 Sam. 5:1–5) and ruled from Jerusalem. (Jebus, as an ancient name for Jerusalem, occurs in Jgs. 19:10–11 and 1 Chr. 11:4–5. Although later passages, they probably preserve an ancient name for the Jebusite city.) Josh. 15:63 reads: "But the Jebusites who lived in Jerusalem the Judahites could not drive out; so the Jebusites dwell in Jerusalem beside the Judahites to the present day." David purchased the threshing floor from Araunah the Jebusite to build an altar to the Lord on it (2 Sam. 24:16–25; see 1 Chr. 21:15–30). His son Solomon would later build the Jerusalem temple there. David's capture of Jerusalem would mark the first recorded siege of the Holy City.

961–922 = Solomon, son of David, proclaimed king of the united Israelite tribes (1 Kgs. 1:11–2:46). The empire he built for himself marked the Golden Age of Israel in the biblical period. Solomon's architectural accomplishments in Jerusalem included the rebuilding of the walls, his palace on the Millo, and especially the Temple on Mt. Moriah, thus ushering in the First Temple period in Jewish history. The Temple was completed around 950 B.C. A description of this structure is given in 1 Kgs. 6:1–8:13.

922 = Schism in Judaism caused by King Rehoboam's speech at Shechem. The monarchy was divided into two kingdoms: Judah in the south, including Jerusalem its capital, and Israel in the north with its capital at Tirzah and then Samaria, later known as Sebaste.

4. Divided Monarchy (922–587 B.C.) List of the Kings of Judah.

922–915 = Rehoboam, son of Solomon (1 Kgs. 11:43; 1 Chr. 3:10; 2 Chr. 9:31). During his reign Pharaoh Shishak (Sheshonk I, 935–914) attacked Jerusalem and plundered the palace and Temple (1 Kgs. 14:21–31). 2 Chr. 11:5–12 lists the cities Rehoboam fortified to protect Judah against hostile invasions.

915–913 = Abijah (Abijam), son of Rehoboam, who allowed pagan worship on high places (1 Kgs. 15:1–8). 2 Chr. 13:1–22 recounts his war against Jeroboam of Israel.

913–873 = Asa, son of Abijah, who, under the influence of his grandmother Maacah, rejected the Canaanite fertility cults in Jerusalem (1 Kgs. 15:9–24; 2 Chr. 14:1–16:14).

873–849 = Jehoshaphat, son of Asa, depicted as a man of zeal for the Law (1 Kgs. 15:24; 22:41–51; 2 Chr. 17:1–19). His was a long, prosperous, and peaceful reign.

849–842 = Jehoram, son of Jehoshaphat, described as an evil ruler who murdered his own brothers. His kingdom was attacked by Philistines and Arabs (2 Kgs. 2:16–24; 2 Chr. 21:1–20).

842 = Ahaziah, youngest son of Jehoram, who with his father fought against Hazael of Damascus. During his flight from Jehu of Israel (842–815) he was wounded near Ibleam but managed to escape as far as Megiddo where he died. (2 Kgs. 8:25–29; 2 Chr. 22:1–10 states that he was killed by Jehu at Samaria.)

842–837 = Athaliah, mother of Ahaziah. When she discovered that her son had been assassinated, she murdered all royal offspring of the house of Judah, save for the infant Joash (Jehoash), who, after Athaliah's execution six years later, was installed as king of Judah (2 Kgs. 11:1–20; 2 Chr. 22:10–23:21).

837–800 = Jehoash, only survivor of Ahaziah's sons; crowned king of Judah by the priest Jehoiada. In the first part of his reign, described as prosperous, he made repairs on the Jerusalem temple. But when Jehoiada the priest died, Jehoash turned to the worship of pagan divinities (2 Kgs. 12:1–22; 2 Chr. 24:1–27).

800–783 = Amaziah, son and successor of Jehoash. He was twenty-five years old when installed as king of Judah, and he reigned twenty-nine years. Both the author of Kings and the Chronicler describe him in favorable terms. He was assassinated by Jehoash of Israel, who "tore down four hundred cubits of the city wall, from the Gate of Ephraim to the Corner Gate" (2 Kgs. 14:13; cf. vv. 1–22; 2 Chr. 25:14–16).

783–742 = Uzziah (Azariah), son of Amaziah. His long reign in Judah is described as peaceful and prosperous, but this is largely due to Assyrian weakness at the time (2 Kgs. 14:21–15:7; 2 Chr. 26:22). It was during the days of Uzziah of Judah and Jeroboam of Israel that Amos of Tekoa (Amos 1:1; 7:14) prophesied in Israel. (For Uzziah's works see 2 Chr. 26:1–15.)

742–735 = Jotham, son of Uzziah, who became his father's regent from ca. 750, when Uzziah contracted leprosy, until 742. He is responsible for building the upper gate of the Temple (2 Kgs. 15:32–36; 2 Chr. 27:1–9).

735–715 = Ahaz, son of Jotham, despised by Isaiah and the authors of Kings and Chronicles. His sixteen-year reign in Judah was an impious one: 2 Kgs. 16:3 says that he acted like the kings of Israel, even immolating his son to the pagan gods; 2 Kgs. 16:10 mentions that he erected an altar modeled after that in Damascus; and 2 Chr. 28:23 quotes him as saying that "since it was the gods of the kings of Aram who helped them, I will sacrifice to them that they may help me also" (2 Kgs. 16:1–20; 2 Chr. 28:1–27). The Assyrian Sargon II captured Samaria in 721 B.C.

715–687 = Hezekiah, son of Ahaz, who ruled for twenty-nine years in Jerusalem. He inaugurated religious and political reforms, and thus was very much unlike his father. Hezekiah accomplished much in Jerusalem, for which he is praised by the writers of Kings and Chronicles. During his reign the famous tunnel in Jerusalem was hewn through the Ophel spur (2 Kgs. 20:20; 2 Chr. 32:30; cf. *ANET*, p. 321; 2 Kgs. 18:1–20:21; 2 Chr. 28:27–32:33). Isaiah prophesied during his reign, warning Jerusalem to prepare itself against an invasion from the north.

687–642 = Manasseh, the son of Hezekiah, who conducted himself very much like his grandfather Ahaz, if not worse. As J.L. McKenzie describes it, "The record of Manasseh (2 Kgs. 21:1–17) is the blackest of all the kings of Judah" (*Dictionary of the Bible*, p. 540). He began his reign when he was twelve years old and ruled for fifty-five years in Jerusalem. For the details of this dark period in Jerusalem, see 2 Kgs. 21:1–18; 2 Chr. 33:10; 2 Chr. 33:11–20, however, records his conversion to the Lord.

642–640 = Amon, who continued the heathen practices of his father and great-grandfather, for which he was assassinated (2 Kgs. 21:19–26; 2 Chr. 33:21–25).

640–609 = Josiah, son of Amon. Josiah lived up to his beautiful personal name, which means "may Yahweh give." During his reign the much needed spiritual reforms in Judah and Jerusalem took place, especially following the discovery of the Book of the Law (most probably the original text of Deuteronomy) by the high priest Hilkiah (2 Kgs. 22:8–13) and interpreted as authentic by the prophetess Huldah (2 Kgs.

22:14–17). This interpretation encouraged Josiah to carry out the most complete spiritual and political transformation ever experienced by Judah (2 Kgs. 23:1–30; 2 Chr. 34:1–35:26). He met his death at the hands of Necho II (609–594 B.C.), Pharaoh of the Twenty-sixth Dynasty: 2 Kgs. 23:29 relates that Josiah died at Megiddo; 2 Chr. 35:22–24, however, says that he was brought wounded to Jerusalem where he died and was interred in the tombs of his forefathers. Josiah was a contemporary of Jeremiah, who eulogized the king in his praise for the restoration of Israel (Jer. 3:11–17).

609 = Jehoahaz, son of Josiah, whom Jeremiah called Shallum (Jer. 22:11). He ruled Judah for only three months (2 Kgs. 23:30–34; 2 Chr. 36:1–4). Necho II deposed him and took him to Egypt, where he died.

609–598 = Jehoiakim, also a son of Josiah. Necho II enthroned him as king of Judah in Jerusalem and changed his name from Eliakim to Jehoiakim. He was a wicked ruler: what his father Josiah had accomplished in Jerusalem, Jehoiakim brought to ruin (2 Kgs. 23:14–24; 2 Chr. 36:5–8).

598–597 = Jehoiachin, son of Jehoiakim, also known as Jeconiah or Joiakin. He did not have sons who would be heirs to the throne. Kings and Chronicles agree that "he did evil in the sight of the Lord, just as his forebears had done" (2 Kgs. 24:9; 2 Chr. 36:9). During his reign Nebuchadnezzar of Babylon (604–562 B.C.) besieged Jerusalem: he took to Babylon all the precious treasures of the Temple and the palace, and deported "ten thousand in number" of the upper class, but left the poor behind. Jehoiachin died in Babylon (2 Kgs. 24:6–17; 2 Chr. 36:8–10).

597–587 = Zedekiah, nephew of Jehoiachin ben Josiah. Nebuchadnezzar placed him on the throne of Judah, and changed his name from Mattaniah to Zedekiah. A feeble king, Nebuchadnezzar had him deported to Babylon where he died in prison. Zedekiah was the last king of the Davidic family to rule in Jerusalem over Judah. The period of the Exile (587–537) began with Nebuchadnezzar's deportation of thousands of Jews from Judah to Babylon. This was also the period during which the Babylonian Talmud, written in

Eastern Aramaic, was prepared by the Jews in captivity.

5. *Persian Rule* (586–333 B.C.)

550–530 = Cyrus II the Great, Persian monarch who came to power in the fourteenth year of Hiram III of Phoenicia. He united the Persians and Medes and defeated the Lydians. He captured Babylon in 539 B.C. Known as the founder of the Persian Empire, Cyrus was quite benevolent towards the Jews living in his country. His decree, recorded in Ezra 6:3–5, was promulgated in 539 B.C., allowing the Jews to return to Judah and to rebuild the City of the Temple (2 Chr. 36:22–23; Ezra 1:1–4; 6:3–5).

538– = Zerubbabel, son of Shealtiel and of the royal house of David through King Jehoiachin. He was governor of Judah after the return of the exiles. His principal endeavor was the rebuilding of the Jerusalem temple, which he began around 520 B.C. (Ezra 3–6).

515 = Second Temple period (515–520/19 B.C.). Zerubbabel built the second temple on the site where the Solomonic "House of the Lord" once stood (Ezra 3:1–13; 5:1–17; 6:14–18). Ezekiel gives an apocalyptic description of the "New Temple" (Ezek. 40–43), but it is very likely based on factual evidence.

445–432 = Nehemiah, appointed governor of Judah by Artaxerxes I, king of Persia (465–425). The book of Nehemiah narrates his journey to Jerusalem (ch. 1–2), his reparations on the city gates (ch. 3) and the building of its walls (ch. 4–6), the reading of the "Book of the Law" before all the people (ch. 7–8), the Covenant and the dedication of the city's ramparts (ch. 9–12), and the close of Nehemiah's work in Jerusalem (ch. 13). It is said that Nehemiah rebuilt the city's defenses in fifty-two days (Neh. 6:15).

6. *Hellenistic Rule* (336–63 B.C.)

357–323 = Alexander the Great, son of Philip of Macedon, who conquered the Persian Empire after his accession to the throne established by his father, *ca.* 336 B.C. Greek culture and language were spread throughout the Middle East, which also caused profound changes in some branches of Judaism. Alexander is mentioned only in 1 Macc. 1:1–9; 6:2. Josephus' account that Alexander visited Jerusalem, prostrated himself before the high priest, and offered sacrifice in the Temple (*Ant.* xi. 329–339) is probably not historical. The Hellenistic period began with Alexander's conquests. After his death the empire was divided between his two generals: Ptolemy I (304–283 B.C.), founder of the Ptolemaic dynasty that ruled Egypt from 323 to 30 B.C., and Seleucus I (312–280 B.C.), who founded the Seleucid dynasty of Syria which included Syria, Babylonia, Asia Minor, and eventually Palestine. The Seleucids ruled from 323 to *ca.* 125 B.C.

175–164 = Antiochus IV Epiphanes, Seleucid king of Syria. He captured Jerusalem, plundered the city, and desecrated the Temple by introducing in it the worship of the Olympian Zeus (1 Macc. 1:10–63; 2 Macc. 5:1–7:42).

165 = Judas Maccabaeus, who restored the cult of Yahweh in Jerusalem by purifying and rededicating it after the abomination of desolation by Antiochus IV. The Akra fortress, however, remained under Seleucid control (1 Macc. 4:36–60).

135–63 = Rule of the Hasmonaeans, descendants of Mattathias Maccabaeus and his sons. This period coincides with the growing parties of the Pharisees, Sadducees, and Essenes in Palestine, but especially in the City of the Temple. There greater emphasis on the observance of the Mosaic Law was put, but interpreted in different ways by these parties and their scribes.

135–104 = John Hyrcanus, son of Simon. He extended Jewish rule over the land east of the Jordan River as far south as Edom. He imposed circumcision upon the Idumaeans and besieged Samaria, culminating with the destruction of the Samaritan temple on Mt. Gerizim. The Pharisees then abandoned the Hasmonaean party.

103–76 = Alexander Jannaeus, called Jonathan, who extended his reign over Philistia in the southwestern corner of Palestine. He then proceeded to take over those parts east of the Jordan which had not as yet been subjected to Jewish control, but he was defeated by the Nabataean king of Damascus, Obodas I (95–87 B.C.). The Nabataeans, an Arab people from southern Arabia, formed one of the most remarkable civilizations of ancient Near Eastern history. Theirs is the historical setting employed in Matthew's account of the Magi (Matt. 2:1–12). Nabataean king Aretas IV (9 B.C.–A.D. 40) is mentioned in Paul's second letter to the Corinthians (2 Cor. 11:32; cf. Acts 9:23–25; in Gal. 1:17 Arabia equals the territory of the Nabataeans.

7. *Roman Rule* (63 B.C.–*ca.* A.D. 325)

63 = Pompey, conqueror of Palestine. The years from 63 to 37 B.C. witnessed the finalization of Roman rule in the country and the end of the Hasmonaean dynasty. *Ca.* 47 B.C. John Hyrcanus II became ethnarch of Palestine, and the Idumaean Herod was appointed governor of Jerusalem.

37–4 = Herod the Great appointed king of Judaea by Caesar Augustus. He established his capital in Jerusalem.

20/19 = Beginning of the Third Temple period. In order to ingratiate himself among the Jews, Herod began a vast building program in Judaea, but especially in Jerusalem. The ancient temple was in serious need of restorations, so Herod decreed that a new one be built. "He removed the old foundations and replaced them with new ones, and upon these he constructed the Temple" (*Ant.* xv. 391). Herod the Great's reign corresponded to a certain extent with that of his patron, Augustus Caesar, Emperor of Rome from 31 B.C. to A.D. 14. This was the age of the Pax Romana, when the whole world was at peace.

6± = Jesus of Nazareth born in Bethlehem of Judaea (Matt. 1:18–25; Luke 2:1–20).

A.D. 6 = Jesus' celebration of the Passover festival in the City of the Temple at age twelve (Luke 2:41–50). He returned with his parents to Nazareth, where we can picture him assisting Mary, working with Joseph, and attending the synagogue school where he would have learned all that was required of pious Jews to know and live out the Mosaic Law and its various interpretations.

27 = Jesus baptized by his cousin John the Baptizer at the Jordan River "in the fifteenth year of the rule of Tiberius Caesar, when Pontius Pilate was procurator of Judaea, Herod tetrarch of Galilee, Philip his brother tetrarch of the region of Ituraea and Trachonitis, and Lysanias tetrarch of Abilene, during the high-priesthood of Annas and Caiaphas" (Luke 3:1–2). Jesus then made his first public appearance in Jerusalem, according to our interpretation, for the fifteenth year of Tiberius corresponded to the forty-sixth year of the building of the Jerusalem temple (John 2:20).

27–30 = Jesus' public ministry in Galilee, Judaea, and Jerusalem. (The Synoptic Gospels [Matthew, Mark, and Luke] would telescope these three years of Jesus' preaching into one. John, believably, preserves the three journeys to Jerusalem during this period.)

30 = Jesus' triumphal entrance into Jerusalem (Mark 11:1–10; Matt. 21:1–9; Luke 19:28–40; John 12:12–29); last Seder meal with his disciples on the Feast of Passover (Mark 14:1–31; Matt. 26:17–35; Luke 22:1–38; John 11:55–57; 13:1–17:26; 1 Cor. 11:17–34); agony in the Garden of Gethsemani and arrest by the Jews (Mark 14:32–52; Matt. 26:36–56; Luke 22:39–62; John 18:1–18); trial before the Sanhedrin (Mark 14:53–72; Matt. 26:57–75; Luke 22:63–71; John 18:19–27); appearance before Pilate and condemnation to capital punishment (Mark 15:1–20; Matt. 27:11–31; Luke 23:1–25; John 18:1–19:16a); carrying his cross to Calvary where he was crucified and died (Mark 15:21–41; Matt. 27:32–56; Luke 23:26–49; John 19:16b–37); burial in the garden tomb (Mark 15:42–47; Matt. 27:57–66; Luke 23:50–56; John 19:38–42); and glorious resurrection from the dead (Mark 16:1–8 [1–20]; Matt. 28:1–20; Luke 24:1–53; John 20:1–21:25). All of these events happened in the springtime during the great pilgrim festival of Passover and Unleavened Bread.

30 = Pentecost event. Fifty days after the Feast of Passover Jesus' disciples were gathered in the Upper

Plate 148 *"Jesus said, 'Do you see these great buildings? There will not be left here one stone upon another that will not be thrown down!'" The column bears a Latin inscription of the Tenth Roman Legio Fretensis, one of the legions that devastated Jerusalem in A.D. 70.*

✝ ————————————————————————— ✝

Plate 149 *The boar was the symbol of the Tenth Roman Legion; this coin was struck during the emperorship of Antoninus Pius (A.D. 138–161), after Jerusalem had been razed and rebuilt as Aelia Capitolina by his predecessor, Hadrian.*

Room, and the Holy Spirit descended upon them. This date marks the birth of Christianity (Acts 1:12–2:47).

34 = Departure from Jerusalem of Paul of Tarsus, a devout Jew, educated under the famous Rabbi Gamaliel, to persecute the (Judaeo-)Christians in Damascus. He was converted to Christianity, however, even before arriving in the city (Acts 9:1–19; 22:3–16; 26:2–18).

37± = Josephus Flavius (Joseph ben Matthias) born in Jerusalem. A Jewish general and later an historian who wrote the *Jewish Wars* and *Jewish Antiquities*, Josephus knew Jerusalem well. He died *ca.* A.D. 100.

41–44 = Herod Agrippa I, king of Jerusalem. He built the "third wall" of Jerusalem.

50 = Jerusalem Council (Gal. 2:1–10; Acts 15:1–29), regarded by some theologians as the first Ecumenical Council.

66–70 = Fall of Jerusalem. The total destruction of the Temple by the Roman legions under Titus ended the First Jewish Revolt against Rome. It also marks the end of the Third Temple period in the history of Judaism. Titus had the treasures of the Temple carried off to Rome, as can be seen on the Arch of Titus there.

135 = Roman emperor Publius Aelius Hadrianus (76–138), nephew of Emperor Trajan. He reigned from 117 to 138 and crushed the Second Jewish Revolt against Rome, led by Bar Kokhba. Hadrian razed Jerusalem and rebuilt it according to Roman city planning (quadrata), which plan can still be discerned in the Old City today. He built a public square (forum) and a temple of Venus over the site of Calvary, and had a statue of himself erected on the quadra, the former site of the Jewish temple. He also built a public square and arch in the northeastern section of the city, covering the ancient Strouthion pool in the process. Under Hadrian Jerusalem received a new name: Colonia Aelia Capitolina decurionum decreto.

Plate 151 "For nation will rise against nation, and kingdom against kingdom; there will be earthquakes in various places; there will be famines; this is but the beginning of sufferings." These Jewish silver shekels were struck in Jerusalem ca. A.D. 68/69, the year before its fall and destruction by the Roman armies under Titus.

Plate 150 (left) Coin of Vespasian I wearing a victory wreath. Vespasian was Roman emperor when the general Titus, his son and successor, captured Jerusalem in A.D. 70.

Plate 152 "But when you see Jerusalem surrounded by armies, then know that its desolation has come." In honor of Titus' victory over Jerusalem, a triumphal arch was erected on the Sacred Way at the entrance into the Roman forum. This famous relief inside the arch pictures the triumphal procession entering Rome. The soldiers, wearing victory wreaths, carry the seven-branched candelabra, the table of the shewbread (or the altar?), and the sacred vessels from the Jerusalem temple. (Rev. Raymond V. Schoder, S.J., Loyola University of Chicago)

313 = Constantine the Great's Edict of Milan, which legalized Christianity in his empire.

325 = Council of Nicaea in Asia Minor. Bishop Makarios of Jerusalem was present at this council convoked by Constantine and which decided to preserve the Holy Places in Jerusalem. Queen Helena, Constantine's mother, later visited the Holy City. Work on the Anastasis (the Rotunda over the Holy Sepulchre) and the Martyrion (the place of witness, identified with the Basilica in front of the Tomb of Jesus) was completed by 335. Descriptions of various types have been recorded by the Pilgrim of Bordeaux, who visited Jerusalem *ca.* 333, by Eusebius of Caesarea (*ca.* 337), and by the adventurous pilgrim nun Aegeria who came to Jerusalem *ca.* 380.

362 = Julian the Apostate's attempt to rebuild the Temple and again introduce the cult of Yahweh in Jerusalem.

386-417 = Building of the great church of Hagia Sion, the "Mother of All Churches," by John II. Scholars dispute whether the Cenacle had been incorporated into this magnificent church or whether it stood adjacent to it on its south side.

390 = Emperor Theodosius I's construction of a large hospice for the sick and poor near the present St. Stephen's Gate (Bab Sitti Miryam).

8. Byzantine Period in Jerusalem (395–638)

395 = Division of the Roman Empire between the East and West.

435 = Special pilgrimage to Jerusalem by Empress Eudokia, wife of Theodosius II. She erected St. Stephen's basilica and monastery, restored the ramparts and the Golden Gate, and built a shrine at the Pool of Siloam, among many other structures in the Holy City.

451 = Decree by the Council of Chalcedon that Jerusalem be a Patriarchal City, which it has remained since.

500± = Jerusalem (Yerushalmi) Talmud completed by the rabbinic schools in Galilee.

529 = Great church of the Nea (Sancta Maria Nova) constructed during the reign of Emperor Justinian.

614 = Burning on May 4 by the Persian Chosroes Parviz of the Constantinian structures of the Holy Sepulchre and destruction of many other churches, shrines, and monasteries in Jerusalem and environs.

622 = Year of the Hegirah. The Islamic prophet (more properly, "messenger") Muhammed (*ca.* 570–632) escaped assassination in Mecca and fled to Medinah where he was warmly received and thus able to establish a theocratic state based on his revelations from Allah. Muhammed's flight marks the first year of the Islamic calendar. He is also believed to have made a night journey to Jerusalem (Koran, Surah xvii), whence he ascended into the seventh heaven. Jerusalem, *el-Quds,* "the Holy [city, sanctuary]," is thus the third most holy city in Islam.

628 = Heraclius' recapture of Jerusalem from the Persians. He triumphantly brought back the relic of the True Cross of Jesus, which Chosroes had taken to Ctesiphon near modern Baghdad in Iraq. Patriarch Modestos, former abbot of the Monastery of St. Theodosius (Deir Dosi) in the Judaean desert south of Jerusalem, restored the Holy Sepulchre according to its original plan.

9. Early Muslim Arab Period (638–1099)

638 = Capture of Jerusalem for Islam by Caliph Omar Ibn el-Khattab. Under Islamic domination Jerusalem, especially the former Temple Mount, would become an especially holy place, because of its association with Muhammed's night journey to the "farther temple in Jerusalem" (Surah xvii). Patriarch Sophronios submitted to Omar. At the Muslim hour of prayer Omar visited the Church of the Holy Sepulchre, but did not pray in it for fear that his followers would convert the Holy Place into a mosque. Had he done so, the fourth-century Constantinian monument would still be preserved, as is the Hagia Sophia in Istanbul.

661–750 = Palestine governed by the Omayyad Caliphs in Damascus.

685 = Pilgrimage of Arculf, a French bishop, to the Holy Land. On his visit to Jerusalem he set in writing a description of Modestus' restorations.

691 = Abdul Malik Ibn-Marwan built the Dome of the Rock on the previous temple site, now called the Haram esh-Sharif, the "Noble Enclosure." This con-

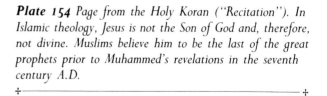

Plate 154 Page from the Holy Koran ("Recitation"). In Islamic theology, Jesus is not the Son of God and, therefore, not divine. Muslims believe him to be the last of the great prophets prior to Muhammed's revelations in the seventh century A.D.

struction took place only seventy-two years after Muhammed's Hegirah.

750–868 = Rule of Palestine by the Abbasid Caliphs in Baghdad.

780 = el-Aqsa Mosque, most important mosque in Jerusalem, completed, probably by Walid, son of Ibn-Marwan. (This is the el-Aqsa el-Qadimeh beneath the present structure.)

768–814 = Charlemagne (Charles I the Great, 742–814), king of the Franks, crowned Roman emperor in 800. He ordered the church and monastery of Sancta Maria Latina (St. Mary of the Latins) built near the Church of the Holy Sepulchre. The present Lutheran Church of the Holy Redeemer (Erlöserkirche) stands on the site.

969–1000 = Palestine ruled by the Fatmid Caliphs of Cairo.

975 = Southern rampart, restored by Eudokia, given up by Caliph Azziz, thus giving Jerusalem its present general outline along the southern wall.

1009 = Jerusalem razed by Sultan Hakim. In the process he ravaged many churches and shrines and systematically destroyed the Church of the Holy Sepulchre, especially the Tomb of Jesus.

1048 = Rotunda (Anastasis) of the Holy Sepulchre rebuilt by Constantine Monomachos after Ibn Abi Daher's systematic destruction of the grotto with hammer and pickaxe.

10. Latin Kingdom of Jerusalem (1099–1187) Period of the Crusades.

1070–1090 = Seljuk Turkish invasion of the Holy Land from Nicaea, Seljuk capital in Asia Minor.

Plate 155 " 'Put your sword back into its place; for all who take the sword will perish by the sword.' " Sword and spurs, allegedly those of the Crusader Geoffrey de Bouillon, displayed in the Church of the Holy Sepulchre near columns dated to the eleventh century.

✝ ———————————————————————— ✝

1099 = First Crusade. The defense of Christianity, elaborated at the court of Charlemagne in the ninth century, became the traditional responsibility of the Latin kings. Geoffrey de Bouillon, a descendent of Charlemagne on both sides, took Jerusalem and was elected first king of the Latin Kingdom of Jerusalem (1099–1100). He is known as the Defender of the Holy Sepulchre. A new basilica of the Holy Sepulchre was constructed and consecrated on July 17, 1099. Baldwin I (1100–1118) was appointed second king of Jerusalem and extended his reign as far north as Beirut. Baldwin II (1118–1131) extended the Latin Kingdom to its widest frontiers. During the Crusader period the Dome of the Rock was converted into the Templum Domini, the Temple of the Lord, and the el-Aqsa Mosque was given over to the Order of the Templars.

1147–1149 = Second Crusade, led by Louis VII of France. Nothing of importance was accomplished. The Holy Sepulchre Church was completed on July 15, 1149.

1187 = Triumph of Sultan Salah ed-Din (Saladin) over the Crusaders at the battle of the Horns of Hattin in Galilee. He then took the Holy City, terminating the Latin Kingdom of Jerusalem in the Holy Land. Many Christian shrines (e.g., the Templum Domini and the Church of the Ascension) were transformed into mosques, which purpose they serve to this day.

1189–1192 = Third Crusade, led by three great Christian monarchs: Richard the Lionhearted of England, Frederick Barbarossa of Germany, and King Philip II of France. This expedition to regain the Holy Land for Christianity witnessed the end of the golden age of the Crusades.

1202–1221 = Fourth and Fifth Crusades, which ended in failure, shocking Christian Europe.

1228–1229 = Sixth Crusade, led by Emperor Frederick II of Germany. Jerusalem was given to the Franks after a short-lived accord between Frederick and Sultan Malik of Egypt.

1248–1254 = Seventh Crusade, the first initiated by King Louis IX of France. Led by Theobald of Navarre (despite opposition from both the Pope and Christians in Europe), its poor organization terminated in failure.

1270 = Eighth Crusade, headed by Louis IX of France and Edward of England. It achieved nothing permanent.

1291 = Fall of Acre (biblical Ptolemais) to Sultan Qalawun, ending the Crusader adventures in the Holy Land. Jerusalem remained in Muslim possession; and the Christians returned to Europe.

11. *Mameluke Period in Jerusalem* (1250–1517)

1250–1381 = Jerusalem ruled by the Bahri Mamelukes of Cairo.

1382–1517 = Almost the entire Middle East governed by the Burji Mamelukes in Cairo.

12. *Ottoman Empire* (1517–1917)

1516–1517 = Jerusalem captured by Turkish Sultan Selim I (1512–1520) for the Ottoman Empire, under which it remained for four hundred years. In 1517 the Protestant Revolution was begun in Europe by Martin

Luther (1483–1546), a former German Augustinian monk.

1520–1566 = Sultan Suleiman I, "The Magnificent," son of Selim, considered the greatest Ottoman Turkish ruler. In year 945 of the Hegirah (1538–1539), as attested in the inscription on the original Jaffa Gate of the Old City, he erected the present walls and gates of Jerusalem. Suleiman I expanded the Ottoman empire to its greatest extent.

1838 = Arch discovered by E. Robinson in the outer western wall of the Temple. He believed it to have been part of the bridge that spanned the Tyropoeon Valley from the Temple Mount to the Upper City. B. Mazar's excavations begun in 1968 proved that this was the spring of the arch which belonged to the monumental staircase described by Josephus.

1853–1856 = Crimean War. In 1853 Turkey, joined by Britain and France (1854) and Sardinia (1855) declared war against Russia. The cause was twofold: Russia's expansion into the Balkans and the dispute over the guardianship of the Holy Places in Palestine. The status quo, still in effect, was imposed on Greek Orthodox and Latin Catholics regarding their rights in the Christian shrines as a result of this war.

ca. 1865 = Another arch that spanned the Tyropoeon Valley identified by C. Wilson. It starts at Bab es-Silsileh of the Haram esh-Sharif and projects westwards towards the Khalidi Library. The arch was probably built in the Hasmonaean period, but restored and embellished under Herod the Great.

1867–1870 = First archaeological excavations in Jerusalem undertaken by Sir C. Warren on behalf of the Palestine Exploration Fund.

1881 = Eastern hill explored by H. Guthe for the Deutsche Verein zur Erforschung Palästinas, founded in 1877.

1883 = Attempt by Gen. C. Gordon to locate sites of Calvary and the Tomb of Jesus. He erroneously identified both places north of the sixteenth-century walls of the city.

1894–1897 = Western hill explored by F.J. Bliss and A.C. Dickie, who detected segments of the first south wall of Jerusalem. The Gate of the Essenes was located and the complex Gihon hydraulic system observed.

1898 = Visit of Kaiser Wilhelm II to Jerusalem. The Turkish government opened the new Jaffa Gate for his entry. His benefactions included the Lutheran Erlöserkirche near the Muristan inside the city, the Dormition Abbey and Monastery on Mt. Zion, and the Augusta Victoria Hospital on Mt. Scopus. This was also the year that T. Herzl (1860–1904), a Hungarian-born Austrian Jew, visited Palestine. Author of the pamphlet *Der Judenstaat* (1896) which proposed the founding of a Jewish national state, Herzl is the founder of the modern Zionist movement. He died in Vienna but is interred on Mt. Herzl in West Jerusalem.

1909–1911 = Gihon water tunnel thoroughly reexamined by M. Parker.

1913–1914 = Pre-Israelite remains on the eastern hill identified by R. Weill. This he did again in 1923–24.

1916–1918 = Leading role in the Arab revolt against the Turks by T.E. Lawrence, "Lawrence of Arabia," during World War I.

1917 = British Gen. E.H. Allenby's entry of Jerusalem on foot after the Battle of Megiddo, thus ending the four hundred years of Ottoman Turkish rule over Palestine. The Balfour Declaration was issued on Nov. 2.

13. *British Mandate over Palestine* (1920–1948)

1920 = Palestine and Transjordania placed under the British Council on April 25 by the supreme council meeting at San Remo; approved by the League of Nations on July 24, 1922. This was a period of much hostility between the Arab and Jewish citizens of Jerusalem and throughout Palestine.

1923–1925 = Large sections (*ca.* 400 feet) of Jerusalem's ancient defense wall uncovered by R.A.S. Macalister and J.G. Duncan. They assigned the material to the

Plate 156 *"If a kingdom is divided against itself, that kingdom cannot stand. And if a house is divided against itself, that house will not be able to stand." The Hinnom Valley was a "No Man's Land" which divided Jerusalem from 1948 to 1967.*

Davidic period, but later archaeological explorations have identified the walls as Hellenistic.

1927 = Trench cut by J.W. Crowfoot and G.M. Fitzgerald across the Tyropoeon Valley revealing a large gate opening from the Ophel towards the central valley. Digging on behalf of the Hebrew University of Jerusalem, E.L. Sukenik and L.A. Mayer discovered remains of a wall much farther north of the present Old City walls and claimed it to be the third north wall of Josephus. The course of Josephus' third wall is still disputed. In our estimation the sixteenth-century defense walls of Suleiman the Magnificent were built along the lines of the first-century rampart of Agrippa, just over a decade after the crucifixion of Jesus, thus enclosing the sites of Calvary and the Holy Sepulchre of Jesus.

1948 = British Mandate over Palestine terminated on May 14, when Zionist Jews proclaimed independence and founded the State of Israel. Immediately war erupted between Palestinians and Israelis, which ended in a 1949 armistice: East Jerusalem became part of the Hashemite Kingdom of Jordan; West Jerusalem remained under Israeli administration. Jerusalem was a divided city.

1961–1967 = Ophel excavated by K.M. Kenyon and R. de Vaux, O.P., uncovering structures dating to about 1800 B.C. Others were identified as belonging to the Judahite monarchy. B. Hennessy excavated at the Damascus Gate, where he also discovered remains of the first-century north gate of the city. As the Latin inscription above it testifies, this was also used by Hadrian in the second century. On behalf of the Royal Ontario Museum A.D. Tushingham directed

the archaeological excavations in the garden of the Armenian Orthodox Patriarchate in Jerusalem.

14. *Reunification of Jerusalem* (1967–)

1967 = Third Arab-Israeli war, the Six-Day War, June 5–11, bringing Jerusalem under Jewish administration after over two thousand years. On June 29 the Israeli Knesset (Parliament) declared the unification of the city.

1968+ = East Jerusalem explored by Israeli archaeologists of the Hebrew University. B. Mazar directed operations along the western and southern sides of the Haram esh-Sharif outer wall, identified as the original first-century Herodian temple enclosure. N. Avigad excavated the Jewish Quarter of the Old City prior to its rebuilding. M. Broshi discovered remains of Herod's palace and Pilate's Praetorium in the Armenian garden south of the Citadel. R. Amiran directed excavations in the area of the Citadel. In a first-century Jewish necropolis at Gib'at ha-Mibtar, north of Jerusalem, V. Tzaferis exhumed remains of a crucified man. Large sections of ancient walls, opulent villas, portions of a Byzantine street following the lines of Hadrian's cardo maximus, are only some examples of how modern archaeology has brought to light the history and civilization of the Holy City. The el-Aqsa Mosque was burned by Australian D.M. Rohan; the mosque is still in the process of restoration and reembellishment. The Jewish quarter with its important synagogues and fine buildings is also being restored. Christians are in the (final?) stages of restorations on the Church of the Holy Sepulchre.

Notes

CHAPTER I   *The Roads to Jerusalem*

1. For a more detailed geographical explanation of this phrase, see J. Jeremias, *Jerusalem in the Time of Jesus,* pp. 51–54.

2. R. T. O'Callaghan, S.J., in *Dictionnaire de la Bible, Supplément* 5, cols. 627–704, esp. cols. 656–666; M. Avi-Yonah, *The Madaba Mosaic Map* (Jerusalem: IES, 1954), pp. 50–60; V. R. Gold, "The Mosaic Map of Madeba," in E. F. Campbell and D. N. Freedman, eds., *The Biblical Archaeologist Reader* 3 (New York: Doubleday, 1970), pp. 366–389, esp. 383–89.

3. Biblical Dothan was excavated by J. P. Free for Wheaton College in seven seasons (1953–1956 and 1958–1960). For excavation reports see *BASOR* 131 (1953): 16–20; 135 (1954): 14–20; 139 (1955): 3–9; *ADAJ* 3 (1956): 79–80; *BA* 19 (1956): 43–48; *BASOR* 143 (1956): 11–17; 147 (1957): 36–37; 152 (1958): 10–18; 156 (1959): 22–29; 160 (1960): 6–15; *ADAJ* 6–7 (1962): 117–120.

4. For the background of this tradition see E. H. Maly, "Genesis" in *JBC* pp. 37–38, Nos. 142–45.

5. Tell Balatah was excavated by E. Sellin and others for the Vienna Academy of Science in 1913–1914, 1926–1928, 1931, and 1934; and again by G. E. Wright *et al.* for the American Schools of Oriental Research in 1956–1957, 1960, 1962, 1964, 1966; Wright, *Shechem: The Biography of a Biblical City* (New York: McGraw-Hill, 1965).

6. The huge mound of biblical Ai (et-Tell) was excavated in 1933–1935 by J. Marquet-Krause for the Baron Edmond de Rothschild Expedition, and then again by J. A. Callaway in 1964, 1966, 1968, and 1969 for the Southern Baptist Theological Seminary. See Marquet-Krause, "et-Tell," *QDAP* 4 (1935): 204–5; Callaway, "New Evidence on the Conquest of Ai," *JBL* 87 (1968): 312–320; "Ai," *RB* 77 (1970): 390–94; P. W. Lapp, *Biblical Archaeology and History* (New York: World, 1969), pp. 74, 109, 118; G. E. Wright, "The Significance of Ai in the Third Millennium B.C.," pp. 299–319 in A. Kuschke and E. Kutsch, eds., *Archäologie und Altes Testament* (K. Galling Festschrift; Tübingen: Mohr, 1970).

7. Bethel (Beitin) was excavated by W. F. Albright in 1934 and J. L. Kelso in 1954, 1957, and 1960, both for the American Schools of Oriental Research. Regarding the capture of Bethel, see R. de Vaux, O.P., in *Ancient Israel: Social*

Institutions (New York: McGraw-Hill, 1965), pp. 217, 236; this should be read with the understanding that Joshua, which describes the capture of Ai, is a postexilic composition, while Judges, which mentions the taking of Bethel, belongs to the Deuteronomic period.

8. The exact location of Kiriath-yearim is unknown. It is traditionally identified with the present village of Abu Ghosh near Tell el-Azhar, a few miles west of Jerusalem on the Jerusalem-Tel Aviv highway.

9. J. B. Pritchard excavated biblical Gibeon (el-Jib) for the American Schools of Oriental Research in 1956–1957, 1959–1960. See Pritchard, *Gibeon: Where the Sun Stood Still* (Princeton: Princeton University, 1962); "The Water System of Gibeon," *BA* 19 (1956): 66–75.

10. The Herodium was excavated by V. C. Corbo, O.F.M., for the Italian Foreign Ministry from 1962 to 1967. See "L'Herodion di Giabal Fureidis," *Liber Annuus* 13 (1963): 219–277; 17 (1967): 65–121; "Gebel Fureidis (Herodium)," *RB* 75 (1968): 424–28.

11. M. F. Unger, *Archaeology and the Old Testament,* pp. 114, 190, 205; J. Prawer, *The Latin Kingdom of Jerusalem,* pp. 18, 133, 146 note 22, 165–66, 184–85, 291; E. J. Mackay, L.-H. Vincent, O.P., and F.-M. Abel, O.P., *Sépulture des Patriarches* (Paris: Leroux, 1923); also Supreme Awqaf Council, *Al-Haram Al-Ibrahimi Al-Khalil: A Brief Guide* (al-Khalil [Hebron], 1966), pp. 6–8.

12. For a brief history of the Nabataeans see S. Cohen, *IDB* 3: 491–93; also N. Glueck, *Deities and Dolphins* (New York: Farrar, Straus, and Giroux, 1965); E. Pax, O.F.M., "Spuren der Nabatäer im Neuen Testament," *Bibel und Leben* 3 (1974): 193–206. The Nabataean Aretas IV was ruler of Damascus *ca.* A.D. 39, when Paul spent some time in that city (2 Cor. 11:32–33; cf. Acts 9:19b–22); cf. *Ant.* xvii. 287.

13. Excavations were directed by H. D. Colt for the British School of Archaeology in Jerusalem from 1934 to 1938; cf. "Discoveries at Auja Hafir," *PEFQS* (1936), pp. 216–220; Colt Archaeological Institute, *Excavations at Nessana* 1 (Princeton, N.J.: Princeton, 1950); 3 (1958); N. Glueck, *Rivers in the Desert,* rev. ed. (Philadelphia: Jewish Publication Society, 1968), pp. 26, 29, 262–63.

14. "H. D. Colt archaeological expedition for the British School of Archaeology, 1935-1936," *PEFQS* (1935), pp. 9–11, 171–181; (1936), pp. 14–27; N. Glueck, *Rivers in the Desert*, pp. 71, 519–525; M. Evenari, L. Shanan, and N. Tadmor, *The Negev* (Cambridge: Harvard, 1971), pp. 161, 168–171.

15. Avdat was excavated by the Department for the Preservation of Landscape and Conservation of Antiquities of Israel under M. Avi-Yonah, A. Negev, and Y. Cohen from 1958 to 1960. See Avi-Yonah and Negev, "A City in the Negeb: Excavations in Nabataean, Roman and Byzantine Eboda," *ILN* 26 (1960): 944–47; N. Glueck, *Deities and Dolphins*, pp. 6–7, 332–33, 520; *Rivers in the Desert*, pp. 271–76.

16. Ancient Mampsis (Kurnub) was excavated by A. Negev for the Hebrew University and the National Parks Authority in Israel from 1956–1970; see S. Applebaum, "Mampsis," *IEJ* 6 (1956): 262–63; A. Biran, "Kurnub," *CNI* 17 (1966): 19–20; Negev, "Kurnub," *IEJ* 16 (1966): 145–48; "The Excavations at Kurnub," *Qadmoniot* 2 (1969): 17–22 (Hebrew); "Mampsis: A Report on Excavations of a Nabataeo-Roman Town," *Archaeology* 24 (1971): 166–171; N. Glueck, *Rivers in the Desert*, pp. 207–210.

17. Old Testament Jericho was one of the earliest mounds excavated in Palestine. C. Warren (*PEFQS* [1869], pp. 14–16) and F. J. Bliss (*PEFQS* [1894], pp. 175–183) excavated Tell es-Sultan for the Palestine Exploration Fund, as did

E. Sellin for the Kaiserlichen Academie der Wissenschaften in Wien and the Deutsche Orient-Gesellschaft in 1907 and 1908; cf. Sellin and C. Watzinger, *Jericho, die Ergebnisse der Ausgrabungen* (Leipzig: Hinrichs, 1913). J. Garstang excavated from 1930 to 1936 for the Marston-Melchett Expedition, University of Liverpool, and the British School of Archaeology in Jerusalem; cf. *PEFQS* (1930), pp. 123–132; (1931), pp. 105–7; (1931), pp. 186–196; (1932), pp. 149–153. The Byzantine church and synagogue were excavated by D. C. Baramki for the Department of Antiquities, Palestine, in 1934; cf. *QDAP* 5 (1936): 82–89; 6 (1937): 73–77. From 1952 to 1958 K. M. Kenyon excavated Jericho on behalf of the British School of Archaeology; cf. *Digging Up Jericho* (New York: Praeger, 1957).

18. *ANET*, pp. 242–43; *ANEP*, Nos. 5, 349, 544.

19. In a discussion of the two authentic sites of Emmaus—that of the Book of Maccabees and that of the New Testament—we have identified the latter with Qalunieh, near modern Motza, about seven miles northwest of Jerusalem on the Jerusalem-Tel Aviv highway. R. M. Mackowski, S.J., "Where Is Biblical Emmaus?" *Science et Esprit* 32 (1980): 93–103.

20. *Autobiography of St. Ignatius Loyola*, trans. J. O'Callaghan, ed. J. C. Olin (New York: Harper & Row, 1974), p. 49.

CHAPTER 1   *The Geology of the Holy City*

"Khalit el-Fûl," *RB* 76 (1969): 572–76.

1. We have learned this interpretation from our Hebrew teacher, M. Uchen of the Hebrew University of Jerusalem.

2. For an exciting account of W. Dever's search and discovery of this Middle Bronze I necropolis, see "The Great Tomb Treasure Hunt," *Jerusalem Post Magazine* (May 24, 1968), pp. 16–17. See also the summary excavations report

3. O. Tufnell, *et al.*, *Lachish IV: The Bronze Age*, 2 vols. (London: Oxford, 1958). See also G. L. Harding, *Guide to Lachish: Tell ed-Duweir* (Jerusalem: Palestine Department of Antiquities, 1943).

CHAPTER 2   *The Hills of Jerusalem*

1. It is difficult, if not impossible, to give exact population statistics for first-century Jerusalem. In his *Contra Apionem* Josephus states that there were about 120,000 Jerusalemites in the Holy City just before its destruction in A.D. 70 (i. 197). In *Jewish Wars*, however, he gives the following: 97,000 were taken captive; 1,100,000 perished in the war, including pilgrims; and there were 2,700,000 dinners for 255,600 victims on the Feast of Passover (vi. 422–26). Modern scholars naturally contest these figures. M. Avi-Yonah suggests 90,000 for Herodian Jerusalem, and 100,000 just before the city's destruction by the Romans. J. Wilkinson estimates 36,280 for the former and 70,398 for the latter. In reply to Wilkinson, M. Broshi calculates 38,500 for the number of Jerusalem's citizens at the beginning of the first century A.D., and 82,500 for the city's population *ca.* A.D. 70. For a study of these scholars' investigations, see Wilkinson, "Ancient Jerusalem: Its Water Supply and Population," *PEQ* 106 (1974): 33–51, especially 46–51; and Broshi's response, "La Population de l'Ancienne

Jerusalem," *RB* 82 (1975): 5–14, especially 10–11 and the maps and charts on 12–13.

2. The extraordinary discovery of Ebla by University of Rome scholars P. Matthiae and G. Pettinato was announced at a number of academic conferences in the United States and abroad. News of the discovery may be read in the *Chicago Tribune* (Aug. 28, 1976); *Archaeology* 29 (1976): 271; *Time* (Oct. 18, 1976); and *Jerusalem Post* (Nov. 26, 1976), in which A. Rabinowich states that "local scholars . . . are excited by the discovery but reserved about its bearing in history," p. 10. See especially Matthiae, "Tell Mardikh: The Archives and Palace," *Archaeology* 30 (1977): 244–253.

3. *ANET*, p. 329.

4. *Ibid.*, p. 488.

5. J. Jeremias, *Jerusalem in the Time of Jesus*, pp. 13–14 (especially for the citations to Josephus and the Mishnah), 29.

6. H. Shanks, *The City of David: A Guide to Biblical Jerusalem* (Jerusalem: Bazak, 1973), pp. 103–4 and note 47.

See also R. Hestrin, Y. Israeli, and Y. Moshorer, *Inscriptions Reveal: Documents from the Time of the Bible, the Mishnah and the Talmud* (Jerusalem: Israel Museum, 1973), no. 182, p. 83; for plate and Hebrew text see p. 182.

7. The forms Bezetha, Bezetho', etc. may be popular contractions or perhaps misunderstandings of the original significance of the name. For a critical study of the manuscript evidence see B. M. Metzger, *et al.*, *Textual Commentary on the Greek New Testament* (London: United Bible Societies, 1971), p. 208 and note 2. Despite the variant readings we remain convinced, in view of the history of the site, that the original name of the northeastern hill during the first century was actually Bethesda, derived either from the Hebrew or, more likely, Aramaic.

8. See ch. 1—Geology of the Holy City, note 1 above. For the various etymologies of Zion (Sion) see *IDB* 4: 959; W. J. MacDonald, ed., *New Catholic Encyclopedia* (New York: McGraw-Hill, 1967) 13: 255; C. Roth, ed., *Encyclopaedia Judaica* (New York: Macmillan, 1972) 16: 1030. Compare also the explanations given in F. Brown, S. R. Driver, and C. A. Briggs, *A Hebrew and English Lexicon of the Old Testament* (Oxford: Clarendon, 1962), p. 851, and Marcus Jastrow, comp., *A Dictionary of Talmud Babli and Talmud Yerushalmi, Targum and Midrash* (Tel-Aviv: Shalom, 1972) 2: 1275.

9. It is difficult to define biblical G(h)areb. We suggest that it is derived from the Semitic root *ʿ-r-b* (Hebrew *ʿ-r-b*, Arabic *ǵ-r-b*), denoting "the west," the place where the sun sets. It is linguistically possible that Hebrew *g* in *grb* (Jer. 31:39) eventually took on a softer guttural sound, like the Arabic *ǵ*. (The Modern Greek pronunciation of *g*, which we believe was also the Ancient Greek pronunciation, is a much softer sound than the hard English *g*, the equivalent of *gk* in Modern Greek.)

10. *BJ* v. 133. Its height is implied in v. 55, 147, 149.

11. *BJ* v. 468; see also v. 115. The battle and capture of Jerusalem is related by Josephus in v. 304–375; the attack on the Upper City is described in vii. 392–408.

12. There is no historical foundation that Scopus is derived from the name of one of Titus' generals.

13. See also Talmud *Parah* iii. 6, and the commentary by Rashi on v. 9. Cf. Mishnah *Middoth* i. 3; ii. 4.

14. Jesus' ascension into heaven must have taken place from that part or quarter of the Mount of Olives popularly called "the Galilee," probably because Jews from that region gathered there on the occasion of the three great pilgrim feasts in Jerusalem. See the excellent explanation concerning this tradition in A. Storme, *Le Mont des Oliviers* (Jerusalem: Franciscan, 1971) 7: 148–152.

15. *Ibid.*, pp. 72–100; J. Prawer, *The Latin Kingdom of Jerusalem*, pp. 170–71. For texts relating to the Church of the Ascension and other monuments, see D. Baldi, O.F.M., *Enchiridion Locorum Sanctorum* (Jerusalem: Franciscan, 1955), Nos. 604–652, pp. 384–426.

16. D. Ussishkin, "The Necropolis from the Time of the Kingdom of Judah at Silwan, Jerusalem," *BA* 33 (1970): 34–46; compare with the later dating by S. Loffreda, O.F.M., "Typological Sequence of Iron Age Rock-Cut Tombs in Palestine," *SBFLA* 18 (1968): 244–281; see also *SBFLA* 16 (1965–66): 85–126; and Ussishkin, "A Recently Discovered Monolithic Tomb in Siloam," pp. 63–65 in *JR*.

17. Cf. C. Warren and C. R. Conder, *The Survey of Western Palestine: Jerusalem* (1884); reprint ed. (Jerusalem: Kedem, 1970), p. 397.

18. Josephus describes the funeral preparations and the funeral cortege to Herod's mausoleum in the Herodium (*Ant.* xvii. 196–99; see *BJ* i. 419–421, 673).

Valleys of the Holy City

1. Bettir (Bittir) is not mentioned in the Hebrew Bible (MT), but the Septuagint of Josh. 15:59 renders the name as Baither or Bether (Thether), sometimes doubling the medial *theta (th)*, and lists it as one of the towns assigned to the clan of Judah. Bettir is identified with Khirbet el-Yehud, approximately 7 miles southwest of Jerusalem. According to the historian Dio Cassius (Díōn ho Kássios or Cassius Dio Cocceianus, A.D. 155–164) some 580,000 Jews were massacred in this part of Judaea by Hadrian's soldiers, after a three and a half year siege involving fifty-two battles before the final victory over the province. For an account of the slaughter cf. Dio Cassius *Roman History*, trans. E. Cary, LCL (Cambridge: Harvard, 1925), lxix *Epitome* 12–14. See also Eusebius *Historia Ecclesiastica* iv. 6; Tosefta *Yebamot* 14.15. For an account of the ancient remains on the site see W. D. Carroll, "Bittir and Its Archaeological Remains," *AASOR* 5 (1925): 77–104.

2. See p. 31, notes 16–17.

3. *Ibid.*, and the excellent discussion of these tombs in K. Baedeker, *Palestine and Syria* (Leipzig: Baedeker, 1898), pp. 94–96.

4. Column 8 describes various places where treasures were supposed to have been hidden, including the so-called tomb of St. James. Cf. J. M. Allegro, *The Treasure of the Copper Scroll* (Garden City, N.Y.: Doubleday, 1960). See the responses to Allegro by R. de Vaux, O.P., *RB* 68 (1961): 146; J. T. Milik, *ADAJ* 4 (1960): 137–155; see also *RB* 66 (1959): 321–357.

5. The custom of whitewashing tombs is still practiced among Jews and Muslims today. It dates back to the New Testament period and is based on Num. 19:11–21 (see Mishnah *Temurah* i. 5).

6. *Géenna* occurs twelve times in the Greek New Testament, but see especially Matt. 23:27–28 in this context. Cf. J. L. McKenzie, *Dictionary of the Bible* (Milwaukee: Bruce, 1965), pp. 299–300.

7. As early as 1959 J. T. Milik suspected a Jewish necropolis in this area; *RB* 99 (1959): 345.

8. See also M. Broshi, "The Expansion of Jerusalem in the Reigns of Hezekiah and Manasseh," *IEJ* 24 (1974): 21–26.

9. On the "plural of majesty" of *teraphim* see *Gesenius' Hebrew Grammar*, ed. E. Kautzsch, rev. A. E. Cowley (New York: Oxford, 1962), pp. 399 § 124 h., 429 § 133 h. For Molech (Moloch) see *IDB* 3:422–23, along with the bibliography. For further examples of how Hebrew and Aramaic words were incorporated into the Koine Greek of the New Testament, see R. M. Mackowski, S.J., *What Mark Said: A Philological Analysis of the Special Vocabulary* (ΑΠΑΞ ΛΕΓΟΜΕΝΑ) *of the Gospel According to St. Mark* (Ph.D. diss., Hebrew University of Jerusalem, 1971), pp. 163–202.

CHAPTER 3

First Wall

1. K. M. Kenyon, *Jerusalem: Excavating 3000 Years of History* (New York: McGraw-Hill, 1967), pp. 24–25; *Digging Up Jerusalem* (New York: Praeger, 1974), pp. 76–106 on pre-Israelite and Davidic Jerusalem. See also the more popular treatment in B. Mazar, *The Mountain of the Lord: Excavating Jerusalem* (Garden City, N.Y.: Doubleday, 1975), pp. 31–32.

2. See pp. 35, 36, notes 7–8 above; also Mazar, *Mountain*, pp. 55–57, especially the map on p. 56, indicating the site of these tombs below the southwestern corner of the sixteenth-century battlements of Suleiman the Magnificent; compare with the plan on p. 43 of *JR*.

3. *JR*, pp. 41–51, but especially pp. 43–44.

4. C. N. Johns, "Recent Excavations at the Citadel," *QDAP* 14 (1950); K. Kenyon, *Jerusalem*, pp. 135, 142; R. Amiran and A. Eitan, "Excavations in the Jerusalem Citadel," *JR*, pp. 52–54; M. Avi-Yonah, ed., *Encyclopedia of Archaeological Excavations in the Holy Land*, 2 (1976): 599–603.

5. Compare the following: Hebrew University of Jerusalem, *Atlas of Jerusalem* (New York: de Gruyter, 1973), Sheet 7, Map 3.7; A. Sharon, *Planning Jerusalem: The Old City and Its Environs* (London: Weidenfeld & Nicolson, 1973), p. 19; M. Avi-Yonah, ed., *Encyclopedia of Archaeological Excavations* 2 (1976): 598; D. Bahat, *Carta's Historical Atlas of Jerusalem: A Brief Illustrated Survey* (Jerusalem: Beit Hadar, 1973), p. 13; A. Negev, ed., *Archaeological Encyclopedia of the Holy Land*, p. 171; L. H. Grollenberg, O.P., *Atlas of the Bible*, trans. and ed. J. M. H. Reid (London: Nelson, 1963), p. 115, Map 33; P. Lemaire and D. Baldi, O.F.M., *Atlante Biblico: Storia e Geografia della Bibbia* (Torino: Marietti, 1964), pp. 247, No. 52; 275, No. xxi; Y. Aharoni and M. Avi-Yonah, *The Macmillan Bible Atlas*, rev. ed. (New York: Macmillan, 1967), p. 149, Map 236.

6. On several occasions we have discussed our map with P. Benoit and wish to express our indebtedness for his suggestions and critique. We take full responsibility for departures made in view of our study and personal convictions derived therefrom.

7. *BJ* v. 144; see vi. 354; cf. Mishnah *Middoth* v. 4.

8. See 1 Chr. 22:2; 1 Esdr. 6:9; Sir. 22:17 (A B S¹); Amos 5:11 (A); 1 Macc. 13:27 (S R).

9. *Geschichte des jüdischen Volkes im Zeitalter Jesu Christi*, 3rd ed. (Leipzig: Hinrichs, 1901) 2:211. See *BJ* v. 144, LCL, pp. 242–43, note e. Such philological accommodation appears to have been a quite common practice among the ancient Jews, as it is today. For example, the Arabic Musrarah quarter northwest of the Damascus Gate is called Morasha, meaning "inheritance" (Ezra 11:15) in Hebrew. El-kas, the splendid ablution fountain in the Haram esh-Sharif (between the Dome of the Rock and the el-Aqsa Mosque) is known as ha-Kôs, "the cup." The Government Tourist (*thayarim*) Office is derived from the Hebrew root *thur*, "to travel, tour, explore." Mamillah, formed from the Arabic *ma' 'aman 'Allah*, "with Allah's confidence or security," is rendered *mamila'* today. There are many other examples, some of which, however, are either transla-

tions or transcriptions of the original Arabic, Hebrew, etc. The suburb of Qatamon, for example, is generally accepted to be an abbreviation of the Greek *kata to monasterion*, "in relation to (close by) the monastery." (A wordplay may be intended in the change from Musrarah to Morasha, if the Hebrew root *m-r-sh*, referring to a [musical] march, is meant, for the root may point to either a triumphal or funeral march.)

10. For example, Gen. 19:1; 23:10; Deut. 21:19; 25:7; 2 Sam. 15:2–6; 1 Kgs. 22:10; Amos 5:10, 12, 15. See R. de Vaux, *Ancient Israel* 1:152–57, and the bibliography on p. xxxvii.

11. D. Bahat and M. Broshi, "Excavations in the Armenian Garden," *JR*, pp. 55–56. The 1975–76 excavations have brought to light even more segments of this wall.

12. L.-H. Vincent, O.P., and A.-M. Steve, D.P., *Jérusalem de l'Ancien Testament: Recherches d'Archéologie et d'Histoire* (Paris: Gabalda, 1954–56) 2:244.

13. G. Dalman, *Jerusalem und sein Gelände* (Gütersloh: Bertelsmann, 1930), pp. 86–87.

14. F. J. Bliss, "Third Report on the Excavations of Jerusalem," *PEQ* 27 (1895): 9–13.

15. Philo Judaeus *Quod omnis probus liber sit* xii–xiii. 75–91; Josephus *BJ* ii. 119–161; Pliny the Elder *Naturalis Historia* xv. v. 73 (or v. 17, 73); Hippolytus *Refutatio* ix. 20. 13–23. Cf. J. Murphy-O'Connor, O.P., "The Essenes and Their History," *RB* 81 (1974): 215–244; F. M. Cross, "The Dead Sea Scrolls and the People Who Wrote Them," *BAR* 3 (1977): 1, 23–32, 51; *Ancient Library of Qumran and Modern Biblical Studies*, 2nd ed. (New York: Doubleday, 1961). For the best English translation of the Dead Sea Scrolls see G. Vermes, *The Dead Sea Scrolls in English* (Baltimore: Penguin, 1962), especially the selected bibliography, p. 253. Particularly worthwhile are B.-G. Pixner, O.S.B., "An Essene Quarter on Mount Zion?" *SH* 1 (1976): 245–284, especially 247–264, 264–275; Y. Yadin, "The Gate of the Essenes and the Temple Scroll," *JR*, pp. 90–91.

16. Mishnah *Mikvaoth* i–x, especially i. 4–8.

17. See p. 41, note 1 above.

Second Wall

1. The fact that Nehemiah "bequeathed the walls of Jerusalem as his everlasting memorial," as Josephus states (*Ant.* xi. 183), would not apply to the second wall of Herodian Jerusalem. The northern defenses did not extend this far north in the fifth century B.C. See N. Avigad, "Excavations in the Jewish Quarter of the Old City, 1969–1971," *JR*, pp. 43 (and plan), and 42 (plate); also "Excavations in the Jewish Quarter of the Old City of Jerusalem, 1969/70 (Preliminary Report)," *IEJ* 20 (1970): 1–8; "Second Preliminary Report," *IEJ* 20: 129–140.

CHAPTER 4

1. Thus, we would agree with M. Avi-Yonah's equation, for which see *IDB* 2: 854 (especially the maps); P. Lemaire and D. Baldi, *Atlante Biblico*, p. 277. Compare with the plans in Y. Aharoni and M. Avi-Yonah, *Macmillan Bible Atlas*, Maps 114, p. 74; 170, p. 108.

2. N. Avigad, *IEJ* 20 (1970): 132–33.

Fountain Gate

1. K. Kenyon, *Jerusalem*, p. 24.

2. *ANEP*, pp. 275 (85), 280. See *Inscriptions Reveal*, No. 75, p. 82 (Hebrew) and p. 40 (English); K. Kenyon, *Jerusalem*, p. 70. Our translation is based on these sources. See also C. Warren and C. R. Conder, *Survey: Jerusalem*, pp. 345–371.

"Casemate-wall" Gate

1. R. Weill, *La Cité de David*, 2 vols. (Paris: Geuthner, 1920, 1947), p. 21.

Potsherd Gate

1. F. J. Bliss and A. C. Dickie, *Excavations at Jerusalem 1894–1897* (London: Palestine Exploration Fund, 1898); cf. K. Kenyon, *Jerusalem*, p. 14.

2. J. W. Crowfoot, "Excavations in the Tyropoeon Valley, Jerusalem 1927," *Annual of the Palestine Exploration Fund*, 5 (1929). See C. Warren and C. R. Conder, *Survey: Jerusalem*, pp. 86–97 for a brief history of the explorations in Jerusalem; D. W. Thomas, *Archaeology and Old Testament Study* (New York: Oxford, 1967), pp. 279–293 for a further history of the archaeology of the Holy City, with notes and bibliography on pp. 293–95; and *JR*, especially pp. 21–24, 41–59.

3. Pliny *Natural History* xii. 25. 54 § 116; xxix. 6. 39 § 134.

4. Livy *History of Rome* xxxiv. 4. 4; cf. Pliny xxxiv. 7. 16 § 34; xxxv. 12. 45 § 157.

5. B. Mazar, *Mountain of the Lord*, pp. 194–95.

6. In reality, this refers to one of the three stones upon which a cooking pot was placed; hence, a "fireplace."

Gate of the Essenes

1. Josephus himself states that "When I was sixteen years old, I decided to learn from personal experience about the various sects into which the nation was divided. As I have already mentioned [*BJ* ii. 119; *Ant.* xiii. 171; xviii. 11], there are three of them: the Pharisees are the first, the Sadducees are the second, and the Essenes are the third. For thus I thought that I would be in a good position to choose the finest. Therefore, I submitted to the rigorous discipline and arduous tasks (of the Essenes) and so advanced through the three states (of

Gate of Ephraim

formation)" (*Vita* 10–11). In this section Josephus also reports that he went into the desert to live with a certain Bannus, and thus become his disciple. Bannus wore clothes made of leaves and ate only what the desert produced. To observe ritual cleanliness, Josephus performed the prescribed ablutions in cold water, day and night. He lived here for three years. Josephus' thorough knowledge of the Essenes can also be detected in his other works: *BJ* i. 78; ii. 119–161, 567; iii. 11; v. 145; *Ant.* xiii. 298, 311; xv. 371–73, 378; xvii. 346; xviii. 18–22.

2. See "Survey of Palestine: Lt. C. R. Conder's Reports; No. 22 (Oct. 1, 1874)," *PEQ* (1875), pp. 7–11; and L.-H. Vincent, *Jérusalem*, pp. 66, p. 68 note 1. See also G. A. Smith, *History of Jerusalem: The Topography, Economics and History of Jerusalem from the Earliest Times to A.D. 70* (1907), reprint ed. (New York: Ktav, 1970)2: 71–72.

3. Y. Yadin, "The Gate of the Essenes and the Temple Scroll," *JR*, pp. 90–91; *Megillath Hammiqdash* (Jerusalem: IES, et al., 1977) 1: 233–35.

4. B.-G. Pixner, "An Essene Quarter on Mount Zion?" *SH* 1 (1976): 255–57. See also War Scroll (1QM) vii. 7: "A distance of two thousand cubits is to be set in every case between the camp and the latrine, and no uncleanliness is ever to be in evidence in the precincts of the camp." Cf. T. H. Gaster, *The Dead Sea Scriptures in English Translation* (Garden City, N.Y.: Doubleday, 1956), p. 290; G. Vermes, *The Dead Sea Scrolls in English*, p. 133. The original Hebrew text is quoted by Pixner, *op. cit.*, p. 255, note 14, citing Y. Yadin, *Jerusalem Through the Ages* (Jerusalem: IES, 1968), p. 82.

5. "Two" is usually employed in the sense of a few (Num. 9:22; 1 Kgs. 17:12) or simply as an approximation (2 Kgs. 9:32; Job 33:29; Isa. 17:6; Matt. 18:20), while "three" designates either a small number (Gen. 30:36; Exod. 2:2; Lev. 19:23; Dan. 1:5) or, as in cultic matters, completeness (Gen. 15:9; Exod. 23:14; Num. 19:12; 31:19). Hyperbole is achieved by multiples of one thousand, which itself is not to be interpreted literally, as in 1 Kgs. 19:18; Lev. 26:8; Deut. 32:30; Ps. 3:6; Hos. 8:13.

6. Mishnah *Mikwaoth* i. 7 and *passim*; 1 *seah* = 2.67 gallons (800.9 c. in., 13,222 cc.).

7. See B.-G. Pixner, *SBF* 22 (1976): 266, and compare with the discussion of J. Murphy-O'Connor, *RB* 81 (1974): 215–244, especially 224–29; see also F. M. Cross, *BAR* 3 (1977): 1, 23–24, 29–32, 51. The site of Khirbet Qumran was excavated by G. L. Harding, R. de Vaux, O.P., and A. K. Dajani for the Palestine Archaeological Museum, the Jordanian Department of Antiquities, and the École Biblique et Archéologique Française in several seasons from 1949 to 1967: R. de Vaux, "Fouille au Khirbet Qumran," *RB* 60 (1953): 83–106; 61 (1954): 206–236; 63 (1956): 533–577; F. M. Cross, *Ancient Library of Qumran and Modern Biblical Studies* (New York: Doubleday, 1961).

Garden Gate

1. Job 6:5; 1 Sam. 6:12. The term *go'ah* in Aramaic, Mishnaic Hebrew, and Syriac means "the low (of cattle)." The

LXX of Job 6:5 renders it *phōnēn boús* but it is left untranslated in the LXX of 1 Sam. 6:12. See also Brown, Driver, and Briggs, *Hebrew and English Lexicon*, p. 171, but perhaps the word is related to the root *g-w-ʿ* meaning to "expire, perish, die," suggesting in some way the Vale of Hinnom.

2. Concerning the problems of identifying the line of the Third Wall, see M. Avi-Yonah, "The Third and Second Walls of Jerusalem," *IEJ* 18 (1968): 98–125; and P. Benoit, "Où en

est la Question du 'Troisième Mur'?" *SH* 1 (1976): 111–126.

3. ii. 219 (Agrippa began the building of the wall but died at Caesarea before its completion); v. 151–52 (Agrippa desisted after merely laying the foundations, because he feared that Emperor Claudius would suspect him of subversion); xix. 326 (Agrippa fortified the ramparts of Jerusalem by increasing their height and width, but he stopped when Claudius transferred him to another place).

CHAPTER 5

1. Isa. 14:31; Jer. 1:14; 4:6; 6:22; 10:22; 16:15; 25:9; Ezek. 26:7; etc.

2. The translation is taken from K. Kenyon, *Jerusalem*, p. 70. See also *ANET*, p. 321 and *Inscriptions Reveal*, No. 75, pp. 82 (Hebrew) and 40 (English). For the history and the description of the tunnel see K. Baedeker, *Palestine and Syria*, pp. 23, 97–98.

3. Cf. K. Baedeker, *Palestine and Syria*, p. 97.

4. See Neh. 3:15 in contradistinction to the steps leading down from the City of David. These should be identified with the steps at the southern tip of Ophel, which are still discernible in the rocky ascent at this point.

Reservoirs

1. Lev. 23:33–44; Deut. 16:13–15. H. Schauss, *The Jewish Festivals: History and Observance* (New York: Schocken, 1974); Y. Vainstein, *The Cycle of the Jewish Year: A Study of the Festivals and of Selections from the Liturgy* (Jerusalem: Haomanim, 1971).

2. F. J. Bliss and A. C. Dickie, *Excavations at Jerusalem 1894–1897*, pp. 178–210.

3. ii. 340; v. 140, 252, 410, 505; vi. 363, 401.

4. *BJ* vi. 358–362 (the Jews rushed up to loot the palace in the Upper City); 374–408 (but the Romans finally captured it and the rebels).

5. P. Benoit, "L'Antonia d'Hérode le Grand et le Forum Oriental d'Aelia Capitolina," *HTR* 64 (1971): 135–167; see especially 145–47.

6. For the various meanings of *strouthíon*, the diminutive of *strouthós*, see L&S, p. 1655.

7. Jgs. 2:13; 10:6; 1 Sam. 7:3, 4; 12:10; 31:10; 1 Kgs. 11:5, 33; 2 Kgs. 23:13.

8. J. Wilkinson, *PEQ* 106 (1974): 39–45. The reservoirs in the northeastern corner of the city could have been built much earlier, but it seems that Birket Israïn along with the entire water system in this area was not completed until the early part of Herod the Great's reign, sometime between 18 and 10 B.C.

9. Private discussion with P. Benoit.

10. See K. Baedeker, *Palestine and Syria*, p. 53.

11. J. L. McKenzie, *Dictionary of the Bible*, p. 92; G. Cornfeld, *Archaeology of the Bible: Book by Book*, pp. 289–290.

12. Early manuscript evidence seems to prefer this name. B. M. Metzger, *et al.*, *Textual Commentary on the Greek New Testament*, pp. 207–8.

Spring Gihon

13. See the articles in *BTS* 86 (1966), and the small guide to the site, *Jérusalem, Sainte-Anne* in French and English, pp. 2–5 and 50–52.

14. Cf. A. Pelletier, S.J., *Lettre d'Aristée à Philocrate, Introduction, Texte Critique, Traduction et Notes, etc.* (Paris: Éditions du Cerf, 1962), Nos. 89–90, pp. 147–48.

15. Because of the decorative crosses found in the mosaic floor, some authorities date the construction to sometime before A.D. 427, since it was in that year that Emperor Theodosius II issued an edict forbidding the use of this sacred symbol in a pavement. Some scholars, however, disagree.

16. R. T. O'Callaghan, S.J., "Madaba (Carte de), Études des Légendes," *Dictionnaire de la Bible, Supplément* 5: 627–704, particularly 660–61. O'Callaghan is followed by M. Avi-Yonah, *The Madaba Mosaic Map* (Jerusalem: IES, 1954), p. 58. For an earlier study of the map, see H. Leclerq in *Dictionnaire d'Archéologie Chrétienne et de Liturgie* (Paris: Librairie Letouzey) 10 (1931): 806–885, especially 847–49. For a more recent study, see V. R. Gold, "The Mosaic Map of Madeba," in E. F. Campbell and D. N. Freedman, eds., *Biblical Archaeologist Reader* 3: 366–389, especially 387. The church was destroyed by Chosroes but restored by Modestus. The present Church of St. Anne dates back to the Crusader period of the twelfth and thirteenth centuries. Cf. E. Hoade, O.F.M., *Guide to the Holy Land*, 8th ed. (Jerusalem: Franciscan, 1976), pp. 57–59, 250–57, for a good historical conspectus of the Crusader church on this site.

17. Cf. *BTS* 86 (1966): 6 and note 3, citing L.-H. Vincent, *RB* 15 (1908): 527.

18. The discovery of an Asclepios temple at Saqqarah south of Cairo was made by the British Egyptologist Prof. W. Emery. In this structure he found a statue of Imhotep, the ancient Egyptian divinity of medicine and architecture. This deified sage was adviser to King Zoser of the Third Dynasty (*ca.* 2800 B.C.), the builder of the famous Step Pyramid at Saqqarah. Imhotep, whom the Greeks called *Imoúthēs*, is to be equated with Asclepios (Joannes Stobaeus [A.D. 5] *Eclogue* i. 485; see also i. 41, 44). Emery's other discoveries here include papyri written in demotic, the popular script of ancient Egypt, and Aramaic. Like Asclepios in the Greek and Roman worlds, the cult of Imhotep was very popular in Egypt: temples dedicated to him were also found in Upper Egypt at Karnak, Deir el-Madina and Deir el-Bahri, as well as on the island of Philae near Aswan, where Ptolemy V Epiphanes (203–181 B.C.) built a temple in his honor.

19. Some authorities dispute as to whether the two portions of this "shrine" fit together. However, upon close exam-

ination we believe that they do belong to each other, thus forming a single votive offering to Asclepios. (It is unfortunate that archaeological discoveries have not as yet uncovered the missing piece or pieces.)

20. On the two *demosía* built by Hadrian in Jerusalem, see E. Hoade, *Guide to the Holy Land*, p. 259.

21. Cf. *Damascii Vitae Isidori Reliquiae*, ed. C. Zintzen (Hildesheim: G. Olms, 1967); cf. *Frag.* No. 348; *Epitoma Photiana* 302, 4, 11, p. 283.

22. M. Astour, *Hellenosemitica: An Ethnic and Cultural Study in West Semitic Impact on Mycenaean Greece* (Leiden: Brill, 1967), pp. 236–39. However, we suggest that the name *Shadrapha* or *Shedrapha* can also be construed in a wider sense. Rather than translating it as the personal name of the divinity, it can also be interpreted as a general appellative or title of the god of medicine, meaning "the one who heals" or simply "he who heals (cures)," from the Semitic (Hebrew and Aramaic) *sh(e)*, "he"; *d(i)*, relative "who"; *r-p(h)-'*, "heal (cure)." It would be of special interest, perhaps, if Astour could also discover a phonetical or etymological relationship between *Shedrapha* and *Asclepios*. The linguistic transition from one consonant to another can be accounted for in all cases except in the case of the middle dental *d* becoming a smooth palatal *k*. Thus, sibilant (or spirant) *sh* = *s*; liquid *r* = liquid *l*; rough labial *ph* = smooth labial *p*. The Semitic glottal stop (*aleph*) acquires the Indo-European (Greek and/or Latin) declension ending *(i)os/(i)us*, which is common. (Linear-B Greek, for instance, shows this to be true in the case of the development of the Greek language. Linear-B nouns ending in *o* receive a final *s*. See J. Chadwick, "The Prehistory of the Greek Language" in I. E. Edwards *et al.*, *The Cambridge Ancient History*, 3rd ed. [Cambridge: Cambridge University, 1964], 2: 5–8; and L. R. Palmer, *The Interpretation of Mycenaean Greek Texts* [New York: Oxford, 1963], pp. 36–46.) According to M. Da-

hood, S.J., of the Pontifical Biblical Institute in Rome, there is only one instance where a middle dental *d* becomes a middle palatal *g* between Biblical Hebrew and Ugaritic. The word for a camel's hump, which occurs as a hapax legomenon in the Old Testament (Isa. 30:16) is the feminine *dabesheth*, which in Ugaritic appears as *g-b-t-t* (*t* = *sh*, *t* = feminine *th*).

23. *Ant.* xi. 329–339. See J. Gray, *A History of Jerusalem* (New York: Praeger, 1969), note on p. 123 and the chronological table on p. 312.

24. For the celebration of the festival of Hanukkah see H. Schauss, *The Jewish Festivals: History and Observance* (New York: Shocken, 1974), pp. 208–236; and Y. Vainstein, *The Cycle of the Jewish Year: A Study of the Festivals and of Selections from the Liturgy* (Jerusalem: Haomanim, 1971), pp. 129–131.

25. For example, see the plans in the guides to the site: E. Hoade, *Holy Land*, p. 258; *Ste. Anne*, p. 3; D. Auscher *et al.*, *Itinéraires Bibliques* (Paris: Éditions du Cerf, 1974), p. 201. The site of the Asclepieion is indicated in *BTS* 86 (1966): 7, which shows the relationship between the twin pools and the excavated section of the shrine.

Aqueducts

1. See L. H. Feldman, *Josephus*, LCL, (Cambridge: Harvard, 1965) 9:47, note c. Josephus here gives the length as 200 stadia.

2. Thus, J. Gray, *Jerusalem*, p. 175. But see Mishnah *Nedarim* i. 2–4; also *BJ* ii. 175; compare *Contra Apionem* i. 167; see *Ant.* iv. 73; Matt. 27:5–7.

3. See P. Germer-Durand, *Echos d'Orient* 4 (1900–1901): 9–11; 5 (1901–1902): 139–141.

4. Cf. F.-M. Abel, "Chronique," *RB* 33 (1926): 284–85.

5. *BTS* 86 (1966): 12; J. Wilkinson, *PEQ* 106 (1974): 45–46.

CHAPTER 6

1. *BJ* v. 238–247, on the Antonia; v. 176–183, concerning the palace. Both palace-fortresses are mentioned in *Ant.* xv. 292.

Fortress Antonia

1. There is scholarly disagreement concerning the origin of Araunah's name. In 1 Chr. 21:14–30 it appears as Ornan (*'rnn*). Given the biblical text of 2 Samuel, the Kethib (*'rnyh*), and the Qere (*'rwnh*), J. L. McKenzie explains it as a possible Hittite name (*Dictionary*, p. 51; see also H. B. Rosen, "Arawna—Nom Hittite?" *VT* 5 [1955]: 318–320). E. A. Speiser believes that the Kethib (*h'wrnh*; Qere *h'rwnh*) in 2 Sam. 24:16 is Hurrian and should not be translated as a personal name, Araunah, but rather as an ordinary Hurrian noun or title, *iwirne*, signifying a "ruler" or "chieftain" ("Introduction to Hurrian," *AASOR* 20 (1940–41): 98–99; see also W. Feiler, "Hurritische Namen im Alten Testament," *ZA* 45 (1939): 222–25).

2. For the explicative *waw* see E. Kautzsch, ed., *Gesenius'*

Fortress Jerusalem

Hebrew Grammar, rev. A. E. Cowley, 2nd ed. (London: Oxford, 1962), § 154, n. 1(b), p. 484. On the waw adaequationis see § 161, note 1, p. 499.

3. K. Kenyon, *Jerusalem*, pp. 14–15; it was known by Josephus as *Ophlas*; cf. *BJ* ii. 448; v. 145, 254; vi. 354.

4. K. Kenyon, *ibid.*, p. 50; cf. p. 49.

5. For example, see *ml'* in Koehler and Baumgartner, *Lexicon*, p. 552, and *mlw'* on p. 556. Other explanations are offered by J. Simons, S.J., *Jerusalem in the Old Testament: Researches and Theories* (Leiden: Brill, 1954), pp. 131–157; see especially p. 132: "from Millo and inwards," which we interpret to indicate the area south of the natural platform in the northwest corner of the Haram; p. 133: "it might be a solid tower... which had huge substructures of solid stone," which we identify with the same rocky terrace; *ibid.*, n. 1. Simons offers the Assyrian *milu* in the same sense as we interpret it in relation to the northwestern elevation on which the Omariyyeh School stands today; p. 133: the reference to the LXX regarding the translation of *mlw'* into Greek *akra* (2 Sam. 5:9; 1 Kgs. 9:15 [LXX^A]: *tén Melō kaí tén ákran*, which *kaí* we construe as expletive of *Melō*; 1 Kgs. 10:22 [LXX^B] contains

only *ákra* for Hebrew *mlw'*; 1 Kgs. 11:27). The phrase *byt mlw'* in 2 Kgs. 12:21 can possibly be interpreted to mean the "terrace house" or the house on the terrace. Furthermore, the Hebrew verb *bnh* does not only mean to "build" or "rebuild," but can also denote "build up"; so it is in this sense that Solomon built (up) his palace on the preexisting platform that serves as David's house (watch post) overlooking the Israelite settlement around the altar of Yahweh on the upper part (Mt. Moriah) of the Ophel spur.

6. 2 Sam. 5:9; 1 Kgs. 9:15, 27; 2 Kgs. 12:21; 1 Chr. 11:8; 2 Chr. 32:5.

7. Koehler and Baumgartner, *Lexicon;* see above, note 5.

8. According to Brown, Driver, and Briggs, Hebrew *byrh* ("a castle or palace") is late and probably a loanword (Assyrian *bîrtu,* "fortress"; Persian *bâru;* Sanskrit *bura, bari*); *Lexicon,* p. 108. According to Liddell and Scott, however, Greek *báris* was originally an Egyptian word, which first identified a type of flat-bottomed boat and later came to mean a "large house" or "tower"; L&S, p. 307. Cf. A. Gardiner, *Egyptian Grammar,* 3rd ed. (New York: Oxford, 1964), p. 75; see also pp. 614–15, 620. Thus "Pharaoh" (*pr,* "house," and '3', "large").

9. Y. Tsafrir has written an interesting article on "The Location of the Seleucid Akra in Jerusalem," *RB* 82 (1975): 501–521, but we find his hypothetical and "largely theoretical" (p. 510) proposal of the location of the Seleucid *akra* to the southeast of the Temple quite unconvincing. He presents an argument that is largely a priori and that contains a number of non sequitur statements as, for example, n. 6 in relation to the text on p. 503, his conclusion stated on p. 510, and a number of other statements that cannot be substantiated either by a careful reading of the sources or a thorough examination of the site itself, especially since archaeological excavations have not been made in the area of the Haram esh-Sharif.

10. Sr. M. Aline, *La Forteresse Antonia à Jérusalem et la Question du Prétoire* (Jerusalem: Franciscan, 1956); L.-H. Vincent and A.-M. Steve, *Jérusalem de l'Ancien Testament 1:* 193–221; M. Avi-Yonah, ed., *Encyclopedia of Archaeological Excavations in the Holy Land 2* (1976): 607; *The Holy Land* (Grand Rapids: Baker, 1976), pp. 53–54, 80, 89, 273.

11. As, for example, J. Comay, *The Temple of Jerusalem* (New York: Holt, Rinehart & Winston, 1975); and M. F. Unger, *Archaeology and the New Testament* (Grand Rapids: Zondervan, 1962).

12. See pp. 94–95 above.

13. Cf. B. Bagatti, O.F.M., "Resti romani nell'area della Flagellazione in Gerusalemme," *SBFLA* 8 (1957–58): 309–352.

14. For the siege and fall of Jerusalem, see v. 468–vi. 1–434; vi. 435–443 is a summary of the previous captures of the Holy City.

15. See i. 54; v. 304, 356; vi. 169.

16. See M. Aline, *La Forteresse, passim,* and the small tourist guide, *Antonia Lithostrotos* (Jerusalem: Franciscan, 1962).

17. The game of *basilicus* is mentioned by the Latin comedian T. Maccius Plautus (184 B.C.) in his play *Curculio* ii. 3. 80.

18. See above p. 76, and note 4.

19. Cf. *BJ* vii. 280–85 on Masada.

20. Cf. *Ant.* ii. 231, where it is translated "stature" with reference to Moses' height.

21. W. S. Caldecott, *Herod's Temple: Its New Testament Associations and Its Actual Structure* (Philadelphia: Union, 1914). Another unfounded localization for the Antonia is that of J. Fergusson, *The Temples of the Jews and the Other Buildings in the Haram Area at Jerusalem* (London: J. Murray, 1878), p. 173.

22. "La posizione del tempio erodiano di Gerusalemme," *Biblica* 46 (1965): 431.

23. For example, P. Benoit, *HTR* 64 (1971): 158–166; "The Archaeological Reconstruction of the Antonia Fortress," *JR,* pp. 87–89; also cited in B. Mazar, *Mountain of the Lord,* p. 36; cf. p. 80. According to L.-H. Vincent, Herodian masonry was also supposedly detected in the northeastern corner of the Haram; cf. *Jérusalem, Pl. 2,* and check his explanation regarding the difficulty in precisely identifying the material "excavated" at the northeast corner of the Islamic enclosure, p. 532. J. Simons states that "the south wall of this pool [*birket israïn*] has nothing in common with the massive, old masonry of the Haram walls, though . . . this wall may be only a facing to the Haram wall proper"; *Jerusalem in the Old Testament,* p. 374. However, "it is theoretically possible, that such a wall is hidden behind the plastered masonry on the southern side of *birket israïn,* but this is not probable, because if it existed the plaster would more probably have been applied to that ancient wall itself"; p. 413. This wall is post-Herodian, as first proposed by Simons himself; cf. p. 413, note 2. The only conclusion, for lack of archaeological evidence at the northeast corner of the Haram, is that it is possible but not probable that the Herodian wall extended as far north as the Pool of Israel, then turned westwards to join the Antonia complex. If such a wall extended up to this point, we suggest that it would have surrounded the entire acropolis on which the Royal Basilica (*hanuyoth*), the Porch of Solomon, the Temple, and the Antonia stood; but we cannot be certain of the exact use of the open northeastern section of the enclosure, especially since it was near the sheep market.

24. That is, practically all those who would hold that the four towers of the Antonia extended beyond the northern enclosure of the present Haram esh-Sharif. Apparently, this was the common view towards the end of the last century, as explained by K. Baedeker, *Palestine,* p. 76; E. Hoade still maintains this identification (*Holy Land,* p. 261), whence we also learn the name of the former mosque.

25. For the use of the Greek preposition *prós* with the accusative, see L&S; H. W. Smyth, *Greek Grammar* (Cambridge: Harvard, 1973), p. 385, No. 1696. 3. a.

26. For the use of *anábasis,* cf. Herodotus ii. 125; Aristotle *Oeconomica* 1347ᵃ; Dio Cassius lxv. 21; for *katábasis,* cf. Herodotus i. 186; vii. 223; Isocrates x. 20; Strabo viii. 6, 12 (cf. Herodotus ii. 122).

27. *Eumenides* 919; see IG 1². 93. 17.

28. During a private interview our colleague Fr. B.-G. Pixner, O.S.B., disclosed to us his hypothesis ("conviction") that the location of Pilate's Praetorium should be much farther to the east, down the Zion slope at or near the site of the Byzantine church of St. Sophia. See his article, "Noch einmal das Prätorium Versuch einer neuen Lösung," *ZDPV* 95 (1979):

24-43. In fact, as is evident from the early pilgrim accounts of Theodosius (A.D. 530), the *Breviarius de Hierosolyma* (530), Anonymus Placentinus (570), (St. Sophronius, Patriarch of Jerusalem [635]), the *Kalendarium Ecclesiae Hierosolymitanae* of the seventh and eighth centuries (for September 21), the site of Jesus' condemnation took place in Pilate's Praetorium located in the Tyropoeon Valley. For these texts see P. Donatus Baldi, O.F.M., *Enchiridion Locorum Sanctorum: Documenta S. Evangelii Loca Respicientia*, 2nd ed. (Jerusalem: Franciscan, 1955), Nos. 889-893, pp. 584-85. Cf. B. Bagatti, O.F.M., "La Tradizione della Chiesa di Gerusalemme sul Pretorio," *RivB* 21 (1973): 429-433.

29. Cf. D. Baldi, *Enchiridion*, Nos. 900-9, pp. 587-591. The footnote on p. 587 is worthy of being quoted in the original: "Statim post adventum Cruciferorum situs praetorii apud S. Sion monstrabatur... Post medium saec. XII Praetorium monstratum fuit in viciniis Antoniae." Translated it reads: "Immediately after the arrival of the Crusaders, the Praetorium was indicated on Mt. Sion.... After the middle of the twelfth century the Praetorium was pointed out in the vicinity of Antonia."

Herod's Palace and Pilate's Praetorium

1. Cf. D. Baldi, *Enchiridion*, especially Nos. 892 (St. Sophronius, Patriarch of Jerusalem, A.D. 635), 894 (an Armenian description of the Holy Places in the seventh century), 895-96 (Epiphanius Monachus, ninth century), 897-98 (Anonymus I, 1098), 901 (*De situ urbis Jerusalem*, 1130), 903 (Anonymus VII, 1145), 904 (Theodoricus, 1172).

2. *Ibid.*, Nos. 886, 889, 891, 893. See also p. 101, notes 28-29 above.

3. But see R. North, S.J., *Stratigraphia Geobiblica: Biblical Near East Archaeology and Geography*, 3rd ed. (Rome: 1970), p. 270c. See especially the reference to J. Simons, *Jerusalem in the Old Testament*, p. 38 and notes 1-3.

4. Popular tradition from earliest times until today locates David's tomb on Mt. Zion. Scholars seriously question this identification.

5. See M. Broshi, *IEJ* 24 (1974): 21-26; see also *JR*, especially pp. 52-53, 57.

6. G. Dalman, *Jerusalem und sein Gelände* (Gütersloh: C. Bertelsmann, 1930), pp. 86, 264-65; "Zion, die Burg Jerusalem," *PJB* 11 (1918): 39-84. Dalman is perhaps following an earlier monograph by F. Speiss, *Das Jerusalem des Josephus: Ein Beitrage zur Topographie der heiligen Stadt* (Berlin: 1881), p. 23.

7. See "Pretoire, Lithostroton et Gabbatha," *RB* 59 (1952): 531-550; *HTR* 64 (1971): 135-167. According to Benoit, the trial and condemnation of Jesus took place in the area of the present citadel and Christ's "way of the cross" followed the present line of David Street eastwards as far as Suq el-'Attarin. We have obtained this information from Benoit's lecture at the Ecumenical Institute for Advanced Theological Research at Tantur, Jerusalem, followed by a walk through the Old City from the Citadel towards the Church of the Holy Sepulchre, on February 6, 1975. In view of our study of both the Citadel and the more probable line of the Via Crucis,

Benoit's identifications are in need of serious modifications.

8. This evidence has been beautifully summarized in *JR*, especially pp. 54-56, 57-59.

9. More likely, Josephus is describing the exquisite Herodian masonry of pure white (cenomanian or turonian) limestone, rather than genuine marble, especially since the Holy Land has no marble quarries, and to import so large an amount of the expensive stone would have been doubly costly.

10. G. A. Smith, *History of Jerusalem. The Topography, Economics and History of Jerusalem from the Earliest Times to A.D. 70* (1907; reprint ed. New York: Ktav, 1970) 1: 55.

11. C. N. Johns, "Recent Excavations at the Citadel," *PEQ* 72 (1940): 53; "The Citadel, Jerusalem," *QDAP* 14 (1950): 121-190; see J. Simons, *Jerusalem in the Old Testament*, p. 269 and notes 1-2 for observations on Johns' conclusions. Cf. R. Amiran and A. Eitan on Johns' wall, "Excavations in the Courtyard of the Citadel, Jerusalem, 1968-1969 (Preliminary Report)," *IEJ* 20 (1970): 10-11.

12. Cf. *JR*, pp. 55-56.

13. J. Wilkinson, "The Streets of Jerusalem," *Levant* 7 (1975): 118-136, but especially p. 122 and the pertinent grid figures 7-8, 10-12.

14. N. Avigad casts much light on the lifestyle of the Jews in this quarter of Herodian Jerusalem; *IEJ* 20 (1970): 1-8, 129-140; 22 (1972): 193-200; see also M. Avi-Yonah, *Encyclopedia of Archaeological Excavations in the Holy Land* 2 (1976): 599-606; and N. Avigad, "Excavations in the Jewish Quarter of the Old City, 1969-1970," *JR*, pp. 44-51.

15. Greek *praitórion* is technically defined as a "Latinism," the Latin noun *praetorium* transliterated directly into Greek. Originally, Latin *praetorium* defined the "tent" or "headquarters" of the *praetor* or general in a Roman camp (Livy x. 33; Julius Caesar *Bellum Civile* i. 76). By extension it could also point to a "war council" held in the tent (Livy xxx. 5; xxviii. 5). Secondly, it indicated the official "residence" of a provincial governor in a subjugated province, whether his title was *praetor*, *proconsul*, general, or prince (Cicero *Actio in Verrem* ii. 4. 28 § 65; ii. 5. 35 § 92; cf. Matt. 27:27). In the New Testament period and afterwards the *praitórion* or *praetorium* designated either a "palace" (Juvenal x. 161; cf. Acts 23:35, though in Phil. 1:13 the term referred more specifically to the "imperial household" or even better to the "praetorian guard" rather than the "praetorian camp or barracks"), or a magnificent villa or building (Suetonius *Augustus* 72; *Caligula* 37; *Tiberius* 39). Tacitus calls it the imperial body guard, *praefectus praetorii* (*Historia* i. 19; iv. 26; see also Pliny vii. 20. 19 § 82, and Suetonius *Nero* 9). For its meaning "the praetorian guard" in the papyri, see *OGI*, 707 (from Tyre, second century A.D.) and *IG*, 14. 911, etc.). The western (Latin or grecized) *praitórion* translates the oriental (Greek) *stratégion* or *stratēgeíon*, which Sophocles uses in the sense of "general's tent" (*Ajax* 721); at Athens it was the place where the *stratēgioi* conducted their meetings (Aeschines ii. 85; iii. 147). In Egypt it defined the "business office" of the *stratēgós* (P. Petr. 2, p. 26, third century A.D.). For its use in the sense of Latin *praetorium*, cf. Philo *Belopoeica* 102. 5; Polybius 31. 1, and Dionysius of Halicarnassus *Antiquitates Romanae* v. 28; ix. 6. In the New Testament *praitórion* is always employed to identify the (former) palace (*aylé*) or the official residence of the pro-

curator, as, for instance, in Mark 15:16 (where the Evangelist clearly explains the term) and Acts 23:35. This is also the meaning assigned in the Johannine account of Jesus' public trial and condemnation (John 18–19 *passim*); cf. parallels of this usage in the papyri: *BGU* i. 288[14] (A.D. 138–161); P. Oxy iii. 471[110] (second century A.D.); *BGU* i. 21[1.16] (A.D. 340); P. Oxy ix. 1190[16] (A.D. 347), and viii. 1116[2] (A.D. 363). It is of special interest to know that Greek *aylḗ* originally meant a "farmyard," or "sheepfold" (as also in John 10:1, 16), a "courtyard" or an uncovered place around the house enclosed by a wall or one within the house, and finally a "(royal) court" or "palace." It is in this last sense that Mark uses the word: *ésō tḗs aylḗs, hó estin praitórion* (15:16). For these and other sources see L&S; J. H. Moulton and G. Milligan, *The Vocabulary of the Greek New Testament* (Grand Rapids: Eerdmans, 1949); W. Bauer, *A Greek-English Lexicon of the New Testament,* trans. and rev. W. F. Ardnt, F. W. Gingrich, and F. W. Danker (2nd ed., Chicago: University of Chicago, 1979); G. W. H. Lampe, *Patristic Greek Lexicon* (London: Oxford, 1968); C. T. Lewis and C. Short, *Latin Dictionary* (1879; reprint ed., London: Oxford, 1962). See also P. Benoit, *RB* 59 (1952): 531–550.

16. The precise nature of ritual defilement or impurity which the Jews would have incurred in this case cannot be established. Perhaps it is related to either the lesser degrees of impurity mentioned in Lev. 11:24–25, 27, or to the greater in 12:2. In any event, cultic terminology is involved here. For more thorough studies see R. E. Brown, S.S., *The Gospel According to John* (Anchor Bible; Garden City, N.Y.: Doubleday, 1970) 2: 845–46; E. Schürer, *Geschichte des jüdischen Volkes im Zeitalter Jesu Christi,* 4th ed. (1905) 1.1: 54, 92; G. Kittel, *Theological Dictionary of the New Testament,* trans. G. W. Bromiley (Grand Rapids: Eerdmans, 1968) 4: 644–47; see also *IDB* 1: 644–48; "Purity and Impurity," *Encyclopaedia Judaica* 13: 1405–1414. Note the parallel between John 18:28 and 1 Macc. 1:63.

17. For the most part Roman trials were public, held in public squares or in a basilica. Cf. A. N. Sherwin-White, *Roman Society and Roman Law in the New Testament* (New York: Oxford, 1963), pp. 24–47. Quoting T. Mommsen from *Zeitschrift für die neutestamentliche Wissenschaft* 3 (1902): 24, P. Benoit explains why Jesus' trial was also public: *RB* 59 (1952): 535. See also *BJ* ii. 172; *Ant.* xviii. 57. For a most recent study of Jesus' trial and condemnation see E. Bammel, ed., *The Trial of Jesus,* C. F. D. Moule Festschrift, *Studies in Biblical Theology* 13 (Naperville, Ill.: Allenson, 1970), especially pp. 78–90.

18. So P. Benoit. See p. 102, note 7 above.

19. Cf. *BJ*, ii. 169–171; *Ant.* xviii. 55–59.

20. Gessius Florus ruled as procurator A.D. 64–66. His ruthless rule over Judaea is recorded by Josephus; *BJ* ii. 277–79, 287–292, 293–343, but especially 301–332.

21. For scourging as a prelude to crucifixion see A. N. Sherwin-White, *Roman Society and Roman Law in the New Testament,* p. 27; W. J. MacDonald, ed., *New Catholic Encyclopedia* 5:955–56; J. L. McKenzie, *Dictionary,* p. 778; N. G. L. Hammond and H. H. Scullard, eds., *The Oxford Classical Dictionary,* 2nd ed. (New York: Oxford, 1970), p. 300. See also articles by McKenzie and B. Vawter in *JBC,* p. 112, No. 196, and p. 460, No. 164, for the exegesis of the passages related to the scourging of Jesus.

22. *Ibid.* Sometimes the beating was so horrible, particularly in the case of slaves, that the victim expired after having been flogged.

23. Mainly the Franciscan school and Israeli scholars who maintain that the material below the Convent of the Sisters of Sion belongs to the Antonia continue the post-Crusader tradition regarding the direction and lines of the Via Dolorosa. P. Benoit, following such German scholars as F. Speiss and G. Dalman (though he does not mention them), is the main proponent of this theory. He is followed by M. Broshi and others of the Israeli school. Our study shows that a new direction and line is much more convincing.

24. J. Wilkinson, *Levant* 7 (1975): Figs. 7–8.

CHAPTER 7

1. Y. Yadin, ed., *Megillath Hammiqdash* (Jerusalem: IES, Hebrew University Institute of Archaeology, and Shrine of the Book, 1977) 1:145–214, especially pp. 153, 159, 195; *BA* 30 (1967): 167.

2. *PG* 92, p. 613.

3. E.g., D. Baldi, *Enchiridion,* Nos. 675–681, pp. 444–454; Z. Vilnay, *The Holy Land in Old Prints and Maps* (Jerusalem: R. Mass, 1965), pp. 86–89; but see also the plans and illustrations of Jerusalem in general, pp. 42–87. The oldest pictorial map of Jerusalem is the fourth-century mosaic in the apse of the Church of St. Pudentiana in Rome, though it is not clear whether the Jerusalem temple can be identified among the structures depicted. For an explanation of the history of the church and the mosaic, see R. U. Montini, *Santa Pudenziana* (Proprietà Letteraria Riservata), especially pp. 69–81. The famous mosaic Madaba Map describes the Jerusalem of the sixth century A.D.

4. It would be quite impossible to list all of the writers, scholarly and popular, on the Jerusalem temple. Abundant

Temple Site

bibliographies exist in such works as: J. Simons, *Jerusalem in the Old Testament,* pp. 505–7; E. K. Vogel, "Bibliography of Holy Land Sites," *Hebrew Union College Annual* 42 (1971): 47–48; J. M. Landay, *Dome of the Rock: Three Faiths of Jerusalem* (New York: Newsweek, 1972), p. 168; J. Comay, *The Temple of Jerusalem,* pp. 267–68; M. Avi-Yonah, ed., *Encyclopedia of Archaeological Excavations in the Holy Land* 2: 580, 591, 597, 627. We have publicly defended our thesis that the Jerusalem temple area was square. R. M. Mackowski, S.J., "Jerusalem 30 A.D.—A New Map," *Report of the Third Archaeological Conference* (Jerusalem, 1975).

5. We learned this from Prof. Yadin during public lectures and private discussions shortly after his having read and studied the recently discovered Temple Scroll.

6. K. Kenyon, *Jerusalem,* pp. 54–55. Kenyon continues, "Solomon's Temple lasted down to the time of the Exile in Babylon that followed the capture of the city by Nebuchadnezzar in 586 B.C. Though most of the important inhabitants were carried away to Babylon, the city was not deserted, and

the exiles even sent offerings to the ruined temple. When the first exiles were allowed by the Persian conquerors of Babylon to return *ca.* 538 B.C., their immediate concern was the rebuilding of the Temple, concerning the site of which no doubt could have risen in this interval. The postexilic temple suffered damage and destruction at intervals in the next five hundred years, but never obliteration, and it was to render this postexilic temple more worthy and glorious that Herod the Great built his temple, beginning in *ca.* 20 B.C. Much of Herod's work can still be traced in the great platform that supports the Dome of the Rock, so from the present structure back to Solomon there is no real break."

7. For a thorough study of the Crusader period in Jerusalem, see J. Prawer, *The Latin Kingdom of Jerusalem.* See also S. Runciman, *A History of the Crusades,* 3 vols. (Baltimore: Pelican, 1971).

8. Nos. 675–79, pp. 444–47.

9. For a brief but eloquent history of this period see A. Eban, *My People: The Story of the Jews* (New York: Behrman House, 1968), ch. 9, "The Rise of Christianity," pp. 100–7; ch. 10, "New Centers of Diaspora," pp. 108–123; ch. 11, "The Age of Islam," pp. 124–160.

10. This tradition is beautifully expressed in J. M. Landay, *Dome of the Rock: Three Faiths of Jerusalem,* particularly ch. 1, 3–7. See also the summary of A. el-Aref, *A Brief Guide to the Dome of the Rock and Haram al-Sharif* (Jerusalem: Supreme Awqaf Council, 1966), pp. 1–98.

11. See p. 99, note 23 above.

12. Cf. F. J. Hollis, *The Archaeology of Herod's Temple* (London: Dent, 1934), pp. 118–122. See also J. Simons' study of the various measurements of the Haram, *Jerusalem in the Old Testament,* pp. 344–48; and B. Bagatti, *Biblica* 46 (1965): 430–35. See also C. Warren, *Underground Jerusalem: An Account of the Principal Difficulties Encountered in Its Exploration and the Results Obtained* (London: 1876), p. 80, where he gives the following measurements of the Haram walls: "The outer courts of Herod are defined by the east, west, and south walls of the present Noble Sanctuary, and by the northern edge of the raised platform of the Dome of the Rock. These walls, measuring respectively 1090, 1138, 922, and 997 feet, give an average of 593 cubits, a very close approximation to the 600 cubits which I suppose to have been the dimension intended by Josephus."

13. N. Avigad, "The Architecture of Jerusalem in the Second Temple Period," *JR,* pp. 14–17.

14. However, during a private discussion in November 1976, we received the impression that perhaps Benoit was modifying his position.

15. B. Mazar, *The Excavations in the Old City of Jerusalem: Preliminary Report of the First Season, 1968* (Jerusalem: IES, 1969), pp. 2–3, see Fig. 1; *Mountain of the Lord,* pp. 119–120 (with his temple plan), and compare this plan with his "conjectural plan" of the Solomonic temple, p. 97; M. Avi-Yonah, "Jerusalem of the Second Temple Period," *JR,* pp. 9–13, with his plan on p. 10; K. Kenyon, *Jerusalem,* Figs. 6, p. 56; 11, p. 109; 14, p. 144; J. Wilkinson, *PEQ* 108 (1974), follows the above-mentioned plans, for which see especially Figs. 5, p. 40; 6, p. 41; *Levant* 7 (1975): Figs. 4–6; J. Comay, *The Temple of Jerusalem,* for the plans on pp. 151, 214.

16. B. Bagatti, *Biblica* 46 (1965): 428–444; E. Vogt, S.J., "Das Wachstum des alten Stadtgebietes von Jerusalem," *Biblica* 48 (1967): 337–358; "Vom Temple zum Felsendom," *Biblica* 55 (1974): 23–64 and plan.

17. Cf. W. S. Caldecott, *Herod's Temple;* see drawing on p. 119; C. Warren, *Underground Jerusalem;* note plan on p. 98. Our reexamination of the sources in light of the above-mentioned materials convinced us of the square plan of the Temple.

18. Cf. Ezek. 42:16–20 where the identical measurements are stated in connection with the size of the temple area.

19. See p. 62, note 1 above.

20. For religious reasons, the Jews would not have planted trees here (cf. Deut. 16:21), for they were symbolic of the pagan cult of Asherah (Hebrew *'asherah,* "sacred pole," is to be equated with the *maṣṣebah* of Gen. 28:18; Exod. 23:24; 34:13). Moreover, trees required fertilizer to grow and thus would have defiled the consecrated ground (cf. Deut. 23:10–15).

21. Much more Herodian masonry does exist north of this east-west line, north of the Golden Gate on the east, and north of Bab en-Nadhir on the west. Bagatti interprets the entire northern section of the Haram as part of the huge compound of Fortress Antonia, but this is only partially correct (see p. 99 and note 22).

22. Citing Jerome (*In Matt.* 4:24; cf. *PL* 26, 180f.; *Enchiridion,* No. 445) in "Il 'Tempio di Gerusalemme' dal II all' VIII Secolo," *Biblica* 43 (1962): 13–14.

23. M. Avi-Yonah, *Madaba Map,* p. 59, note 79.

24. See above p. 116, note 4; p. 118, and notes 12, 16, and 17.

Porticoes

1. It was supposed to have been built by Solomon (1 Kgs. 6:1–38 [see Acts 7:47]; Josephus *Ant.* xv. 396, 398) and restored and embellished by many of his successors (*Ant.* xv. 402; xx. 220–22).

2. See above, pp. 122–23.

3. Use of the silver Tyrian shekel as a census tax may be a later (postexilic) legislation (Neh. 10:32) for the upkeep of the Jerusalem sanctuary; see Exod. 30:11–16; Lev. 27:25; Num. 3:47; 18:16. Minted coins seem to have been introduced into Palestine probably during the Persian period (1 Chr. 29:7; Ezr. 7:12–20; 8:24–30; cf. Ezr. 2:69; Neh. 7:70–72) when the Jewish exiles were permitted to return from Babylon. See W. J. Fulco, S.J., "Money in Biblical and Early Christian Times," *The Bible Today* 56 (1971): 530–34. Longer discussions appear in *IDB* 3: 423–436; J. D. Douglas, ed., *New Bible Dictionary,* pp. 836–841.

4. B. Gerhardsson has an excellent monograph, *The Tempting of God's Son: Mt. 4:1 and Parallels,* trans. J. Toy (Lund: Gleerup, 1966).

5. See D. Baldi, *Enchiridion,* Nos. 228–237, pp. 200–4; also K. Baedeker, *Palestine and Syria,* pp. 50–51.

6. D. Baldi, *Enchiridion,* No. 228: "lapis angularis magnus." Could this be the huge stone discovered by Israeli archaeologists at the southwestern corner of the Temple Mount (see note 7)? Perhaps the stone fell or was thrown down at a

later period, when the Muslims were restoring the walls and converting the area into the present-day Haram. "... Ubi Salomon palatium habebat." A long tradition, which many scholars still accept, places Solomon's palace either directly opposite the Dome of the Rock or some place to the southwest of it. No. 230: "Et inde [a S. Sophia] venis ad illam pinnam templi... et est ibi basilica in cruce posita." This describes the walk from the church of St. Sophia, situated in the Tyropoeon Valley below the Temple Mount towards a cruciform church on the esplanade, built upon large vaults and substructures. A visit to the el-Aqsa el-Qadimeh (the ancient el-Aqsa Mosque) proves the existence of vast subterranean rooms and supports. These are particularly noticeable in the southeastern corner, above which are built several mosques, one named in honor of Zechariah (see No. 231). No. 231: "où se trouve la qib-lèh... une mosquée souterraine... le mihrab de Meriem ... à Zékéria." This seems to indicate the southeastern corner of the Mahed 'Isa alluded to in this text; but perhaps the "qiblèh, mosquée souterraine" and "Zékéria" could also point to the ancient material in the el-Aqsa el-Qadimeh. No. 234: "in angulo civitatis, est cubiculum (cunabula) Christi." The fact is that the southwestern, not the southeastern, corner has always faced the city. (Was the "cradle of Jesus" thought to be here in the twelfth century?) No. 235: "Juxta idem palatium Salomonis milites templarii habent plurima adjuncta aedificia magna et ampla." The Knights Templars had their monastery (cf. J. Prawer, *The Latin Kingdom of Jerusalem*, p. 171) in the el-Aqsa Mosque on the southwestern part of the temple esplanade.

7. The Hebrew reads: *lbyt htqy' h lhk[ryz?]*: "To the place of the trumpeting...." Cf. *Inscriptions Reveal*, No. 168, p. 165 [Hebrew], p. 76 [English]. See also *JR*, pp. 26-27 (see plate on p. 35), and B. Mazar, *Mountain of the Lord*, p. 138. This huge block of limestone measures 243 cm. long, 104 cm. wide, and 100 cm. high.

8. A magnificent example of opus sectile is the floor of the Curia in the Forum Romanum in Rome. Many Byzantine churches and public, as well as private, buildings contain this type of flooring. Opus sectile was also used in the Renaissance period. The upper church of the Annunciation Basilica in Nazareth displays the same artistry and workmanship.

9. K. Kenyon, *Jerusalem*, p. 188; see index, p. 210.

Temple Gates

1. Huldah was a prophetess who lived in Jerusalem during the reign of Josiah (640-609 B.C.). She was consulted, according to 1 Kgs. 22:14-20; 2 Chr. 34:22-28, concerning the Book of the Law that had been discovered during the restorations on the Temple. She supposedly identified the scrolls as authentic and prophesied disaster for Judah because of its disobedience to the Law.

2. J. Comay, *Temple*, p. 158: "In the Western Wall Josephus refers to four gates and the Mishnah to only one. In fact two have been found. One of them, the Priests' Gate, opened on to the bridge across the Tyropoeon Valley, of which Wilson's Arch is a remnant. The other, Barclay's Gate (named after its American missionary discoverer), is low down near the southwestern corner, just below the stairway leading up to the present Moors' Gate...." Actually, four gates can be identified with a high degree of certainty; the Mishnah (unfortunately, Comay does not cite her source) never refers to this gate as the Priest's. It is explicitly called the Kiphonos (Gate) [*qypwnws*] in *Middoth* i. 3.

3. Plautus *Poenulus* 1298; cf. Aeschylus *Fragm.* 323; Josephus *Ant.* xv. 410.

4. Cf. B. Mazar, *Excavations* (1971), pp. 13-19, especially p. 17, col. 1; Figs. 10, 11a, 11.

5. Cf. R. A. Markus, *Christianity in the Roman World* (New York: Scribner's, 1974), note b, pp. 198-99, namely, that the precise location of the two gates that led to the suburb (*Ant.* xv. 410, LCL) cannot be identified. We disagree; Warren's Gate is Bab el-Mat-hara and Barclay's Gate is that below Bab Harat el-Maghariba.

6. C. Warren and C. R. Conder, *Jerusalem*, pp. 212-15.

7. See above, p. 100.

8. G. Cornfeld, *The Mystery of the Temple Mount* (Jerusalem: Bazak, 1972), p. 38.

9. See p. 118, note 16 above.

10. Mishnah *Middoth* i. 3; *Parah* iii. 6; *Shekalim* iv. 2. The reference is to Lev. 16:1-34, specifically vv. 20-22.

11. See above, pp. 162-66.

12. *Protevangelium* iv. 8. Cf. *The Lost Books of the Bible and the Forgotten Books of Eden* (New York: World, 1948), pp. 24-37.

13. Mishnah *Shekalim* v. 6. Any donor could enter the Chamber of Utensils to deposit his gift.

14. See p. 93, note 9.

15. Cf. also *BJ* vi. 282; *Ant.* xix. 294; Mishnah *Shekalim* iii. 2 (cf. ii. 5); v. 6 (cf. ii. 1); *Middoth* v. 3-4; *Tamid* iii. 3-4 (*Shekalim* v. 4).

16. Mishnah *Shekalim* ii. 1; vi. 1, 5; see Mark 12:41; Luke 21:1; cf. *BJ* v. 200.

17. See also *OGIS* 54[22] (of the second half of the third century B.C.); cf. *gazophylákion*, "a military treasury," in *OGIS* 225[16] (also third century B.C.).

CHAPTER 8

1. M. Broshi, *IEJ* 24 (1974): 21-26; see also *JR*, pp. 52, 57-59.

2. M. Broshi in *JR*, pp. 57-58.

3. B.-G. Pixner, *SH* 1 (1976): 245-275.

4. Cf. 11QPs[a] in J. A. Sanders, *The Psalms Scroll of Qum-*

Upper Room

rân Cave 11, DJD 4 (Oxford: Clarendon, 1965): 43, 85-87; *The Dead Sea Psalms Scroll* (Ithaca, N.Y.: Cornell, 1967), pp. 123-27 and *passim*; "Palestinian Manuscripts 1947-1972," in F. M. Cross and S. Talmon, eds., *Qumran and the History of the Biblical Text* (Cambridge: Harvard, 1976), pp. 401-413, especially p. 410 for an up-to-date bibliography on the psalmlike Apostrophe to Zion; Y. Yadin, ed., *Megillath Hammiqdash* 1:233–35.

5. D. Baldi, *Enchiridion*, Nos. 728–787, pp. 473–531; B.-G. Pixner, *SH* 1: 276–284; J. Wilkinson, "The Streets of Jerusalem," p. 128, and compare the following grids: Figs. 7–8 for the streets leading to the Hagia Sion, and Figs. 9–10 for the contours of Mt. Zion and the remains of the other streets in relation to the grid.

6. Arabic *nebi'* equals Hebrew *nabi'* meaning "prophet," while *Daud*, or *Dahood*, is the Arabic name for David (*Dawid*, probably meaning "beloved"). For an account of the surrender of Jerusalem to Salah ed-Din, see S. Runciman, *History of Crusades*, Vol. 2, *Kingdom of Jerusalem*, pp. 463–68. For the Islamic tradition of the tombs of David and Solomon on Mt. Zion, see H. Z. Hirschberg, "The Tombs of David and Solomon in Moslem Tradition," *Eretz Israel* 3 (1954): 213–220.

7. M. Broshi in *JR*, p. 59; compare his plan with the grids by J. Wilkinson in note 6.

8. Cf. *PG* 43. 259–260; D. Baldi, *Enchiridion*, No. 733, p. 478. The quotation is from Isa. 1:8; Greek *hyperóon*, "upper room," occurs in Acts 1:13; 9:37, 39; 20:8.

9. Cf. the sources quoted by D. Baldi, *Enchiridion*, Nos. 728–732, pp. 473–77.

10. Cf. *PG* 33. 924; D. Baldi, *Enchiridion*, No. 730, p. 475.

11. Cf. *PG* 22. 43; D. Baldi, *Enchiridion*, No. 728, p. 474.

12. The Syrian Orthodox community in Jerusalem claims that their church on St. Mark's Street in the Old City stands on the site of St. Mark's house, the Upper Room, mentioned in Acts 12:12, and that a number of other biblical events took place at this site. But the tradition is of very recent vintage, based on the 1940 discovery of a sixth-century Syriac inscription next to the door on the west wall of the structure. "This is the house of Mary, mother of John, called Mark. Proclaimed a church by the holy apostles under the name of Virgin Mary, mother of God, after the ascension of our Lord Jesus Christ into heaven. Renewed after the destruction of Jerusalem by Titus in the year 73 A.D." The provenance of this inscription cannot as yet be ascertained. The monks of St. Mark's Convent also hold that they possess a picture of Our Lady and Jesus, "painted [or "believed to have been painted"] by St. Luke himself."

13. Archaeologists have uncovered one of the earliest surviving examples of Christian painting in an above-ground building, a baptistery in a house converted into a church. Both the nearby Jewish community house (built *ca.* A.D. 200 and rebuilt in 245) and the Christian community house, which was in use in 231, were destroyed in 257 during the reinforcement of the wall against attacks by the Persians.

14. The church of Santa Pudentiana was built over the house of the Senator Pudens of whom the Apostle Peter was a guest in the first century.

15. Cf. B. Bagatti, O.F.M., *Gli scavi di Nazaret*, Vol. 1: *Dalle origini al secolo XII* (Jerusalem: Franciscan, 1967). For more general works on primitive Christianity in the Holy Land, see B. Bagatti, "Resti Cristiani in Palestina anteriori a Costantino?" *Revista di Archeologia cristiana* 26 (1950): 117–131; *L'Église de la Circoncision*, trans. A. Storme (Jerusalem:

Franciscan, 1965), pp. vii–286; *L'Église de la gentilité en Palestine* (*Ier–XIe siecle*) (Jerusalem: Franciscan, 1968). For more general works on primitive Christian churches and early Christianity, see under "Églises" in *Dictionnaire d'Archéologie Chrétienne et de Liturgie* 4:2279–2304, especially 2282–85 ("Synagogues"), 2285–88 ("Habitations privées"), and 2292–2304 ("Éxistence d'Églises Chrétiennes": "Ephese," 2295; "Antioche," 2297; "Syrie et Palestine," 2298; "Rome," 2298–99); R. A. Markus, *Christianity in the Roman World*, especially the first four chapters, pp. 13–96; M. Goguel, *The Primitive Church*, trans. H. C. Snape (London: Allen and Unwin, 1963); R. M. Grant, *Augustus to Constantine: A Thrust of the Christian Movement into the Roman World* (New York: Harper & Row, 1970); J. G. Gager, *Kingdom and Community* (Englewood Cliffs, N.J.: Prentice-Hall, 1975); J. Daniélou and H. Marrou, *Nouvelle Histoire de l'Église* (Paris: Éditions du Seuil, 1963), Vol. 1: *Des Originines à Grégoire le Grand*, especially chs. 1–3, pp. 31–289; K. Baus, *A Handbook of Church History*, Vol. 1: *From the Apostolic Community to Constantine* (New York: Herder & Herder, 1965), with bibliography, pp. 435–505.

16. J. Pinkerfeld, "David's Tomb: Notes on the History of the Building," *Bulletin Rabinovitz* 3 (1960): 41–43; this preliminary report was edited by M. Avi-Yonah (see note p. 43). In general, we agree with its conclusions; however, we note a rather serious discrepancy between the author's or editor's statements concerning the orientation of the important niche and the plan of the structure; cf. p. 41: "the niche pointed north with an eastern deviation of several degrees, i.e., exactly towards the Temple Mount," and p. 43: "the niche of the heightened apse points toward the Temple Mount." But see Fig. 1, p. 42. The plan clearly indicates that the entire structure, including the niche, is oriented rather towards the northwest and not the northeast or directly ("exactly") towards the Temple Mount. Our examination of the site of the alleged tomb of David on Mt. Zion has also proved the northwest orientation.

17. Philo Judaeus *Quod omnis probus liber sit* 75–91; *Hypothetica* xi. 8–13; cf. *Apologia pro Judaeis*; Eusebius *Praeparatio Evangelica* viii. 2, *PG* 24.21.

18. Hippolytus *Refutatio omnium haeresium sive Philosophoumena* ix. 20. 12–23, cf. *PG* 16. 3017; and see Eusebius *Praeparatio evangelica* viii. 2; cf. *PG* 21. 21.

19. *New Catholic Commentary*, Nos. 714a, p. 909; 771e, p. 998; 795e, p. 1029. See also J. A. T. Robinson, *Redating the New Testament* (Philadelphia: Westminster, 1976), p. 284 and note 147; "The Baptism of John and the Qumran Community," *HTR* 50 (1957): 175–191; E. F. Sutcliffe, S.J., *The Monks of Qumran* (London: Burns & Oates, 1960), pp. 123–24; K. Stendahl, ed., *The Scrolls and the New Testament* (New York: Harper, 1957), especially W. H. Brownlee, "John the Baptist in the New Light of the Ancient Scrolls," pp. 33–53. D. Flusser, "The Dead Sea Sect and Pre-Pauline Christianity," *Scripta Hierosolymitana* 4 (1958): 215–266.

20. See above, p. 62, note 1.

21. Fr. Pixner's interpretation of the biblical text, communicated to the author in a number of discussions, sounds convincing, but it must be studied in greater detail.

CHAPTER 9

Church of the Holy Sepulchre

1. *PG* 20. 1035–1102; see D. Baldi, *Enchiridion*, No. 924, pp. 619–623.

2. See C. Coüasnon, O.P., *The Church of the Holy Sepulchre*, Schweich Lectures, 1972 (New York: Oxford, 1974), pp. 38–40. It was our privilege to have attended Coüasnon's lectures at both the École Biblique and the site itself.

3. From Coüasnon's lectures at the site; cf. *The Church of the Holy Sepulchre*, pp. 41–44. Cf. V. Corbo, O.F.M., *La Basilica del S. Sepolcro* (Jerusalem: Franciscan, 1969); M. T. Petrozzi, *Dal Calvario al S. Sepolcro* (Jerusalem: Franciscan, 1972); J. Wilkinson, "The Church of the Holy Sepulchre," *Archaeology* 31 (1978): 6–13.

4. Cf. on Matt. 27:32 in *PG* 13. 1777.

5. Cf. *PG*.

6. Cf. *PL* 22. 581.

7. C. Coüasnon, *The Church of the Holy Sepulchre*, p. 11.

Calvary

1. Lectures and private discussions; cf. Coüasnon, *Church of the Holy Sepulchre*, pp. 39–40; also 7–8; M. Du Buit, "Les Rochers se Fendirent," *BTS* 149 (1973): 7–8; and Coüasnon, "Le Golgotha. Maquette du sol naturel," *BTS* 149 (1973): 10–18. Coüasnon studies the maquette or clay model, made by his colleague M. T. Ball, of the topography of the quarry foundations of the Church of the Holy Sepulchre in relation to the present Crusader structure, for which see pl. 1–8, pp. 10–15.

2. *Ibid.* Cf. M. Piccirillo, "La Roca del Calvario y el Golgota," *Tierra Santa* (1979): 93–97.

3. *Ant.* xii. 240–41; cf. *BJ.* i. 32; *Ant.* xii. 247. Cf. Daniel's prophecy (11:31) in *Ant.* x. 276. Cf. J. A. Fitzmyer, S.J., "Crucifixion in Ancient Palestine, Qumran Literature, and the New Testament," *CBQ* 40 (1978): 493–513.

4. O. Thenius of Dresden (1845) seems to have been the first to suggest another site for Golgotha and the tomb of Jesus north of the present sixteenth-century battlements of the Old City. In 1883 British General C. G. Gordon, Governor-General of the Sudan (1874–1879) and of Khartoum fame, was supposed to have examined this other candidate most carefully and thus arrived at the conclusion that Calvary should be identified with a skull-shaped hillock just north of the Damascus Gate. However, there is absolutely no foundation—in history, archaeology or even tradition—for this equation. The booklet, *Where is Calvary?* by L. T. Pearson, 5th ed. (Worthing: Walter, 1972) should be read with prudence, particularly in light of the many previous studies of the sites of Calvary and Jesus' tomb within the Old City of Jerusalem.

BIBLIOGRAPHY

Abel, F.-M., O.P. *Géographie de la Palestine*. Vol. 1. *Géographie physique et historique*. Vol. 2. *Géographie politique. Les Villes*. 3rd ed. Paris: Gabalda, 1967.

———. *Jérusalem nouvelle*. Paris: Gabalda, 1922.

Amiran, A., and Eitan, A. "Excavations on the Courtyard of the Citadel, Jerusalem, 1968–1969 (Preliminary Report)." *IEJ* 20 (1970): 10–11.

Avigad, N. *Archaeological Discoveries in the Jewish Quarter of Jerusalem, Second Temple Period*. Jerusalem: IES and Israel Museum, 1976.

———. "Excavations in the Jewish Quarter of the Old City, 1969–1970 (Preliminary Report)." *IEJ* 20 (1970): 1–8.

———. "Second Preliminary Report." *IEJ* 20 (1970): 129–140.

Avi-Yonah, M. *The Madaba Mosaic Map*. Jerusalem: IES, 1954.

———. "The Third and Second Walls of Jerusalem." *IEJ* 18 (1968): 98–125.

Bagatti, B. *L'Église de la Gentilité en Palestine (Ier-XIe siecle)*. Ed. A. Storme. *SBFLA* 4 (1968).

———. "La Pozizione del tempio erodiano di Gerusalemme." *Biblica* 46 (1965): 428–444.

Bahat, D. *Carta's Historical Atlas of Jerusalem: A Brief Illustrated Survey*. Jerusalem: Beit Hadar, 1973.

Baldi, D., O.F.M., ed. *Enchiridion Locorum Sanctorum: Documenta S. Evangelii Loca Respicientia*. 2nd ed. Jerusalem: Franciscan, 1955.

Bammel, E., ed. *The Trial of Jesus*. Festschrift C.M.D. Moule. *Studies in Biblical Theology* 13. Naperville, Ill.: Allenson, 1970.

Barrett, C.K., ed. *The New Testament Background: Selected Documents*. New York: Harper & Row, 1961.

Ben-Dov, M. "Herodian Jerusalem Revisited." *CNI* 26 (1978): 138–142.

Benoit, P. "L'Antonia d'Hérode le Grand et le Forum Oriental d'Aelia Capitolina." *HTR* 64 (1971): 135–167.

———. "Où en est la question du 'Troisième Mur'?" *SH* I. *SBF* 22. Jerusalem: Franciscan, 1976, pp. 111–126.

———. "Pretoire, Lithostroton et Gabbatha." *RB* 59 (1952): 531–550.

Bliss, F.J., and Dickie, A.C. *Excavations at Jerusalem 1894–1897*. London: Palestine Exploration Fund, 1898.

Broshi, M. "Estimating the Population of Ancient Jerusalem." *BAR* 4 (1978): 10–15.

———. "The Expansion of Jerusalem in the Reigns of Hezekiah and Manasseh." *IEJ* 24 (1974): 21–26.

———. "La Population de l'Ancienne Jerusalem." *RB* 82 (1975): 5–14.

Brown, R.E. *The Gospel According to John*. Anchor Bible. Garden City, N.Y.: Doubleday. II (1970): 845–46.

Brownlee, W.H. "John the Baptist in the New Light of the Ancient Scrolls." Pp. 33–53 in K. Stendahl, ed., *The Scrolls and the New Testament*. New York: Harper, 1957.

Busink, T.A. *Der Tempel von Jerusalem: Von Solomo bis Herodes*. Leiden: Brill, 1970.

Chen, D., Margalit, S., and Soler, C. "Antica Strada Scoperta a Gerusalemme." *La Terra Santa* (1979): 116–19.

Comay, J. *The Temple of Jerusalem*. New York: Holt, Rinehart and Winston, 1975.

Conder, C.R., *et al. The Survey of Western Palestine*. 3 vols. 1881. Reprint ed. Jerusalem: Kedem, 1970.

Corbo, V. *La Basilica del S. Sepolcro*. Jerusalem: Franciscan, 1969.

Cornfeld, G. *The Mystery of the Temple Mount*. Jerusalem: Bazak, 1972.

Coüasnon, C., O.P. *The Church of the Holy Sepulchre in Jerusalem*. 1972 Schweich Lectures. London: Oxford, 1974.

Crowfoot, J.W.V. *Excavations in the Tyropean Valley, Jerusalem 1927. Annual of the Palestine Exploration Fund* (1929).

Dalman, G. *Jerusalem und sein Gelände*. Gütersloh: Bertelsmann, 1930.

Diez, F. "El Testimonio del Arqueolege." *Tierra Santa* (1979).

Donner, H., and Cuppers, H. *Die Mosaikkarte von Madeba* I. Wiesbaden: Harrassowitz, 1977.

Fergusson, J. *The Temples of the Jews and Other Buildings in the Haram Area at Jerusalem*. London: Murray, 1878.

Gibb, H.A.R. *Mohammedanism: An Historical Survey*. 2nd ed. New York: Oxford, 1969.

Gilbert, M. *Jerusalem History Atlas*. New York: Macmillan, 1977.

Gray, J. *A History of Jerusalem*. New York: Praeger, 1969.

Hebrew University of Jerusalem, Department of Geography. *Atlas of Jerusalem*. New York: de Gruyter, 1973.

Hoade, E., O.F.M. *Guide to the Holy Land*. 8th ed. Jerusalem: Franciscan, 1976.

Hollis, F.J. *The Archaeology of Herod's Temple*. London: Dent, 1934.

Ignatius of Loyola. *Autobiography*. Trans. J. O'Callaghan. Ed. J.C. Olin. New York: Harper and Row, 1974.

Israel Museum. *Inscriptions Reveal: Documents from the Time of the Bible, the Mishnah, and the Talmud*. Ed. R. Hestrin, Y. Israeli, and Y. Meshorer. Jerusalem: Israel Museum, 1973.

Jaubert, A. "La calendier des Jubilés et de la secte de Qumrân, les origines bibliques." *VT* 3 (1953): 250–264.

Jeremias, J. *Jerusalem in the Time of Jesus*. Philadelphia: Fortress, 1969.

Johns, C.N. "The Citadel, Jerusalem." *QDAP* 14 (1950): 121–190.

Kenyon, K.M. *Digging Up Jerusalem*. New York: Praeger, 1974.

_____. *Jerusalem: Excavating 3000 Years of History*. New York: McGraw-Hill, 1967.

Kopp, C. *The Holy Places of the Gospels*. New York: Herder and Herder, 1963.

Landay, J.M. *Dome of the Rock: Three Faiths of Jerusalem*. New York: Newsweek, 1972.

The Lost Books of the Bible and the Forgotten Books of Eden. New York: Collins-World, 1948.

Mackowski, R.M., S.J. "Jerusalem A.D. 30—A New Map." In *Report of the Third Archaeological Conference*. Jerusalem, 1975.

_____. "Where Is Biblical Emmaus?" *Science et Esprit* 32 (1980): 93–103.

Mazar, B. *The Excavation in the Old City of Jerusalem near the Temple Mount: A Preliminary Report of the Second and Third Seasons, 1969–1970*. Jerusalem: IES, 1971.

_____. *The Excavations in the Old City of Jerusalem: Preliminary Report of the First Season, 1968*. Jerusalem: IES, 1969.

_____. *The Mountain of the Lord: Excavating Jerusalem*. Garden City, N.Y.: Doubleday, 1975.

Murphy-O'Connor, J. "The Essenes and Their History." *RB* 81 (1974): 215–244.

Negev, A., ed. *Archaeological Encyclopedia of the Holy Land*. Jerusalem: Weidenfeld & Nicolson, 1972.

Orni, E., and Efrat, E. *Geography of Israel*. 3rd rev. ed. Jerusalem: Israel Universities, 1971.

Pax, E. "Spuren der Nabatäer im Neuen Testament." *Bibel und Leben* 3 (1974): 193–206.

Pearson, L.T. *Where Is Calvary?* 5th ed. Worthing: Walter, 1972.

Petrozzi, M.T. *Dal Calvario al S. Sepolcro*. Jerusalem: Franciscan, 1972.

Pixner, B.-G. "An Essene Quarter on Mount Zion?" *SH* 1 (1976): 245–284.

_____. "Retracing the Dolorosa." Unpublished article, with permission of the author.

Prawer, J. *The Latin Kingdom of Jerusalem*. London: Weidenfeld and Nicolson, 1972.

Robinson, J.A.T. "The Baptism of John and the Qumran Community." *HTR* 50 (1957): 175–191.

Rupprecht, K. *Der Tempel von Jerusalem: Gründung Salomos oder jebusitisches Erbe?* New York: de Gruyter, 1977.

Schürer, E. *Geschichte des jüdischen Volkes im Zeitalter Jesu Christi*. 3 vols. 4th ed. Leipzig: Hinrichs, 1891–1909.

_____. "The History of the Jewish People in the Age of Jesus Christ (175 B.C.–A.D. 135)*. Ed. G. Vermes and F. Millar. Edinburgh: Clark, 1973–.

Shanks, H. *The City of David: A Guide to Biblical Jerusalem*. Jerusalem: Bazak, 1973.

Sharon, A. *Planning Jerusalem: The Old City and Its Environs*. London: Weidenfeld and Nicolson, 1973.

Shiloh, Y. "Jerusalem: The City of David," *IEJ* 28 (1978): 274–76.

Simons, J., S.J. *Jerusalem in the Old Testament: Researches and Theories*. Leiden: Brill, 1954.

Smith, G.A. *History of Jerusalem: The Topography, Economics, and History of Jerusalem from the Earliest Times to A.D. 70*. 2 vols. 1907. Reprint ed. New York: Ktav, 1970.

Speiss, F. *Das Jerusalem des Josephus: Ein Beitrage zur Topographie der heiligen Stadt*. Berlin, 1881.

Storme, A. *L'Église de la Circoncision*. Jerusalem: Franciscan, 1965.

_____. *Gethsemane*. Trans. G. Bushell, O.F.M. Jerusalem: Franciscan, 1972.

Sukenik, E.L., and Mayer, L.A. *The Third Wall of Jerusalem: An Account of Excavations*. London: Oxford, 1930.

Tsafrir, Y. "The Location of the Seleucid Akra in Jerusalem." *RB* 82 (1975): 501–521.

Universitas Booksellers of Jerusalem Atika. *The Holy Land in Ancient Maps*. 3rd ed. Jerusalem, 1965.

Ussishkin, D. "The Necropolis from the Time of the Kingdom of Judah at Silwan, Jerusalem." *BA* 33 (1970): 34–46.

Vilnay, Z. *The Holy Land in Old Prints and Maps*. Jerusalem: Mass, 1965.

Vincent, L.-H., O.P., and Steve, A.-M. *Jérusalem de l'Ancien Testament: Recherches d'Archéologie et d'Histoire*. Paris: J. Gabalda, 1954–56.

Vogel, E.K. "Bibliography of Holy Land Sites." *Hebrew Union College Annual* 42 (1971): 47–48.

Vogt, E. "Das Wachstum des alten Stadtgebietes von Jerusalem." *Biblica* 48 (1967): 337–358.

Warren, C. *Underground Jerusalem: An Account of the Principle Difficulties Encountered in Its Exploration and the Results Obtained*. London, 1876.

Weill, R. *La Cité de David*. 2 vols. Paris: P. Geuthner, 1920–1947.

Wilkinson, J. "Ancient Jerusalem: Its Water Supply and Population." *PEQ* 106 (1974): 33–51.

_____. *Jerusalem As Jesus Knew It*. London: Thames and Hudson, 1978.

_____. "The Streets of Jerusalem." *Levant* 7 (1975): 118–136.

Yadin, Y. *Jerusalem Through the Ages*. Jerusalem: IES, 1968.

_____, ed. *Jerusalem Revealed: Archaeology in the Holy City 1968–1974*. New Haven: Yale, 1976.

_____. *The Temple Scroll (Megillath Hammiqdash)*. 3 vols. Jerusalem: IES, Hebrew University of Jerusalem Institute of Archaeology, and the Shrine of the Book, 1977.

GLOSSARIES

Arabic

ʾAllah	God (Allah), akin to Hebrew ʾel, ʾeloah.
ʿamud	column, pillar; Bab el-ʿAmud, the Gate of the Column (Damascus Gate)
ʿAqṣa	the farther (temple or mosque); cf. Koran, Surah xvii.
ʾaqwas	pillared arches (as in the Haram esh-Sharif).
ʾasbat	tribes: name of the northeastern gate of the Haram.
ʿatem	darkness, obscurity, the name of a northern gate of the Haram.
ʿaṭṭarin	spices; the Suq el-ʿAttarin follows the Roman cardo maximus.
ʾawqaf	property belonging to a mosque; all that belongs to the Supreme Muslim Council.
bab	gate (with the same meaning as Hebrew shaʿar); also door.
bashurah	Annunciation; name of a quarter in the Old City of Jerusalem.
beit	house (equivalent to Hebrew baith).
beqaʿ	a (small) valley.
bir	a well, like Hebrew beʾer.
Bir-ʿAyyub	Job's Well situated south of Spring Gihon in the Wadi en-Nar.
birqeh	pool, cistern.
Caliph	see Khalifeh.
dabbagha	tannery; name of a street in the Old City.
ḍaheriyeh	probably meaning "back" or the quarter or part where the city ends.
daraj (darag)	step
Daud	David (Hebrew dawid).
deir	a monastery.
dirweh	a protective screen, a wall; a parapet; a hiding-place, porch.
diwan	office; government department.
Dosi	Arabic corruption of Theodosius; name of a monastery (Deir Dosi) in the Judaean desert near Bethlehem.
ʿein	spring; eye. A spring is the eye of the earth.
ʾel	the definite article "the." The "l" frequently receives the form of the following consonant, e.g., er-ram, es-salam, etc.
furdeis [fureidis]	written and pronounced furdaus in Koranic Arabic; the word means "paradise" and is of Persian origin (see below), meaning "an enclosed garden or park."
gebel (jebel)	a mountain, as in Gebel et-Tur, Arabic for the Mount of Olives.
ghassul	from the root "to wash," hence the name of a plant from which soap was produced, and the name of the Chalcolithic site Tuleilat Ghassul.
Ghawanimeh	an Arabic family surname; name of a minaret in the Haram.
gib (jib)	a pocket (in its various senses, e.g., in clothes, in a mountain range, etc.).
ḥadid	iron; name of a western gate in the Jerusalem Haram.
ḥaram	enclosure, as in Haram esh-Sharif, the Noble Enclosure.
ḥaret	a lane, street; Haret en-Nasara, Christian Quarter Street.
ḥasan	excellent, beautiful, etc.
Hegirah (Hejirah)	the Hegirah; Muhammed's flight from Mecca to Medina in A.D. 622. This event marks the year one in the Islamic calendar.
ḥelu	sweet, soft; name applied to a type of limestone in the Jerusalem area.
ḥuṣṣor	a straw mat; name of a street in the Old City following the southern portion of Hadrian's cardo maximus.
ḥuṭṭa	repentance; one of the northern gates of the Haram in Jerusalem is called the Gate of Repentance (Bab el-Hutta).
ʾIbrahim	Abraham, equivalent to Hebrew ʾabraham.

'Isa (Saiyidna 'Isa)   Jesus (Our Lord Jesus).

janneh   paradise; name of the northern door of the Dome of the Rock.

Ka'aba   the Black Rock in Mecca, venerated by Muslims as the House of Abraham (Koran, Surah xxii, see v), the most holy shrine of Islam.

kas   a cup; the name of the ablution fountain between the Dome of the Rock and el-Aqsa Mosque in the Haram esh-Sharif.

Khalifeh (Caliph)   from the verb to succeed; hence, the Successor to Muhammed.

Khalil   friend, like *haber* in Hebrew; the Arabic name for Hebron.

khan   of Turkish origin, meaning an "inn, hostel," etc.

khanqa   an inn or hostel; name of a street in the Old City; also used of a school attached to a mosque.

khirbeh (khirbet-)   a ruin, as in Khirbet Qumran.

Koran   see *Qur'an*; from the verb "to read, recite."

mahed   a cradle.

masjid (masgid)   a mosque.

masharif   eminences; also the outskirts of a city.

mathara   ablution; name of a western gate in the Haram.

meleke   royal; from the root "to be king"; name of a type of limestone in the Jerusalem area.

mihrab   the prayer niche in a mosque, pointing in the direction of Mecca.

minbar   a pulpit.

mi'raj (mi'rag)   Muhammed's night journey from Mecca to Jerusalem, as related in the Koran, Surah xxii. In Islamic theology Muhammed was transported through the seven heavens from Jerusalem up to the throne of God (Allah). Muslims venerate the sacred rock beneath the Dome of the Rock as the point of departure of Muhammed's miraculous ascent.

Miryam   Mary; the title of Surah xix in the Koran; this chapter relates and explains the birth of Jesus from a Muslim point of view.

mizze   hard, durable; a kind of limestone in the Jerusalem vicinity.

mojahidin   the fighters for the sake of God; name of a street in the Old City.

Moslem   see *Muslim*.

mosque   see *masjid*.

mugharah   a cave or grotto.

Muhammed   Muhammed, prophet and founder of Islam, born in Mecca *ca.* 570, fled to Medina in 622, and died at Medina in 632; *h-m-d*, to praise.

mukabber   from the root *k-b-r*, big; hence, magnified or telescoped; name of the mountain directly south of Jerusalem.

Muslim   Muslim or Moslem; derived from Arabic *'aslama*, to submit, or to convert to Islam; a follower or believer in Islam.

nadhir (nazir)   principal; the principal of a school.

nar   fire; name of a valley, Wadi en-Nar (the Kidron Valley), running in a southeasterly direction from Jerusalem to the Dead Sea.

Nasara   Christians; the meaning is obviously taken from Nazareth.

nebi   a prophet, equivalent to Hebrew *nabi'*.

'Omariyyeh   adjective formed from *'Omar*, the second Caliph or successor to Muhammed. The Omariyyeh School in the northeastern part of the Old City occupies the rocky spur on which the palace-fortress proper of the Antonia was built, although its entire compound embraced some portion of the northwestern corner of the Haram. The school is the site of the traditional First Station of the Cross.

qaber   grave.

qadimeh   old, ancient; name of the ancient el-Aqsa Mosque beneath the present structure, built over the Double Huldah Gates of the Temple.

Qait-bai   name of an Egyptian Mameluke Sultan after whom the beautiful Sebil Qait-bai, erected *ca.* 1445 in the Harma, was named. It probably stands on or near the site where the Yahweh temple once stood.

qala'a   citadel, castle, or fortress.

Qelt   a valley (Wadi el-Qelt) running from Jerusalem in a northeasterly direction towards Jericho. The course of the ancient Roman road from Jerusalem to Jericho followed, in general, this valley.

qibleh   a technical term in Islam, referring to the direction of Mecca towards which the *mihrab* (prayer niche) of a mosque is oriented.

qishleh   from the Turkish word for barracks (*kışle*); the present site of the police station to the right of Jaffa Gate.

qubbeh (qubbet-)   dome; *qubbet-* is the construct case, meaning "dome of . . . ."

Quds   Holy, specifically Jerusalem; the Sanctuary, the Holy City, etc. The root is identical with Hebrew *qodesh*, holy.

Qur'an   the Koran, the most holy book in Islam, believed by Muslims to have been dictated or recited (hence the name is from the root *q-r-'* to read, recite, etc.) by the archangel Gabriel to Muhammed. The book contains

114 chapters revealed to Muhammed at Mecca and Medina.

rababeh	a one-stringed musical instrument resembling a violin; the present name of the Hinnom Valley (Wadi er-Rababeh).
raḥmeh	mercy; the name of the southern entranceway of the Golden Gate in the Haram esh-Sharif.
ṣāḥweh	a hill, crest; a mountain range.
ṣāḥyun	Ṣion (Ṣiyon or Zion).
ṣakhra	rock, as in Qubbet es-Sakhra, the Dome of the Rock.
Ṣalaḥiyyeh	an adjective formed from the name Salah, as in Salah ed-Din (Saladin); the Arabic word means interest, good, welfare; hence, Salaḥ ed-Dîn, the good (welfare) of religion.
sebil	an ablution fountain in the mosque area.
sharaf	noble, as in the name Haram esh-Sharif, the Noble Sanctuary.
sharif	noble, highborn; descendant of the Prophet Muhammed, as in the case of Sharif Hussein, grandfather of King Hussein, of the Hashemite family.
silsileh	chain; the name of the street and gate leading to the Haram from the west, over the Tyropoeon Valley (el-Wad).
suq	market or marketplace, equivalent to Hebrew *shuq.*
Suleiman	the Arabic form of Solomon, as in the name of the Hebrew King Solomon or the Turkish Sultan Suleiman the Magnificent, the builder of the present Old City's ramparts dating back to the sixteenth century.
Surah	chapter, a division in the Koran.
ṣurar	small stones; the name of a valley southwest of Jerusalem, Wadi es-Surar.
ṭanṭur	a tiara or the crown of an Egyptian Pharaoh.
ṭariq	a street or road.
tell	equivalent to Hebrew *tel,* hill or mound, employed in the technical sense to refer to an artificial mound composed of occupational layers or strata.
tobeh	repentance; the name of the northern gate or passageway inside the Golden Gate of the Haram esh-Sharif; see *raḥmeh.*
tuleilat	small hills, as in the name of the Chalcolithic site Tuleilat Ghassul situated in the Jordan Valley northeast of the Dead Sea.
wadi	a valley, sometimes defined as a dry riverbed, though torrential rains in the winter months may cause deep flooding and considerable damage to roads, etc. built in or across them.
weli	an Islamic holy man or saint, as Nebi Saleḥ.
yehudi	Jewish; name used for a type of limestone in the Jerusalem region.
Yesuʿ (Yesuʿ il-Mesiḥ)	Jesus (Jesus the Messiah, the Christ).
zeit	oil; *zeit zeitun,* olive oil; the word appears in the name of the northern half of the principal north-south street in the Old City, following the course of the Hadrianic cardo maximus as Suq Khan ez-Zeit, the market of the oil caravansary.

Greek

agorá	a marketplace, a public square (*piazza, place, Platz*) of a Greek city; Latin forum.
ákanthos	a plant whose leaves were used in Corinthian capitals; acanthus leaves, thorns, etc.
Akeldama (Acheldama)	Akeldama or Haceldama, from Aramaic *demaʾ,* blood, and *haqel,* field, hence, the Field of Blood (*agròs haímatos*).
ákra	end, point, the highest point; Latin arx.
Amýgdalon	almond; the name of a reservoir in Jerusalem, taken from the tower close by, hence from Hebrew *hammigdal,* the tower.
anábasis (ana-baínein)	an ascent, steps (leading upwards).
anabathmós (ana-baínein)	steps (leading upwards), an ascent.
anágaion (anṓgaion, anṓgeon)	an upper room, a room on the second floor.
anástasis (anístēmi)	a rising, resurrection; name of the Rotunda of the Holy Sepulchre.
anástēma	height, prominence, erection; building, protuberance, tower.
anatoliké	east, eastern; hence Anatolia (Turkish Anadolu).
Aphrodíte	the goddess of love and beauty; Latin Venus.
apó	preposition meaning "from, away from," etc.
Asklēpieíon	an Asclepium: a religious sanitorium in honor of Asklēpios, the god of medicine and of healing, corresponding to the Semitic Eshmun of Phoenicia and Shedrapha' of Syria.
Athena	tutelary goddess of Athens; Latin Minerva, goddess of wisdom, the arts, and sciences.
aylé	farmyard, courtyard; court, palace, e.g., Herod's palace in Jerusalem, as distinguished from the Antonia (*phroúrion*). The Hero-

dian palace was later called the Praetorium or the residence of the Roman procurator in Jerusalem.

azýmōn (ta ázyma) unleavened bread; the Feast of Unleavened Bread; cf. *maṣṣoth* in Exod. 12:8, 15, etc.

Bāris considered originally to be an Egyptian word for a flat-bottomed boat; later meaning a "large house" or "tower"; name of the fortress in the northwestern corner of the Temple during the Maccabean period, which Herod rebuilt and renamed Antonia.

basilikós (from *basileús*, king; diminutive *basilískos*), kingly, royal; name of a game; Latin basilica equivalent to Greek *stoá*.

béma (baínein) the speaker's platform, as in Corinth and the forum in Rome; Latin tribunale.

Bēthesdá (Bēthzathá, Bēzathá, Belzathá, Bēthsaidá, Bezethá, Bethzaith) from the Aramaic *beith-ḥesda* or Hebrew *beith-ḥesed*, both meaning the "Place [House] of (divine) Mercy." Bethesda was the name of the northeastern (hill) quarter of Jerusalem, which took its name from the healing cult practiced here during the Old Testament period (of Eshmun or Shedrapha) and during the Graeco-Roman, New Testament, and Hadrianic periods (Aesculapium; see also *Asklēpieíon* above).

Bēthsō latrine, from Hebrew *beith*, house, and *ṣoʾah*, excrement; latrines of the Essenes; cf. BJ v. 145.

Charseíth from Hebrew *ḥarsiyth*, rendered as a proper name by the Septuagint translators for the Potsherd Gate in the southeastern part of Jerusalem.

chómata (plural of *chóma*) a siege ramp.

diakonikón room in a Byzantine church where the sacred vessels and vestments were kept; a sacristy or vestry. The term is still used in the Greek Orthodox tradition.

diasporá (dia-speírein) a scattering; the Dispersion of the Jews from Palestine throughout the Graeco-Roman world.

diástēma (diastēnai) extension, dimension; interval.

dístegos (stégos, roof) a second story; a two-storied structure; a room or a chamber (upstairs).

eis preposition meaning "to, towards, into."

Ekklēsía (from ek-kaleín, ékklētos) an assembly (of citizens called together), a meeting; a church; Hebrew *qahal*, a gathering, community, congregation.

eleutherópolis (eleútheros, free, pólis, city) free city; name of biblical Mareshah (LXX *Máris(s)a, Márēsa*) after emperor Septimius Severus had granted it special rights and privileges; "Libertyville."

enkaínia (ta enkaínia) Feast of the Dedication of the Temple, equivalent to the Jewish festival of Hanukkah.

epí preposition meaning "at, by, near," etc.

ex preposition meaning "out of, from within," etc.

éxō adverb signifying "outwards, outside"; Latin foris.

gazophylákion (gazophylakeíon) treasury, storeroom; from Persian *ganuǵ*, treasury, and Greek *phylakeín*, to guard.

géenna gehenna, grecized from Hebrew *gey' ben-hinnom* and Aramaic *Geyhinnam*; the Hebrew means "the valley of the son of Hinnom," probably the name of the first (Jebusite) owner of the property.

Gennáth name of a gate in ancient Jerusalem; derived from Aramaic *ginnaʾ*, Hebrew *gan*, meaning "garden."

hagía holy, sacred.

hápax legómenon once mentioned; a technical expression for a word or form occurring only once in literature or in a given author, as, for example, the hapax legomena *alektorophōnía, apódēmos, nounechós, smyrnízein*, etc. in Mark.

Héra Hera, sister and wife of Zeus, who was also the queen of the Greek pantheon.

hierón holy (with reference to the sacred treasury of the Temple; see *chrēmátōn*).

himátion an outer cloak, cape, worn above the *chitón*, like the Roman toga.

ho definite article "the."

hōraía (hōraíos, from hóra, season) beautiful; seasonable.

hósios holy. According to some scholars this is a possible explanation of the etymology of Essene, although others offer *ísos*, meaning "egalitarian," as another possibility. We do not consider the name Essenes of Greek origin.

hyperóon an upper room, a second story; used of the Cenacle or the upper chamber in which Jesus celebrated his last Passover meal, and the place of the Pentecost event.

kainópolis new city or new town; from *kainós*, new

(temporal, as distinguished from *néos* which refers to the quality of the thing), and *pólis*, city; *Kainopolis* was the popular name of the new quarter of Jerusalem which developed north of the city walls during the first century A.D.

kápēlos   a retail dealer, huckster, tavernkeeper.

katà méson   right through the middle.

katábasis (*katá*, down + *baínein*, to go)   a descent or a flight of steps going down (opposite of *anábasis*).

kermatistḗs (plural *kermatistaí*)   moneychanger(s); see *kollybistḗs* below.

kḗrygma   a proclamation (from *kērýssein*, to announce as a herald).

kinýra   a harp; related to Hebrew *kinnor*, a cithara (*kithára*); hence, Gennesaret (*Gennēsarét*, *Gennesár*; Hebrew *gennesar*), relating to the shape of the Sea of Galilee; *kinýresthai*, to utter a plaintive sound; to lament or moan.

koinḗ   common, ordinary; Koiné Greek was the common language or lingua franca of the Middle East during the first centuries before and after Christ, although Aramaic was also spoken in this region.

kokkínēn   red (the color of the cloak, according to Matthew, which the Roman soldiers placed on Jesus after the flagellation).

kollybistḗs (plural *kollybistaí*)   moneychangers; *kóllybos*, a small coin.

kolymbḗthra   a pool, a swimming pool, a water reservoir, as in John's account of the miracle at the Sheep (Bethesda) Pool in the northeastern corner of Jerusalem.

Kōpónios   Coponius, the first Roman procurator of Palestine (A.D. 6–9); also *Kiphōnos*.

kopría   dunghill.

kráspedon   the hem or border of a garment; the tassel (*ṣiṣith*) which the true Jew is supposed to wear on the four corners of his outer garment, as prescribed in Numbers and Deuteronomy.

kremannýnai   to hang up (as a shield or as a votive offering in the Temple); to suspend from; of persons the verb means "to be hanged"; Deut. 21:22 with Gal. 3:13, which quotes the passage from Deuteronomy, "Accursed is anyone who is hanged on a tree."

krínon   a lily.

laúra   a narrow way, lane; a defile or a ravine; in Byzantine Greek also a monastery or a group of monks' cells (sometimes caves or grottos) grouped together under a single leader; e.g., the Great Laura of Mar Sabas deep in the Kidron (Wadi en-Nar) Valley, southeast of Jerusalem.

léschē   a public building; perhaps etymologically related to Hebrew *lishkah*.

lithóstrōtos   a pavement (derived from *líthos*, stone, and *strṓnnymi*, to spread); apparently a technical word in the Johannine Gospel describing the place of judgment, the stone pavement upon which the judge's chair was placed, translated into English either as the Lithostrotos or the Pavement.

Magoí   a Magus or wise man, derived from Persian *magush* meaning "magician." We agree that the Matthaean account of the wise men who came from the east to adore the infant Jesus in Bethlehem can be explained against the background of the great Nabataean Arab kingdom of the first centuries before and after Christ.

martýrion   a proof or testimony, from *mártys* meaning a "witness." The Martyrion or "place of witness" of the Constantinian basilica was related to the Anastasis or rotunda over the Tomb of Jesus. The remains of the Constantinian structure were discovered beneath the present Katholikon of the Church of the Holy Sepulchre.

neá   new (in a qualitative rather than temporal sense, as distinct from *kainós*). The Byzantine *Neá*, recently discovered by Israeli archaeologists in the Jewish Quarter of Jerusalem, was erected by Emperor Justinian and consecrated around 542. Its full title was "The New Church of the Mother of God." The appearance of this church on the Madaba Map assists in dating the famous mosaic to the sixth century A.D.

nekrópolis   a city of the dead, a necropolis, cemetery, or burial ground; derived from *nekrós* (*nékys*), a dead body or corpse, and *pólis*, city.

nóton   hill or mound.

óchlos   crowd, tumult, multitude.

Ophlás   Ophel, the southeasternmost spur of Jerusalem. Ophel translates Hebrew ʿ*Ophel*, from the root "to swell," meaning a mound or hill.

órganon   instrument, implement, tool; a war engine (perhaps similar to the battering ram [*helopóleis*] employed by the Romans in the capture of Jerusalem).

pantòs lógou kreíssōn   defying all description, simply amazing; Josephus' description of Herod's palace (*aylḗ*) in the northwestern part of the Upper City.

parembolḗ   barracks; the royal military barracks in the courtyard of the Antonia, situated in the

passaleúein northwestern part of the esplanade of the present Haram esh-Sharif.

to fasten, peg, pin; *diapassaleúein*, to stretch out by nailing the extremities (Herodotus vii. 33) and *prospassaleúein*, to nail up or hang on a peg (Herodotus i. 114).

pentēkostē Pentecost (from fifty [*pentēkonta*] days), equivalent to the Jewish festival of Shebuôth or Feast of Weeks, celebrated seven weeks after Passover in the spring.

períbolos an enclosure (from *perí*, around, and *bállein*, to throw); a wall around a town or a sacred area; the precinct of a temple.

pétra rock, translating Aramaic *kephaʾ*, from which Peter's name Cephas is derived.

phroúrion a fortress, rendering Hebrew *meṣudah*.

porphyroun (porphýran) purple.

praitórion Latin loanword meaning, in post-Augustan Greek, "palace," the equivalent of *aylē* (see above). A praetorium first referred to the general's tent or headquarters in a battlefield; secondly it signified a war council; and thirdly it meant a palace. The Latin military term praetorium corresponds to Greek *stratēgion*. As used in the New Testament, this is a technical term defining the procurator's residence, the former palace of Herod the Great, in the Upper City of first-century Jerusalem.

proásteion suburb; literally, before the city (*pro - ásty*, a city or town).

probatikós pertaining to sheep (*próbaton*, flock of sheep [or cattle]; literally "anything that goes before"), frequently rendered "probatic" (with reference to a gate or reservoir in Jerusalem) as, for example, the Probatic Pool in John's Gospel, sometimes also called the Pool of Bethesda.

prós a preposition with the accusative case meaning "towards, in the direction of," etc.

pýlē gate (of a city wall, as distinct from *thýra*, the door of a house).

pyramídion the diminutive of *pyramís* meaning a "pyramid" (or, secondly, a kind of cake). Its derivation from Egyptian *pr-m-wś* is dubious; the Egyptian word for pyramid is *mer*.

pyrgoeidés towerlike, derived from *pýrgos*, tower, and *eídos*, figure, form, image, or shape.

skopós an observer or lookout man (in time of war); hence, Mt. Scopus, the name of the mountain north of Jerusalem from which the Holy City could be observed (surveyed); derived from *skopeín*, *sképtesthai*, meaning "to see, observe," etc.

spoudaíoi zealous ones; in Byzantine Greek it denoted a "scholar"; these were also the ones who attached themselves to certain holy places in

order to protect them, to provide pilgrims with devotional practices, etc. in them.

stádion a fixed unit of measurement equivalent to about 607 feet; the Roman stadium (stade or furlong); the length of a Greek running-stadium

stauróō to crucify (as a means of punishment), from the noun *staurós*, an upright stake or pale, also defined as a cross, an instrument of torture.

stoá a portico, a colonnaded building or promenade; also a *basilikē* (*oikía*), hence Latin basilica, signifying (a) a porticoed public building or (b) a church in the Byzantine period, as also today with reference to the special status of a Christian church.

stratēgion the commanding general's tent in a field of battle; the eastern (Greek) term for the western (Latin) praetorium.

strouthíon diminutive of *strouthós*, a large bird, like the ostrich; any species of bird, like the sparrow. Strouthion is the name of the large reservoir which supplied water for Fortress Antonia; it can still be viewed beneath the Convent of the Sisters of Sion in Jerusalem. See the text for our explanation of this term in light of Hebrew ʿ*Ashtoreth*; Strouthion, then, could possibly point to the place where this foreign divinity had been worshiped in Jerusalem.

synagōgē a synagogue; a meeting place (*sýn*, with, and *ágein*), which corresponds to the Hebrew ʿ*edah*, congregation, but frequently equivalent to Hebrew *qahal*, assembly. The Modern Hebrew word for synagogue is *Beith-Kneseth*, the house (place) of assembly or convention.

témenos the temple precinct; in general, any piece of property cut off (*témnein*, to cut) for a set purpose; in a religious context it defines the area considered sacred to a divinity.

tetrágōnos square or four-cornered (*téssares*, four, *tetrás*, in four ways, and *gōnía*, corner or angle). The Jerusalem temple is delineated as a square, according to Josephus and exegeted from various passages in the Old Testament and the Qumran Temple Scroll.

tetrápylon a single structure composed of four archways or entrances, like Latin quadrivium; technical term, derived from *tetrás*, and *pýlē*, meaning a "city gate."

Theós God; *theós*, also a foreign or pagan god or divinity.

Theotókos the "Mother of God," composed of *Theós*, and *tókos* (*tíktein*, to beget), meaning "parturition" or "childbirth." For the Church of the Theotokos in Jerusalem, see *Neá* above.

thermaí hot springs, public baths, like Latin balneum or thermae.

thēsaurós	treasure, treasury; see also under *gazophylákion* above with reference to the treasury of the Temple.
thymiatérion	a censer or incense burner, as depicted on the coin of Herod the Great (p. 116).
thýra	the door of a house, as distinct from *pýlē*, a city gate.
Tyropoión	Tyropoeon, the name of the central valley in Jerusalem, rendered the Valley of the Cheesemakers, which we explain as a type of linguistic accommodation from Hebrew *teraphim*, the word for pagan idols.

Hebrew and Aramaic

Note on transcription: Though there might have been differences, we remain convinced that the ancient Hebrews, at least in Palestine, did not distinguish between כ = K and כ, ך = Kh, although פ, ף could have had two sounds, that of a P and an aspirated Ph. ב was always pronounced B. Students of Hebrew are aware that there exist at least two pronunciations of Hebrew, excluding Modern Israeli Hebrew which is still undergoing phonetic changes; the Ashkenazic pronunciation of East European Jews differs from the Sephardic pronunciation of the Oriental Jews. Finally, to facilitate transcription and pronunciation we have vocalized all of the "pointing" with full vowels, which also contributes to an easier reading of the word or phrase.

HEBREW

ʿ*ain*	spring, eye (the human eye or the eye [spring] of the earth); construct ʿ*ein-*, sometimes also transliterated *en-*; equivalent to Arabic ʿ*ein*.
ʿ*alah*	to go up, ascend. The noun ʿ*aliah* may signify either a pilgrimage (to Jerusalem) or, as in Modern Israeli Hebrew, immigration (a going up or return to Zion).
ʾ*alleluiah* (*hallelu-yah*)	"Praise God!" The original probably read *hallelu eth-YHWH*, with the verb in the Piel or intensive form meaning "to shine, boast, praise, or celebrate."
ʾ*allon*	oak, as in Oak of Moreh. The Aramaic is ʾ*ilan*, rendered *balluṭ* in Arabic, hence the name of the site identified as Shechem Balatah near modern Nablus on the West Bank.
ʾ*asherah*	Asherah for Ishtar or Astarte, a Semitic goddess, and a sacred pole, a cult object (e.g., in Genesis with respect to a pillar, standing post (of wood or stone); feminine plural ʾ*Asheroth* (see ʿ*Ashthoreth*).
ʾ*ashpath*	dung, excrement; ʾ*ashpôth*, dungheap.
ʿ*Ashthoreth*	Ashthoreth (Ashtoreth), Hebrew vocalization of the Canaanite goddess of fertility after *bosheth*, shame or disgrace.

Tyropoeon is made up from *tyrós*, cheese, and the verb *poieín*, to make.

xystós	(a) that part of a gymnasium in which athletes exercised; (b) a colonnaded promenade, like that over the bridge (Wilson's Arch) in Jerusalem; rendered xystus in Latin literature.
Zeús	Zeus, the Latin Iupiter, the father of the Greek pantheon.

ʿ*ashin*	powerful; equivalent to Aramaic *ḥisnaʾ*, power, force; *ḥesen*, (royal) power.
ʾ*asyaʾ*	physician, surgeon; used in the Targum for a thaumaturg, and a possible etymological explanation for the name Essene.
ʿ*azarah*	an enclosure; derived from the root ʿ*azar*, to help, assist, succor; see *haʿazarah* below.
baʿal	lord; Baal, a Canaanite god.
baith	house or place; construct *beith-*; Arabic *beit*.
bedeq	treasury (with *lishkah*, see below), but literally meaning a "breach or fissure" (of a building, like the Temple).
bēthṣoʾah	Greek *bēthsō*; latrine, derived from *baith*, house or place, and *ṣoʾah*, filth, human excrement.
birah	fortress, castle, palace; capital in Modern Israeli Hebrew; see Greek *Bāris*.
debir	the Holy of Holies of the Jerusalem temple; the innermost chamber of the Temple, corresponding to Greek *Adyton* (Latin *Adytum*); the inner sanctuary of the House of God from which he spoke to man, like the seat of an oracle (*manteíon*) of a pagan shrine. In the Jerusalem temple the *debir* was the place of the Ark of the Covenant and the throne room of Yahweh. The term is probably derived from the word for back part of a room (like Arabic *dabir*), not from the root *dabar*, to speak.
ʿ*ebed*	servant, slave; Isaiah's ʿ*ebed-YHWH* should not only be translated as "the servant of Yahweh," but especially as "the one who worships or adores God"; note the Arabic personal name Abdullah (ʿ*abed* + ʾ*Allah*).
ʾ*Elohim*	God; considered to be the plural of majesty of ʾ*el*, ʾ*eloah*; related to Arabic ʾ*Allah*.
ʾ*ephod*	a sacerdotal garment like an apron or scapular worn by the priests, as described in the Old Testament.
ʾ*eshdathayin*	(see Aramaic Glossary). Hebrew ʾ*ashedah*, from ʾ*ashed*, foundation, bottom, or the lower slope of a hill or mountain, can perhaps have been the older name of that

part of northeastern Jerusalem called Bethesda, along whose slope was built a huge double water reservoir, hence the dual *beth-'eshdathayin,* the place in the twin pool, known in the New Testament period as the Sheep (Probatic or Bethesda) Pool, correctly identified by J.T. Milik with the large double watercatchers on the property of St. Anne's Church in Jerusalem.

gan — garden or enclosure; Aramaic *ginna'*; the Gennath or Garden Gate is derived from this word.

gazith — a cutting or hewing (of stones for a building); the *lishkath-hagazith* is the name of one of the chambers of the Temple; phonetically related to Greek *xystós.*

genizah — a storeroom or hiding place (from Hebrew and Aramaic *g-n-z,* to hide, conceal, store) wherein worn-out scrolls of the Law were placed; for example, the famous Cairo Genizah yielded thousands of documents in Hebrew, Aramaic, Arabic, Greek, and Samaritan, when it was discovered in the Qaraite Ben-Ezra Synagogue around 1894 in Old Cairo.

Gethsemani — an oil press, from *gath,* a vat for pressing wine and/or oil(?), and *shemen,* oil (see Aramaic glossary).

gey' — valley, as in the Valley of the Son of Hinnom (Gey' Ben-Hinnom), the present Wadi er-Rababeh, running along the western and southern slopes of the Jerusalem promontory; see Greek *géenna.*

Ghareb — Gareb or Ghareb (if derived from *'arab*), which we identify with the northwestern hill of Jerusalem. The interchange between Hebrew and Greek *g,* which was actually pronounced more like a *gh* (a guttural sound almost similar to Hebrew and Arabic '), can be linguistically explained in the variant readings of the Hebrew and Greek texts of Jeremiah where it refers to a hill in the western part of Jerusalem.

Gihon — Gihon Spring, probably derived from Hebrew *giah,* to gush or burst forth; Hebrew and Aramaic *g-h-n,* to bend or to curve, may also be used to explain the name of this water source, deriving its name from the curving of the tunnel (especially that of Hezekiah) at or from this important spring on the eastern slope of Ophel.

golal — a rolling stone (see Aramaic glossary).

Golgotha — (pronounced *Gulgoleth*); the place of crucifixion in Jerusalem (see Aramaic glossary); from *galal,* to roll.

ha — the definite article "the." Its pointing depends on the preceding consonant.

ha'azarah — the sacred precinct or enclosure of the Jerusalem temple; *'azar,* to help or aid; hence, enclosure, a ledge surrounding (e.g., Ezekiel's altar). It can also refer to the outer court of the Temple.

Halakah — from the verb *halak,* to walk; the official or lawful way according to which a Jew ought to conduct his life. The Jewish Halakah contains various moral laws and ritual prescriptions, embracing the entire corpus of Judaism's teachings based on the Bible.

Hallel — to praise [the Lord]. The Hallel in the technical sense refers to Pss. 113–118, songs of praise sung on each of the three great pilgrim feasts to Jerusalem (Passover, Pentecost or Weeks, and Tabernacles or Booths).

Hanukkah — the Feast of the Dedication (*hanak,* to dedicate) of the Temple. John refers to it as *ta enkaínia*; Josephus calls it the Feast of Lights. It occurs on the twenty-fifth day of the month of Kisleb (see *Kislew*).

hanuyoth — (plural of *hanuth*); shops or stores. The Royal Basilica or Stoa along the southern part of the Court of the Gentiles served as a place where pilgrims could exchange their municipal money, minted with the emperor's image on it, for typical Jewish coins which did not represent such a figure, and thus purchase the necessary items for a feast or sacrifice in the temple area proper.

har — mountain.

hasid — kind, godly, pious; from the root *hesed,* kindness, mercy, etc.; its Aramaic equivalent is *hasan,* as also *hesda',* meaning "mercy."

Hebron — literally, the place of the friend (*haber*), the city of Hebron (Arabic el-Khalil), where God's friend Abraham was interred in the Cave of Machpelah according to Genesis.

heres — sun (also *shemesh*); the root also points to the abode of the Amorites.

heres — an earthen vessel, earthenware, potsherd, sherd; perhaps similar in its root-meaning to Arabic *harash,* to scratch, lacerate, or irritate.

hesed — kindness, mercy; Aramaic *hesda'*; New Testament Greek *eulabés* (Luke 2:25; Acts 2:5; and 8:2) translates this root in describing the "pious ones," the devout Jews who lived in Jerusalem.

heykal (hekal) — a palace or temple; from Assyrian *ekallu,* palace, temple; originating from Sumerian *e-gal,* a great house. Ancient temples were generally divided into three parts: the first was called the *'ulam,* the entrance or forecourt; the second was the *hekal,* the main room or sanctuary; and the third was the *debir,* the Holy of Holies, the innermost chamber of the Temple (see also *'ulam* and *debir*).

Hinnom — Hinnom; etymologically, the name cannot be proven to have originated from a root meaning "to wail or to cry," like the Arabic "cries of children" (with reference to the infant sacrifices that took place in the Valley of Hinnom). The full name of the valley, Gey' Ben-Hinnom, the Valley of the Son(s) of Hinnom, suggests the original Jebusite owner of the land here; see also *géenna*, *gey'*, etc.

ḥomoth — (plural of *ḥomah*); walls (of a city, as distinct from *qir*, the walls of a house).

Hosanna — "Save us, please!" The form is causative (hiphil) with the suffix interjection *-na'* indicating an entreaty, prayer, etc. The Great Hosanna (Ps. 118:25; Mark 11:9; Matt. 21:9; John 12:13) was recited on the Feast of Tabernacles, once daily for six days and seven times on the seventh day.

ḥoshen — breastpiece, sacred pouch (of decision) which was worn by the high priest while ministering in the Temple. The root probably indicates something excellent or beautiful; hence, the *ḥoshen* was either the principal ornament of the *'ephod* (see above) or the most precious vestment of the priest's garments. (Since the majority of the Essenes were described as priests, we could also derive their name from this root rather than those suggested by scholars.) But see *Ṣion* below.

Israel — the new name of one of the patriarchs (Isaac's son Jacob) and later predicated of the people called the Israelites. The etymology is uncertain. The following are generally proposed: *sarah*, to strive, which can therefore mean "El contends," "Let El strive," or "He strives with El"; *śar*, prince, which can then imply that "El is prince," "the prince of El," or "Let El be prince"; *yashar*, straight, right, pleasing, which would signify "El is right or pleasing," "Pleasing to El," "Let El be pleased." We would suggest that the name is a contraction of *'ish-ra'ah-'el*, "the man who saw El," and would relate it to the name of the place *Penu'el* meaning the "Face of El," which we consider more plausible in view of the account in Gen. 32:22–31. The site of Penuel is generally identified with Tulul edh-Dhahab (Tell edh-Dhahab esh-Shariyeh) east of the Jordan River in Wadi ez-Zerqa, equated with the River Jabbok.

Jacob — *Ya'aqob*, from the root *'aqab*, to be devious; see *Israel* above.

Kidron (*Qidron*) — valley or brook between Jerusalem and the Mount of Olives, along the eastern flank of the city; sometimes rendered *Cedron* after the Greek *Kedron*; root *q-d-r*, to be dark; to cause to mourn.

kinnereth — (from *Kinnor*, a harp); a place name in the territory of Naphtali in Galilee; Hebrew name for the Sea of Galilee (see Greek *kinýra*).

Kislew (**Kisleb** or **Kislev**) — ninth month of the Jewish calendar, corresponding to December.

kokim (**kokhim**) — from the singular *kok*, a niche, crypt, or sepulchral chamber.

kothel — wall, the Western (Wailing) Wall, as distinguished from *ḥomah*, a city wall, and *qir*, the wall of a house. The basic meaning of the verb *kathal* seems to be to join together, make compact, make into blocks (in which sense it can also signify the wall[s] of a house).

le — to, for, belonging to.

lehem — bread (staple nourishment); Arabic *laḥm*, meat. The word for war (*milḥamah*) is derived from the same root meaning "to fight" (for one's break or survival), perhaps related to a god or goddess Laḥami, as seen in the name of Bethlehem (*beith-lehem*), generally interpreted to mean the House of Bread.

libnoth — to build, rebuild, reconstruct, etc.; from the root *banah*.

lishkah — a public building; a room, shrine, or chamber; see Greek *léschē*.

lo' — no, not.

Lubban — from *laban*, meaning "white"; name of a biblical site, preserved in the Arabic place name, in the hills of Ephraim north of Jerusalem.

ma'alah — an ascent; from the root *'alah*, to go up; akin to Arabic *qa'alah*.

magharabi (**ma'arabi**) — western; from the root *'arab*, to cross.

mahaneh — camp, encampment, quarter (sector) of a city, like the Quarter of the Essenes on Mt. Zion in Jerusalem; from *ḥanah*, bend down, decline, encamp.

maṣṣoth — matzoth, unleavened bread; the plural of *maṣṣah*, derived from the root *m-ṣ-ṣ* to drain out, press out, suck, referring to the unleavened bread or cake eaten by the Jews at Passover, also known as the Feast of Unleavened Bread.

menorah (plural **menoroth**) — seven-branched candelabra, derived from *nor* meaning "light." The term may also signify a candlestick or lampstand, but used only in the technical sense, as defined above, in the Old Testament.

meṣudah — a fortress situated on a hill, rock, or prom-

	ontory; derived from *ṣadah*, to lie in wait.
mibṣar	a fortress. The verb *baṣar* means to "cut off, make inaccessible (by means of a fortification)," hence also "an enclosure."
Middoth	a tractate of the Jewish Mishnah (see below) meaning "measurements." It deals specifically with the measurements of the Jerusalem temple.
millo'	frequently rendered "Millo" and explained as a "filling in," derived from the root *malē'* to fill (in). However, we prefer to translate the word "terrace or platform" and explain it in relation to Assyrian *mulû (tamlû)*, which, we think, also explains the biblical usage. This suggestion has already been offered; the location of the Millo in the northwest corner of the original Temple Mount is based on our own study of the word in relation to the history and geography of the area.
min	a preposition meaning "from."
migdal	a tower, derived from the root *gadal* meaning "big." (See also Greek *Amýgdalon*.)
miqva'oth	plural of *miqveh*; a Jewish ritual bath, a body of water, a pool or reservoir; derived from the root *q-w-h*, to gather (together); also the title of a tractate in the Mishnah.
Mishnah	from the verb *shanah*, to repeat. The work is a compilation of Jewish religious and legal teachings as taught in Palestine by the rabbis and orally handed down until they were compiled by Judah ha-Nasi (A.D. 135–*ca.* 220). In this it is distinct from the written documents called the Miqra' or "reading." The Mishnah is composed of six orders termed Sederim, which in turn are divided into tractates or treatises known as the Massekthoth, such as *Middoth, Rosh ha-Shanah, Miqvaoth*. The Mishnah is the first part of the Talmud (see below).
mishneh	derived from *shanah*, but also meaning "new" or "second." The Mishneh was a new quarter of Jerusalem, which, according to some scholars, is to be located either along the eastern slope of Mt. Zion or a northern extension of the city in the Tyropoeon Valley along the Temple Mount. We prefer the latter location, as it seems more logical that the city would extend itself along the Temple Mount rather than across the Tyropoeon, which would make it less defensible, given the much higher top of Mt. Zion above it.
mishpaṭ	judgment, derived from *shapaṭ*, to judge.
Molek (Molekh or Molech, also Moloch)	(from *malak*, to rule, be king); god of the Ammonites, whose shrine, Topheth (see below) was located in the Hinnom Valley, and to whom the Israelites sacrificed their chil-

	dren, especially during the reigns of kings Ahaz, Manasseh, and Amon in the late eighth and early seventh centuries B.C. The noun takes its vocalization from the Hebrew *bosheth*, shame, as explained with reference to ʿAshthoreth above.
moqed	from *yaqad*, to burn, be kindled, hence "hearth" or a "fireplace." The Beith ha-Moqed was a chamber in the Temple where the perpetual fire was maintained.
moriyyah	Moriah or Mt. Moriah. Neither the exact location nor the precise etymology of this name can be ascertained. Both the etymology, as explained in the book of Genesis, and the identification of Mt. Moriah with the Temple Mount are based on popular tradition, in antiquity as also today.
negeb	from the root meaning "dry" or "parched"; hence the southern parched land of Palestine, geographically called the Negeb.
nephesh	life, soul, living being, person; the word is also used to define a funerary monument or tombstone as, for example, the Tomb of Absalom in the Kidron Valley.
niṣoṣ	the "Nitzotz," the subterranean gallery which led from the inner courts of the Temple to the Tadi Gate in the north. The word appears in Isa. 1:31 where it means a "spark," derived from the root *n-ṣ-ṣ*, to shine, sparkle, glitter, be enkindled. The secret passageway probably derived its name from its destination, the Moqed or "hearth" where the priests on duty spent the night.
ʿOphel	hill, mound; derived from the root meaning "to swell." The Ophel is the southeasternmost spur of Jerusalem, called the City of David. Josephus knows it as Ophlas. It is also the oldest part of Jerusalem, dating back to the third millennium B.C. Jebusites occupied it in the second and first millennia B.C.
'oṣar	a treasury or storehouse.
parah	a cow; the (red) heifer sacrificed on the Mount of Olives. It is also the name of the ramp leading from the northeastern gate, the present Golden Gate, towards Mt. Olivet.
qiryah (qiryath)	city, as in Kiriath-yearim, "Forest-ville."
rab (rabbah)	great, derived from *rabab*, to be great; hence, Rabbi, my master (teacher); in Greek transcription appears as *rabbí* and *rabbeí*; title of an ordained Jewish teacher of the Law or leader of a Jewish community.
ramah	from *r-m-h*, to be high, exalted; hence, a high place or height; construct *ramath*, as in the place name Ramath-Rachel, a site be-

tween Jerusalem and Bethlehem, identified with the biblical Beth-hakkerem, Khirbet Salih.

reḥob a street; from the root r-ḥ-b, to be wide; distinguished from *derek*, a way, from *darak*, to tread (in, upon), to walk, go.

Rogel a fuller; a watchman or spy; a wanderer. Ein-Rogel, equated with modern Bir-ʿAyyub near the junction between the Kidron and Hinnom Valleys, indicated the boundary line between the territories of Benjamin and Judah south of Jerusalem.

ṣaphon the north. In addition to its theological significance in Canaanite and other literature, it was also the origin of fear and catastrophe for the Israelites, for the enemy would come down "from the north" as the prophets Isaiah and Jeremiah warned.

seder from the verb "to order, arrange," hence, the Jewish Seder or Passover meal.

śaʿir the scapegoat named Azazel which was sent into the desert on the Day of Atonement, according to the prescriptions of Leviticus.

shaʿar a gate, equivalent to Arabic *bab*.

Shabbath the Sabbath or the Jewish day of rest. The root of the word seems related to *sh-b-th*, meaning "to cease (from work)," "to rest," although scholars do not agree with regard to the history of the institution of the day as a holy day in Judaism. In general, Mosaic origins are sought in this respect.

shaphath from *sh-p-h*, to sweep bare or to set on the pot; see also *'ashpôth* above and the following.

shaphoth dung, excrement.

sheqel a Shekel, from the root meaning "weight," a Jewish silver coin equal to the Greek silver *statér*, a standard coin in the ancient Greek and Roman world. The *sheqel* was equivalent to about half an ounce of silver.

shephodim a Midrashic Hebrew word for "spears," with reference to the eight spears found in the Temple, variously explained in the story of the Dedication of the Temple.

shiloaḥ Siloam, referred to in Isaiah as "the waters of Siloam" (*mei shiloaḥ*), an ancient hydraulic system related to the Gihon Spring on the eastern slope of Ophel. The name is interpreted to mean "the sender" or "the one who was sent." It appears in Greek, in the Septuagint and in John's Gospel, as *Siloám*, *Siloá*, and *Seiloám*, and in the Latin as *Siloë*. The Arab village Silwan, opposite Ophel, takes its name from and preserves the site of the ancient aqueduct.

shophar (shopharoth) a shofar or ram's horn, used to announce the beginning or end of certain Jewish feasts. It is certainly the most common instrument of music mentioned in the biblical text. Its function corresponded to that of the *teqiʿah* in some respects. Both instruments are translated *salpínx* by the Septuagint authors (see also *teqiʿah* below).

shopheṭ a judge, derived from the verb *shapaṭ* meaning "to judge or to govern."

shoshan a lily; probably a generic word describing any lilylike flower; considered an Egyptian loanword, from *shoshen* (*sššen*) meaning "a lily."

Shushan Susa, a great city in Persia, the winter villa of the Persian kings. This was also the name of the northeastern gate of the temple precinct, which depicted this royal city on its lintel, probably in appreciation to the Persians who allowed the Jews to rebuild the Temple in the sixth century B.C.

Ṣidqiyahu Zedekiah, king of Judah from 597–587. This is also the name, though only rarely used today, of the multichambered cave, now called Solomon's Quarries, beneath Bethesda hill, between the present Damascus and Herod's gates in the north wall of Jerusalem.

ṣinnor a tunnel, conduit, or pipe; probably derived from *ṣ-n-r*, referring to a waterfall or cataract. The *ṣinnor* at the Gihon Spring was the Jebusite water conduit which brought water from the spring up into the city and through which David's armies captured Jebusite Jerusalem.

Ṣion (Ṣiyon) Sion or Zion. The etymology of the word is disputed; see pp. 65–66; see also Arabic *ṣāhyun*. As explained in the text, in our view the word (name) Essene (*haṣṣionîm* = those who lived on Mt. Sion [Zion]) is very plausibly derived from this root (and word).

ṣophim scouts (singular *ṣopheh*). "Mountain of Scouts" is the more recent Hebrew name for Mt. Scopus (see Arabic glossary) in the north of Jerusalem.

soreg derived from *s-r-g*, to strap, gird, interlace. The Soreg in the temple area was the latticework fence (railing) which surrounded the Temple proper and through which no Gentile was allowed to pass under penalty of death. Stone markers were placed at strategic places along this balustrade warning Gentiles not to enter beyond this line. See p. 121.

Sukkoth the Feast of Tabernacles or Booths, a fall festival commemorating the vintage harvest. This feast, along with the spring holy days of Passover and Pentecost, was one of the three great pilgrim feasts which brought the Jews to the City of the Temple.

Ṭadi the Tadi Gate; the name of the northern gate of the temple precinct, according to

	Mishnah *Middoth*, which describes the gate and states its position; however, the source disagrees with regard to its function: i. 3 says that it was either not used or perhaps unknown; i. 9 mentions that it was used by the young priests on duty for certain purposes.
Ṭalith	the Tallith or prayer shawl, prescribed in Numbers for devout Jewish males to wear at prayer time; compare also Greek *kráspedon* or tassel (see also p. 65).
talîh	from the verb *talah* meaning "to hang, suspend, or execute," as in Deut. 21:22. The Modern Hebrew term for cross is *ṣelab*, and "to crucify" is *haṣleb*, which appears to be a late Hebrew word. Compare the use of *kremannýnai, passaleúein,* and *stauróō* in the Greek glossary.
Talmud (*Talmud*)	comprises the Mishnah and Gemara, which are additional interpretations to the Jewish Torah. Its period of composition is between Ezra in the Old Testament period and the middle of the sixth-century-A.D. Roman period. The Palestinian Talmud (Talmud Yerushalmi) was compiled at Caesarea, Sepphoris, and Tiberias; the Babylonian Talmud (Talmud Babli) dates to the Jewish captivity in Babylon and is written in Eastern Aramaic. The Halakah, the legal material of the Talmud, should be studied in relation to the Haggadah, which deals with Jewish ethics and religion. The Talmud is, in fact, the entire corpus of Jewish law and teachings. The title is derived from the Hebrew root *l-m-d,* to learn, teach, or instruct.
tel	a mound, equivalent to Arabic *tell,* a hill, mound; a technical term in archaeology defining an artificial mound with occupational layers buried within it.
teqiʿah (tqiaʿ)	a trumpet, used for sounding signals, especially for the gathering of an assembly; sometimes confused with the *shofar* which was, in fact, a ram's horn, the most common biblical musical instrument.
teraphim	a pagan "idol" (in the plural of majesty); also household gods, something like Latin penates. The etymology is uncertain: it may be related to either Assyrian *tarpû,* spectre, or Semitic *r-ph-ʾ,* healing, health, etc. The term appears in Greek as either *eídōla,* idols, or simply transliterated *theraphín.*
Topheth	Tophet, a high place opposite the Potsherd Gate in the Hinnom Valley. The word is derived from Aramaic *taphaʾ* signifying a hearth or a fireplace which, in fact, describes the sanctuary of Molek to whom the Israelites offered child sacrifices. The word receives its pointing from *bosheth,* a shameful thing, and its location is to be sought in the neighborhood of the Potter's Field (see *Akeldama*). The Greek form appears as *Taphes, Taphéth,* and *Thaphphéth.*
ʾulam	the entrance hall, vestibule, or porch of the Temple. The word is Akkadian in origin: *ellamu,* in front (porch), although some scholars see in it the root *ʾ-w-l,* to be first, chief. The *ʾulam* may also refer to the forecourt or gate of the Temple.
yad	hand; power; strength; by metonymy it can mean "person"; also a monument. The expression *yad washem* (literally a hand and a name) signifies, in Isa. 56:5, "a monument and a memorial." Yad Vashem is the Jewish memorial in West Jerusalem, commemorating those who perished during the Nazi persecution in Europe during World War II.
Yahweh (YHWH)	the Divine Name, pronounced only once by the high priest in the Holy of Holies on the Day of Atonement; also called the tetragrammaton or the "four letters." The form of the word, derived from Hebrew *h-w-h,* to fall, to come into being, to become, to exist, or to be, appears to be in the hiphil or causative state, meaning "he who causes... to come into existence."
yam	sea or, in general, any body of water. Its Assyrian equivalent is *iâmu,* and it may be rendered into Greek by either *thálassa,* sea, or *pélagos* (Latin pelagus), the high sea or any large body of water.
yeʿar (plural *yeʿarim*)	a forest. The word appears in the name of the biblical city Kiryath-yearim (Qiriath Yeʿarîm), "the City of Forests" (Forestville), identified with the present village of Abu Ghosh, about seven miles west of Jerusalem en route to Tel Aviv-Jaffa.
yom	day, as distinguished from *laylah,* night, and as it appears in the Day of Atonement (*Yom Kippur*).
Zion	see *Ṣion* above.

ARAMAIC

baith	house; *beith-,* house of (construct); same as Hebrew *baith.*	*dam (demaʾ)*	blood, as in Haqel-demaʾ, Akeldama, the Field of Blood.

'eshda' — from *sheda'*, to pour out (water), to shed (blood), equivalent to Hebrew *shadah*. *'Eshdathayin*, dual of *'eshda'* (biblical Hebrew = *'eshdah*). The dual *byt-'shdthyn* of the Copper Scroll of Qumran Cave 3 has been identified by J.T. Milik as the double pool (Sheep Pool or Pool of Bethesda) in the northeastern corner (outside the second north wall) of Jerusalem.

Gethsemani (Greek Gethsemane í) — an oil vat; from *gath*, a press, and *mashah*, oil, unguent, although etymologically Hebrew *shemen*, oil, is much clearer in the name.

golal — a rolling-stone (as for a tomb); a stone too heavy to be carried. Both the Aramaic and Hebrew are derived from the same root *g-l-l*, to roll, be round. Aramaic *gelal* may also describe a square stone (*lapis quadratus*).

Gulgoltha' — Golgotha; derived from the root *g-l-l*, transcribed into Greek *Golgothá* and translated *kraníon*, Calvaria in Latin.

haqel — field (see *dam, dema'* above).

harsutha' — potsherd, like Hebrew *harsith*.

hazia' — connotes "seeing as a seer" in an ecstatic state; Hebrew *hozen*, a worshiper or watcher.

kepha' — rock. Hebrew *keph* is perhaps an Aramaic loanword (the Hebrew term for rock being *sela'*) whence Peter's name Cephas, translates Greek *pétra* (rock or stone), but with the masculine termination (*Pétros*).

sheda' (shedah) — to pour; see *'eshda'* above.

'ushshin — the foundations of a building; from the singular *'ushsha'*. The word is derived from *'osh*, which may be a loanword from Assyrian *ushshu*. The emphatic plural is *'ushshayya'*. The basic meaning of the word is foundation.

Latin

Ad — a preposition meaning "to, towards, at," etc.

Aesculapium — a temple or shrine in honor of Aesculapius, the god of medicine and healing; a kind of religious sanitorium.

Agrippeum — one of the large halls of Herod's palace, named after Vipsanius Agrippa.

Ampulla — a flask or bottle; a Byzantine, silver pilgrim flask with an impression of the shrine of the Holy Sepulchre on it, like those of Bobbio and Monza in Italy.

Aurea — golden.

Balneum — a bath, bath house (like Greek *thérmai*, hence Italian *terme*).

Caesareum — one of the large halls of Herod the Great's palace, named after Caesar Augustus.

Calvarium — Calvary or the "place of the skull," from Calvaria meaning "skull."

Cardo — a hinge (related to Greek *kradaínō*, to swing).

Cardo maximus — the principal street of a Roman city, usually running from north to south, as in Jerusalem.

Cauponius — an innkeeper (from Caupere, Copere); metaphorically "knavish, huckster."

Coenaculum (or Caenaculum; more commonly Cenaculum) — a dining room; usually the upper story of a house. Greek *hyperóon*, a room upstairs. The Cenacle or Upper Room in which Jesus celebrated his last Passover meal.

Columbarium — a dovecot; a tomb with niches into which were placed urns or ossuaries, especially in the case of secondary burials (Latin columba, a dove).

Curulis — the official seat of a magistrate, consul, etc. (cf. Sella curulis below).

Decumanus — a boundary line drawn from east to west; the main (east-west) street of a Roman city cutting through the Cardo maximus, as also in Jerusalem of the second century A.D.

Deus — god, a divinity; God; etymologically related to Greek *theós*.

Dolorosa — an adjective signifying "sorrowful."

Dominus — a lord or the Lord; like Greek *Kýrios* for Hebrew *YHWH*. For "Dominus flevit," see Luke 19:41: "the Lord wept over Jerusalem."

Ecce — interjection meaning "Behold! Look!," like French *voici!*

Enchiridion (Greek encheirídion) — a manual.

Ex voto — a votive offering to a divinity in fulfillment of a promise.

Fictilia — an earthen vessel (from ficticilis).

Figlinum — an earthen vessel, jar (pertaining to a potter).

Forum — a public square (Greek *ágora*), commonly translated "marketplace."

Fretensis — from the adjective fretum, strait, channel. Here it pertains to the Strait of Sicily or the

Strait of Messina. The Tenth Roman Legion (Legio Decima Fretensis) was from this area.

Galilaeus a Galilaean; a person from Galilee, the northern district of first-century Palestine.

Gaudium joy; gaudii in the possessive case.

Gallicantu cock-crowing; from gallus, rooster, and cantus, song. St. Peter-in-Gallicantu is a small chapel on the eastern slope of Mt. Zion, believed by some to have been the house of Caiaphas.

Homo man, as distinguished from vir, a male person; homo can also denote "mankind."

In situ a technical term in archaeology, meaning that the remains are exactly in the place or position in which they were discovered.

Itinerarium an itinerary, sometimes also called a diary; frequently a pilgrim's diary.

Iuno (Juno) Roman goddess, the wife of Jupiter, equivalent to Greek Hera.

Iupiter (Jupiter) the father of the Roman pantheon, identical with Greek Zeus.

Lapis a rock; the Lapis Pertusis, the "perforated rock," is identified with the Sacred Rock beneath the Dome of the Rock in the Haram esh-Sharif.

Legio a legion; a division of the Roman army, consisting of ten cohortes (troops) and containing from 4000 to 6000 milites (soldiers).

Manipulus a division of the Roman army, a company of foot soldiers; from manus and plere, to fill; a handful.

Maximus the largest or biggest; the principal, as in the phrase cardo maximus, which identified the principal street of a Roman city.

Minerva a Roman goddess identified with the Greek Athena, the goddess of wisdom, etc.

Mons a mountain, as in the Crusader expression "Mons Gaudii," the present Nebiʾ Samwil.

Opus reticulatum a technical term describing a netlike arrangement of bricks in a Roman structure, as at Herodian Jericho (Tulul Abu el-ʿAlaiq; retes, a net).

Opus sectile a technical expression depicting a mosaiclike pattern (but composed of much larger pieces) of a Roman floor design, a good example of which may be seen in the Flavian palace on the Palatine Hill in Rome (sectilis, from secare, to cut, refers to a pavement made up of small pieces of colored stone).

Patibulum the upper, horizontal crossbeam to which those condemned to crucifixion were tied and which they were forced to carry through the streets of a city. The person was then nailed to it and hoisted up to hang on the upright beam already fixed in its place, as on Golgotha in Jerusalem.

Pertusus perforated (see Lapis above).

Pinnaculum a pinnacle, wing of a building, a peak; a corner (?), structure (?), or some architectural design of the Jerusalem temple, as used in the New Testament.

Porta as in "in portarum exitibus quae in Siloam ducunt," "at the gates which lead towards Siloam (pool)."

Praefectus a civil or military official or superintendent; a commander.

Praetorium (a) the general's headquarters in a Roman camp; (b) the official residence of a Roman governor in a subjugated province; (c) the military palace of a Roman governor or procurator; grecized praitórion, as in the New Testament.

Procurator a manager, viceroy, governor, or procurator, such as Coponius or Pontius Pilate in Palestine.

Quadra a square.

Quadrata squared or square; the grid or layout of a Roman city was in square sections, divided from north to south by the cardo maximus and from east to west by a decumanus. Hadrian's Jerusalem, Aelia Capitolina, was quadrata, as can still be discerned in the principal streets of the Old City today.

Quadrivium a crossroads; that part of a Roman street plan where four roads met, as at Palmyra or Latakia in Syria.

Scopus from Greek skopós (skopeín or sképtesthai) signifying a watchman, guardian, observer. Mt. Scopus, north of Jerusalem, is the high point from which invading armies could survey the city below.

Sella curulis the judgment seat of a Roman magistrate, as that from which Pontius Pilate condemned Jesus to crucifixion.

Sicarius a murderer or an assassin; a nationalistic band of Jews in ancient Jerusalem who stabbed certain persons for their lack of observance of the law. Judas, one of Jesus' apostles, had probably belonged to this group, hence his name Iscariot formed from Hebrew ʾish qarioth.

Speciosa beautiful; one of the Temple Gates was called the Porta Speciosa in the New Testament, as also by the Crusaders.

Stadium a unit of measurement of approximately 607 feet; derived from Greek stádion, sometimes translated "furlong."

Studium zeal, study; institute, academy, or school;

like the Studium Biblicum Franciscanum in Jerusalem.

Templum   a place cut off (*témenos*) from the rest of the city or region and dedicated to a divinity; hence, temple, shrine, or asylum.

Thermae   see Balneum.

Tribunale   the speaker's platform, equivalent to the Greek *béma* as in Corinth and Rome.

Venus   a Roman goddess of love, whose counterpart in the Greek world was Aphrodite. Hadrian built a temple in honor of Venus on the site of the Holy Sepulchre.

Vetus   old; the old Latin version of the Bible which St. Jerome used is called the Vetus Latina, though he seems to have used the Hebrew text for his translation of the Old Testament. Jerome himself admits that in his day there were numerous versions and a multiplicity of manuscripts in Latin translations of the Sacred Scriptures.

Via   way, road.

Vir, pl. viri   man, men; Viri Galilaei..., Men of Galilee....

Xystus   a promenade, a colonnade walk (see Greek *xystós*, Hebrew *gazith*).

Other Near Eastern Words and Phrases

AKKADIAN

ekallu   palace or temple, hence Hebrew *heykal*.

ishdu   foundation; also connotes a mountain slope.

'L'   root of the verb "to go up"; compare Hebrew *'alah* and Arabic *'alla*.

malikum   a name related etymologically to *m-l-k* (*molek, melek*, etc.); Hebrew *molek*, Arabic *malaki*.

mi-il-kí-li   a name etymologically related to Molek.

shupat   a fireplace or hearth.

tamlû   a terrace (something artificially built up, from *mulû*, to build up).

tarpû   a spectre (see Hebrew *teraphim*).

ulamu   a gateway or gate.

urusalimmu   Jerusalem (as it appears in the Amarna correspondence of the mid-fourteenth century B.C.; see p. 26).

EBLAITE

urusalim   Jerusalem, as it occurs on a cuneiform tablet recently discovered at Tell Mardikh (Ebla) near Aleppo in northern Syria; the archaeological material discovered on this site is dated to the third millennium B.C.

EGYPTIAN

'3a   big, great; see "Pharaoh" below, from the verb *aai*, to be great.

baru   a type of flat-bottomed boat; the word in later Egyptian came to mean "a large house or tower," hence, Greek *Baris*, the name of the palace which Herod the Great rebuilt and renamed Antonia in the northwest corner of the Temple Mount.

Pharaoh (*pir-*)   originally meaning "great house," from *pir (pr)*, house, and *a*, large, great, or big. Its usage is similar to that of the American "White House." *Pir - a*, Pharaoh (Hebrew *par'oh* and Greek (*Pharaó*) was later predicated of the Egyptian king or ruler (who lived in a large house from which he governed his country).

pir (pr)   house (see Pharaoh and *'3a (aai)*, above).

urusalim   Jerusalem (as transliterated from an Egyptian Execration Text of the early second millennium B.C.; see p. 26).

PERSIAN

ganuǵ   a treasure; hence, Greek *gazo(phylákion)*, a sacred or military treasury.

maguš   a Persian priest or wiseman experienced in astrology and the interpreting of dreams, omens, etc. The root *mag* appears in such words as Greek *mégas* and Latin *magnus*, both meaning "great, large, big," etc. The Old Persian "Magian" was in fact also esteemed as an enchanter, wizard, or magician. The Matthaean account of the birth of Jesus uses the term *mágoi*, the wisemen from the east, in this sense but, in view of our research, most probably against the background of the great Nabataean kingdom east of the Jordan. It is incorrect to translate *mágoi* as "kings," and only partially accurate to describe them as "astrologers," for the term does not imply kingship, and the Nabataeans were much more than astrologers.

pairidaēza   an enclosure or wooded park, especially that of Persian monarchs and noblemen. The word has come into Greek, probably through Xenophon, as *parádeisos (parádisos)*, describing a "pleasure ground," then internationalized into Hebrew *pardes*, also found in Latin *paradisus*, hence English "paradise"; see Arabic *furdeis (fureidis)*.

SYRIAC

ṣehyûn   a mound or hillock; hence, Hebrew Ṣiyyôn, Zion, like Arabic *ṣāhyun* (see Arabic glossary).

TURKISH

Anadolu   Anatolia; Turkish corruption of Greek *anatolé*, east, with reference to Asia Minor, modern Turkey.

caravansary   an inn; for the derivation of the word see below, *kervan* and *saray*.

han   an inn or hostel, hence Arabic *khan*, as in Khan es-Sultan or Suq Khan ez-Zeit.

kervan   a caravan. The expression *kervana katılmak* means "to go with the rest" or "to join a procession."

kışla   barracks; see Arabic *qishleh*, a police post or station east of the Jaffa Gate in the Old City.

Kurnub   a Nabataean, Roman, and Byzantine site in the Negeb, identified with Mampsis (perhaps biblical Meshash). Arabic *Qurnub* is apparently derived from *karnibahar*, meaning "cauliflower." There is no clear connection between the meaning and the name of the historic site.

saray   a palace or mansion, but also referring to a government building or office. The word is used as a compound in the English word "caravansary" (see above).

Sultan   Sultan, an Islamic ruler, more specifically identified with the former emperors of Turkey.

INDEX

Colophon

PUBLISHER	WM. B. EERDMANS PUBLISHING COMPANY
EDITOR	ALLEN MYERS
DESIGN AND PRODUCTION	JOEL BEVERSLUIS
PRODUCTION MANAGER	CHARLOTTE ELLISON
TYPESETTER	THE COMPOSING ROOM OF MICHIGAN
TYPE FACES	10/12 GOUDY OLD STYLE (TEXT)
	14/14 PERPETUA ITALIC (CAPTIONS)
	GOUDY THIRTY (DISPLAY)
MAPS AND FIGURES	PETER KRAFFT, DAN MALDA
COLOR SEPARATIONS AND FILM	BLACK DOT
PAPER	70# WARREN L.O.E.
PRINTER	R.R. DONNELLEY AND SONS COMPANY

DATE DUE

GAYLORD   PRINTED IN U.S.A.

AELIA CAPITOLINA
(A.D. 135)

Letters A–P refer to the same sites in each of the three periods shown. Numbers correspond to those on maps of Jerusalem in the time of Jesus.

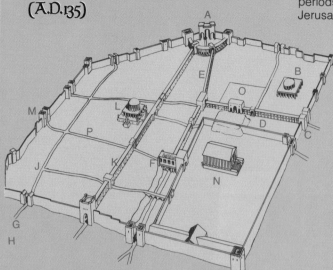

LEGEND

A.(1) North Gate
B.(3) Asclepeion
C.(5) East Gate
D. East-west street
E. North-southeast colonnaded street
F. Houses
G. Ruins outside city wall
H.(43) Ruins outside city wall
J. Street
K.(41) Cardo maximus
L.(33) Venus (Aphrodite) Temple
M. West Gate
N.(10–13) Quadra, site of Capitolium
O.(2) Roman Forum and Hadrian's Arch
P. Decumanus and Tetrapylon (Quadrivium)

THE MADABA MAP
(6TH CENT. A.D.)

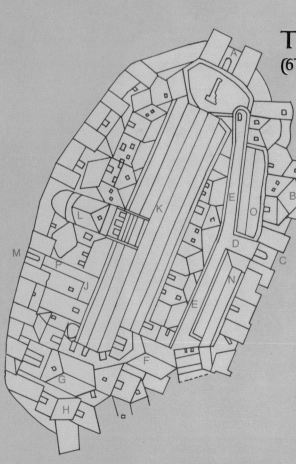

LEGEND

A.(1) St. Stephen's Gate (Porta Neapolitana)
B.(3) Basilica Sanctae Mariae and Piscina Probatica
C.(5) East (Benjamin) Gate
D. East-west street
E. North-southeast colonnaded street
F. Nea (New Church of the Mother of God)
G. Hagia Sion (Mother of All Churches)
H.(43) Coenaculum
J. Street leading to the Hagia Sion
K.(41) Porticoed street and shops
L.(33) Anastasis and Martyrion (Holy Sepulchre Basilica)
M. Porta Purgu (Tower Gate)
N.(10–13) (Not visible on map, area possibly deserted)
O.(2) Buildings (ecclesiastical and public)
P. Street